Forensic Investigations

Forensic Investigations
An Introduction

Brent E. Turvey
*Forensic Solutions, LLC, Sitka, Alaska, United States;
Director, The Forensic Criminology Institute
(USA & Mexico)*

Stan Crowder
Kennesaw State University, Georgia, GA, United States

AMSTERDAM • BOSTON • HEIDELBERG • LONDON
NEW YORK • OXFORD • PARIS • SAN DIEGO
SAN FRANCISCO • SINGAPORE • SYDNEY • TOKYO

Academic Press is an imprint of Elsevier

Academic Press is an imprint of Elsevier
125 London Wall, London EC2Y 5AS, United Kingdom
525 B Street, Suite 1800, San Diego, CA 92101-4495, United States
50 Hampshire Street, 5th Floor, Cambridge, MA 02139, United States
The Boulevard, Langford Lane, Kidlington, Oxford OX5 1GB, United Kingdom

Copyright © 2017 Elsevier Inc. All rights reserved.

No part of this publication may be reproduced or transmitted in any form or by any means, electronic or mechanical, including photocopying, recording, or any information storage and retrieval system, without permission in writing from the publisher. Details on how to seek permission, further information about the Publisher's permissions policies and our arrangements with organizations such as the Copyright Clearance Center and the Copyright Licensing Agency, can be found at our website: www.elsevier.com/permissions.

This book and the individual contributions contained in it are protected under copyright by the Publisher (other than as may be noted herein).

Notices

Knowledge and best practice in this field are constantly changing. As new research and experience broaden our understanding, changes in research methods, professional practices, or medical treatment may become necessary.

Practitioners and researchers must always rely on their own experience and knowledge in evaluating and using any information, methods, compounds, or experiments described herein. In using such information or methods they should be mindful of their own safety and the safety of others, including parties for whom they have a professional responsibility.

To the fullest extent of the law, neither the Publisher nor the authors, contributors, or editors, assume any liability for any injury and/or damage to persons or property as a matter of products liability, negligence or otherwise, or from any use or operation of any methods, products, instructions, or ideas contained in the material herein.

Library of Congress Cataloging-in-Publication Data
A catalog record for this book is available from the Library of Congress

British Library Cataloguing-in-Publication Data
A catalogue record for this book is available from the British Library

ISBN: 978-0-12-800680-1

For information on all Academic Press publications
visit our website at https://www.elsevier.com/

Publisher: Sara Tenney
Acquisition Editor: Elizabeth Brown
Editorial Project Manager: Joslyn Chaiprasert-Paguio
Production Project Manager: Lisa Jones
Designer: Matthew Limbert

Typeset by TNQ Books and Journals

Contents

List of Contributors... xiii
Preface xv

CHAPTER 1 **Forensic Investigations: A Primer** 1
Brent E. Turvey, Stan Crowder
Corpus Delicti.. 3
Forensic Necessity: Everybody Lies... 5
The Forensic Investigator.. 7
    Forensic 7
    Forensic Science... 8
    Forensic Scientists/Forensic Examiners................................... 8
    Investigators/Investigations... 9
    Forensic Investigators.. 10
    Data Integrity.. 10
Forensic Investigations: The Big Picture 11
Forensic Facts Versus Political Reality 12
Conclusions 16
Endnotes 16
References 17

CHAPTER 2 **Law and Evidence** 19
Brent E. Turvey
The Pillars of the Criminal Justice System 20
    Academia... 21
    Law Enforcement 21
    Forensic Services... 21
    The Judiciary 22
    Corrections... 22
The Adversarial System.. 23
    The Prosecution... 23
    The Defense 23
Scientific Fact Versus Legal Truth 24
Experts, Evidence, and Admissibility 26
    Evidence 26
    Chain of Custody... 27
    Expert Evidence 27

Constitutional Rights..30
    The Right to Due Process..31
    Brady v. Maryland (1963)..33
    The Right to "Effective" Counsel 35
    Melendez-Diaz (2009)..37
Conclusion 41
Endnotes...41
References..41

CHAPTER 3 Investigative Ethics...45
Brent E. Turvey, Stan Crowder
Understanding Ethics 46
    Ethics and Morality..46
    Ethical Dilemmas 47
    Professional Ethics...51
Duty of Care...52
    The Forensic Investigator..54
    Employers and Fitness for Duty 54
Bias..59
An Ethical Canon for the Forensic Investigator......................62
Conclusion 64
Endnotes...64
References..64

CHAPTER 4 Investigators and the Scientific Method 67
Brent E. Turvey, Stan Crowder
Reflection and Metacognition 69
Critical Thinking 72
    The Polygraph..73
    The FBI 74
    The Problem...75
The Availability Heuristic and the Problem With Experience ...76
Science Versus Scientific Method...77
Science as Falsification..79
Logical Fallacies 81
    Poisoning the Well...82
    Suppressed Evidence or Card Stacking..........................82
    Appeals to Authority...82
    Appeal to False Authority 83
    Appeal to Tradition...84
    Argumentum ad Hominem, aka "Argument to the Man"......84

Emotional Appeal 84
Circulus in Probando, aka Circular Reasoning 85
Cum Hoc, Ergo Propter Hoc, or "With This, Therefore
Because of This" 85
Post Hoc, Ergo Propter Hoc, or "After This, Therefore
Because of This" 85
Hasty Generalizations 86
Sweeping Generalization 86
False Precision 86
Conclusion 87
Endnotes 88
References 88

CHAPTER 5 Crime Scene Investigation and Analysis 91
Brent E. Turvey, Jodi Freeman
The CSI Effect 92
The FBI Effect 95
Crime Scene Investigation, Reconstruction, and Analysis 98
Crime Scene Investigation 98
Crime Reconstruction 99
Crime Scene Analysis 105
Forensic Relevance 105
Corpus Delicti 106
Modus Operandi 107
Signature Behavior 108
Linking the Suspect to the Victim 109
Linking a Person to a Crime Scene 109
Disproving or Supporting Witness Testimony 109
Identification of Suspects 110
Providing Investigative Leads 112
Endnotes 120
References 122

CHAPTER 6 Crime Scene Processing 125
Brent E. Turvey, W. Jerry Chisum
Crime Scenes 126
Primary Crime Scene 127
Secondary Crime Scene 129
Intermediate Crime Scene 129
Dumpsite/Disposal site 129
Tertiary Crime Scene 131

Crime Scene Processing...131
Crime Scene Processing: A Descriptive Tiered System..........133
    Police: Level 1..134
    Scientist: Level 1..135
    Police: Level 2..135
    Scientist: Level 2..135
    Police: Level 3..136
    Scientist: Level 3..136
Crime Scene Processing Protocols.....................................140
    Checklists..140
    Inside the Tape..140
    National Institute of Justice Guidelines..........................141
    Evidence Recognition..146
    Evidence Documentation..148
    Evidence Collection and Preservation............................151
    Evidence Transportation...154
Conclusion..154
Endnotes...155
References..155

CHAPTER 7 Forensic Victimology..157
Brent E. Turvey, Jodi Freeman
Forensic Victimology: Evidence of Context.......................159
Goals...161
Victim Exposure Analysis...164
    Categorizing Victim Exposure..164
    Lifestyle Exposure...165
    Situational/Incident Exposure..168
Victimology Guidelines...174
    Creating a Timeline: The Last 24 h.................................178
Conclusion..179
Endnotes...179
References..179

CHAPTER 8 The Sexual Assault Examination...........................181
Brent E. Turvey, Charla Jamerson
The Role of Reconstruction..182
The "Team"..183
Forensic Nursing...187
    Time Constraints...188
    Consent Forms..189
    The Intake Form..191
Sexual Assault Examination Protocols...............................192
    History...193

    Physical Examination: Head to Toe 197
    NIJ Guidelines: Forensic Medical Examination
    and Evidence Collection Procedures 197
        Full Body Photos 204
        Physical Injuries 204
        Bruise and Other Injury Patterns 205
        Genital Examination 210
Evidence of Sexual Activity 211
    Semen and Sperm 212
    Saliva 213
    Fecal Matter 213
    Condoms 213
Clothing 214
False Positives: Conditions That Mimic Abuse 215
Toxicology 216
    Mental Incapacity 216
    Substance Abuse 217
Presentation of Findings 217
Endnotes 218
References 218

CHAPTER 9 Medicolegal Death Investigation: Protocols and Practice 221

Stan Crowder, Brent E. Turvey

Terms and Definitions 223
    Medicolegal 223
    Medicolegal Death Investigator 225
    Medical Doctor 225
    Medical Opinions 225
    Forensic Pathology 225
    Medical Examiner 226
    Coroner 226
    Autopsy 227
    Cause of Death 230
    Manner of Death 231
Protocols for Medicolegal Death Investigators 233
    Chain of Custody 233
    Death Investigation Protocols 236
Autopsy Protocols 249
    The National Academy of Sciences Report 249
The National Association of Medical Examiners
Standards 250
    Contents 255

Medicolegal Failures: A Top 10 List 256
Conclusion 258
Endnotes 259
References 259

CHAPTER 10 **Forensic Interviews...261**
Paul J. Ciolino, Brent E. Turvey
Terms and Definitions..262
Goals...263
Stakes and Consequences...264
Interview Preparation and Checklists...............................265
    Investigative Tasks Prior to Any Interview 266
Documentation and Recording 267
Interview Protocols..269
Generic Interview Questions: A Starter Kit 270
    General Interview Questions for All Witnesses 270
    Eyewitness Questions...270
    Alibi Witness Questions..271
Advice and Discussion 271
    Physical Evidence..272
    Conduct and Tone...272
    Investigator Dress and Presentation..............................272
    Promises 273
False Confessions 273
Continuing Education and Professional Development..........275
Endnotes 275
References..275

CHAPTER 11 **The Polygraph: Uses and Misuses 277**
Michael McGrath
The Test..278
Polygraph Research..280
Summary..289
Endnotes 290
References..291

CHAPTER 12 **Investigating Allegations of Police Torture: Forensic Protocols and Psychological Assessment 295**
Aurelio Coronado Mares, Brent E. Turvey
Prevalence..297
    Torture by Government Agents in Mexico.....................297
    Torture by Government Agents in the United States........302

Role of the Forensic Investigator 310
Defining Torture 312
Coercive Interrogation v. Torture 312
    Coercive Interrogation 313
    Torture: The Rationale 313
Behaviors Constituting Torture 314
Diagnostic Categories Related to Torture 315
The Psychological Effects and Impact of Torture 316
    Cognitive and Behavioral Manifestations 316
Torture: Forensic Interview Protocols for the Mental Health Professional 320
Conclusion 325
Endnotes 325
References 326

CHAPTER 13 Forensic Investigations for Court: Probation, Sentencing, Mitigation Issues in Capital Cases 329
Ronald J. Miller
Juvenile Court Probation Systems 330
Adult Probation 332
Capital Murder Mitigation Investigations 336
References 342

CHAPTER 14 Oklahoma v. Elvis Thacker: Evaluating Victimology, Victim Sexual Assault Evidence, Suspect Torture by Law Enforcement, and the Quality of a Forensic Investigation 343
Brent E. Turvey
The Plea and the Confession 345
The Evidence, the Confession, and Suspect Torture 345
The State of the Case 385
Endnotes 385

Index 387

List of Contributors

W. Jerry Chisum
California Department of Justice (ret.), Elk Grove, CA, United States

Paul J. Ciolino
Paul J. Ciolino and Associates, Inc., Chicago, IL, United States

Stan Crowder
Kennesaw State University, Georgia, GA, United States

Jodi Freeman
Forensic Solutions, LLC, Sitka, Alaska, United States; University of Western Ontario, London, ON, Canada

Charla Jamerson
Forensic Nurse, Fayetteville, AR, United States

Aurelio Coronado Mares
Forensic Psychologist, Cienca Aplicada, Aguascalientes, Mexico

Michael McGrath
Forensic Psychiatrist, Unity Healthy Systems, Rochester, NY, United States

Ronald J. Miller
Behavioral Forensics, Washington State, United States

Brent E. Turvey
Forensic Criminology Institute, Sitka, Alaska, United States and Aguascalientes, Mexico

Preface

Brent E. Turvey and Stan Crowder

> *If the law has made you a witness, remain a man of science. You have no victim to avenge, no guilty or innocent person to convict or save — you must bear testimony within the limits of science.*
> Dr. P.C.H. Brouardel, 19th-Century French Medicolegalist
> (quoted in Helpern, 1979, p. 66).

We have been friends and colleagues for almost 20 years. We have taught classes and seminars together; we have worked cases together; and this is our third textbook collaboration. It will not be our last.

Our personal and professional backgrounds could not be more different. One of us is a civilian forensic scientist; the other is a former military investigator. But we both teach and we both believe in the importance of leadership. We believe that our students are an investment for the future of the investigative and forensic community, as the best mechanism for change. Everything else we do is just cleanup: casework and analysis are written up after a crime has happened; lessons and protocols are written after mistakes have been made and after the damage has been done; and sometimes expert testimony is needed to explain it. We do these things, and they are made meaningful through their use in crafting lessons.

In teaching students, whether it is through textbooks, in the classroom, or by professional example, there is the opportunity to be proactive. There is the opportunity to tell them the future—and give them the tools to change it. That is why writing is so important to us. It lays down the mistakes of the past to render a roadmap for some of what will happen in the future.

The reason behind this current teaching volume, titled *Forensic Investigation*, is deceptively simple. It has to do with the changes in the law enforcement and forensic science communities. In short, the character of law enforcement has changed dramatically since the 1990s and the certainty of forensic science conclusions have been challenged and reigned in. Unfortunately, the courts, the public, and the ranks of criminal justice educators have failed to acknowledge these changes in a meaningful fashion. That is, if they are aware of them at all.[1]

---

[1] Suffice it to say that both professionals and regular citizens across the board are reading or comprehending less. Or they are hyperfocused on their own immediate environments without concern or appreciation for how global or national events effect them. Either way, they are less informed and less literate. This is a subject for another book entirely; one that need not be written because those it concerns would not likely read it or anything else.

A brief explanation is necessary, as any dedicated law enforcement professional will rise to defend the character in their particular agency and many state employed forensic personnel will immediately do the same.

A SHIFT IN LAW ENFORCEMENT CHARACTER

Through our casework and related experiences over the past two decades, we have witnessed and documented a decline in the character of those in law enforcement. This is owing to *negligent hiring* practices (e.g., the hiring of those with criminal records, little formal education, or a history of misconduct with other agencies and/or clear mental health issues); *negligent supervision* (e.g., refusal investigate complaints against officers; refusal to regiment drug testing; or just absentee management; see Crowder & Turvey, 2013); and *negligent retention* (e.g., refusal to suspend or terminate officers for continuous excessive use of force; sleeping with confidential informants and prostitutes; and other criminal violations, including evidence theft, drug trafficking, and illegal drug use; see Crowder & Turvey, 2015). We have also observed an influx of a former military into law enforcement, too often with untreated and even unidentified mental health issues. This to say nothing of the *Officer Shuffle*, and the problem of Gypsy Officers, which forces honest police to work alongside (and protect) criminals in uniform, or those that have been otherwise discredited (Gottschalk, 2011; Middleton-Hope, 2003; Shockley-Eckles, 2011; see also Chapter 12). And there is even a move within some police agencies to deprofessionalize and return to hiring those without a basic college education—ensuring substandard levels of legal, administrative, and ethical literacy. It is, without exaggeration, the unraveling of everything that was set in motion by August Vollmer more than a century ago to make law enforcement a trusted and respected occupation.

This context has created a reality in which law enforcement officers and investigators are documenting less, and doing less evidence-related inquiry, all for fear of what a complete and scientifically transparent forensic investigation might reveal. That reality is reflected in the findings of a 2016 audit of the frequently embattled Houston Police Department. Specifically, with respect to their Crime Scene Unit, the audit "found several deficiencies. Missteps included a lack of written documentation and overreliance on photographs; stopping short of fully investigating scenes because a homicide detective felt the crime scene unit had done 'enough'; and writing that something 'makes sense' because it matched the account of an officer who fired his gun" (Flynn, 2016). These tendencies, which become the norm for many police agencies nationwide, are not the hallmarks of competent, comprehensive, or scientific investigations. More importantly, they cannot provide a foundation for honest police work.

A SHIFT IN FORENSIC SCIENCE INTERPRETATIONS

The limits of evidence interpretation have always been understood by actual scientists (see generally Chisum & Turvey, 2005, 2011). In fact, that is how to identify a scientist. They are the first to admit and explain any limitations with their findings. It will be a part of their reports and conclusions.

However, the confidence of forensic science interpretations can fluctuate greatly when delivered by law enforcement—employed examiners. When a finding tends to help the prosecution, it is reported with great certainty—and even more so in later expert testimony. When a finding tends to erode or eradicate prosecution theories, it is too often minimized, if not ignored then made obscure (Kozinski, 2015; Turvey, 2013).

Recognition and acceptance of this reality was the reasoning behind a major finding of the National Academy of Sciences (NAS) Report on Forensic (Edwards & Gotsonis, 2009): that law enforcement and forensic science must be separated to preserve the objectivity, and trustworthiness, of the scientific endeavor. In other words, that law enforcement influence has had the tendency, and therefore the ongoing potential, to corrupt objective scientific findings. Whether or not this has been intentional is irrelevant. It has been going on for a long time, and it needs to stop.

Recommendations in the NAS Report, and revelations about false forensic testimony from FBI examiners over the past 30 years, led the Department of Justice to partner with the National Institute on Standards and Technology (NIST) to create a National Commission on Forensic Science. They in turn conducted a "Forensic Science Discipline Review," and recently published draft language regarding the majority of forensic science disciplines, with respect to the acceptable limits of findings, reporting, and related expert testimony (see DOJ, 2016). For example, with respect to latent prints, the following draft language has been suggested by the scientific community (Latent Print Discipline, 2016):

Statements Approved for Use in Latent Print Examination Testimony and/or Laboratory Reports

Identification

1. The examiner may state or imply that an identification *is the determination that two friction ridge prints originated from the same source because there is sufficient quality and quantity of corresponding information such that the examiner would not expect to see that same arrangement of features repeated in another source. While an* identification *to the absolute exclusion of all others is not supported by research, studies have shown that as more reliable features are found in agreement, it becomes less likely to find that same arrangement of features in a print from another source.*

Inconclusive

2. An examiner may state or imply that an inconclusive *result is the determination that there is insufficient quality and quantity of corresponding information such that the examiner is unable to identify or exclude the source of the print.*

Exclusion

3. An examiner may state or imply that an exclusion *is the determination that two friction ridge prints did not originate from the same source because there is sufficient quality and quantity of information in disagreement.*

Statements Not Approved For Use in Latent Print Examination Testimony and/or Laboratory Reports

Exclusion of All Other Sources

1. An examiner may not state or imply that two friction ridge prints originated from the same source to the absolute exclusion of all other sources.

Absolute or Numerical Certainty

2. An examiner may not state or imply a level of certainty in his/her conclusion that is absolute or numerically calculated.

Zero Error Rate

3. An examiner may not state or imply that the method used in performing a friction ridge print comparison has a zero error rate or is infallible.

In other words, latent print examiners may no longer state that a fingerprint match is a conclusive or absolute match, necessarily originating from a single or specific individual. They may say that a positive identification suggests a likely source, but not to the exclusion of all others. This is because there are no scientific research to support such a claim, and the error rates of examiners and their fingerprint examination methods must be taken into account.[2]

Similar language has been drafted for other forensic sciences as part of the Commission's "Forensic Science Discipline Review." They generally include requirements for clarity about the nature of tests and examinations performed; the limitations of those tests; and the clear acknowledgment that inconclusive results must be reported as findings—not buried as irrelevant (see DOJ, 2016).

That is to say, just about everything that the FBI and police-employed forensic scientists have been testifying to over the past century is fraught with overconfidence and error. And the scientific community has, at long last, stepped in to say "enough." Enough with the exaggerations; enough with the lack of transparency; and enough with the pretending that supporting research exists when it actually does not. In other words, enough with the lack of science in forensic science.

OUR GOALS

With the publication of this volume, we hope to give students a chance. As future professionals, we hope to give them a chance to recognize any limitations in the

---

[2]There is no way to overemphasize the significance of this single revelation to the forensic science community. Long the gold standard for forensic identifications, the problems with fingerprint comparisons are many and the public failures have been undeniable. There is, furthermore, supporting documentation and references for setting limits on interpretations with respect to each of the major forensic disciplines available at https://www.justice.gov/dag/forensic-science.

investigative and forensic geography within their corners of the justice system as they encounter them. And we hope to give them a chance to deal with them on some level. This volume can serve as a platform, or a framework, for scientific decision-making in that regard.

Professionals, whether they are new to forensic investigation or not, will find this volume of tremendous value as a map to the limitations, and questions, they will be confronted within forensic contexts. These limitations, and the issues they raise, are not going away. They are going to come up in response to reports, depositions, and expert testimony—past, present, and future. As attorneys become more attenuated, so will their efforts and cross-examination. The professional forensic operative must be prepared for this eventuality, and willful blindness is no longer an option.

Ultimately our goals are intended to serve the justice system through truth seeking. We believe that this is best accomplished through fact-based scientific investigations and testimony. This requires recognition and acceptance of the aforementioned issues and some careful study of them. It does not matter what readers want or choose to believe; in the forensic realm, what matters is the evidence and whether it supports those beliefs.

We proceed with these goals in mind.

REFERENCES

Chisum, W. J., & Turvey, B. (2005). *Crime Reconstruction* (1st ed.). San Diego: Elsevier Science.

Chisum, W. J., & Turvey, B. (2011). *Crime reconstruction* (2nd ed.). San Diego: Elsevier Science.

Crowder, W. S., & Turvey, B. (2013). *Ethical justice*. San Diego: Elsevier Science.

Crowder, W. S., & Turvey, B. (2015). *Anabolic steroid abuse in public safety personnel: A forensic manual*. San Diego: Elsevier Science.

DOJ. (2016). *"Forensic science" United States Dept. of Justice*. https://www.justice.gov/dag/forensic-science.

Edwards, H., & Gotsonis, C. (2009). *Strengthening forensic science in the United States: A path forward*. Washington, DC: National Academies Press.

Flynn, M. (2016). *HPD wants its crime scene unit back. Crime lab's civilian leadership says no*. Houston Press. http://www.houstonpress.com/news/hpd-wants-its-crime-scene-unit-back-crime-labs-civilian-leadership-says-no-8682790.

Gottschalk, P. (2011). Management challenges in law enforcement: the case of police misconduct and crime. *International Journal of Law and Management, 53*(3), 169–181.

Helpern, M. (1979). *Autopsy*. New York: Signet.

Kozinski, A. (2015). "Criminal Law 2.0" Georgetown law review. *Annual Review of Criminal Procedure, 44*, iii–xliv.

Latent Print Discipline. (2016). *Department of Justice: Proposed uniform language for testimony and reports for the forensic latent print discipline*. United States Dept. of Justice. https://www.justice.gov/dag/forensic-science.

Middleton-Hope, J. (2003). Misconduct among previously experienced officers: issues in the recruitment and hiring of gypsy cops. *Saint Louis University Public Law Review, 22*, 173–183.

Shockley-Eckles, M. (August 2011). Police culture and the perpetuation of the officer shuffle: the paradox of life behind 'the blue wall'. *Humanity & Society, 35*, 290–309.

Turvey, B. (2013). *Forensic fraud.* San Diego: Elsevier Science.

CHAPTER 1

Forensic Investigations: A Primer

Brent E. Turvey[1], Stan Crowder[2]
Forensic Criminology Institute, Sitka, Alaska, United States and Aguascalientes, Mexico[1];
Kennesaw State University, Georgia, GA, United States[2]

CHAPTER OUTLINE

Corpus Delicti 3
Forensic Necessity: Everybody Lies 5
The Forensic Investigator 7
    Forensic 7
    Forensic Science 8
    Forensic Scientists/Forensic Examiners 8
    Investigators/Investigations 9
    Forensic Investigators 10
    Data Integrity 10
Forensic Investigations: The Big Picture 11
Forensic Facts Versus Political Reality 12
Conclusions 16
Endnotes 16
References 17

The terms *forensic investigator* and *forensic investigation* are part of our cultural identity. They can be found in the news, on television, and in film. They are invoked, generally, to imply that highly trained personnel will be collecting some form of physical evidence with eventual scientific results that cannot be questioned or bargained with. In other words, they are invoked to imply the reliability, certainty, and authority of a scientific inquiry.

This can be a good thing, the authors would agree, when there are well-educated and properly trained professionals involved in the process. Primarily because everyone lies—some intentionally and some unintentionally, gathering and examining physical evidence is the only way to ensure that lies are exposed and kept from the gates of justice. As a mechanism for this effort, the forensic investigator is meant to be an objective truth seeker.

There are some problems, however. First, not everyone knows what these terms actually mean, so their use can be inappropriate or even misleading. This means there are those in the justice system using these terms to create a false impression about what has or will be done with the evidence.

Second, not everyone involved in the justice systems wants the facts or evidence on the record. As one gains experience with criminal investigation and the courts, one learns there are those who would prefer certain evidence not be documented, examined, or made public. Motives vary, including apathy, incompetence, politics, and fear of consequences (e.g., jail time, civil liability, or both). For those that might not appreciate the severity, or the reality of the problem, they need but reference the public facts relating to any one of the following national conditions:

- the existence of tens of thousands of unexamined rape kits in police custody (Reilly, 2015)[1];
- the frequency and timing with which law enforcement dash cams have been intentionally switched off, usually at key moments during police contact with civilians (Rubin, 2014);
- the frequency and timing with which officer body cams and audio have been intentionally disabled by those wearing them—to deliberately prevent a record from being created (Main & Dumpke, 2015);
- the intentional destruction of "decades of records" that detail law enforcement misconduct and disciplinary actions (Berg, 2015);
- the frequent refusal of law enforcement agencies to open criminal investigations into illegal steroid rings involving their own, and to mandate officer drug testing (see Crowder & Turvey, 2015).
- the continuous stream of cases involving police and prosecutorial misconduct related to lying about, hiding, or destroying evidence that should have been collected, preserved, or merely turned over to opposing counsel during criminal and civil proceedings (Kosinksi, 2015; Volokh, 2015).

For example, one of the authors (Turvey) testified as an expert during a sexual assault case in the State of Oregon[2]. The case involved negligent failure to collect, document, and test an array of physical evidence—let alone to attend or process the alleged crime scene in any real fashion (among many other investigative and forensic shortcomings). The judge in that case ruled that the police had no duty to conduct a forensic investigation at that level, and that there was subsequently no need for testimony from anyone to explain (and make a public record of) these deficiencies before the jury. The judge further ruled that the police had no duty to conduct a thorough investigation in accordance with policies outlined by the State of Oregon's Attorney General's Sexual Assault Task Force; and no duty to consider or collect evidence that might tend to bear on the defendant's innocence. Once an accusation of rape was made, the police were within their duties to assume it was true and move forward without considering the physical evidence. The author, testifying before the court under oath, asked the judge whether he intended to explain this ruling to the jury. And then the author asked why the state employed forensic scientists and operated crime labs if law enforcement had no such duty—what was the point if they could simply ignore all of the physical evidence? The judge did not answer, as was his privilege.

Such examples are just the tip of the iceberg, but they demonstrate how common the problem of evidence suppression is, even among those who swear an oath to ensure its identification and investigation.

These concerns have been ever present motivators in the authors' casework and teachings. They have also served to drive the completion of this project. Our belief is simple: as more people understand what a forensic investigation is, and what it requires, there will be fewer capable of abusing or ignoring the evidence that it puts on the record. We understand that this will take some explaining. And those readers who do not yet fully understand the landscape of what we have experienced in the justice system are about to.

The purpose of this textbook is to help students and professionals rid themselves of the myths and misconceptions they have accumulated regarding forensic investigators, and the subsequent forensic investigations they help to conduct. This text will help the reader understand the role of the forensic investigator; the nature and variety of forensic investigations that take place in the justice system; and the mechanisms by which such investigations become worthy as evidence in court. The goals are no more lofty than that. However, they could not be more necessary to our understanding of what justice is, how it is most reliably achieved, and how it can be corrupted by those who are burdened with apathy and alternative motives.

CORPUS DELICTI

The investigation of reported crimes is the statutory and jurisdictional province of law enforcement agencies; the agency in charge depends on which laws have been reported broken and where[3]. Nobody else has the legal authority to respond, interview witnesses and suspects, collect evidence, or make arrests in these cases. Consequently responding law enforcement agencies have a duty of care—an obligation to be competent custodians of the criminal investigations they initiate and any evidence that supports or refutes allegations of criminal activity against accused suspects.

Investigators may not assume what happened based on the statements of one party; they may not assume that a crime has actually occurred until the facts have been established; and they must impartially place the cuffs on anyone they determine has broken the law when their investigative work is complete. As explained in Bryden and Lengnick (1997, pp. 1230–1231):

> *As with all crimes, the police decide whether a reported rape actually occurred, and attempt to determine who committed it. If they want the case to go forward, they "found" the complaint and transmit the file to the prosecutor's office... The*

police must investigate, a task that cannot easily be combined with offering the emotional support that the victim needs. The detective presumably wishes to avoid an injustice to a wrongly accused individual. In addition, for reasons of professional pride, he does his best to avoid looking naive by falling for a story that turns out to be false. Experienced investigators also know that many rape complainants ultimately decline to press charges, sometimes to the dismay of a detective who has worked hard to build a case.

Meeting these responsibilities is best accomplished with a comprehensive investigation. By comprehensive investigation, the authors mean a detailed assessment of witness and suspect statements, along with the diligent collection and examination of any physical evidence. All of this must be completed before making determinations regarding whether a crime has been committed, and whether probable cause exists to arrest any suspects. Specifically they must establish the elements of the crime.

The corpus delicti, literally translated as "body of the crime," refers to those essential facts which demonstrate that a crime has taken place, not the criminal statute that has been broken. Rather, this is a reference to the facts, and the supporting evidence making up the elements of a crime. If there is no corpus delicti, there is no evidence of a crime, and there can be no arrests or criminal proceedings.

To establish the crime of burglary, for instance, a forensic analysis of the crime scene for physical evidence could include searching for items of evidence such as, but not limited to, the following:

- Tool marks and fingerprints at the point of entry
- Broken doors or windows
- Direction of the broken glass (inside or outside) to establish an element of scene staging
- Glass in the burglar's shoes and pants from broken glass at the scene
- Missing valuables found in the possession of the suspect
- Footwear impressions on the ground outside of the residence at the point of entry

To establish a rape or sexual assault, a forensic analysis of the crime scene for physical evidence could include searching for items of evidence such as, but not limited to, the following:

- The victim's blood at the crime scene
- The rapist's semen/sperm in the victim's mouth, vagina, or rectum
- A weapon with biological transfer evidence of some kind
- Wound patterns on the victim
- Torn items of victim clothing
- The rapist's pubic hair on the victim or vice versa

While none of the aforementioned proves that sexual assault must have occurred, they may be help support or refute different versions of events that may be provided in witness, victim, or suspect statements.

To establish the crime of homicide in a gunshot case, a forensic analysis of the crime scene for physical evidence could include searching for items of evidence such as, but not limited to, the following:

- The victim's body with a gunshot wound
- A projectile matching the suspect's gun found in the body or at the scene associated with the shooting
- The suspect's gun found in his or her possession or care
- Gunshot residue on the suspect's hands indicating that he or she fired a gun
- A determination of homicide as the result of a shooting incident reconstruction and the autopsy findings
- Security camera footage of the suspect shooting the victim

As becomes clear, it is a host of facts and evidence acting together which prove whether a crime actually occurred, and whether a given suspect is responsible. It is not just one thing. Consideration of the physical evidence is a vital part of that effort, and ignoring it is not just irresponsible, it is investigatively negligent.

FORENSIC NECESSITY: EVERYBODY LIES

The evidence gathered by forensic investigators is meant to provide the most reliable and objective record of the crime and any related activity (Chisum & Turvey, 2011). As explained in Kirk (1953, p. 4):

> *This is evidence that does not forget. It is not confused by the excitement of the moment. It is not absent because human witnesses are. It is factual evidence. Physical evidence cannot be wrong; it cannot perjure itself; it cannot be wholly absent. Only its interpretation can err.*

This is important because people get confused or forget details; they can be biased or pressured by external influences; and they can lie for personal or professional gain. This includes suspects, witnesses, and even victims. All are potential sources of false and misleading information which the investigator has a responsibility to identify and block.

The investigator must also be aware of the possibility that law enforcement reports and testimony can be similarly tainted, as detailed in the research compiled in Turvey (2013). Many criminal justice scholars make the argument that deception, and outright lying, are integral to law enforcement culture. One such view is presented in Slobogin (1997), which offers a continuum of falsity that runs from the somewhat justifiable to the utterly inexcusable (pp. 775–776):

> *Many police, like many other people, lie occasionally, and some police, like some other people, lie routinely and pervasively. Police lie to protect innocent victims, as in hostage situations, and they tell "placebo lies" to assure or placate worried citizens. They tell lies to project nonexistent authority, and they lie to suspects in*

the hopes of gathering evidence of crime. They also lie under oath, to convict the guilty, protect the guilty, or frame the innocent.

Some of these lies are justifiable. Some are reprehensible. Lying under oath is perjury and thus rarely permissible. On the other hand, lying that is necessary to save a life may not only be acceptable but is generally applauded (even if it constitutes perjury). Most types of police lies are of murkier morality, however.

A more chilling perspective of law enforcement deception is reported in the research compiled by Dorfman (1999, pp. 460–461):

Police officers can be expected to omit, redact, and even lie on their police reports, sworn or unsworn; they will conceal or misrepresent to cover up corruption and brutality; they are trained to deceive citizens during investigations as part of good police practice; they will obscure facts, and even lie, to cover up the misconduct of fellow officers. Additionally, command practice and policy gives officers every incentive to lie to cover for lack of productivity or to aggrandize themselves for recognition and promotion. And yes, police officers will commit perjury in our courts of law.

Perhaps the most damning account in recent years comes from Alex Kozinski, the chief judge of the United States Court of Appeals for the Ninth Circuit. He wrote of systemic failures in our justice system across the board sparing none. He argued that one of the myths on which our justice system is predicated is that law enforcement agencies "are objective in their investigations" (2015; p. x). He went on to explain that this "bedrock assumption" of the justice system is has been all but eroded (pp. x–xi):

Police investigators have vast discretion about what leads to pursue, which witnesses to interview, what forensic tests to conduct and countless other aspects of the investigation. Police also have a unique opportunity to manufacture or destroy evidence, influence witnesses, extract confessions and otherwise direct the investigation so as to stack the deck against people they believe should be convicted. And not just small-town police in Podunk or Timbuktu. Just the other day, "[t]he Justice Department and FBI formally acknowledged that nearly every examiner in an elite FBI forensic unit gave flawed testimony in almost all [of the 268] trials in which they offered evidence against criminal defendants over more than a two-decade period before 2000." Do they offer a class at Quantico called "Fudging Your Results To Get A Conviction" or "Lying On The Stand 101"? How can you trust the professionalism and objectivity of police any-where after an admission like that?

There are countless documented cases where innocent people have spent decades behind bars because the police manipulated or concealed evidence, but two examples will suffice:

In 2013, Debra Milke was released after 23 years on Arizona's death row based entirely on a supposed oral confession she had made to one Detective Saldate *who was much later shown to be a serial liar. And then there is the case of Ricky Jackson, who spent 39 years behind bars based entirely on the eyewitness identification of a 12-year-old boy who saw the crime from a distance and failed to pick Jackson out of a lineup. At that point, "the officers began to feed him information: the number of assailants, the weapon used, the make and model of the getaway car."*

Working in the justice system, the authors encounter these kinds of circumstances every day, if not every hour. Eventually the experienced forensic operative learns not to take anyone at their word. Not supervisors, not colleagues, not friends, and none of those involved in their casework. They learn the most important components of a forensic investigation are well-honed critical thinking skills and a healthy dose of skepticism. As explained in Brookfield (1987), critical thinking requires strict adherence to logical analysis, and the discipline to scrutinize the strengths, weaknesses, and overall rationality of all arguments and assertions. It also requires (p. 6) "continual questioning of assumptions"; (p. 8) "challenging the importance of context"; (p. 9) "imagining and exploring alternatives" and "reflective skepticism"; and (pp. 11–12) "the ability to distinguish bias from reason and fact from opinion." Critical thinking necessitates doubt and proof, no matter the source of data or the strength of assertions about the integrity of findings.

This mind-set is a good scientific practice, and therefore it is a necessity for the successful completion of any forensic investigation.

THE FORENSIC INVESTIGATOR

Scientific truths can only be revealed by the examination of facts in the context of reality. There are no shortcuts. This is the challenge of the forensic investigator: to help emancipate justice by providing facts, information, and context to forensic examiners and to the court.

It is at this point where we encounter a barrier to scientific truth—the confusion of roles and goals within the criminal justice community. Forensic investigators are NOT necessarily forensic scientists; and consequently they are NOT necessarily qualified to interpret the evidence. This will likely come as a surprise to many poorly educated and improperly trained forensic personnel.

To ensure that justice is served, these kinds of limitations must be made clear when present, otherwise there is confusion and the potential for injustice. Consequently the following terms and definitions must be attended with great care, and not used as synonyms. They mean, and imply, very different things.

FORENSIC

In a legal context, the term *forensic* means court[4]. It is not a reference to *science* or anything *scientific* necessarily[5]. However, this is sometimes what the use of the term is intended to imply. The term forensic is merely a descriptor, meaning whatever profession or subject matter comes next is intended to be of and for the courtroom.

To be more precise, a forensic analysis and a scientific analysis are not always the same thing. This is because not all forensic analyses are scientific (e.g., conducted in accordance with the scientific method, established scientific principles, and the published literature). However, all forensic analyses are conducted in anticipation of courtroom admissibility. Otherwise the descriptor forensic would not apply.

Consider the Police Practices Expert, often used in court to give expert testimony regarding law enforcement policies and procedures. They are allowed to provide forensic opinions regarding whether the policies in place within a given agency were adequate, whether they were properly followed, and whether related officer training was sufficient. Such an expert is employed to conduct a forensic analysis of the governing policies, facts, and evidence relating to cases of wrongful officer termination; whistleblowing; in-custody deaths; and officer use of force—to name but a few.

Analyses conducted under such circumstances are not governed by scientific techniques or principles, but rather by the expert's education, training, research, and experience with the subject matter in question. They can be qualified by the court as an expert simply by virtue of their knowledge and repetition with analogous facts and circumstances. This was established in *United States v. Romero* (1999), a ruling which recognizes that expert testimony from experienced investigators has proven to be useful to juries in cases containing certain fact patterns. Expertise from experience combined with helpfulness is the basis for this kind of courtroom admissibility—without addressing the scientific validity of the expertise.

Again, this is still a forensic analysis because it is done with the expectation of expert courtroom testimony.

FORENSIC SCIENCE

Forensic science is the application of scientific methodology, knowledge, and principles to the resolution of legal questions, whether criminal or civil (Chisum & Turvey, 2011; Houck & Seigal, 2010; James & Nordby, 2003; Saferstein, 2010; Thornton & Peterson, 2007). This definition, generally consistent across the forensic science literature, is intentionally broad. There are, in fact, many different forensic subdisciplines, including (but certainly not limited to) criminalistics, crime reconstruction, forensic pathology, forensic anthropology, forensic toxicology, forensic entomology, forensic mental health (psychology and psychiatry), and forensic criminology (Chisum & Turvey, 2011; Houck & Seigal, 2010; James & Nordby, 2003; Saferstein, 2010; Seigel, Saukko, & Knupfer, 2000; Turvey & Petherick, 2010).

FORENSIC SCIENTISTS/FORENSIC EXAMINERS

The terms *forensic examiner* and *forensic scientist* will be used interchangeably throughout this text. They generally refer to any professional who examines and interprets facts, evidence, or data with the expectation of courtroom testimony. As explained in Turvey (2011; p. xxii):

Criminal investigators are tasked with serving the criminal justice system by establishing the objective facts and evidence of a given case. Forensic examiners are tasked with analyzing the evidence and interpreting the facts objectively.

Forensic examiners are defined by the fact that they anticipate courtroom testimony. As explained in Thornton and Peterson (2007, p. 3):

The single feature that distinguishes forensic scientists from any other scientist is the certain expectation that they will appear in court and testify to their findings and offer an opinion as to the significance of those findings. The forensic scientist will testify not only to what things are, but to what things mean.

This provides that forensic scientists do not just test or examine evidence and then record the results; they are meant to explore, understand, and explain its significance to an attorney, judge, or jury. The defining quality of forensic examiners is the possibility that they will be called on to present their findings, under penalty of perjury, in a court of law. Subsequently they will be asked to explain to the court what those findings mean and how they came to them. This can be as straightforward as recording information about drug identifications, weights, and cash amounts; or it can be as complex as reconstructing a crime scene and determining cause and manner of death.

Forensic examiners, therefore, exist across a broad spectrum of professions. This would include criminalists and other forensic scientists such as forensic pathologists, forensic toxicologists, firearm and tool mark examiners, crime reconstructionists, criminal profilers, forensic criminologists, forensic psychologists, and even forensic victimologists.

INVESTIGATORS/INVESTIGATIONS

An *investigator* is someone who is charged with carrying out a formal inquiry. This may be done on behalf of a law enforcement agency or the judiciary, where the designation is also a job title or rank; it may be done on behalf of a private company; or it may be done on behalf of private citizens. The investigators' role in this regard is dictated by their client or their employer, and the work they do is not necessarily conducted with the anticipation of public disclosure.

An *investigation* is a systematic or directed inquiry into a person, group, organization, or question. In the broadest sense, it involves the formation and asking of questions; and the collection of statements and physical or documentary evidence that might help to answer them. There are subsequently criminal investigators and criminal investigations; there are administrative investigators and administrative investigations; and there are private investigators and private investigations. As will be discussed throughout this work, each is conducted by a different kind of investigator, with specific roles and obligations, under specific employment conditions.

FORENSIC INVESTIGATORS

Forensic investigators are those with the ability to ensure that the statements, recordings, and/or evidence they collect will be sufficiently reliable for the forensic examiner to analyze. They attend all the details necessary to provide what the scientific community refers to as data integrity.

Subsequently the forensic investigator ensures their evidence and eventual analytical findings will be admissible in court. They provide what the forensic scientists need to conduct their examinations in good faith. The scientific community calls it *data integrity*, but it is referred to in the forensic sciences as a *chain of custody*[6].

DATA INTEGRITY

Data integrity is required because scientists of every kind are prohibited from blindly accepting what they are told by anyone. They have an obligation to be critical and openly skeptical of everything they find. The importance of this scientific reality is explained in Gardenier (2011, p. 3):

> *[a]nalytic methodology cannot be divorced from the data. Both must be specifically congruent in structure, relevance, and assumptions. Even more important than any measure of confidence or significance in the output is the logic that the conclusions follow from the data…*
>
> *Scientists may mistakenly consider it an ethical obligation to accept data from colleagues or superiors for statistical analysis without detailed attention to all of the considerations above. That is incorrect. Without data integrity, it is impossible to achieve research integrity.*

Data integrity is not a suggestion. It is a scientific requirement. It must be earned and established at all junctures, never to be presumed. When weaknesses are identified with the evidence, they must be acknowledged, considered, and then reported as a function of limits set against any reliable interpretation. Not side-stepped, ignored, or denied.

Data integrity is provided in forensic investigations by virtue of demonstrating trustworthy character along with a solid chain of custody for any evidence that is being offered. Government agencies and the judiciary tend to have a zero-tolerance policy with respect to bad character, false testimony, and lying. This means they are likely to terminate anyone who is shown to have made false statements, or to have given false evidence, in the course of dispatching their official duties. This includes those engaged in criminal activity. Those who lie to investigators and the court cannot be trusted to give evidence under oath—which is a central investigative function. As explained in Noble (2003, p. 101): "In law enforcement, there are no second chances when it comes to the integrity of our officers and ourselves. In law enforcement, malicious deceptive conduct is untenable and cannot be tolerated at any level in the organization."

FORENSIC INVESTIGATIONS: THE BIG PICTURE

A *forensic investigation* is one that is conducted to address case-related questions about the evidence, and then meet the challenges of courtroom admissibility. The forensic investigation is every part of the inquiry; it includes the work of all forensic professionals, including investigators and examiners alike. It includes the following component parts:

1. Crime scene investigation (evidence collection, examination and reconstruction)
2. Forensic interviews
3. Forensic victimology
4. Medicolegal investigation (e.g., sexual assault examination, toxicology, and/or autopsy)
5. Crime lab analysis (e.g., criminalistics)
6. Forensic mental health assessments

Forensic investigators recognize, document, collect, preserve, and even transport evidence to forensic examiners so they can do the work of examination and interpretation. That is the nature of the relationship. The quality and reliability of one depends entirely on that of the other. As described in Edwards and Gotsonis (2009, p. 55):

> *Forensic investigations involve intelligence and information gathering, crime scene investigation, laboratory analysis, interpretation of tests and results, and reporting and communication with members of law enforcement and the judicial system. Law enforcement agencies within the United States vary in organizational structure regarding how forensic science examinations are conducted and evidence is admitted into court... Variations are attributable to the geographical size and population served by the jurisdictional authority, the types and level of crimes encountered, the funding source, and local tradition. In general, however, the forensic science community includes crime scene investigators; state and local crime laboratories; medical examiners; private forensic laboratories; law enforcement identification units; resources such as registries and databases; professional organizations; prosecutors and defense attorneys; quality system providers (i.e., accrediting and certifying organizations); and federal agencies that conduct or support research as well as provide forensic science services and training.*

For example, a medical examiner's office will employ forensic investigators. These investigators are charged with attending the death scene on behalf of the medical examiner taking photographs and recording their observations. They do this on behalf of the medical examiner; so the medical examiner does not have to do it themselves; so that the medical examiner can focus on the larger picture. The forensic investigator gathers information and evidence; the medical examiner examines everything together, including autopsy-related findings and provides interpretations. Both may be called to testify in court, to verify the nature and quality of their work.

But only the medical examiner is a scientist, and only the medical examiner is going to be qualified as a forensic expert and then allowed to give interpretations.

By contrast, consider the misnomer "forensic polygraph examination," which is often used by polygraph examiners. The reality is that the results of a polygraph examination are, across the board, unreliable because they have no scientific basis. This is why polygraph results are generally not admissible in court during the guilt phase of a trial[7]. Consequently use of the term "forensic" in association with the term "polygraph" is highly misleading, if not potentially fraudulent—at least in the United States.

As we have made clear in this and following chapters, forensic investigations are not minor tasks. They must be attended with every ounce of ethics and seriousness that the forensic investigator can bring to bear, and they do not generally survive incompetence or apathy. At least not in the long term.

FORENSIC FACTS VERSUS POLITICAL REALITY

Forensic investigation is about documenting and revealing facts that establish truths, both inconsequential and horrific. However, many forensic investigators work for elected officials, or those appointed by elected officials. This means they are susceptible to pressure. Pressure to conform to a political landscape that may be adverse to revealing the unblemished evidence in their custody.

Consequently honest forensic investigators working for the government can, from time to time, feel the squeeze. Sometimes, under this kind of pressure, they can be compelled by supervisors and prosecutors to overlook evidence; to change the words or confidence used describe evidence; to leave observations and evidence out of reports entirely; or maybe to just shove evidence in a drawer and hope that nobody ever asks about it. This is not a remote or even an unlikely scenario.

Consider the FBI—heralded around the world as being the gold standard in both criminal and forensic investigations. In 2015, the United States Department of Justice admitted what the independent forensic science community had been reporting for decades. FBI agents had been giving false forensic testimony to help prosecutors secure convictions against innocent defendants for years. This was not one bad apple, but almost all of the FBI's forensic examiners that had ever given expert testimony regarding hair comparison evidence, as reported in Hsu (2015):

> *The Justice Department and FBI have formally acknowledged that nearly every examiner in an elite FBI forensic unit gave flawed testimony in almost all trials in which they offered evidence against criminal defendants over more than a two-decade period before 2000.*
>
> *Of 28 examiners with the FBI Laboratory's microscopic hair comparison unit, 26 overstated forensic matches in ways that favored prosecutors in more than 95 percent of the 268 trials reviewed so far, according to the National Association*

> of Criminal Defense Lawyers (NACDL) and the Innocence Project, which are assisting the government with the country's largest post-conviction review of questioned forensic evidence.
>
> The cases include those of 32 defendants sentenced to death. Of those, 14 have been executed or died in prison, the groups said under an agreement with the government to release results after the review of the first 200 convictions…
>
> The admissions mark a watershed in one of the country's largest forensic scandals, highlighting the failure of the nation's courts for decades to keep bogus scientific information from juries, legal analysts said.

Clearly this was not a mistake, but rather these consistently "overstated" confidence levels with respect to hair evidence were policy, dictated by lab supervisors. And it took many years of external investigation to force the FBI to come clean, taking a serious hit to their public image and global forensic clout.

Consider further the scandal at Washington DC Department of Forensic Sciences Crime Lab. The 220 million dollar facility was opened in 2012. Early on, the lab's director, retired FBI agent Max Houck, publicly denied any problems with his lab's procedures or with the quality of his people. Then he was abruptly forced to resign and two of his supervisors were "let go." As reported in Alexander and Zauzmer (2015):

> The embattled director of the District's first independent DNA lab resigned Thursday, a week after two audits found that the lab's procedures were inadequate, thereby forcing a national accreditation body to suspend all of the lab's DNA testing.
>
> Max M. Houck has been the director of the District's Department of Forensic Sciences since the lab opened its $220 million facility in Southwest Washington three years ago.
>
> In addition to Houck's resignation, two other senior officials, the chief scientist for the lab and the senior manager for DNA testing, were let go…
>
> Last week, the ANSI-ASQ National Accreditation Board determined in its audit that analysts at the lab were "not competent and were using inadequate procedures." The authors of the audit, which was ordered by the District, gave the lab 30 days to address the concerns…
>
> Prosecutors stopped sending DNA evidence to the lab earlier this year.
>
> Houck had a year and a half left in his four-year contract with the city as director of the lab.
>
> Local prosecutors have ordered the review of 182 cases as a result of the errors they said they discovered in the lab's DNA results. Prosecutors, as well as the accreditation board, had problems with the interpretation in DNA mixtures cases, those in which more than one person's DNA is present in the evidence.

> It remains unclear how many cases have been affected by the lab's problems. The prosecutors said the errors have not resulted in the dismissal of any cases or in any exonerations…
>
> In a brief interview Thursday, Houck praised his colleagues at the lab and called them the "finest people" he had ever worked with. He also said the employees were doing the "best-quality work" they can do with "the resources that they are given." He declined to elaborate.
>
> Houck has repeatedly defended the lab's operations, even after prosecutors said they found numerous flaws in the analyses. Houck argued that his lab technicians followed the same protocol that many city and state labs across the country use in interpreting evidence…
>
> The audit by the DNA-lab accreditation board criticized the D.C. lab's practices as not in compliance with FBI standards. It ordered "at a minimum" the revalidation of test procedures, new interpretation guidelines for select DNA cases, additional training and competency testing of the staff.

One could argue that this is a case reflecting a failure of leadership and examiner training, resulting in a much needed change. However, according to a member of the Scientific Advisory Board for Washington DC's Department of Forensic Science, this was the result of political pressure. The board member, Jay Siegel, sent in a letter of resignation in response to the lab shake-up alleged just that, as reported in Fatzick (2015):

> In the letter obtained by The DCNF, Jay Siegel called the recent firing of administration members at the lab "hasty and unwarranted," and alleged scientific issues had little to do with it.
>
> Max Houck, who had been the director of the lab since it opened three years ago was allowed to resign, though two other top officials, the chief scientist for the lab and the senior DNA testing manager, were fired.
>
> Siegel told The DCNF he believes the closing of the lab and the firing of top management personnel was purely political, because Mayor Muriel Bowser and prosecutors in the United States Attorney's Office for the District of Columbia couldn't control what happened in the laboratory…
>
> At issue was the protocols the lab used when interpreting DNA data to determine matches, which Siegel told The DCNF were "quite esoteric and quite controversial."
>
> "It is well known in the forensic science community that there are no standards for the statistical interpretation of such mixtures," Siegel wrote in his resignation letter. "The DNA unit of the DC Forensic Science Laboratory was using methods that represent a consensus among many forensic science DNA units nationwide."

Only time will tell the truth, which will ultimately be forced into the light by either civil litigation from one of the terminated lab employees, or via testimony from one of the analysts that is compelled as part of their work on a criminal matter. Either way, this was pressure from above being exerted on forensic evidence and its interpretation, to influence the forensic investigation into fact.

Consider also recent revelations from the Michigan State Police Crime Lab. Prosecutors are reported to have exerted pressure on forensic examiners to report their findings with specific language. This resulted in a lab policy change with respect to forensic interpretations that allows prosecutors to levy felonies instead of misdemeanors, as reported and discussed in Neher (2016):

In 2013, the Michigan State Police quietly changed a policy at its crime labs.

It instructed its lab technicians to change how they handle samples containing THC. That's the chemical in marijuana responsible for its psychological effects.

It used to be that if it was obvious that a crime lab sample came from a marijuana plant, the lab report would say that. Now, unless there's visible plant material in the sample, the lab must say the origin is unknown.

That's important. It means prosecutors can pursue felony charges because they can argue in court that the drugs police found are synthetic. Possessing synthetic THC carries tougher penalties than possessing marijuana from a plant. It's the difference between a felony and a misdemeanor…

A number of forensic scientists are now speaking out against the policy, saying there's no way most or any of the samples in question contain synthetic THC.

"It is unreasonable to make any qualifying statements that this stuff might be synthetic. It is not a reasonable scientific conclusion that one could reach," said Dr. Jay Siegel, a professor emeritus of forensic science at Michigan State University who has worked in crime labs across the country.

Siegel also instructed many technicians in the State Police crime lab, including its current director who oversaw the implementation of the THC policy. He says samples that come from marijuana hold obvious clues — such as other chemicals that come from marijuana plants. He says those would be extremely difficult if not impossible to create in a lab — and there's no reason anyone would want to.

Siegel says the only explanation he can come up with for the policy change is political pressure. "And if that's the case, that's deplorable. All the things I ever taught those students was that you have to be a scientist here. You have to be true to the science and not the political or any other kind of pressure," he said.

The former director of the state crime lab agrees. "You're really getting into an ugly area that really gets into professional ethics as far as the reporting of testing results. And my understanding is, having looked at this, is that that line was crossed," said John Collins, who is also a former student of Siegel's.

Collins says he quit as head of the crime lab in part because of what he calls "tremendous" pressure from prosecutors to present evidence in a way that's beneficial to them. "There are some that really I think view forensic science as being a prosecution business as opposed to a science business," he said.

What these examples demonstrate is the political landscape of forensic evidence and the overall struggle for control of forensic investigations by those hoping to abuse them.

As will be discussed in subsequent chapters, it takes an unyielding commitment to professional ethics to resist this kind of pressure. And there are many other temptations awaiting the forensic investigator yet to be considered.

CONCLUSIONS

The forensic investigators understand what they need to do to identify, document, collect, and preserve forensic evidence of all kinds—and to do so in a fashion that ensures its reliability and admissibility. They also understand they will be challenged, from all sides, which they embrace because this is how it should be. It also means they are capable of giving courtroom testimony to explain the nature of their evidence and why it should be trusted by anyone.

The forensic investigator serves as one component within the overall forensic investigation, ensuring evidence with the requisite integrity to allow forensic examinations. They are not necessarily scientists, and they are not necessarily experts qualified to make interpretations. However, they must have sufficient good character to give sworn reports, affidavits, and testimony. In this way, their work serves to establish or refute the elements of the crime, otherwise referred to as the corpus delicti.

The overall forensic investigation is vital to the mission of truth seeking, because the forensic evidence does not lie. Moreover, gathering and examining forensic evidence is the only way to ensure that false information is exposed, and ultimately kept from the gates of justice. The forensic evidence, the forensic investigator, and the forensic examinations are all linked in the service of these objectives.

ENDNOTES

1. To say nothing of the number of times that a rape kit is not collected when it should be.
2. *Oregon v. Kevin Driscoll*; the jury ultimately found the defendant innocent of any and all charges—in large part due to the forensic and investigative failings detailed in a report provided by the author to the defense. That and the demonstrably false statements of the accuser in light of the known physical evidence.
3. This section is adapted from Savino and Turvey (2012).
4. This term is not to be confused with the subject of "forensics," which relates to the art of arguing and debating, with no relationship to the issues of courtroom admissibility or expertise. Most people

confuse the terms, and this is a quick way to distinguish those who are properly educated and trained as forensic practitioners from those who are not.
5. The relationship between forensic investigators, science, and the scientific method will be detailed in Chapter 4: Forensic Investigators and the Scientific Method.
6. This cornerstone concept of forensic investigations will be discussed in subsequent chapters.
7. Specific problems with the polygraph will be discussed in Chapter 13: The Polygraph: Use and Abuse.

REFERENCES

Alexander, K., & Zausma, J. (April 30, 2015). *Director of D.C.'s embattled DNA lab resigns after suspension of testing*. Washington Post. https://www.washingtonpost.com/local/director-of-dcs-embattled-dna-lab-resigns-following-suspension-of-testing/2015/04/30/1c619320-ef80-11e4-8666-a1d756d0218e_story.html.

Berg, A. (December 14, 2015). *Chicago police unions fight to destroy decades of records*. The Rock River Times. http://rockrivertimes.com/2015/12/14/chicago-police-unions-fight-to-destroy-decades-of-records/.

Brookfield, S. (1987). *Developing Critical Thinkers*. San Francisco: Jossey-Bass.

Bryden, D., & Lengnick, S. (Summer 1997). Rape in the criminal justice system. *Journal of Criminal Law and Criminology, 87*, 1194−1384.

Chisum, W. J., & Turvey, B. (2011). *Crime reconstruction* (2nd ed.). San Diego: Elsevier Science.

Crowder, W. S., & Turvey, B. (2015). *Anabolic steroid abuse in public safety personnel: A forensic manual*. San Diego: Elsevier Science.

Dorfman, D. (1999). Proving the lie: litigating police credibility. *American Journal of Criminal Law, 26*, 455−503.

Edwards, H., & Gotsonis, C. (2009). *Strengthening forensic science in the United States: A path forward*. Washington, DC: National Academies Press.

Fatzick, J. (May 27, 2015). *DC adviser resigns claiming massive foul play in DNA lab management firings*. The Daily Caller. http://dailycaller.com/2015/05/27/dc-adviser-resigns-claiming-massive-foul-play-in-dna-lab-management-firings/.

Gardenier, J. (2011). Data integrity is earned, not given. *Office of Research Integrity Newsletter, 19*(3), 3.

Houck, M., & Seigal, J. (2010). *Fundamentals of forensic science* (2nd ed.). San Diego: Elsevier Science.

Hsu, S. (April 18, 2015). *FBI admits flaws in hair analysis over decades*. The Washington Post. https://www.washingtonpost.com/local/crime/fbi-overstated-forensic-hair-matches-in-nearly-all-criminal-trials-for-decades/2015/04/18/39c8d8c6-e515-11e4-b510-962fcfabc310_story.html.

James, S., & Nordby, J. (2003). *Forensic science: An introduction to scientific and investigative techniques*. Boca Raton, FL: CRC Press.

Kirk, P. (1953). *Crime investigation*. New York, NY: Interscience.

Kosinski, A. (2015). Criminal law 2.0. *Georgetown Law Review, Annual Review of Criminal Procedure, 44*, iii−xliv.

Main, F., & Dumpke, M. (December 19, 2015). *22 police shootings in Chicago this year — and no audio in any*. Chicago Sun-Times. http://chicago.suntimes.com/news/7/71/1190969/22-police-shootings-audio.

Neher, J. (January 18, 2016). *Forensic scientists blast State Police crime lab THC policy as man fights to get son back*. Michigan Radio. http://michiganradio.org/post/forensic-scientists-blast-state-police-crime-lab-thc-policy-man-fights-get-son-back#stream/0.

Noble, J. (2003). Police officer truthfulness and the Brady decision. *The Police Chief, 70*(10), 92—101.

Reilly, S. (July 16, 2015). *Tens of thousands of rape kits go untested across USA*. USA Today. http://www.usatoday.com/story/news/2015/07/16/untested-rape-kits-evidence-across-usa/29902199/.

Rubin, J. (April 07, 2014). *LAPD officers tampered with in-car recording equipment, records show*. Los Angeles Times. http://articles.latimes.com/2014/apr/07/local/la-me-lapd-tamper-20140408.

Saferstein, R. (2010). *Criminalistics: An introduction to forensic science* (10th ed.). Upper Saddle River, NJ: Prentice Hall.

Savino, J., & Turvey, B. (2012). *Rape investigation handbook* (2nd ed.). San Diego: Elsevier Science.

Seigel, J., Saukko, P., & Knupfer, G. (2000). *The encyclopedia of forensic science* (Vols. 1—3). London: Academic Press.

Slobogin. (Winter 1997). Deceit, pretext, and trickery: investigative lies by the police. *Oregon Law Review, 76*, 775—816.

Thornton, J., & Peterson, J. (2007). The general assumptions and rationale of forensic identification. In D. Faigman, D. Kaye, M. Saks, & J. Sanders (Eds.), *Modern scientific evidence: The law and science of expert testimony* (Vol. 1). St. Paul, MN: West Publishing Group.

Turvey, B., & Petherick, W. (2010). An Introduction to Forensic Criminology. In B. Turvey, W. Petherick, & C. Ferguson (Eds.), *Forensic Criminology*. San Diego: Elsevier Science.

Turvey, B. (2011). *Criminal profiling: An introduction to behavioral evidence analysis* (4th ed.). San Diego: Elsevier Science.

Turvey, B. (2013). *Forensic fraud*. San Diego: Elsevier Science.

United States v. Romero (1999) 189 F.3d 576, 584, 7th Circuit.

Volokh, E. (July 17, 2015). *Judge Kozinski on reforms that can help prevent prosecutorial misconduct*. The Washington Post. https://www.washingtonpost.com/news/volokh-conspiracy/wp/2015/07/17/judge-kozinski-on-reforms-that-can-help-prevent-prosecutorial-misconduct/.

CHAPTER

Law and Evidence[1]

2

Brent E. Turvey
Forensic Criminology Institute, Sitka, Alaska, United States and Aguascalientes, Mexico

CHAPTER OUTLINE

The Pillars of the Criminal Justice System 20
    Academia 21
    Law Enforcement 21
    Forensic Services 21
    The Judiciary 22
    Corrections 22
The Adversarial System 23
    The Prosecution 23
    The Defense...23
Scientific Fact Versus Legal Truth 24
Experts, Evidence, and Admissibility 26
    Evidence 26
    Chain of Custody 27
    Expert Evidence 27
        The Federal Rules of Evidence 28
Constitutional Rights 30
    The Right to Due Process 31
    Brady v. Maryland (1963) 33
    The Right to "Effective" Counsel 35
Conclusion 41
Endnotes 41
References 41

Justice, in a legal sense, is the result of forging the rights of individuals with the government's corresponding duty to ensure and protect those rights. Legal justice is intended to be the proper administration of due process and the law, with the equal, fair, and impartial treatment of all individuals by agents of the justice system. Lady Justice, a Greco-Roman blend of the goddesses of justice, is commonly used to symbolize these ideals. She holds the balanced scales of truth and fairness in her right hand and a double-edged sword in her left that is never sheathed. She is also blindfolded, representing the promise to rule dispassionately—without influence from personal feelings, beliefs, politics, or money.

The sword of justice is meant to swing when compelled by admitted *evidence*; facts and information which combine to validate or repudiate legal arguments, properly accepted by the court. The evidence is collected by investigators and forensic professionals; it is collated by attorneys attempting to craft legal positions; and it is evaluated by the court for admissibility before being seen or heard by a jury. Sometimes evidence is introduced by itself (e.g., a document, a recording; or a photograph); sometimes it must be accompanied by expert testimony; and sometimes it is excluded for lack of relevance, reliability, or authenticity.

The purpose of this chapter is to discuss the relationship of the courtroom, and the law, to evidence. This will require a discussion of the structure and function of the justice system, and the role of the court with respect to admitting or excluding evidence. It will conclude with discussions of related constitutional rights and legal rulings.

THE PILLARS OF THE CRIMINAL JUSTICE SYSTEM

The criminal justice system is a network of government and private agencies charged with the management of accused and convicted criminals. It also includes agencies meant to provide basic assistance to crime victims, in terms of legal protection, financial aid, and medical care. However, victim assistance is not a guarantee.[2]

The criminal justice system is frequently described as being composed of "agencies responsible for enforcing criminal laws, including legislatures, police, courts, and corrections" (Reid, 2003, p. 355). A similar portrayal is offered in Sullivan (1977, p. 157): "The general view of criminal justice reflects a system of three separately organized functions: the police, the courts, and corrections. Each has a distinct role, yet they are interrelated." These and similar explanations, while they are somewhat accurate and representative of the literature, are prosecution oriented. As such, they fail to account for the full balance of professionals responsible for ensuring justice in an adversarial system.

A prosecutorial point of view dominates the criminal justice landscape. Consequently texts and courses on the subject have not, historically, acknowledged the value of the many components of the criminal justice system that are not aligned with law enforcement or the prosecution. In some instances, these elements have been neglected entirely. That is to say, the literature tends to gloss over, or ignore, the necessary roles fulfilled by academia, the legal defense community, and private or independent forensic examiners working in and for the criminal justice system. This leaves students uninformed and unprepared.

In reality, the modern criminal justice system consists of the following major interrelated and interdependent pillars: academia, law enforcement, forensic services, the judiciary, and corrections. This is in accordance with the US Constitution and related court rulings.

ACADEMIA

Academia is the pillar of the criminal justice system comprised of those criminal justice researchers and educators working in colleges, universities, academies, and institutions around the world—anywhere that criminal justice professionals seek information, knowledge, formal education, or specific training. These researchers and educators combine to form a vital support for those employed by or seeking employment within the criminal justice system. At their best, they provide coordinated knowledge and structured learning to those who seek it, often to fit the needs of a particular agency, profession, or community.

Although disorganized in many circles, and routinely neglected, this pillar has been and remains essential to the professional development and overall effectiveness of those employed in the criminal justice system (Edwards & Gotsonis, 2009; Morn, 1995; Vollmer, 1971).

LAW ENFORCEMENT

Law enforcement is the pillar of the criminal justice system that deals with reported crime. Law enforcement agencies are intended to enforce the law—to ensure that citizens act lawfully and to investigate the nature and extent of unlawful acts (Vollmer, 1971). In this capacity they serve as "peace officers," preventing or deterring crime and generally working to keep the peace (see, generally, Kleinig, 1996). However, they are also obligated to investigate any criminal complaints and establish the events that actually caused it to happen in the first place (Savino & Turvey, 2011). When the agents of law enforcement believe a crime has been committed, they are obligated to investigate, identify and arrest available suspects. In some cases this will also involve the recognition, collection, storage, and transportation of physical evidence by crime scene investigators. As explained in Sullivan (1977, p. 149):

> *It is the job of the police to enforce the law. Thus, officers must remember that they are primarily fact-finders for their department and have no authority or control over the judicial or legislative branches of government. If the police effectively enforce the law, they have done all that is expected.*

Law enforcement officers and investigators work for government agencies as dictated by jurisdiction and statute, to include federal, state, county, and municipal (e.g., city, village) authorities, and are supported by a variety of civilian personnel in various administrative and specialist capacities.

FORENSIC SERVICES

A number of essential forensic services form the pillar of the criminal justice system that deals with the collection, examination, and interpretation of evidence—whether it is physical, behavioral, and testimonial.

Government-employed analysts, technicians, criminalists, pathologists, and forensic mental health experts perform a wide variety of forensic services on behalf of the state, generally for the police and prosecution.

In the United States, however, there is also a large community of independent forensic examiners. These private sector professionals are regularly engaged to perform examinations, and audits, for the prosecution and the defense alike. When brought in to examine a case, they provide the necessary counterbalance and independent review required in an adversarial system.

The availability of forensic science, technology, and expertise is a sore issue within the justice system, as these are scarce resources. In most jurisdictions, private labs are limited or nonexistent. Consequently attorneys on both sides may be forced by geographic and budgetary constraints to rely on variably qualified government-employed analysts for the bulk of examinations and interpretations. It is fair to say that the lack of available government services, private practitioners, and related funds for either has caused serious case backlogs, delays, and even miscarriages of justice (see generally: Cooley & Turvey, 2014).

THE JUDICIARY

The judiciary is the pillar of the criminal justice system that deals with the adjudication of criminal defendants, to include exoneration, punishment, treatment, and efforts to reform. As explained in Black's Law Dictionary (Black, 1990), it is the role of the judiciary to "interpret, construe, apply, and generally administer and enforce the laws" (p. 847).

A short list of those involved in the judiciary includes government prosecutors and public defenders, private defense attorneys, magistrates, judges, investigators for the prosecution, investigators for the defense, investigators for the court, paralegals, court reporters, court clerks, bailiffs, and the juries (drawn from the local citizenry). Each has a specific duty that is explicitly decreed and governed by the law—perversions of which result in violations of due process.

CORRECTIONS

Corrections is the pillar of the criminal justice system that deals with the probation, incarceration, management, rehabilitation, treatment, parole, and in extreme cases the execution of convicted criminals.

Many law enforcement agencies and courthouses have on-site jail facilities to enable short-term incarceration of offenders involved in lesser crimes, or to accommodate the local court appointments of felons "visiting" from other correctional institutions. However, federal, state, and county penitentiaries are designed to accommodate the long-term sentences of convicted felons. Additionally there are hospitals outside of correctional institutions that have forensic units providing court-mandated mental evaluations, treatment, and defendant residency. Some of these institutions are government owned and operated (county, state, and federal), whereas others are privately contracted.

A short list of those professionals involved in corrections includes probation officers, corrections officers, corrections investigators, corrections counselors, parole officers, intelligence officers, social workers, forensic psychologists, forensic psychiatrists, and the members of various parole boards.

THE ADVERSARIAL SYSTEM

In an adversarial system, criminal defendants are entitled to an adequate defense and due process of law, while the burden of proving guilt is on the state or government (i.e., the prosecution). Such systems are grounded firmly in the principle that defendants are presumed innocent until proven guilty. Consequently there are always at least two sides in each criminal dispute: a prosecution representing the government and its citizens, and a defense representing the accused. As defined in Black's Law Dictionary (Black, 1990, p. 53):

> *[An adversary system is a] jurisprudential network of laws, rules and procedures characterized by opposing parties who contend against each other for a result favorable to themselves. In such a system, the judge acts as an independent magistrate rather than prosecutor; distinguished from an inquisitorial system.*

Ultimately, each side of a legal dispute works to convince a judge or a jury that its position is the most correct—ostensibly within a set of specific rules for conduct. In other words, each side must avoid conduct that is illegal or unethical when making their case.

THE PROSECUTION

In the United States, attorneys for the prosecution work exclusively for the government at the city, county, state, or federal level. They are charged with seeking the truth in criminal matters on behalf of the citizenry, and work with the benefit of law enforcement resources and personnel from both state and federal agencies. Unfortunately, prosecutors are often elected, appointed, promoted, or otherwise advanced based on political considerations or their conviction rate. This can cause some to be less interested in "truth seeking" and more interested in what they can prove in court to obtain a politically desirable legal outcome.

The state has the greater burden of proof, and must prove a defendant's guilt beyond a reasonable doubt. This means that before a defendant can be found guilty of any crime, the state must prove every element of that crime and also that the defendant was the person responsible. However, the prosecution also controls a vast pool of government resources, as well as its related punitive powers, to assist in the pursuit of their desired legal outcomes—which the defense does not.

THE DEFENSE

Attorneys for the defense are not necessarily interested in truth seeking, but rather are ethically bound to zealously advocate for the best interests of the accused—their client. Some defense attorneys work for the government as county, state, or federal public defenders, while others work in private practice. With only a few exceptions, the defense enjoys limited resources, and has no authority to broker deals with witnesses in exchange for testimony.

Defendants with the financial means may hire a private attorney. However, doing so can be prohibitively expensive. Indigent defendants, being unable to afford private counsel, are represented by a public defender. In states or counties without a dedicated public defender system, the court appoints legal representatives to indigent defendants from a list of available local attorneys, referred to as "appointed counsel." The defense rarely enjoys the same resources, experts, and funding available to prosecutors.

The defense is not required to prove innocence in an adversarial justice system. In fact, the defense is not required to prove or disprove anything. The defense needs to only demonstrate that there is a reasonable doubt with respect to the prosecution's theories to prevail. The limited burden of proof required by the defense is founded in the right to be presumed innocent until convicted in a court of law. The fact that a person has been arrested and put on trial may not be considered as evidence of guilt, despite any personal beliefs to the contrary.

If convicted of a serious felony, a defendant is further entitled to state and federal appeals that can be based on demonstrable errors and misconduct during trial; ineffective assistance by defense counsel; lack of evidence sufficient to support a conviction; newly discovered evidence; and actual innocence.

SCIENTIFIC FACT VERSUS LEGAL TRUTH

Before we can discuss how evidence gets admitted in court, it is necessary to explain the relationship between scientific facts and legal truths. They are not the same thing. Anyone suggesting otherwise is ignorant of both science and law, or attempting a not-so-clever deception.

Scientific fact refers to information and events that have been established based on a broad factual record to a reasonable degree of scientific certainty by scientists using the scientific method. Legal truth refers to information and events that have been established by a court ruling based on a narrow factual record—at the discretion of either a judge or a jury. Scientific fact is the result of objective and analytical deliberation; legal truth is the result of something else entirely, as explained in Thornton and Peterson (2002, p. 149):

> *Scientific "truths" are established when the validity of a proposition is proven to the satisfaction of a prudent and rational mind. Legal "truths" are not established by the exercise of the scientific method, but by the processes of the adversary system.*
>
> *The role of physical evidence in the administration of justice may reasonably be described as follows: Science offers a window through which the law may view*

the technological advances of our age. Science spreads out a smorgasbord of (hopefully) valid facts and, having proudly displayed its wares, stands back. The law now picks out those morsels that appear most attractive to it, applying selection criteria that may or may not have anything to do with science. These selection criteria may appear sensible, even obligatory to the law, but may appear illogical or even whimsical to science.

Scientific fact and legal truth are therefore very different propositions. Not only are they established by entirely different means, they are also sought for what can be incompatible ends. Science seeks to find out what happened and why; the law seeks just resolution of legal conflict.

This reality often places scientific fact and legal truth at cross-purposes. It is not made one bit easier by the fact that while the scientist must respect the courts and the law, the opposite is not also true. This is noted in Thornton (1994, p. 483): "Every scientist understands that there are courts of law. By and large, they are accorded respect. I am not as certain that every lawyer understands that there are courts of science as well."

It is also necessary to explain that forensic practitioners are at a terrific disadvantage when they practice within the justice system. This must be conceded at the outset of any forensic endeavor, to recognize the potential for abuse. A useful discussion is found in Thornton (1983, pp. 86–88):

Basic conflicts that influence the practice of forensic science become apparent at the interface of law and science. Law and science on occasion have conflicting goals, each having developed in response to different social attitudes and intellectual needs. The goal of law is the just resolution of human conflict, while the goal of science traditionally has been cast, although perhaps too smugly, as the search for "truth."

Certainly there is nothing intrinsically dichotomous in the pursuit of these goals; the court or jury strive in good faith to determine the truth in a given situation as a way to resolve conflicts. But proof is viewed somewhat differently by law and science, as is the application of logic and the perception of societal values…

How, then, do these differences between law and science lead to abuse of forensic science? They do simply because all the players want to win and are likely to use any ethical means at their disposal to do so. The attorneys in a case are aligned with only one side, and it is entirely appropriate under the adversary system for them to advocate a particular point of view, even without full and fair disclosure of all relevant facts. Subject only to the rules of evidence, the rules of procedure, and the Code of Professional Responsibility, attorneys are free to manipulate scientific evidence to maximize the opportunity for their side to prevail. Not only is behavior of this sort countenanced by the law, it is the ethical responsibility of counsel to attempt to do so.

In all reality, the domains of science and law are so divergent, and so foreign to each other's purpose, that some argue forensic experts can only be abused in legal proceedings. In other words, they have no legitimate role to play, and their evidence can only be distorted. For example, according to Ingraham (1987, p. 179), "[t]he adversary 'game' is not a procedure whose underlying purpose is to communicate facts or determine truth but rather to communicate position statements about reality, and ultimately the expert witness is forced into the role of a coadvocate selling a partisan position to the trier-of-fact rather than an impartial source of information."

The subordination of science to attorneys, the courts, and mercurial interpretations of the law remains a daily occurrence in the criminal justice system. It happens each time a judge makes a legal ruling about the reliability of any scientific evidence, methodology, or related testimony in such a manner as to allow, limit, or preclude its admissibility. Often this will be based on incomplete, uninformed, and erroneous argumentation from counsel with filtered, limited, or no testimony from objective forensic practitioners, and often this will conflict with rulings in another courtroom, whether across the nation or just down the hallway. This practical reality is not going to change anytime soon.

Forensic practitioners accept these contradictions and must do their best to avoid being abused by either side of the courtroom. In doing so, they do well to heed the following cautionary advice from Thornton and Peterson (2007, p. 4): "Forensic science is science exercised on behalf of the law in the just resolution of conflict. It is therefore expected to be the handmaiden of the law, but at the same time this expectation may very well be the marina from which is launched the tension that exists between the two disciplines." To be clear, acting as a handmaid is not necessarily a corrupted role, so long as the correct priorities are being attended. While some jurists will still seek to manipulate the findings of the ethical forensic examiner, at least there will be something scientifically competent of use to those who would seek the truth to defend against such manipulations. Otherwise, science abandons the courts entirely to judges and lawyers—and this is no good solution.

EXPERTS, EVIDENCE, AND ADMISSIBILITY

As discussed, the courtroom is a realm of laws, not science. Science is merely an occasional guest. Barring misconduct, a judge's authority on case-related decisions must be respected and their will conformed to. The judge decides who the experts are, what evidence is admissible, and how and when court will proceed. If one seeks to engage in forensic practice, one must accept this reality and the many disappointments that will necessarily follow.

EVIDENCE

Consider the issue of evidence. Evidence, as explained in Black (1990), is "testimony, writing, material objects, or other things presented to the senses that are offered to prove the existence or non-existence of a fact." This is consistent with Lilly (1987, p. 2), who provides that evidence is "any matter, verbal or physical, that can be used to support the existence of a factual proposition."

Evidence in a forensic context is not a scientific designation: it is a legal construct. Consider that any fact or finding gathered in relation to a legal proceeding is considered evidence until a judge says it is not. For example, documentation of a factual event may exist, such as a taped interview, a written confession, or an exclusionary test result. However, a judge may determine that it is not admissible, for whatever reason, and that fact and related documentation may not be considered as evidence at trial.

As a direct result of this legal reality, the sum total of evidentiary facts under consideration by a judge or jury in a given case generally does not represent the entire picture of known facts or findings; rather, it is the court's interpretation and reduction of the evidence based on its determination of what is and is not admissible. According to Black (1990), admissibility "as applied to evidence...means that the evidence introduced is of such character that the court or judge is bound to receive it; that is, allow it to be introduced at trial." Trial judges have broad discretionary authority with respect to deciding the admissibility of any proposed evidence. It is, in reality, a complex and inconsistently applied legal heuristic whereby a judge determines which facts and circumstances may actually be introduced as evidence based on "material relevance." Such determinations may be standardized for certain kinds of proposed evidence or may require an evidentiary hearing.

However, the trial judge is not the final decider; any case may be overturned by a court of appeals, given sufficient cause from a judge that has improperly excluded evidence or the experts seeking to present it.

CHAIN OF CUSTODY

Every item of evidence that is intended to be admitted in a court of law must have a documented *chain of custody*. This is a record of each person, and agency, who has controlled, taken custody of, examined, tested, or had any other kind of contact with a particular item of evidence from its discovery to the present day—with dates and locations. It includes a clear record of any examinations performed, or any damage caused. This allows others to review and evaluate the quality of a given item of evidence, and make assessments regarding tampering or contamination.

This issue will be discussed more thoroughly in Chapter 6: *Physical Evidence Collection*, where specific protocols will be provided.

EXPERT EVIDENCE

Consider the Federal Rules of Evidence (FRE, 2011), which serve as a guideline for expert evidence admissibility in Federal Court and many States.

The Federal Rules of Evidence (FRE, 2011)

Article VII. Opinions and Expert Testimony

Rule 701. Opinion Testimony by Lay Witnesses

If a witness is not testifying as an expert, testimony in the form of an opinion is limited to one that is:

(a) rationally based on the witness's perception;
(b) helpful to clearly understanding the witness's testimony or to determining a fact in issue; and
(c) not based on scientific, technical, or other specialized knowledge within the scope of Rule 702.
Notes: (Pub. L. 93–595, §1, Jan. 02, 1975, 88 Stat. 1937; Mar. 02, 1987, eff. Oct. 01, 1987; Apr. 17, 2000, eff. Dec. 01, 2000; Apr. 26, 2011, eff. Dec. 01, 2011.)

Rule 702. Testimony by Experts.

A witness who is qualified as an expert by knowledge, skill, experience, training, or education may testify in the form of an opinion or otherwise if:

(a) the expert's scientific, technical, or other specialized knowledge will help the trier of fact to understand the evidence or to determine a fact in issue;
(b) the testimony is based on sufficient facts or data;
(c) the testimony is the product of reliable principles and methods; and
(d) the expert has reliably applied the principles and methods to the facts of the case.
Notes: (Pub. L. 93–595, §1, Jan 02, 1975, 88 Stat. 1937; Apr 17, 2000, eff. Dec 01, 2000; Apr 26, 2011, eff. Dec 01, 2011.)

Rule 703. Bases of Opinion Testimony by Experts

An expert may base an opinion on facts or data in the case that the expert has been made aware of or personally observed. If experts in the particular field would reasonably rely on those kinds of facts or data in forming an opinion on the subject, they need not be admissible for the opinion to be admitted. But if the facts or data would otherwise be inadmissible, the proponent of the opinion may disclose them to the jury only if their probative value in helping the jury evaluate the opinion substantially outweighs their prejudicial effect.

Notes: (Pub. L. 93–595, §1, Jan. 02, 1975, 88 Stat. 1937; Mar. 02, 1987, eff. Oct. 01, 1987; Apr. 17, 2000, eff. Dec. 01, 2000; Apr. 26, 2011, eff. Dec. 01, 2011.)

Rule 704. Opinion on Ultimate Issue.

(a) In General—Not Automatically Objectionable. An opinion is not objectionable just because it embraces an ultimate issue.
(b) Exception. In a criminal case, an expert witness must not state an opinion about whether the defendant did or did not have a mental state or condition that constitutes an element of the crime charged or of a defense. Those matters are for the trier of fact alone.

Notes (Pub. L. 93—595, §1, Jan. 02, 1975, 88 Stat. 1937; Pub. L. 98—473, title II, §406, Oct. 12, 1984, 98 Stat. 2067; Apr. 26, 2011, eff. Dec. 01, 2011.)

Rule 705. Disclosure of Facts or Data Underlying Expert Opinion

Unless the court orders otherwise, an expert may state an opinion—and give the reasons for it—without first testifying to the underlying facts or data. But the expert may be required to disclose those facts or data on cross-examination.

Notes: (Pub. L. 93—595, §1, Jan. 02, 1975, 88 Stat. 1938; Mar. 02, 1987, eff. Oct. 01, 1987; Apr. 22, 1993, eff. Dec. 01, 1993; Apr. 26, 2011, eff. Dec. 01, 2011.)

A forensic expert, according to Federal Rule of Evidence 702 (2011), is qualified to testify by virtue of "knowledge, skill, experience, training, or education" at the discretion of the judge. The entire concept of forensic expertise is a legal one, unrelated to science or scientific practice.

Judges are meant to invoke standards for the admissibility of experts, such as *Frye*, *Daubert*, or *Kumho*, to screen out junk science or unproven methods of analysis.[3] As already mentioned, these are guidelines only and not strict requirements; trial court judges have broad discretion with respect to admissibility of all things—to include experts and expert testimony.

In reality, judicial rulings on expert admissibility are partial to say the least, as discussed in Moreno (2004, pp. 3—4):

Judges routinely admit expert testimony offered by prosecutors, but frequently exclude expert testimony offered by the defense. A review of federal criminal court cases reveals that 92% of prosecution experts survive defense challenges while only 33% of defense experts survive challenges by federal prosecutors. A recent study of federal appellate criminal cases found that more than 95% of prosecutors' experts are admitted at trial, while fewer than 8% of defense experts are allowed to testify. Why do judges consistently fail to scrutinize prosecution experts? Maybe it is the uniform. The most common prosecution expert witness is a police officer or a federal agent. In state and federal criminal trials, law enforcement experts are routinely permitted to testify to opinions and conclusions derived from their on-the-job experience and personal observations. Prosecutors rely on police officer experts most frequently in narcotics cases. In drug cases, law enforcement experts are often asked to interpret ambiguous words or phrases used by the defendant and/or his coconspirators. The purpose of, and problem with, this expert testimony is that it tells jurors precisely which inculpatory inferences they should draw from the factual evidence.

Judges have an ethical duty to refrain from proprosecution bias with respect to qualifying anything with a badge as an expert—as is too often the case. They must evaluate each expert on objective criteria having nothing to do with which side they work for or whether their decision will effect other cases (e.g., disqualifying a law enforcement expert can affect every case that they work on from that point forward).

Despite suggestions that this kind of behavior is uncommon, defense counsel and nonlaw enforcement experts called by the defense in criminal trials are acutely aware that such behavior from a sitting judge is not at all unusual. Hostility toward the defense and anyone seeking to help them is anticipated in the many less than professional courtrooms that exist. This is especially true when the judge is prolaw enforcement. In some instances, judges will actually bar the defense, or their experts, from saying anything that undermines law enforcement credibility—especially if it happens to be true.

While the court rules on admissibility, it has no authority to determine anything in the realm of scientific practice. In other words, forensic professionals determine whether evidence is sufficient and reliable for their examinations. They make the determination as to whether there is enough evidence of sufficient quality to examine; and they determine whether the results of the examination are reliable enough to make conclusions. The courts, at a later point, will determine whether or not any of these things are admissible. But the courts cannot dictate the scientific facts or decide best methods for conducting forensic examinations. That would an abuse of authority, and cause untold distortions in the quality of the evidence being admitted.

CONSTITUTIONAL RIGHTS

The United States Constitution contains amendments that establish the rights of its citizens, the precise meaning of which are a matter of continual public debate and legal reinterpretation. These include, but are in no way limited to, freedom of religion and freedom of the press (First Amendment); the right to "keep and bear arms" (Second Amendment); freedom from "unreasonable searches and seizures" without "probable cause" (Fourth Amendment); the right to adequate legal representation, a "speedy and public trial, by an impartial jury," and to confront of any witness (Sixth Amendment); freedom from "excessive fines" and "cruel and unusual punishments" (Eighth Amendment); and the right to vote (the 15th, 19th, and 26th Amendments).

In addition, the 5th and 14th Amendments contain what are referred to as due process clauses—in that they specifically guarantee citizens the right to due process. The Fifth Amendment states "No person shall be held to answer for a capital, or otherwise infamous crime, unless on a presentment or indictment of a Grand Jury, except in cases arising in the land or naval forces, or in the Militia, when in actual service in time of War or public danger; nor shall any person be subject for the same offense to be twice put in jeopardy of life or limb; nor shall be compelled in any criminal case to be a witness against himself, nor be deprived of life, liberty, or property, without due process of law; nor shall private property be taken for public use, without just compensation."

The 14th Amendment states "All persons born or naturalized in the United States, and subject to the jurisdiction thereof, are citizens of the United States and of the State wherein they reside. No State shall make or enforce any law which shall abridge the privileges or immunities of citizens of the United States; nor shall any State deprive any person of life, liberty, or property, without due process of law; nor deny to any person within its jurisdiction the equal protection of the laws."

These and other constitutional rights are guaranteed to all citizens—they are not entitlements or benefits. Government is drawn from the citizenry and is intended to serve them by first providing and then protecting these rights, as discussed in Kleinig (1996, p. 14) "the chief end of government is the protection of individual life, liberty, and property… The right to government protection against invasions of life, liberty, and property has been reinterpreted to include the government securement or provision of what will enable those rights to be enjoyed, supplemented by other social, political, and welfare rights."

Any government or government agent that does not provide for and protect the rights of its citizens is in violation of due process.

Consider the following constitutionally protected rights and their impact on evidence-related issues: *Due Process*, *Effective Counsel*, and *Witness Confrontation*.

THE RIGHT TO DUE PROCESS

Due process refers to the preservation of federal and state constitutional rights; the rights of citizens as described in these constitutions may not be violated or taken away without strict adherence to the law. It is central to what justice is and means within any legal system. Due process is achieved only when those in the justice system both understand and follow the laws about when and how individual rights can be infringed. When those laws are not followed, individual's rights are infringed and due process is violated. As we will learn, due process violations can result in severe consequences for those responsible.

As explained in Chapman and McConnell (2012), there are two different interpretations of due process (p. 1676):

Some argue that "due process" meant nothing more than judicial procedure. It therefore applied to the courts and, perhaps, to the executive with respect to prosecution and the enforcement of court judgments. Under this reading, due process did not apply to the legislature. Others contend that "due process of law" entailed judicial procedure and natural law norms such as reasonableness, justice, or fairness

In other words, there are those of the opinion that due process requires simply following the letter of legal procedure as written. Others, however, argue that due process has an underlying set of moral requirements that are equally inviolate. For example, Black's Law Dictionary explains that due process requires an underlying theme of fairness (Black, 1990, p. 501): "Embodied in the due process concept are the basic rights of a defendant in criminal proceedings and the requisites for a fair trial."

Regardless of how one interprets the concept of due process, its establishment and interpretation are not the role of the executive branch of government, as explained in Chapman and McConnell (2012, p. 1681):

> *The due process and law-of-the-land clauses of the American state and federal constitutions originate in Magna Charta and the English customary constitution. This is uncontroversial. What commentators have underemphasized is that due process has from the beginning been bound up with the division of the authority to deprive subjects of life, liberty, or property between independent political institutions. In modern parlance, due process has always been the insistence that the executive — the branch of government that wields force against the people — deprive persons of rights only in accordance with settled rules independent of executive will, in accordance with a judgment by an independent magistrate.*

To be clear, the history of due process suggests that the executive branch (e.g., law enforcement) is meant to have no part in deciding what due process entails—otherwise it will inevitably be unbalanced in their favor. The precise elements of due process, and the rights being protected, must be established by the judiciary, legislated by congress, and then only enforced by the executive. But where does the original language come from?

The 5th and 14th Amendments to the *U.S. Constitution* provide that the government may not deprive its citizens of "life, liberty, or property without due process of law." This provision is essentially a fairness requirement. Ideally citizens may only be tried and punished for crimes alleged by the state under the most impartial and unprejudiced conditions. Any condition or treatment that tends to bias a judge, jury, or the process as a whole in favor of the state is considered a violation of due process.

Due process violations are currently understood to include things such as inadequate defense counsel, inadequate access to legal counsel or private experts, failure to admit proffered experts, and failure to disclose exculpatory evidence or witnesses. In reality, the government has more money, more resources to draw from, and often benefits from a presumption of guilt held by ignorant and even partial jurors (and jurists). Under these conditions, due process is an ideal rather than a reality.

To abide the mandates of due process, forensic practitioners employed by the government must conduct forensic examinations in such a way as to be transparent in their methods and findings. As explained in Edwards and Gotsonis (2009, p. 186):

> *As a general matter, laboratory reports generated as the result of a scientific analysis should be complete and thorough. They should describe, at a minimum, methods and materials, procedures, results, and conclusions, and they should identify, as appropriate, the sources of uncertainty in the procedures and conclusions along with estimates of their scale (to indicate the level of confidence in the results). Although it is not appropriate and practicable to provide as much detail as might be expected in a research paper, sufficient content should be provided to allow the nonscientist reader to understand what has been done and permit informed, unbiased scrutiny of the conclusion.*

Some forensic laboratory reports meet this standard of reporting, but most do not. Some reports contain only identifying and agency information, a brief description of the evidence being submitted, a brief description of the types of analysis requested, and a short statement of the results (e.g., "The green, brown plant material in item #1 was identified as marijuana"). The norm is to have no description of the methods or procedures used, and most reports do not discuss measurement uncertainties or confidence limits. Many disciplines outside the forensic science disciplines have standards, templates, and protocols for data reporting. Although some of the Scientific Working Groups have a scoring system for reporting findings, they are not uniformly or consistently used.

Forensic science reports, and any courtroom testimony stemming from them, must include clear characterizations of the limitations of the analyses, including associated probabilities where possible. Courtroom testimony should be given in lay terms so that all trial participants can understand how to weight and interpret the testimony. In order to enable this, research must be undertaken to evaluate the reliability of the steps of the various identification methods and the confidence intervals associated with the overall conclusions.

In other words, forensic scientists must not withhold, conceal, or distort their examinations, methods, and related findings. Reports must be written in a clear fashion so as to be within the intellectual grasp of the layman, while also containing sufficient detail to accurately convey what they did, what they found, and what it means.

Due process and its constitutional origins combine to establish a presumptive requirement for those who seek employment in the criminal justice system at any level—to read and understand not only the U.S. Constitution, but also any subsequent legal decisions that influence its interpretation by the courts.

Any professional or agency that does not fully comprehend or support the U.S. Constitution, along with the individual rights and due process requirements that it guarantees all citizens, will continually be at odds with the moral and ethical requirements of working in the criminal justice system. Failure to take this obligation seriously, or supplanting it with personal ideas and emotions, has been the source of much avoidable injustice.[4]

BRADY V. MARYLAND (1963)

In the United States, law enforcement agencies, government crime laboratories, and prosecutorial agencies are required by law to comply with a well-known (and often ignored) legal standard passed down from the U.S. Supreme Court in *Brady v. Maryland* (1963). This ruling was intended to spell out the government's duty to provide the defense with equal access to inculpatory evidence, to prevent what is generally referred to as "trial by ambush," and to avoid miscarriages of justice by allowing timely independent investigations of the prosecutor's evidence by the defense. As explained in Gershman (2006, pp. 685–686):

Brady's holding is familiar to virtually every practitioner of criminal law: "[T]he suppression by the prosecution of evidence favorable to an accused upon request violates due process where the evidence is material either to guilt or to punishment, irrespective of the good faith or bad faith of the prosecution."

This principle, according to the Brady Court, reflects our nation's abiding commitment to adversarial justice and fair play toward those persons accused of crimes. As the Court observed: "Society wins not only when the guilty are convicted but when criminal trials are fair; our system of the administration of justice suffers when any accused is treated unfairly." Indeed, by explicitly commanding prosecutors to disclose to defendants facing a criminal trial any favorable evidence that is material to their guilt or punishment, Brady launched the modern development of constitutional disclosure requirements.

The idealistic language in Brady requiring timely disclosure of potentially exculpatory evidence stands in contrast to its interpretation and application. It was intended as a clear standard set forth for reasonable minds to appreciate and follow. However, the adversarial nature of the criminal justice system, and the general lack of accountability for even blatant prosecutorial misconduct, has left Brady without the teeth it needs. This was, in fact, the conclusion offered in Gershman (2006, pp. 727–728):

Reflecting on the evolution of Brady v. Maryland, one is struck by the stark dissonance between the grand expectations of Brady, that the adversary system henceforth would be transformed from a "sporting contest" to a genuine search for truth, and the grim reality that criminal litigation continues to operate as a "trial by ambush." The development of the Brady rule by the judiciary depicts a gradual erosion of Brady: from a prospective obligation on prosecutors to make timely disclosure, to the defense of materially favorable evidence, to a retrospective review by an appellate court into whether the prosecutor's suppression was unduly prejudicial. The erosion of Brady has been accompanied by increasing prosecutorial gamesmanship in gambling that violations will not be discovered or, if discovered, will be allowed, and tactics that abet and hide violations. Finally, the absence of any legal or ethical sanctions to make prosecutors accountable for violations produces a system marked by willful abuse of law, cynicism, and the real possibility that innocent persons may be wrongfully convicted because of the prosecutor's misconduct. Indeed, more than any other rule of criminal procedure, the Brady rule has been the most fertile and widespread source of misconduct by prosecutors; and, more than any other rule of constitutional criminal procedure, has exposed the deficiencies in the truth-serving function of the criminal trial.

Balko (2013) agrees reporting that prosecutorial misconduct related to *Brady* is among the most common causes of overturned convictions:

There are a number of ways for a prosecutor to commit misconduct. He could make inappropriate comments to jurors, or coax witnesses into giving false or misleading testimony. But one of the most pervasive misdeeds is the Brady violation, or the failure to turn over favorable evidence to the defendant. It's the most common form of misconduct cited by courts in overturning convictions.

The name refers to the 50-year-old Supreme Court decision in Brady v. Maryland, which required prosecutors to divulge such information, like deals made with state's witnesses, crime scene evidence that could be tested for DNA, information that could discredit a state's witness and portions of police reports that could be favorable to the defendant. But there's very little to hold prosecutors to the Brady obligation.

As a consequence of the lack of accountability surrounding Brady violations, and the terrific advantage that they can afford the prosecution, they are among the most common forms of prosecutorial misconduct.

The original language in Brady has been expanded by the Supreme Court to cover any and all potentially exculpatory information in control of the prosecution, the police, and their agents. This includes government-operated crime labs as well as private labs and private experts contracted into government service. Unfortunately, ignorance regarding Brady remains even within these informed circles, as explained in Giannelli and McMunigal (2007, pp. 1517—1518):

The U.S. Supreme Court has extended Brady to cover exculpatory information in the control of the police. Some courts have explicitly included crime labs within the reach of Brady. In one case, the Supreme Court of California noted that a laboratory examiner "worked closely" with prosecutors and was part of the investigative team. The court concluded that the "prosecutor thus had the obligation to determine if the lab's files contained any exculpatory evidence, such as the worksheet, and disclose it to petitioner." [In re Brown, 952 p. 2d 715, 719 (Cal. 1998)]

In another case, a court wrote that an experienced crime lab technician "must have known of his legal obligation to disclose exculpatory evidence to the prosecutors, their obligation to pass it along to the defense, and his obligation not to cover up a Brady violation by perjuring himself." [Charles v. City of Boston, 365 F. Supp.2d 82, 89 (D. Mass. 2005)] While the expert should have been on notice about perjury, it is less clear that the Brady obligation would be known to lab personnel—without the prosecutor tutoring the lab. How often do prosecutors discharge this duty? Many lab examiners have never heard of Brady.

Ultimately the court's holdings related to Brady make it clear that "the trial courts should order that all information favorable to the defense be produced before trial" by the police and the prosecution (Cary, Singer, & Latcovich, 2011, p. 44; see also the court's rulings in United States v. Acosta, 2005; United States v. Safavian, 2005; and United States v. Sudikoff, 1999). Failure to do so is an invitation by police and prosecutors alike to selectively interpret Brady in their favor, to ignore it when convenient, or to simply claim ignorance all the way around.

THE RIGHT TO "EFFECTIVE" COUNSEL

Criminal defendants have a constitutionally guaranteed right to legal representation. The Sixth Amendment to the United States Constitution provides specifically that "[i]n all criminal prosecutions, the accused shall enjoy the right to a speedy and public trial, by an impartial jury of the State and district wherein the crime shall have been committed, which district shall have been previously ascertained by law, and to be informed of the nature and cause of the accusation; to be confronted with the witnesses against him; to have compulsory process for obtaining witnesses in his favor, and to have the Assistance of Counsel for his defence."

The Sixth Amendment right to counsel is essential for due process in the criminal justice system, because everything else guaranteed to a criminal defendant relies on it and fails without it. More than a requirement for a warm body, the defense attorney must also be competent, as explained in Gershman (2011, p. 560): "A defendant's right to counsel, guaranteed by the Sixth Amendment, has long been understood to include the right to the effective assistance of counsel." Thus, not only are criminal defendants entitled to legal counsel, counsel must also be effective; counsel may not be inadequate or incompetent.

When a criminal defendant cannot afford a legal representative, the state must provide one for him or her to ensure that the defendant is receiving impartial legal advice. This was explained best in the United States Supreme Court's ruling in Gideon v. Wainwright (1963):

> ...[I]n our adversary system of criminal justice, any person haled into court, who is too poor to hire a lawyer, cannot be assured a fair trial unless counsel is provided for him. This seems to us to be an obvious truth. Governments, both state and federal, quite properly spend vast sums of money to establish machinery to try defendants accused of crime. Lawyers to prosecute are everywhere deemed essential to protect the public's interest in an orderly society. Similarly, there are few defendants charged with crime, few indeed, who fail to hire the best lawyers they can get to prepare and present their defenses. That government hires lawyers to prosecute and defendants who have the money hire lawyers to defend are the strongest indications of the widespread belief that lawyers in criminal courts are necessities, not luxuries. The right of one charged with crime to counsel may not be deemed fundamental and essential to fair trials in some countries, but it is in ours. From the very beginning, our state and national constitutions and laws have laid great emphasis on procedural and substantive safeguards designed to assure fair trials before impartial tribunals in which every defendant stands equal before the law. This noble ideal cannot be realized if the poor man charged with crime has to face his accusers without a lawyer to assist him. A defendant's need for a lawyer is nowhere better stated than in the moving words of Mr. Justice Sutherland in Powell v. Alabama: "The right to be heard would be, in many cases, of little avail if it did not comprehend the right to be heard by counsel. Even the intelligent and educated layman has small and sometimes no skill in the science of law. If charged with crime, he is incapable, generally, of determining for himself whether the indictment is good or bad. He is unfamiliar with the rules of evidence. Left without the aid of counsel, he may be put on trial without a proper charge, and convicted upon incompetent

evidence, or evidence irrelevant to the issue or otherwise inadmissible. He lacks both the skill and knowledge adequately to prepare his defense, even though he have a perfect one. He requires the guiding hand of counsel at every step in the proceedings against him. Without it, though he be not guilty, he faces the danger of conviction because he does not know how to establish his innocence."

Further the US Supreme Court has held that legal counsel must also be effective, in Strickland v. Washington (1984): "The Sixth Amendment right to counsel is the right to the effective assistance of counsel, and the benchmark for judging any claim of ineffectiveness must be whether counsel's conduct so undermined the proper functioning of the adversarial process that the trial cannot be relied on as having produced a just result." This was echoed in Martinez v. Ryan (2012), which explains that "[t]he right to the effective assistance of counsel at trial is a bedrock principle in our justice system."

However, this decision does not necessarily provide an immediate remedy for bad or otherwise incompetent lawyering, as discussed in Freedman (2005, p. 918):

…[U]nder Strickland, even grossly incompetent lawyering is not enough to establish ineffective counsel. In addition, the lawyer's incompetence must have caused "prejudice" to his client, meaning that there must be a "reasonable probability that, but for counsel's unprofessional errors, the result of the proceeding would have been different." Thus, even a reasonable possibility that an innocent person might have been wrongly convicted because of his lawyer's established incompetence is not enough to justify a new trial.

Consequently, fulfillment of this obligation may rest entirely on the defense attorney's sense of professional responsibility. In any case, the legal imperatives are clear: the state must provide legal counsel for arrestees, and the lawyers who represent them must be competent. Anything less risks derailing due process and subverts the cause of justice—without remedy in certain cases. Those professionals who do not believe criminal defendants are entitled to, or even deserve, effective representation are at cross-purposes with one of the criminal justice system's most important pillars. Needless to say, such a belief has no place in the cause of justice.

MELENDEZ-DIAZ (2009)

Ake v. Oklahoma (1985) is a landmark U.S. Supreme Court decision which holds that, because the government has overwhelming access to manpower, money, and forensic experts, the defense must be given parity for the adversary system to function fairly. The ruling is, of course, an ideal. The reality is that not every lawyer and court understands and invokes Ake appropriately or consistently, as explained in Findley (2008, pp. 929—931):

…[T]he government has significantly greater access to forensic science services and experts than do most criminal defendants. Crime laboratories exist to provide such services to prosecutors; no corresponding institutions exist for defendants.

> *And, because most defendants are indigent, their ability to hire experts is dependent on public funding of legal services to the indigent, which is abysmally inadequate in virtually every jurisdiction. Because funding for indigent defense is so inadequate, defense services are rationed in ways that put innocents at risk; rationing disfavors expensive, substantive innocence claims (such as expensive litigation about the validity of forensic evidence), and instead favors more inexpensive procedural constitutional claims. While the Supreme Court in Ake v. Oklahoma recognized a constitutional right to publicly funded experts for the indigent, exercise of that right is dependent on the willingness of a local judge to order the expenditure of scarce local resources, and on a cumbersome case-by-case, expert-by-expert process for requesting funding. Any risk of failure of that case-by-case process to provide adequate expert services falls on the defendant, and courts have tended to apply Ake narrowly. That system comes nowhere close to providing the level of forensic sciences assistance that is needed, or that is available to the prosecution.*

The Court's decision in *Ake* changed the forensic landscape in the United States dramatically by requiring the state to fund expert forensic analyses for indigent defendants. It reminded the criminal justice system to live up to that part of its promise of due process. Ake also increased the demand for independent forensic expertise of every relevant type and directly acknowledged the legitimacy of private forensic practice as a necessary agent of balance within the criminal justice system.

Similarly, the U.S. Supreme Court ruling in Melendez-Diaz (2009) further corrected imbalance in relation to government-employed forensic practitioners. In essence, it reasserts that the accused have the right to confront any and all evidence and witnesses against them. This right to confrontation includes forensic scientists who have written reports to be used as evidence against them at trial.

Forensic practitioners testifying about evidentiary tests and findings at trial have not always been the same examiners who performed analyses in the case in question. Because of time and budget constraints, crime labs have been known to send supervisors or, in some cases, any warm body available on the day to satisfy the need for expert testimony during trial.

In anticipation of this practice, certain government agencies have a history of doing one of two things: submitting reports with no name attached; or submitting reports with everyone's name attached. Federal agencies have, for example, engaged in the practice of preparing forensic reports such that it is unclear who actually performed examinations and who wrote the report. In these instances, reports were drafted by a particular unit or section without a specific name attached to them. Another common practice has been to prepare reports with everyone's name on them: multiple supervisors, multiple analysts, and multiple reviewers.

Either practice would allow a crime lab to send just about any employee available from the section that generated the report to satisfy the ever-changing schedule of required courtroom testimony. However, when the agency did not send the actual analyst who performed the actual testing and wrote the actual report to testify, the accused was essentially out of luck. There could be no meaningful inquiry into the nature, quality, and competence of any collection or testing. The available employee could testify only to generalities and could honestly deny any direct knowledge of the testing involved in the given case.

Pretrial evidentiary hearings could be even worse. Prior to trial, some legal jurisdictions have allowed police officers or detectives to bring crime lab reports to the stand and explain their meaning in the absence of testimony from a crime lab scientist. In these cases, oversimplification, misinterpretation, and misrepresentation of scientific findings by law enforcement officers become not just possible, but likely.

This practice has worked in favor of the prosecution for generations. It has allowed government crime labs to put their best foot forward and law enforcement agents to inappropriately copilot scientific testimony. However, as explained in Liptak (2009), *Melendez-Diaz* has made such practices impermissible:

> *Crime laboratory reports may not be used against criminal defendants at trial unless the analysts responsible for creating them give testimony and subject themselves to cross-examination, the Supreme Court ruled Thursday in a 5-to-4 decision.*

> *The ruling was an extension of a 2004 decision that breathed new life into the Sixth Amendment's confrontation clause, which gives a criminal defendant the right "to be confronted with the witnesses against him."*

> *...Noting that 500 employees of the Federal Bureau of Investigation laboratory in Quantico, Va., conduct more than a million scientific tests each year, Justice Kennedy wrote, "The court's decision means that before any of those million tests reaches a jury, at least one of the laboratory's analysts must board a plane, find his or her way to an unfamiliar courthouse and sit there waiting to read aloud notes made months ago."*

> *Justice Antonin Scalia, writing for the majority, scoffed at those "back-of-the-envelope calculations." In any event, he added, the court is not entitled to ignore even an unwise constitutional command for reasons of convenience. "The confrontation clause may make the prosecution of criminals more burdensome, but that is equally true of the right to trial by jury and the privilege against self-incrimination," Justice Scalia wrote. "The sky will not fall after today's decision," he added.*

> *But that is not how prosecutors saw it. "It's a train wreck," Scott Burns, the executive director of the National District Attorneys Association, said of the decision. "To now require that criminalists in offices and labs that are already burdened and in states where budgets are already being cut back," Mr. Burns said, "to travel to courtrooms and wait to say that cocaine is cocaine—we're still kind of reeling from this decision."*

> *Mr. Burns said complying with the ruling would be particularly tough in large rural states with a single crime laboratory and in old cases where the analyst has died or moved away.*

The decision came in the wake of a wave of scandals at crime laboratories that included hundreds of tainted cases in Michigan, Texas and West Virginia. William C. Thompson, a professor of criminology at the University of California, Irvine, said those scandals proved that live testimony from analysts was needed to explore potential shortcomings in laboratory reports.

"The person can be interrogated about the process, about the meaning of the document," Professor Thompson said. "The lab report itself cannot be interrogated to establish the strengths and limitations of the analysis."

…Cross-examination of witnesses, Justice Scalia wrote, "is designed to weed out not only the fraudulent analyst, but the incompetent one as well." He added that the Constitution would require allowing defendants to confront witnesses even if "all analysts always possessed the scientific acumen of Mme. Curie and the veracity of Mother Teresa."

The case arose from the conviction of Luis E. Melendez-Diaz on cocaine trafficking charges in Massachusetts. Part of the evidence against him was a laboratory report stating that bags of white powder said to have belonged to him contained cocaine. Prosecutors submitted the report with only an analyst's certificate.

Jeffrey L. Fisher, a law professor at Stanford who represented Mr. Melendez-Diaz, said perhaps a third of all states follow procedures that comply with Thursday's decision. What that will mean as a practical matter remains to be seen. Criminal defense lawyers may still stipulate that crime lab reports are accurate, fearing that live testimony will only underscore their clients' guilt. Others may insist on testimony in the hope that the analyst will be unavailable. Still others will now be able to prove that an analyst's conclusion was mistaken or inconclusive.

"The defense bar today gains the formidable power to require the government to transport the analyst to the courtroom at the time of trial," Justice Kennedy wrote. "The court's holding," Justice Kennedy wrote, "is a windfall to defendants, one that is unjustified by a demonstrated deficiency in trials, any well-understood historical requirement, or any established constitutional precedent."

Melendez-Diaz (2009) provides that if a lab analyst performed evidentiary analysis and wrote the report of findings, then they alone may offer it as evidence against the accused in a legal proceeding. Detractors of this ruling will groan that it places an inordinate and unbearable strain on overtaxed government crime labs and their employees. No agency has the time or travel budget required to send crime lab employees away for days at a time, to wait for testimony that may ultimately be unnecessary. Casework quality will suffer and backlogs will grow, they will argue.

The authors of this text agree that there will be challenges. However, there are inexpensive workarounds. The simplest and most cost-effective include expert forensic testimony via remote videoconferencing (e.g., Skype). The courts have accepted video depositions and phone testimony from experts and lay witnesses for years, as well as the "phone presence" of attorneys unable to be physically present with their clients during certain court proceedings. Testimony via remote videoconferencing is now becoming more accepted and common.

CONCLUSION

Forensic investigators must accept that they work in service of the law and the courts. This requires understanding the structure and function of the various components of the adversarial system. It also means accepting how, working together, they are intended to create the balance that justice requires.

Their responsibility is to prepare evidence with such reliable providence that it can meet requirements of courtroom reliability and admissibility. This includes a working understanding of the United States Constitution; the individual rights that it guarantees (which they must protect); and related case law. It comes down to being capable of proving integrity of both character and evidence; and accepting that forensic facts help the courts to negotiate justice within the confines of the law.

ENDNOTES

1. This chapter has been adapted from material originally published in Chisum and Turvey (2012) and Cooley and Turvey (2014).
2. The justice system nationwide is plagued by instances of crime victims being billed by the government for rape kits and body bags; and of domestic violence victims being denied protective orders. To say nothing of the courts and government agencies refusing to revoke the parole for those in clear violation, especially when domestic violence or abuse is involved. Moreover, the quality and existence of victim assistance agencies varies from county to county.
3. Frye v. United States (1923) requires that expert testimony be generally accepted by the relevant scientific community; in Daubert v. Merrell Dow Pharmaceuticals, Inc. (1993), the Supreme Court held that Rule 702 superseded Frye, requiring scientific testimony to be "not only relevant, but reliable;" in Kumho Tire Co. v. Carmichael (1999), the Supreme Court held that Daubert "applies not only to testimony based on 'scientific' knowledge, but also to testimony based on 'technical' and 'other specialized' knowledge." Each state has adopted its own guidelines related to some, all, or none of these rulings.
4. This will be discussed more thoroughly in Chapter 12: Investigating Allegations of Police Torture.

REFERENCES

Ake v. Oklahoma (February 26, 1985). US Supreme Court, 470 US 68.

Balko, R. (August 01, 2013). *The untouchables: America's misbehaving prosecutors, and the system that protects them.* Huffington Post. http://www.huffingtonpost.com/2013/08/01/prosecutorialmisconduct-new-orleans-louisiana_n_3529891.html.

Black, H. C. (1990). *Black's law dictionary* (6th ed.). St Paul, MN: West Publishing.

Brady v. Maryland, (1963) 373 U.S. 83.

Cary, R., Singer, C., & Latcovich, S. (2011). *Federal criminal discovery*. Chicago, IL: ABA Publishing.

Chapman, N., & McConnell, M. (2012). Due process as separation of powers. *Yale Law Journal, 121*(7), 1672—1807.

Chisum, W. J., & Turvey, B. (2012). *Crime reconstruction* (2nd ed.). San Diego, CA: Elsevier Science.

Cooley, C., & Turvey, B. (2014). *Miscarriages of justice*. San Diego, CA: Elsevier Science.

Daubert v. Merrell Dow Pharmaceuticals, Inc. (1993). US Supreme Court, 509 US 579.

Edwards, H., & Gotsonis, C. (2009). *Strengthening forensic science in the United States: A path forward*. Washington, DC: National Academies Press.

Findley, K. (2008). Innocents at risk: adversary imbalance, forensic science, and the search for truth. *Seton Hall Law Review, 38*, 893—973.

FRE. (2011). *Federal rules of evidence*. Cornell University Law School. https://www.law.cornell.edu/rules/fre/article_VII.

Freedman, M. (2005). An ethical manifesto for public defenders. *Valpraiso University Law Review, 39*(4), 911—923.

Frye v. United States (1923). 293 F. 1013, DC Cir.

Gershman, B. (Summer 2006). Reflections on Brady v. Maryland. *South Texas Law Review, 47*, 685—728.

Gershman, B. (2011). Judicial interference with effective assistance of counsel. *Pace Law Review, 31*(2), 560—582.

Giannelli, P., & McMunigal, K. (December 2007). Prosecutors, ethics, and expert witnesses. *Fordham Law Review, 76*, 1493—1537.

Gideon v. Wainwright (1963). US Supreme Court, 372 US 335.

Ingraham, B. (1987). The ethics of testimony: conflicting views on the role of the criminologist as expert witness. In P. Anderson, & L. Winfree (Eds.), *Expert witnesses: Criminologists in the courtroom*. Albany, NY: State University of New York Press.

Kleinig, J. (1996). *The ethics of policing*. New York, NY: Cambridge University Press.

Kumho Tire Co. v. Carmichael (1999). US Supreme Court, 526 US 137.

Lilly, G. (1987). *An introduction to the law of evidence* (2nd ed.). St. Paul, MN: West Publishing Co.

Liptak, A. (June 25, 2009). Justices rule lab analysts must testify on results. *New York Times*.

Martinez v. Ryan (2012). 132 S.Ct. 1309, 1317.

Melendez-Diaz v. Massachusetts (June 25, 2009). US Supreme Court, No. 07-591.

Moreno, J. (November 2004). What happens when Dirty Harry becomes an (expert) witness for the prosecution? *Tulane Law Review, 79*, 1—54.

Morn, F. (1995). *Academic politics and the history of criminal justice education*. Westport, CT: Greenwood Press.

Reid, S. (2003). *Crime and criminology* (10th ed.). Boston, MA: McGraw-Hill.

Savino, J., & Turvey, B. (2011). *Rape investigation handbook* (2nd ed.). San Diego, CA: Elsevier.

Strickland v. Washington (1984). US Supreme Court, No. 82-1554, 466 US 668.

Sullivan, J. (1977). *Introduction to police science* (3rd ed.). New York: McGraw-Hill.

Thornton, J., & Peterson, J. (2007). The general assumptions and rationale of forensic identification. In D. Faigman, D. Kaye, M. Saks, & J. Sanders (Eds.), *Modern scientific evidence: The law and science of expert testimony* (Vol. 1). St. Paul, MN: West Publishing Group.

Thornton, J., & Peterson, J. (2002). The General Assumptions and Rationale of Forensic Identification. In D. L. Faigman, D. H. Kaye, M. J. Saks, & J. Sanders (Eds.), *Modern Scientific Evidence: The Law and Science of Expert Testimony* (Vol. 3). St. Paul, MN: West Publishing Co.

Thornton, J. (1983). Uses and abuses of forensic science. In W. Thomas (Ed.), *Science and law: An essential alliance*. Boulder, CO: Westview Press.

Thornton, J. (1994). Courts of law v. courts of science: a forensic scientist's reaction to Daubert. *Shepard's Expert Scientific Evidence Quarterly, 1*(3), 475−485.

United States v. Acosta (2005) 357 F. 2nd 1228, 1233.

United States v. Safavian (2005) 233 F.R.D. 12.

United States v. Sudikoff (1999) 36 F. 2nd 1196.

Vollmer, A. (1971). *The police and modern society.* Montclair, NJ: Patterson Smith.

CHAPTER

Investigative Ethics

3

Brent E. Turvey[1], Stan Crowder[2]
Forensic Criminology Institute, Sitka, Alaska, United States and Aguascalientes, Mexico[1];
Kennesaw State University, Georgia, GA, United States[2]

CHAPTER OUTLINE

Understanding Ethics 46
    Ethics and Morality...46
    Ethical Dilemmas 47
    Professional Ethics 51
Duty of Care... 52
    The Forensic Investigator 54
    Employers and Fitness for Duty 54
Bias 59
An Ethical Canon for the Forensic Investigator 62
Conclusion 64
Endnotes 64
References 64

The first duty of any forensic investigator is to faithfully serve the justice system, as a "forensic" designation naturally suggests. This means they are accountable to the law and the Constitution before anything else. The ability to keep and maintain this professional allegiance is the reason they are hired by any employer, because it will be front and center every time they testify, or give evidence, in court. They must understand this duty and also possess the character to dispatch it in favor of legal justice, no matter the circumstance, while ignoring their personal feelings.

To be very clear, the forensic investigator's first allegiance is not to their place of work, to their supervisors, or to their co-workers. If the forensic investigator is employed by an agency that does not recognize this principal duty to the law or the Constitution, then there will be tension—to put it mildly. The law will require one thing; the agency another. When disagreements occur, the court must be served first or there is no justice.

As should also be clear from previous chapters, referring to a professional as "forensic" has implications, and it has consequences. To be fair, if an operative is not sworn or otherwise required to uphold the law; to abide by the rulings of the court; and to do so with professional integrity (as well as accountability), then they should drop the word "forensic" from any job titles or descriptions. Anything less is going to be misleading to the community of criminal justice professionals—to say nothing of ultimately deceiving the court.

The purpose of this chapter is to explore the means and mechanisms by which the forensic investigator understands, effects, and ultimately demonstrates ethical professional character—that they may be worthy of courtroom service. This is necessary because courtroom testimony requires trust. If one is not trusted, or cannot demonstrate that they are trustworthy, then their testimony will not be believed. It may even be excluded. This requires discussions relating to general ethics, professional ethics, the forensic investigator's duty of care, and concerns regarding bias. Case examples will be provided to illustrate these concepts as needed.

This chapter will then conclude with an ethical canon for the forensic investigator.

UNDERSTANDING ETHICS

There is a great deal of confusion with respect to ethics in the justice system—including what they actually are, how they are achieved, and their relationship to morality. This routinely occurs when those discussing professional ethics inappropriately conflate philosophy with religion. For example, the criminal justice literature is rife with publications treating personal morality, religious dogma, and professional ethics as though they are interchangeable constructs. In reality, they are quite different.

The forensic investigator has a responsibility to understand these distinctions, demonstrated ultimately by the degree of opacity in what they document (and how); what they collect (and leave behind); what they seek to examine (or keep from being examined); and what they report (or fail to report). The forensic investigator is a truth seeker. Any perversion of this service in favor of personal or political agendas is a violation against the cause of justice.

ETHICS AND MORALITY

In philosophy, *ethics* relates to the study of individual or group character. Character is comprised of many different elements, including morality, ideals, values, and virtues (Thornton, 2011).[1] *Morality* is a significant contributor to the development of ethics. It is most commonly associated with individual feelings or beliefs regarding the quality and consequences of actions. Morality provides a foundational basis for determining whether actions or choices are considered right, wrong, good, or bad. Morals are comprised of values and beliefs; ethics are the rules created to ensure the integrity of underlying morals are preserved.

Ethics are the specific situational rules of conduct constructed from morality and other elements of character (e.g., motivation, libido, courage, loyalty, integrity, and empathy); they are, necessarily, the result of reflection and deliberation (Ethics Across the Curricula Committee, 2007). The influence of morality on ethics can be absolute or finite, with shifts dependent on individual or group beliefs. Ethics tend to evolve based on how we view ourselves, as well as the groups and belief systems that we identify with.

Consider the act of killing. A number of groups with differing belief systems consider the act of killing a fellow human being to be immoral. Consequently a *moral imperative* exists within these groups to refrain from killing.[2] However, these same groups recognize there are circumstances under which killing is not only acceptable, but also necessary and expected. This includes killing as an act of self-defense; killing as just and necessary retribution; killing enemies during a time of war; and state-sanctioned killing in the form of capital punishment. The specific circumstances in which killing is permissible might even be referred to as "the ethics of killing."

At this point, it is important to accept that every belief system (e.g., institutional, political, religious, cultural) has its own set of values, morals, and ideals with its own subsequent ethical canon. Consider that in some cultures women can drive a car, wear revealing clothes, own property, get an education, and marry or date whomever they prefer. In other cultures, such conduct by a woman is considered immoral; in extreme cases it may even be a violation of the law. This reality provides that there are no truly universal moral imperatives or obligations: even rape and torture are considered acceptable by some depending on the context (e.g., honor killings, time of war). Right and wrong, it must be understood, are functions of cultural necessity.

ETHICAL DILEMMAS

Ethical dilemmas arise when the available choices and obligations in a specific situation do not allow for an ethical outcome. In such instances, making a choice or taking action is unavoidable. Yet, all of the available alternatives violate an explicit ethical principle or guideline. In other words, a true ethical dilemma is a no-win situation.

Ethical dilemmas are unavoidable when working with or for others that maintain different moral foundations or ethical obligation; or when serving in multiple roles with diverse obligations. This is ever the case for the forensic investigator, who must serve the evidence, the court, and their employer all at once.

Ethical dilemmas commonly occur along one of the following themes:

(1) Truth v. Loyalty: Choosing between personal integrity *and* fidelity pledged to others (e.g., friends, family members, coworkers, employers, and organizations).
(2) Individual v. Group: Choosing between the interests of an individual (self), or a few (profession or agency), *and* those of a larger community (society).

(3) Immediate v. Future: Choosing between present benefits (e.g., money, credit, awards, arrests, convictions, or continued employment) *and* those that are long term (e.g., personal reputation, agency reputation, justice).

(4) Justice v. Compassion: Choosing between fair and dispassionate application of consequences *and* the individual need for mercy.

Ethical dilemmas should not be confused with ignorance of what is ethical, or with the discomfort that often comes from having to make difficult ethical decisions (e.g., when being ethical requires personal sacrifice or harming a friend).

A common ethical dilemma faced by forensic investigators involves *Truth v. Loyalty*. Very often, the forensic investigator will have knowledge that could harm the reputation of their agency or employer if it were to be made public. This includes knowledge that evidence has been contaminated; knowledge that evidence supporting alternative theories has been lost or intentionally destroyed; or knowledge a coworker has given false testimony about their resume or findings. Revealing this information would be in the public interest, and in the interest of justice; but it is also likely to be a violation of agency policy.

The ethical course of action would seem obvious, but it is not. Government (a.k.a. public) institutions, including law enforcement agencies and their respective crime laboratories, generally have written policies that severely restrict the speech of their employees. This includes restrictions on the things they say while working, as well as the things they say about work while in their private life (e.g., talking to the press, posting to Facebook, etc.). These rules are necessary to protect the confidentiality of sensitive issues, to provide for operational authority and to help maintain overall agency effectiveness.[3]

A careful read of a government employee contract, and related institutional policies, usually makes it clear that government employees with concerns or grievances regarding coworkers, supervisors, or other internal matters must report them only within the institutional chain of command. They are generally forbidden from pursuing such matters themselves, and from speaking out about them publicly—lest they harm the "operation of the agency, or perception of the public." Consequently unless a matter of public interest is involved (which is a subjective standard at best), government employees can be punished, and even terminated, for violations (Ronald, 2007).

CASE EXAMPLE: *SPECIAL AGENT MICHAEL P. MALONE, FBI HAIR AND FIBER ANALYST, FBI CRIME LAB*

In 1995, the FBI Crime Laboratory suffered the first of numerous scandals that would plague it until the present day.[a] It came as the result of allegations from within. Dr. Fred Whitehurst, a 20-year FBI veteran holding a Ph.D. in chemistry, reported that FBI investigators and examiners were being pressured to skew findings in favor of police and prosecutors. As explained in Peterson and Leggett (2007, pp. 646–647):

> ...in 1995, Dr. Frederic Whitehurst, a scientist employed in the FBI laboratory, leveled charges of sloppy work, flawed report writing, and perjured court testimony

affecting the explosives, chemistry, toxicology, and materials analysis units of the laboratory. Under the supervision of Michael R. Bromwich, the United States Justice Department's Inspector General, and with the assistance of an external blue ribbon panel, an extensive eighteen-month investigation ensued, which uncovered very serious problems. The investigation did not substantiate most of Whitehurst's allegations but did find numerous instances of "testimonial errors, substandard analytical work, and deficient practices." The Inspector General's final report, issued in 1997, made numerous recommendations aimed at maintaining the independence of scientists in the crime laboratory and at protecting them from the influence of field investigators while conducting laboratory examinations, writing reports, and delivering testimony.

Dr. Whitehurst was fired as a result of his whistle-blowing efforts, and subsequently sued the FBI for wrongful termination. Eventually he reached a $1.46 million settlement agreement. The scandal made public by Dr. Whitehurst, and the Inspector General's investigation that followed, preceded the publication of *Tainting Evidence: Inside the Scandals at the FBI Crime Lab* (Kelly & Wearne, 1998). This detailed book levied a scathing and ultimately accurate indictment of FBI Crime Laboratory culture.

One of the FBI agents involved in this scandal was Michael S. Malone, a hair and fiber analyst in the crime lab. In 1997, Inspector General Michael Bromwich concluded that Malone had "testified falsely" on 27 different points in the impeachment of US District Judge Alcee Hastings (Bromwich, 1997). Malone testified that he had done a lab test that was in fact performed by another examiner. In another case, Malone testified that carpet fibers found on a woman's clothing linked her to defendant's apartment despite his report which stated that his lab findings were inconclusive. Details about Malone's rise and fall in the Bureau were reported in Freedberg (2001):

He grabbed headlines for his work in the "Fatal Vision" appeals of Jeffrey MacDonald, the Green Beret Army surgeon convicted of murdering his wife and children at Fort Bragg, N.C. He won praise for helping with the case against John Hinckley, who shot President Ronald Reagan. And Hillsborough County sheriff's deputies credited him with finding the key evidence—tiny strands of fiber—that put away Bobby Joe Long, a Tampa Bay area serial killer who tied up his victims before raping and strangling them.

The more famous Malone got, the more eager police and prosecutors around the country became for his testimony…

And in time, with all the glory Malone achieved came whispers, whispers that turned to murmurs and then a steady buzz: Mike Malone was sloppy. He was a government shill. He stretched the truth, maybe even made things up…

In 1987 and again in 1988, the Florida Supreme Court threw out murder convictions that hinged on his hair testimony. In 1989, William Tobin, the FBI's chief metals expert, accused Malone of intentionally giving false testimony in a case. It wasn't just any case, either. A judicial panel was deciding whether to recommend the impeachment of then-federal Judge Alcee Hastings of South Florida.

A jury in Miami had acquitted Hastings of taking a bribe to fix a case, but the FBI suspected he lied to win acquittal. The alleged payoff was made in Georgetown, near a leather shop. Hastings had testified he was in Georgetown to find a shop to fix a broken purse.

The FBI asked Malone to test the purse strap to see if it had been broken accidentally by snagging it on something, as Hastings said, or whether it was too strong to break and had been cut. Among other exams, Malone said he performed a "tensile test," measuring the force needed to break an object, and concluded the strap had been cut.

> His testimony, and the judicial panel's subsequent report, helped prompt the U.S. Senate to remove Hastings from the bench. (Three years later, Hastings was elected to Congress.)
>
> Tobin agreed the strap had been cut. But Tobin said he, not Malone, had performed the tensile test, and, in a six-page memo, he detailed 26 other instances where Malone made "false... contrived/fabricated... deceptive" statements under oath. Things looked bad for Malone. "Sad to say, you are right on every point," Tobin's supervisor wrote on a Post-it note.
>
> But when the memo reached a higher up, nothing happened. Instead, the quiet, easygoing Malone kept moving up the FBI's career ladder—nominated twice for the bureau's top award.

Ultimately Malone's false testimony and misconduct costed him his reputation and his place in the crime lab. Despite this, the consequences were not exactly severe, as reported in Earle (2014):

> Although he was never disciplined and got to retire with a pension, Malone's criminal forensics work has come under heavy scrutiny by investigators—including his involvement in a case that sent former DC resident Donald Gates to prison for 28 years for a murder he didn't commit.
>
> "Malone's faulty analysis and scientifically unsupportable testimony contributed to the conviction of an innocent defendant" and at least five other convictions that were later reversed, the IG wrote in its report, released last week.
>
> Malone testified at trial that one of Gates' hairs scientifically matched one found on the body of Georgetown University student Catherine Schilling, 21. DNA evidence later proved him to be wrong...
>
> Independent scientists found 96 percent of Malone's caseload to be "problematic" for reasons such as making statements that "had no scientific basis." Contrary to normal standards, Malone produced lab notes that were "in pencil and not dated."
>
> The prior IG investigation found Malone testified "outside his expertise and inaccurately" and cited him for misconduct.

Special Agent Malone was transferred to the field and then retired in 1999. However, in 2014 it was revealed that he had been working for the FBI as a contract employee conducting background investigations since 2002. Dr. Fred Whitehurst minced no words when he learned of this circumstance, as further reported in Earle (2014):

> "It's absolutely unbelievable considering what the FBI knows about this individual that he's been allowed to continue as an FBI contractor," whistleblower Fred Whitehurst, a former top FBI explosives expert, told The Post.
>
> Early on, the FBI appears not to have considered looking into more systemic problems in its hair and fibers unit. Investigators uncovered a 2002 memo from DOJ's criminal division to Michael Chertoff, then assistant attorney general, raising concerns about "the specter that the other examiners in the [Hairs and Fibers] unit were either as sloppy as Malone or were not adequately conducting confirmations [of his work]. This issue has been raised with the FBI but not resolved to date."

What the case of Michael Malone helps to reveal is a cultural tendency within the FBI to knowingly use flawed methodology; to hide it, ignore it, and deny it as long as possible; to tailor forensic findings to the needs of the prosecution; to reward those who participate in the deception; and to punish those who would speak out against it. All of this acts as a disincentive for anyone from within to break ranks and report similar misconduct.

Restrictions on employee speech have a long-standing tradition within government agencies, and currently enjoy coverage from the United States Supreme Court, which holds that (Garcetti et al. v. Ceballos, 2006) "When public employees make statements pursuant to their official duties, they are not speaking as citizens for First Amendment purposes, and the Constitution does not insulate their communications from employer discipline." In a work environment where punishment, termination, and loss of employee benefits (e.g., wages, medical coverage, and pensions) can result from sharing internal matters outside the chain of command, institutional secrecy is all but assured except in perhaps the most extreme cases (Diehl, 2011; Papandrea, 2010; Wright, 2011).[b]

It is perhaps worth noting that ethical dilemmas are useful in that they can reveal the need for deeper reflection and deliberation about the consequences of actions—which is how we are meant to develop ethical guidelines in the first place.

[a]Refer back to Chapter 1, and the discussion regarding the FBI's present admissions that the vast majority of its hair and fiber analysts have been giving false testimony in favor of the prosecution for decades. This has resulted in numerous wrongful convictions, including several involving the death penalty.
[b]Concern regarding the culture of secrecy within government agencies is something that the U.S. Supreme Court generally acknowledged and warned against when ruling on antiretaliation legislation subsequent to the Garcetti decision in *Crawford v. Metro. Government of* Nashville et al. (2009), arguing: "if an employee reporting discrimination in answer to an employer's questions could be penalized with no remedy, prudent employees would have a good reason to keep quiet about Title VII offenses (e.g., employer retaliation in the form of discrimination, unlawful employment practices and sanction, unlawful investigations of employees, and procedural denial)."

PROFESSIONAL ETHICS

Professional ethics are the specific ideals, principles, values, and constraints imposed on practitioners by the mandates of their profession and workplace. They are generally expressed as an explicit code of ethical conduct (Davis, 1995). It can be said that a profession without a written, comprehensive, and uncompromising code of ethics is no profession at all, as explained in Kleinig (1996) and Sullivan (1977, p. 280):

Without question, a code of ethics is essential in a profession. Without it, a profession could not exist. Moreover, the rules and regulations selected must reach the highest standards. There must be no opportunity for compromise. Professional ethics dictates the application of such absolutes as "always" and "never."

Professional codes of ethics include three different kinds of directives: ideals, principles, and requirements (Davis, 1995).

Ideals are professional aspirations and essentially impossible to achieve with perfection or consistency, such as those related to maintaining unsullied character, showing respect, maintaining dignity, or seeking justice. Professionals are expected to try, but they are also allowed to fail so long as it is not part of an intentional subversive effort.

Principles are specific values or commitments, such as an organizational commitment to a profession, its members, a particular goal, or a particular school of thought; or member commitments to impartiality and integrity. As with ideals, professionals are expected to maintain principles, but they may unintentionally falter without being severely punished—so long as they acknowledge their failings and seek remedy.

Requirements are mandatory rules and obligations that must be followed to the letter. Far from being an ideal or a principle, a requirement is explicit and cannot be negotiated—such as forbidding members from misrepresenting their credentials or mandatory expulsion for members convicted of a felony charge.

Unfortunately professional codes of ethics are often written in such a fashion as to confuse these directives, making some difficult to interpret, abide, and enforce (Davis, 1995; Kleinig, 1996).

DUTY OF CARE

The investigation of reported crime is the statutory and jurisdictional province of various local, state, and federal law enforcement agencies. The specific agencies responding to a criminal complaint, and ultimately in charge, depend on which laws have been reported to be broken and where. Crimes reported in the city generally belong to municipal police (e.g., city, borough, village, or township); crimes reported outside city limits generally belong to the county sheriff; and the state police bureaus are in charge of the highways, investigations of fraud related to state licensure and services (e.g., Medicaid and welfare), coordination of multijurisdictional cases, and providing resources to local agencies on request (these responsibilities vary from state to state). Federal law enforcement agencies [e.g., the FBI, the Bureau of Alcohol, Tobacco, Firearms, and Explosives (B-ATF), and the US Marshals] become involved when federal crimes are suspected or alleged (e.g., terrorism, organized crime, trafficking, civil rights violations, and tax evasion), or when a crime occurs in a federal building or on federal land (e.g., a federal prison, a Native American reservation, or a National Park).

Whichever agency takes charge of a criminal complaint, they alone have the legal authority to respond, interview witnesses and suspects, collect evidence, or make arrests.

A responding law enforcement agency has a duty of care. This refers to the professional and legal obligation to be competent custodians of any victims who are encountered; any criminal investigations that are initiated; and any evidence that supports or refutes allegations of criminal activity against accused suspects. Very often this is a matter of state, or local statute, wherein law enforcement officers are not allowed to turn a blind eye to crime and must respond to protect life and property, and very often it is made part of the formal oath they take when being sworn in. If an agency, or its officers and investigators, do not hold or perceive a professional duty of care to their community, then they are not fit to serve it.

The primary responsibilities of law enforcement, when responding to a criminal complaint, include the following:

(1) Protect themselves; call for back-up when needed.
(2) Establish who is involved.
(3) Ensure that everyone involved is safe.
(4) Get medical assistance for those who need it.

(5) Determine what happened.
(6) Establish who made the complaint and what it is about.
(7) Identify any witnesses.
(8) Seek out, identify, collect, and protect any physical evidence.
(9) Ensure the objective forensic examination of all relevant evidence.
(10) Determine whether or not a crime has taken place.
(11) Identify any criminal suspects.
(12) Establish whether probable cause exists for an arrest.
(13) Arrest any criminal perpetrators.

These tactical issues also reflect an ethical responsibility. Investigators may not assume what happened based on the statements of one party, whether responding to a domestic situation or an alleged sexual assault. They may not assume that any crime has actually occurred until the facts have been established. They must be sufficiently educated to understand what the elements of each crime are and what the probable cause is. They must also impartially place the cuffs on anyone they determine has broken the law. For example, as explained in Bryden and Lengnick (1997, pp. 1230−1231):

> As with all crimes, the police decide whether a reported rape actually occurred, and attempt to determine who committed it. If they want the case to go forward, they "found" the complaint and transmit the file to the prosecutor's office... The police must investigate, a task that cannot easily be combined with offering the emotional support that the victim needs. The detective presumably wishes to avoid an injustice to a wrongly accused individual. In addition, for reasons of professional pride, he does his best to avoid looking naive by falling for a story that turns out to be false. Experienced investigators also know that many rape complainants ultimately decline to press charges, sometimes to the dismay of a detective who has worked hard to build a case.

Meeting these responsibilities is best accomplished with a thorough, diligent, and comprehensive investigation. By comprehensive investigation, the authors mean a detailed review of the complainant and their statements; the careful consideration of witness and suspect statements; and the diligent collection and examination of any physical evidence. All of this must be attended prior to making final determinations regarding whether a crime has been committed and whether probable cause exists to arrest any suspects.

Too often, the police do not comprehend the needs of a criminal investigation, let alone probable cause, and the responsibilities mentioned are implemented in reverse. This is to say that suspects are often arrested first and investigations happen later, if at all. This is backward and may result in the creation of bias, missed suspects and evidence, and then doubt when the results of the investigation begin to point away from the person that was initially arrested.

Investigators have a duty to refrain from becoming invested in their suspects to the point where they consider making an arrest before a sufficient (or any) investigation has been undertaken. Failure to proceed with the investigation first, and ensure that any arrests are a natural result of that process, can lead to a miscarriage of justice (e.g., a failed prosecution of the factually guilty or a successful prosecution of the factually innocent).

THE FORENSIC INVESTIGATOR

The duty of care specific to the forensic investigator includes the following:

1. Seeking out the proper education related to their intended forensic profession;
2. Being knowledgeable of the law and legal rulings related to their areas of expertise and forensic experts in general;
3. Seeking out the most current rulings, literature, and ongoing training opportunities to remain informed regarding developments in their profession;
4. Achieving and maintaining relevant professional certifications;
5. Submitting to a written code of ethics, usually as part membership in a professional association, which forbids them from misrepresenting their professional resume, from misrepresenting their findings, and from working beyond their areas of demonstrated expertise.
6. Documenting and reporting fraud or negligence when it is observed, to ensure that it becomes known by the proper decision makers.

These are the very basics, and essentially require the forensic investigator to know what they are doing; to know why; to understand and follow the law; to be honest; and to discern, then admit, the limits of their abilities and findings. In the forensic community, ignorance is a vice, and less information is not better.

If the forensic investigator does not acknowledge this duty of care, then they are not a professional but something that seeks to exist outside the bounds of forensic accountability. When there is no accountability, there is no science; and when there is no science there can be no trust of subsequent forensic findings. On these points the forensic investigator must not waver.

EMPLOYERS AND FITNESS FOR DUTY

Just as forensic investigators have a duty of care, so also do their employers. In fact, it is not altogether different. Those who employ forensic investigators have a duty of care to hire only the qualified, who are also in possession of good character; to require those in their employ to be current with the scientific literature and methodology relevant to their respective areas of evidence and/or expertise; to achieve and maintain relevant certifications; and to weed out the inept or unethical as they are identified by virtue of a pattern of behavior that indicates apathy, ongoing errors, negligence, or misconduct.

Employers also have a duty to recognize, report, and when necessary sanction or terminate those who are unfit. *Fitness for duty* refers to the ability to safely and effectively perform one's job-related responsibilities with integrity. This means the absence of physical, psychological, and character impediments.

Fitness for duty in a law enforcement or public safety context is important because the consequences of failure, or inability, are high. When public safety employees are not fit for duty, people can be harmed if not killed. Those at risk can include the unfit officer, fellow officers, other public safety personnel, victims, suspects, and any unfortunate bystanders.

The legal responsibilities related to fitness for duty are explained in Fischler et al. (2011, p. 72):

> *Police employers have a legal duty to ensure that police officers under their command are mentally and emotionally fit to perform their duties, and failure to do so can result in significant civil liability to the employer and serious consequences. Occasionally, a law enforcement officer's behavior raises concerns that the officer may be unstable, a physical danger to self and to others, or ineffective in discharging responsibilities. Such behavior may occur on or off duty and may include excessive force, domestic violence, lack of alertness, substance abuse, or other observable counterproductive behaviors.*

Red flags, or indicators, of an employee's lack of fitness include the following (adapted from Fischler et al., 2011):

- Making false statements to supervisors in reports or in testimony
- Observed symptoms of psychological distress (e.g., excessive crying, irritability, or paranoia)
- Making threats against others
- Suicidal threats or attempts
- Admission to any facility for mental health issues
- Irrational behavior
- Delusional behavior
- Consistent failure to complete official duties despite corrective action
- Consistent failure to comply with basic departmental rules and directives despite corrective action
- Disclosure of a significant mental health issue or a mental health diagnosis or treatment by a mental health professional e.g. psychologist, and use of psychotropic medication
- Suspicion of drug abuse (prescription or street drugs). Review of *prescription* drug history
- Multiple citizen or internal complaints
- Involvement in an accident
- Incurring a physical injury
- 911 call to the officer's home
- An arrest for any crime
- A conviction for any felony, or any misdemeanor related to integrity, vice, or violence.
- Positive drug test results

As explained in Fischler et al. (2011), the existence of these red flags should initiate an officer evaluation (p. 72): "When such behavior occurs, and it is reasonably suspected to be attributable, at least in part, to an underlying psychological impairment or condition, a Fitness-For-Duty Evaluation (FFDE) is often necessary to assess the nature of the psychological problem and its impact on job functioning." Failure to acknowledge these indicators and conduct an FFDE would be considered negligence on the part of the employer, and compound liability with respect to leaving an unfit employee on the street, perhaps even carrying a firearm. But indifference is not the worst employer response to unequivocal red flags—as revealed in the case of Deborah Madden (Fig. 3.1).

CASE EXAMPLE: *DEBORAH MADDEN, CRIMINALIST, SFPD CRIME LAB*

In early 2010, the San Francisco Police Department's crime lab suspended all drug testing and was forced to submit to an external audit due to revelations that one of its veteran criminalists, Deborah Madden, had been stealing cocaine for personal use. Apparently, she had been abusing her position at the crime lab for a number of years, to feed a substance abuse problem. As reported in Burack (2012) (Fig. 3.2):

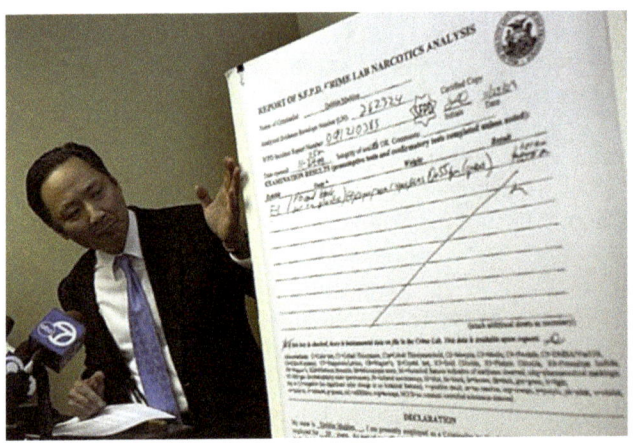

FIGURE 3.1

Pictured Jeff Adachi, San Francisco Public Defender, at a press conference on March 10, 2010. He is holding "an enlargement of a Report of S.F.P.D. Crime Lab Narcotics Analysis filled out by Deborah Madden…" The purpose of the press conference was to discuss the "ramifications of longtime police crime lab technician deborah madden allegedly tampering with drug evidence, as well as the impact of troubling crime lab audit findings" (Van Derbeken, 2010).

> *In 2010, revelations that a department criminalist was pilfering drug evidence led to the dismissal of hundreds of drug cases. And in 2011, more than 100 more drug cases were dismissed after [Public Defender Jeff] Adachi's office discovered videos allegedly depicting officers illegally entering residences and falsifying police reports and stealing suspects' valuables.*

Ms. Madden was not arrested for any crimes by the local government. Instead she was given immunity, allowed to resign, and also allowed to collect a pension while she continued to serve as an expert witness for the state in multiple criminal trials. As reported in Eskenazi (2011):

> *Disgraced former crime lab technician Deborah Madden will not face any criminal charges, despite triggering a scandal that led to millions of dollars in city costs and a literal Get Out of Jail Free card for thousands of accused drug criminals. Madden is now free to begin drawing her city pension; with 29 years on the job, she's entitled to somewhere in the neighborhood of 75 percent of her $63,000 yearly salary.*

Duty of Care   57

FIGURE 3.2

Deborah Madden, formerly a criminalist with the San Francisco Police Department's crime lab, is escorted from her arraignment in 2010.

> *This author experienced the hypocrisy of the prosecutor's office first hand when testifying as an expert for the defense in* California v. Culton *against Deborah Madden. Specifically the district attorney became furious when this author explained, under oath, that he did not seek out information about the homicide scene directly from Ms. Madden, who processed it for evidence. This, the author explained, because she was in fact a known fraud—and therefore unreliable. When the district attorney objected, the trial judge told him to stop asking questions that he did not want the answers to. As reported in Burack (2011):*
>
> *The former San Francisco Police department criminalist whose alleged theft of drugs from the crime lab scandalized the department will be called soon to testify in a nearly 30-year-old murder case. Debbie Madden appeared at a pretrial court hearing Wednesday in the case of Dwight Culton, 61, accused of killing 43-year-old Joan Baldwin at a former auto body shop near the Hall of Justice on April 6, 1984.*
>
> *Madden, 61, will testify at Culton's trial, with immunity from prosecution for any statements she might make about her recently scrutinized activities at the lab, her attorney Paul DeMeester said Thursday. He said this was the first nondrug case in which she had been called to testify since leaving the department in 2009. Madden's alleged admission that she took small amounts of cocaine from evidence at the lab in*

late 2009 could potentially be used by defense attorneys to impeach her credibility as a witness, even in a decades-old murder case.

DeMeester said the relatively recent accusations of Madden's misconduct at the drug lab "have nothing to do with what she did on the case in 1984." Madden was called to the scene of Baldwin's murder to collect blood evidence and later did some of the testing. "She is a material witness in this case, and her testimony is necessary for us to establish chain of custody," District Attorney's Office spokeswoman Erica Derryck said.

When proffering her as a witness for the state, the prosecution routinely attempted to hide Ms. Madden's identity and by extension her duplicitous character. For instance, they placed her on the witness list under a misleading name; they did not initially disclose her criminal history; and they did not disclose her termination for laboratory drug theft. Despite the requirements of discovery set forth in Brady v. Maryland (1963), the prosecution argued that these were lawful tactics, reported in Begin (2010):

The District Attorney's Office had no formal policy regarding releasing the criminal history of its expert witnesses to the defense, prosecutors told a judge Thursday. That information will be used to challenge evidence in a trial. The admission came as Superior Court Judge Anne-Christine Massullo is creating a framework for hundreds of future drug cases that could be revisited after a debacle at the San Francisco Police Department's crime lab that became public March 9.

Documents released this week show top narcotics prosecutor Sharon Woo complained to her superiors in November of "disturbing" problems with the attendance of longtime lab technician Deborah Madden. While the chief attorney in the office, Russ Giuntini, relayed a message of concern to police, it did not include Madden's name.

On Thursday, Massullo ordered the release of more documents to defense attorneys related to the Police Department's investigation into Madden, who is suspected of taking cocaine from evidence samples at the crime lab. Massullo also pressed Woo for District Attorney Kamala Harris' policy on notifying defense attorneys of the criminal history of a witness.

In 2008, Madden was convicted in San Mateo County on a count of misdemeanor domestic violence for throwing a cordless phone at her domestic partner's head. Despite the conviction and a subsequent internal investigation, the Police Department never informed the District Attorney's Office, which it's required to do under California law.

"I don't believe there is a written policy," Woo said. "There is no written procedure. Our policy is to follow the law." The District Attorney's Office relies on the Police Department to provide information about one of its employees, Woo said.

"Saying we rely on the police to tell us really isn't [sufficient] under this court's eyes," Massullo said.

When it became clear that local authorities had lost perspective regarding Ms. Madden's conduct, allowing her to essentially skate on one of the biggest lab scandals in the country at the time, the Federal Government stepped in and charged her with violations of relevant Federal statutes. As reported in Drumwright (2011):

Felony drug charges were filed in federal court Thursday against Deborah Madden, the disgraced former technician at the San Francisco Police Department's crime lab. In a one-sentence indictment, federal prosecutors allege that Madden did "knowingly and intentionally acquire and obtain possession of, by misrepresentation, fraud, forgery, deception and subterfuge" cocaine from the lab.

Madden, who has admitted to taking small amounts of drugs from the lab in 2009, is due to make an initial appearance before U.S. Northern District Court Judge Elizabeth D. Laporte on Wednesday. The drug scandal rocked the crime lab, which was temporarily shut down in March 2010. The incident led to the outsourcing of drug testing to other labs in the Bay Area.

Madden, 61, who has not been jailed on the charge, has never been prosecuted by The City. She did plead no contest in San Mateo County to charges that stemmed from San Mateo police finding 0.09 g of cocaine during a search of Madden's home there.

In October of 2012, the Federal case against of Deborah Madden ended with a mistrial. During a retrial for the same felony charges, she was allowed to plead guilty to a misdemeanor count of cocaine possession in March of 2103, confessing "I knowingly possessed cocaine outside the scope of my employment" (Griffin, 2013). She admitted during interviews with police that she stole the cocaine to manage an ongoing problem with alcohol abuse. It is believed that this plea, and the language involved, was crafted by the defense with an eye to preserving Ms. Madden's government pension.

This case serves to demonstrate that there are those within law enforcement culture willing to tolerate criminality, and also willing to actively conceal it to get what they want. Had the police department and the district attorney's office adopted a zero tolerance policy for criminal conduct by police department employees, Ms. Madden's domestic violence conviction in 2008 would have removed her from the department and from active casework. This would have prevented at least 2 years of misconduct, forensic fraud, and overturned or dismissed criminal cases.

BIAS

Bias refers to prejudice, or preconceived beliefs, for or against a particular person, group, or idea. When asked about bias, the majority of forensic investigators will claim they are entirely objective when performing their analyses, or that they try very hard to be. They also tend to believe their employer, personal emotions, and personal beliefs have essentially no influence on their final conclusions. To admit otherwise would be professional suicide, as objectivity and emotional detachment are prized above all other traits in the course of forensic investigations and related examinations. One could even argue that these are defining traits.[4]

Given the professed objectivity of forensic investigators, and their implied scientific training, it could be asked how bias might persist in their results. This is a perfectly reasonable question. Some claim that bias can be eliminated, and that an objective attitude combined with scientific training is sufficient to cure most of the ills that infect forensic examinations and subsequent results. However, this belief is far from true. It ignores a fundamental principle of cognitive psychology—the pervasive existence of observer effects.

As cognitive psychologists have documented, tested, and repeatedly proven, "[T]he scientific observer [is] an imperfectly calibrated instrument" (Rosenthal, 1966, p. 3). Imperfections stem from the fact that subtle forms of bias, both conscious and subconscious, can easily contaminate what appears outwardly to be an objective process or finding. These distortions are caused by, among other things, observer effects. This particular form of bias is present when results of a forensic investigation are distorted by the context and mental state of the forensic professionals involved to include subconscious expectations and desires.

Acknowledging and managing observer effects is considerable, especially given the forensic community's affiliation with both law enforcement and the prosecution. Specifically, this association has fashioned an atmosphere in which an unsettling number of forensic professionals have all but abandoned objectivity and have become completely partial to the prosecution's objectives, goals, and philosophies. They may even go so far as to regard this association as virtuous and heroic, and believe any alternative philosophy to be morally bankrupt.

So strong is the influence of this association between forensic science and law enforcement that some forensic investigators have deliberately fabricated evidence, or testified falsely, so that the prosecution might prove its case.

CASE EXAMPLE: *DAVID KOFOED, CHIEF CRIME SCENE INVESTIGATOR*

Douglas County Sheriff's Office Crime Laboratory

David Kofoed is the former Chief Crime Scene Investigator for the Douglas County Sheriff's Office in Omaha, Nebraska. In 2010, he was convicted of a felony (tampering with evidence) for falsifying blood evidence against two suspects in a double homicide. Mr. Kofoed spent about a year and a half in jail, failing in his appeal to the Nebraska Supreme court for a new trial, as reported in Kelly (2012) (Fig. 3.3):

FIGURE 3.3

David Kofoed, former Chief Crime Scene Investigator for the Douglas County Sheriff's Office in Omaha, Nebraska, leaves the Cass County Courthouse immediately following his 2010 conviction for charges related to falsifying physical evidence in a double homicide.

Cass County, Neb.: The murder of Wayne and Sharmon Stock

The faulty evidence in this double homicide in Murdock, Neb. landed Kofoed in prison. The Stocks were murdered in their bedroom on Easter night, 2006.

Investigators from the Cass County Sheriff's Department and the Nebraska State Patrol succeeded in getting Matt Livers, the Stocks' nephew, to confess to the crime and implicate another man, Nick Sampson. Before the confession was discovered to be coerced and false, Kofoed claimed he found a small trace of blood in a vehicle owned by Sampson's brother.

Suspicions about the source of that blood peaked when other evidence led police to the real killers, a pair of teenagers from Wisconsin.

When the Nebraska Supreme Court denied Kofoed's request for a new trial, it did not end legal action related to the case. Livers and Sampson filed a civil lawsuit in U.S. District Court claiming their civil rights were denied when they were jailed without reliable evidence.

Along with Kofoed, the case seeks damages from his former employer, the Douglas County Sheriff's Office, the Cass County Sheriff's Department, and the Nebraska State Patrol. Both the organizations and individual officers named as defendants have asked to be dropped from the suit. This spring, the Eighth District Federal Appeals Court convened in Minneapolis to hear arguments. The three-judge panel will decide if any—or all of them—should be included in the lawsuit, and if it should be allowed to proceed.

In his argument before the court, the attorney for Livers, Locke Bowman of MacArthur Justice Center at Northwestern University in Chicago, argued that no one in the case properly shared evidence that could have cleared his client, known in law enforcement as exculpatory evidence.

"This record reflects appalling, massive ignorance on the part of every employee of Douglas County CSI with respect to the obligation to disclose exculpatory evidence," Bowman said. "Kofoed obviously didn't get it." In an interview after the hearing, Bowman said his client wants "his day in court so he can show the world that he was railroaded" and he hopes for some level of compensation.

Douglas County Sheriff Tim Dunning, also named in the lawsuit, told NET News last fall that he had "expected more challenges than I have seen." Dunning initially stood by Kofoed, but by the time the guilty verdict was declared, the sheriff came to believe he and the rest of the CSI unit had been deceived. "He's gone. He's not coming back. We're not doing business like that ever again," Dunning said. "Every piece of what was here that was from him is completely gone."

The decision by the Nebraska Supreme Court did not equivocate regarding what it determined to be Mr. Kofoed's forensic duplicity, as further reported in Kelly (2012):

Writing for the majority, Justice William Connolly wrote: "Kofoed's deceit was amply demonstrated by the false statements that he made in his reports and the inconsistent statements that he made to investigators." Connolly added later: "(Kofoed) was tangled in his own web of deceit."

On his release, Mr. Kofoed was confronted with legal challenges regarding potential falsified evidence in at least two other cases. One involves blood evidence apparently planted in relation to the disappearance of 4-year-old Brendan Gonzalez in 2003. Another involves blood evidence apparently planted in relation to the disappearance of Jessica O'Grady in 2006. In both of these cases, a body was not recovered and Mr. Kofoed was the one who "discovered" trace amounts of evidence of victim blood which were used to associate a defendant with a murder charge. Both cases also resulted in convictions of defendants that are, as of this writing, under review.

In 2014, Mr. Kofoed was held personally liable for almost 6.5 million dollars in damages as the result of a civil rights lawsuit filed against him. As reported in Winchester (2014):

Two Nebraska men who have been awarded a nearly $6.5 million judgment in a civil rights case over evidence-planting could have trouble collecting the money.

A federal judge this week ordered David Kofoed, the disgraced former Douglas County CSI chief, to pay $4.35 million in damages, costs and attorneys fees to Matthew Livers and $2.14 million to Livers' cousin Nick Sampson. Sampson and Livers were wrongly jailed for several months after the 2006 shotgun murders of Livers' aunt and uncle, Wayne and Sharmon Stock of Murdock, Neb...

The county was released from liability, but not the county's insurers, "to the extent those insurers may be deemed responsible for payment of a judgment against Kofoed," according to the settlement reached last fall.

In an email, Sampson's lawyer, Maren Chaloupka, indicated that she might take that route. "Douglas County went to extraordinary lengths to protect Mr. Kofoed for much of this litigation," she said. "Surely this was with the knowledge and consent of its liability insurer. Perhaps it is time for the liability insurer to step from the shadows and cover this judgment."

...Last year, Sampson and Livers settled claims with the other defendants in the lawsuit — the Nebraska State Patrol, Cass County and Douglas County and individual investigators — for $2.6 million. Of that sum, Livers received $1.65 million; Sampson was awarded $965,000...

Kofoed, who maintains his innocence, skipped his trial in the federal lawsuit, saying he couldn't afford the trip back to Omaha. Reached Tuesday at his home in North Carolina, he said the final judgment doesn't change much for him: He's still broke and unemployed.

Ultimately this case demonstrates an investigator, a sheriff's office, and a prosecutorial agency biased by a win at any cost mentality. This includes planting evidence and protecting those that do from any consequences. Kofoed himself is still in denial about the wrong he has done and the harm that it has caused, which is not uncommon in these cases. Those accustomed to wielding this kind of power often have difficulty admitting fault and taking responsibility. It is a stark lesson in the dangers of allowing law enforcement and prosecutors to examine and interpret the forensic evidence.[c]

---

[c]Giannelli (1997) discusses how the forensic community's structural configuration has created many proprosecution forensic investigators and examiners. Further still, The National Academy of Sciences Report on Forensic Science explains that law enforcement and forensic science cultures must be separated because of the very different missions that each undertakes; that because so many forensic personnel work as subordinates within a law enforcement agency or culture, they may forget that they are scientists and instead continually seek to join or at least gain the approval of the prosecution team (Edwards & Gotsonis, 2009).

AN ETHICAL CANON FOR THE FORENSIC INVESTIGATOR

Perhaps one of the most respected criminalists to have retired from profession is Dr. John Thornton. He is an alumnus of multiple crime labs in California, both government and private. He is also the former Director of the Criminalistics Program at the University of California at Berkeley. He has written extensively on intersection of forensic practice, ethics, and the law.

Dr. Thornton recognized the biases that could influence forensic investigators, and the pressures that routinely besieged them (2011; pp. 55–56):

Pressure from attorneys, on both the prosecution and the defense side, may be even more relentless, as their canon of ethics allows them, within bounds, to be insincere. Attorneys are legitimately propagandists of a particular point of view. They are advocates, and they want their views to prevail. Until they are told differently, they may wish to enlist the reconstructionist in their efforts. Apparently no one ever bothers to tell them in law school that the crime reconstructionist is not their trained seal.

This is an aspect of a basic dilemma between law and science. Crime reconstruction is, or certainly it should be, an application of the scientific method. Science takes the establishment of truth as its fundamental goal. Crime reconstruction, as the handmaiden of the legal process, takes the pursuit of justice as its goal. Truth and justice are not enemies, but they are not the same thing, which has caused and will continue to cause a certain tension between the two disciplines…

The way to avoid being pressured by attorneys, investigators, or anyone else to "put the best face" on the evidence—that is, the best face as they perceive that face to be—is not to yield the first time. If the crime reconstructionist demonstrates a manner of professional chastity and does not yield the first time, it will establish the tenor of the relationship between the attorney and the reconstructionist on terms that the attorney will have to accept. Attorneys do not invite others to shape and form their canon of ethics. It is only fair that they should not dictate how crime reconstructionists should approach their own ethical stance.

In furtherance of this goal, Dr. Thornton has offered the following ethical canon for forensic practitioners (specifically for reconstructionists), with the caveat that it be posted publicly (2011; p. 58):

1. *As a practicing crime reconstructionist, I pledge to apply the principles of science and logic and to follow the truth courageously wherever it may lead.*
2. *As a practicing crime reconstructionist, I acknowledge that the scientific spirit must be inquiring, progressive, logical, and unbiased.*
3. *I will never knowingly allow a false impression to be planted in the mind of anyone availing themselves of my services.*
4. *As a practicing crime reconstructionist, it is not my purpose to present only that evidence which supports the view of one side. I have a moral and professional responsibility to ensure that everyone concerned understands the evidence as it exists and to present it in an impartial manner.*
5. *The practice of crime reconstruction has a single professional demand—correctness. It has a single ethical demand—truthfulness. To these I commit myself, totally and irrevocably.*

6. *The exigencies of a particular case will not cause me to depart from the professionalism that I am required to exercise.*

The public display of these guidelines, at the forensic practitioner's desk or on their Website, would serve as a reminder of their precise ethical obligations. Not only to others, but to themselves.

CONCLUSION

Forensic investigators have a professional duty of care that must include adequate education and training; competent practice for which they must be accountable; fitness for duty; and a clearly defined code of professional ethics outlining their obligation to the truth and the law before agencies or politics.

Unfortunately the existing literature suggests the forensic community suffers from an absence of written ethics codes; and when they do exist, either practitioners are not bound to them or they are simply not enforced (Cooley & Turvey, 2014; Edwards & Gotsonis, 2009; Turvey, 2013). This reality has only contributed to the increased number of defendant exonerations (Lozano, 2016); the rise in government liability; and an undeniable loss of faith in forensic evidence and the justice system.

ENDNOTES

1. Ideals are concepts of perfection that may be aspired to but not achieved in reality (e.g., justice, purity, and wisdom). Values are those objects, traits, or ideas that are judged to be significant or important, often regardless of morality (e.g., beauty, money, and intelligence). Virtues are those actions and choices that are considered moral, useful, or otherwise desirable (e.g., chastity, patience, fidelity, and humility). These terms are not mutually exclusive, as one can value an ideal or a virtue.
2. A moral imperative is anything that is deemed vital or essential to maintaining morality.
3. See the "Model Policy on Standards of Conduct" developed by the International Association of Chiefs of Police (IACP, 2012), on which the vast majority of law enforcement agency policies and procedures are based.
4. For instance, according to Dr. Henry Lee (1993), "The adversarial relationship between the state and a defendant tends to place the forensic experts engaged by one side or the other into an adversarial relationship… Nevertheless, most forensic scientists, regardless of who employs them or engages their services, think of their results as entirely objective and try not to allow themselves to be forced into adversarial roles."

REFERENCES

Begin, B. (April 15, 2010). *Policy on expert witnesses lacking*. San Francisco Examiner.
Brady v. Maryland, 373 U.S. 83 (1963).
Bromwich, M. (April 1997). *The FBI laboratory: An investigation into laboratory practices and alleged misconduct in explosives-related and other cases*. Washington, DC: U. S. Department of Justice, Office of the Inspector General.

Bryden, D., & Lengnick, S. (Summer 1997). Rape in the criminal justice system. *Journal of Criminal Law and Criminology, 87*, 1194−1384.

Burack, A. (March 05, 2011). *DUI convictions at risk following SFPD revelations*. San Francisco Examiner.

Burack, A. (April 01, 2012). *Former SF crime lab technician Debbie Madden to testify in murder trial*. San Francisco Examiner.

Cooley, C., & Turvey, B. (2014). *Miscarriages of justice*. San Diego, CA: Elsevier Science.

Crawford v. Metro, Government of Nashville, et al., 2009. U.S. Supreme Court, 555 U.S. 271, 129 S. Ct 846, 172 L. Ed. 2d 650.

Davis, M. (1995). Code of ethics. In W. Bailey (Ed.), *The encyclopedia of police science* (2nd ed.). New York: Garland.

Diehl, C. (2011). Open meetings and closed mouths: elected officials' free speech rights after Garcetti v. Ceballos. *Case Western Reserve Law Review, 61*(2), 551−602.

Drumwright, S. (December 01, 2011). *Feds dish out drug charges to former San Francisco crime lab tech*. San Francisco Examiner.

Earle, G. (July 21, 2014). *Discredited ex-FBI agent hired back as a private contractor years later*. New York Post. http://nypost.com/2014/07/21/discredited-ex-fbi-agent-hired-back-as-a-private-contractor-years-later/.

Edwards, H., & Gotsonis, C. (2009). *Strengthening forensic science in the United States: A path forward*. Washington, DC: National Academies Press.

Eskenazi, J. (January 04, 2011). *Can San Francisco tap into Deborah Madden's pension?* San Francisco Weekly.

Ethics Across the Curricula Committee. (2007). *Ethics 101: A common ethics language for dialogue*. Chicago, IL: DePaul University, Institute for Business & Professional Ethics. http://commerce.depaul.edu/ethics/docs/EthicsManual.pdf.

Fischler, G. L., McElroy, H. K., Miller, L., Saxe-Clifford, S., Stewart, C., & Zelig, M. (2011). The role of psychological fitness-for-duty evaluations in law enforcement. *Police Chief, 78*, 7278.

Freedberg, S. (March 04, 2001). *Good cop, bad cop*. St. Petersburg Times. http://www.sptimes.com/News/030401/Worldandnation/Good_cop__bad_cop_.shtml.

Garcetti, et al., v. Ceballos, 2006. Supreme Court of the United States. No. 04-473, May 30.

Giannelli, P. C. (Spring 1997). The abuse of scientific evidence in criminal cases: the need for independent crime laboratories. *Virginia Journal of Social Policy & the Law, 4*, 439−470.

Griffin, M. (March 20, 2013). Was Deborah Madden's confession a move to keep her city pension? San Francisco Examiner. http://www.sfexaminer.com/sanfrancisco/was-deborah-maddensconfession-a-move-to-keep-her-city-pension/Content?oid=2320991.

IACP, 2012. Model Policy on Standards of Conduct. The International Association of Chiefs of Police; http://www.theiacp.org/PoliceServices/ProfessionalAssistance/Ethics/ModelPolicyon-StandardsofConduct/tabid/196/Default.aspx.

Kelly, J., & Wearne, P. (1998). *Tainting evidence: Inside the scandals at the FBI crime lab*. New York: Free Press.

Kelly, B. (May 29, 2012). *Former CSI Kofoed dogged by legal challenges as jailtime ends*. NET News−NPR. http://netnebraska.org/article/news/former-csi-kofoed-dogged-legal-challenges-jailtime-ends.

Kleinig, J. (1996). *The ethics of policing*. New York: Cambridge University Press.

Lee, H. C. (1993). Forensic science and the law. *Connecticut Law Review, 25*, 1117−1124.

Lozano, J. (February 02, 2016). *Report finds record number of US exonerations in 2015*. Seattle Times. http://www.seattletimes.com/nation-world/record-number-of-us-exonerations-includes-homicide-cases/.

Papandrea, M. (2010). The free speech rights of off-duty government employees. *Brigham Young University Law Review, 6*, 2117—2174.

Peterson, J., & Leggett, A. (Spring 2007). The evolution of forensic science: progress amid the pitfalls. *Stetson Law Review, 36*, 621—660.

Ronald, K. (2007). Garcetti v. Ceballos: the battle over what it means has just begun. *Urban Lawyer, 39*(4), 983—1015.

Rosenthal, R. (1966). *Experimenter effects in behavioral research*. New York: Appleton-Century-Crofts.

Sullivan, J. (1977). *Introduction to police science* (3rd ed.). New York: McGraw-Hill.

Thornton, J. (2011). Crime reconstruction: ethos and ethics. In W. J. Chisum, & B. Turvey (Eds.), *Crime reconstruction* (2nd ed.). San Diego, CA: Elsevier.

Turvey, B. (2013). *Forensic fraud: Evaluating law enforcement and forensic science cultures in the context of examiner misconduct*. San Diego, CA: Elsevier Science.

Van Derbeken, J. (March 15, 2010). Police waited 2 months to investigate lab tech. San Francisco Chronicle. http://www.sfgate.com/bayarea/article/Police-waited-2—months-to-investigate-labtech-3270108.php (Accessed December 2013).

Winchester, C. (April 01, 2014). *Kofoed ordered to pay $6.5M to 2 men wrongly jailed after '06 slayings*. Omaha World-Herald. http://www.omaha.com/news/kofoed-ordered-to-pay-m-to-men-wrongly-jailed-after/article_5fd6bf60-e2aa-55ed-9b46-20b1b37cf92b.html.

Wright, R. G. (2011). Retaliation and the rule of law in today's workplace. *Creighton Law Review, 44*(3), 749—768.

CHAPTER 4

Investigators and the Scientific Method

Brent E. Turvey[1], Stan Crowder[2]

Forensic Criminology Institute, Sitka, Alaska, United States and Aguascalientes, Mexico[1];
Kennesaw State University, Georgia, GA, United States[2]

CHAPTER OUTLINE

Reflection and Metacognition	69
Critical Thinking	72
The Polygraph	73
The FBI	74
The Problem	75
The Availability Heuristic and the Problem With Experience	76
Science Versus Scientific Method	77
Science as Falsification	79
Logical Fallacies	81
Poisoning the Well	82
Suppressed Evidence or Card Stacking	82
Appeals to Authority	82
Appeal to False Authority	83
Appeal to Tradition	84
Argumentum ad Hominem, aka "Argument to the Man"	84
Emotional Appeal	84
Circulus in Probando, aka Circular Reasoning	85
Cum Hoc, Ergo Propter Hoc, or "With This, Therefore Because of This"	85
Post Hoc, Ergo Propter Hoc, or "After This, Therefore Because of This"	85
Hasty Generalizations	86
Sweeping Generalization	86
False Precision	86
Conclusion	87
Endnotes	88
References	88

It is the responsibility of the forensic investigator to assist with establishing whether and how a crime has been committed[1]. Their work will lay the foundation for all legal considerations, including the establishment of probable cause; determining who is the victim and who is the aggressor; measuring the harm that has been inflicted; and suggesting the appropriate charges. It will also help judges and juries to render legal decisions, such as whether or not evidence is reliable enough to be admissible; or whether or not the evidence is sufficient to establish guilt or liability. Forensic investigators make essential contributions to all of these investigative and courtroom determinations, and more, without which the legal process can be left uninformed.

The responsibilities of the forensic investigator are not to be with burdened with personal beliefs, but constructed on the foundation of logical proofs[2]. Forensic investigations require methodical and deliberate reasoning, with firewalls constructed to deaden the impact of emotion, bias, and incompetence. When these firewalls are in place, and made visible to all, they enable the recognition, documentation, collection, and preservation of reliable evidence worthy of subsequent forensic examination.

A word, briefly, on *forensic neutrality*. It is not the function of a forensic investigation to seek out only the evidence which tends to support the theories of a particular institution, employer, or system of beliefs. Or to ignore evidence which tends to work against them. Forensic investigations are intended to help establish scientific facts and their contextual meaning, with no investment in the outcome (DeForest, 2005; Turvey, 2013). The neutrality of this endeavor must not be in question, because demonstrable neutrality gives a forensic investigation the only value it enjoys. The best way to demonstrate neutrality, or objectivity, is by following the scientific method; throughout the history of humankind, this has been the most reliable and accurate way to investigate, build knowledge, and perceive truths. Those who would ignore this reality do so either out of ignorance, or out of a desire to avoid the consequences to that uncomfortable facts tend to require.

Forensic investigations are, when conducted by honest professionals, vital to police inquiries and courtroom proceedings. And they are blight to the dishonest—those who would betray their service to the court with dishonest needs, beliefs, and agendas. The reason is simple. People are inherently unreliable. Sometimes people forget; make mistakes; exaggerate; and sometimes they lie.

The dishonesty of witnesses is found in every context, as experienced criminal justice professionals come to learn. People lie to their friends, to the police, and even to the court while under oath. Government witnesses are capable of making false statements as well—arising from every possible intent. The physical evidence and its scientific examination offer the only objective fact base against which false statements may be compared, considered, and hopefully filtered from proceedings. As explained by the court in People of the Philippines v. Aguinaldo (1999):

> *When physical evidence runs counter to testimonial evidence, conclusions as to physical evidence must prevail. Physical evidence is that mute but eloquent manifestation of truth which rate high in our hierarchy of trustworthy evidence.*

Ultimately, the physical evidence cannot lie; physical evidence can only be misinterpreted and misrepresented by the less knowledgeable, the less competent, and the morally bankrupt (Kirk, 1953).

The purpose of this chapter is to lay out specific warnings, permissions, and tools intended to help the forensic investigator with their decision making and determinations. In other words, it is intended to help think more purposefully, more critically, and more scientifically. This necessitates reviews of critical-thinking strategies, cognitive biases, the scientific method, and will conclude with a discussion of logical fallacies.

REFLECTION AND METACOGNITION

A forensic examination seeks to understand and explain the events related to a crime. It is meant to be based on the evidentiary foundation created during the early stages of an overall forensic investigation. This cannot happen accidentally or thoughtlessly. It must be a deliberate effort, and requires support from the pillars of tested knowledge, careful observation, and the habit of reflection. In other words, an adequate forensic investigation requires investigators to deliberate before they determine, and to think before they act.

Thoughts and reason manifesting without reflection are going to be the result of mental habits, personal beliefs, or prejudices masquerading as insight (otherwise known as intuition). This can be good or bad, without the thinker being capable of understanding the difference. This is where metacognition plays a role.

Metacognition (aka self-monitoring) refers to "the ability to know how well one is performing, when one is likely to be accurate in judgment, and when one is likely to be in error" (Kruger & Dunning, 1999, p. 1121). At the most basic level, metacognition is best described as thinking about the process of thinking. This requires self-awareness: explicit knowledge that one exists separately from other people and full recognition of one's capabilities, strengths, weaknesses, likes, and dislikes. A solid discussion regarding the relationship between metacognition and mindfulness is provided in Preston, Stewart, and Moulding (2014, pp. 1057–1059):

> *Metacognition is a construct that was first articulated by John Flavell, who later defined it as "cognition about cognitive phenomena[.]" Metacognition, so named and defined, has only recently become a focus of cognitive-developmental inquiry. Often described informally as "thinking about thinking," metacognition is the concept that individuals can monitor and regulate their own cognitive processes and thereby improve the quality and effectiveness of their thinking.*
>
> *Teaching metacognitive skills to thinkers is similar to what coaches and athletic psychologists try to teach athletes. They bring to the forefront the awareness of how to maximize, and consistently tap into, all the talent and genius possessed by the player, both inherently and by the process of practice. It is the awareness and then strategic adjustment that pushes someone with flashes of brilliance into a consistently brilliant thinker who can learn, absorb, and apply new material with increasing ease.*

> *Metacognition requires having both awareness of the process and the ability to control learning and thinking. The two components are identified as knowledge and regulation. It appears that metacognitive knowledge and metacognitive regulation develop independently of each other. By the time students reach adulthood, most have fairly well-developed metacognitive knowledge. In contrast, metacognitive regulation, which involves "the monitoring of one's cognition and includes planning activities, awareness of comprehension and task performance, and evaluation of the efficacy of monitoring processes and strategies," is frequently underdeveloped.*
>
> *Understanding metacognition requires distinguishing it from other concepts. Metacognition is different from mindfulness, though they are related concepts. Mindfulness "generally refers to a deliberate, present-moment, non-judgmental awareness of whatever passes through the five conventional senses and the mind: emotions, thoughts, and body sensations." Mindfulness is awareness of in-the-moment thought, while metacognition is awareness and regulation of the process of thinking, reasoning, and learning. The concepts overlap as both mindfulness and metacognition include awareness and, to some extent, self-regulation. Mindfulness is often associated with awareness of the substantive content of a person's thinking and control of emotions while metacognition is thinking of the cognitive strategies and processes used while thinking.*

As this discussion would indicate, believing oneself to be competent is not enough; and awareness of how one is thinking is not enough. These thoughts are too often delusional.

Genuine metacognitive capacity requires active regulation. The forensic investigator must be capable of expressing basic and essential knowledge, skills, and abilities relating to their particular areas of evidence. They must also have some form of external assessment—whether this comes in the form of oversight from supervisors, feedback from colleagues, peer review from the community, or certifications from professional organizations. They must also have the discipline to stop or pause during the performance of their tasks; to reflect on the quality of work and results to that point; and render an honest self-evaluation.

Not everyone is equally capable when it comes to exercising metacognitive dexterity. Some are simply incompetent, perhaps even brazenly so. That is an important reality to accept. As Kruger and Dunning (1999, p. 1121) explain "[W]hen people are incompetent in the strategies they adopt to achieve success and satisfaction, they suffer a dual burden: Not only do they reach erroneous conclusions and make unfortunate choices, but their incompetence robs them of the ability to realize it. Instead … they are left with the mistaken impression that they are doing just fine." Miller (1993, p. 4) explains: "It is one of the essential features of such incompetence that the person so afflicted is incapable of knowing that he is incompetent. To have such knowledge would already be to remedy a good portion of the offense."

It is also cold reality that much forensic investigation occurs under circumstances that do not allow for reflection, contemplation, or the mindfulness of regulation.

Consequently research into forensic casework and related reporting reveals conclusions by modern forensic experts that are sorely lacking in quality, reliability, and objectivity (Edwards & Gotsonis, 2009; Turvey, 2013). Instead, they are too often based on raw experience, incomplete evidence, unchecked assumptions, untested theories, fabricated or misunderstood statistics, poor on-the-job training, and oversimplified or fallacious arguments.

This occurs, and is allowed to occur, because those with vested interests and authority often apply pressure to get forensic results which serve their immediate purposes; and because the court gives preferential trust to government witnesses instead of requiring them to earn it (Moreno, 2004). Under these conditions, where law enforcement and prosecutors are "too wedded to the current 'fragmented' forensic science community, which is deficient in too many respects" (Edwards & Gotsonis, 2009, p. 18), independent thinking is frowned upon. Reflection and deliberation are, under such conditions, considered enemies.

Consider that even as this book goes to press, there are forensic professionals suing for justice, just so they can investigate and report the evidence without fear of sanction, as reported in Virtanen (2016):

Three scientists who worked at the New York State Police crime lab have sued the agency, alleging administrators retaliated against them for finding flaws in processing

DNA evidence and pushing for new testing that would identify past errors. Shannon Morris, Melissa Lee and Kevin Rafferty are seeking unspecified damages in federal court. They cited blowback for supporting the computerized DNA analysis called TrueAllele that state police began implementing then rejected.

The three scientists said that had the system remained in place, it would have exonerated "a small percentage" of suspects who were convicted using evidence involving scenes with mixed genetic material.

"There are people that are very pro-prosecution. They were putting pressure on scientists to reach conclusions that were not scientifically valid," their lawyer, John Bailey, said Friday. "That's what my clients were objecting to."

Morris was the associate lab director until she was fired last year. Lee and Rafferty, both lab supervisors, still work there, but faced disciplinary proceedings and have been reassigned. All worked for the state police for nearly 20 years with otherwise unblemished records, Bailey said.

Their suit alleges that they're protected from retaliation as government employees for speaking out on matters of public importance.

Those working in the forensic science community will be uncomfortably familiar with how common such circumstances are in government-funded crime labs, especially those housed within law enforcement agencies. Actual scientists inside these agencies are keenly aware of deficiencies in their methods and interpretations; they are also mindful of the need to regulate flawed methods and conclusions, to prevent them from harming justice. Yet their employers would keep them silent. The only uncommon thing about this case in New York is that forensic professionals are speaking out, publicly, and they are suing. Normally they can afford to say nothing, as the cost of speaking out requires extensive legal funding enabling the breach of employment contracts (Turvey, 2013).

As long as forensic science is "overseen" by vested individuals and organizations, there will remain little incentive for metacognitive rigor, including mindful reflection, apart from what defines the individual professional compass. There is, consequently, a deep and abiding responsibility to reflect on methods, theories, and findings before ascribing meaning to them, and certainly before putting them into a report (Edwards & Gotsonis, 2009). And to be mindful, despite pressure to do otherwise.

CRITICAL THINKING

There are many definitions for the term *critical thinking*. A unifying concept is that critical thinking involves identifying and questioning the assumptions in arguments that we encounter in any context, and from any authority. Paul and Scriven explain (2004) "critical thinking is the intellectually disciplined process of actively and skillfully conceptualizing, applying, analyzing, synthesizing, and/or evaluating information gathered from, or generated by, observation, experience, reflection, reasoning, or communication, as a guide to belief and action." It requires more information, not less; and it therefore requires lots of reading, to support or temper any prior knowledge that already have (Nelson, 2016).

Most of the students and professionals encountered by the authors have no idea what critical thinking is, what it involves, or how it can be useful in problem solving. This is because their education and/or experience have burdened them with a set of basic assumptions about casework which they are often too lazy or apathetic to question. This is also because it requires them to admit to the possibility of being wrong, which ego and emotionally charged thinking strategies often will not allow.

For example, a recent study from the National Science Foundation and the Cultural Cognition Lab at Yale Law School found that providing someone with factual information which goes against strong personal beliefs (e.g., political views and religious conviction) actually tends to harden those beliefs (Kahan, Peters, Dawson, & Slovic, 2013). This regardless of education or intellectual dexterity. Such propensities are unacceptable, to say nothing of being dangerous.

For the purposes of a forensic investigation, the application of critical thinking to casework means an unflinching refusal to accept any evidence or theories without sufficient proof. It also means skeptical gathering of evidence, skeptical examinations, and the skeptical interpretation of results—no matter the source. This includes the following practices:

1. Scrutinizing the nature and quality of all information and its source
2. Accepting the possibility of bias
3. Separating hard facts from opinions and guesses
4. Distinguishing between primary sources of information (unaltered—direct from the source) and secondary sources of information (altered—interpreted or summarized through someone else)
5. Processing and assembling information

THE POLYGRAPH

For example, a critical thinker would quickly dispense with the notion that polygraph examinations have any forensic value, lacking reliability or validity across the board. The problems with it have been well documented for generations, as will be discussed in a future chapter. Yet law enforcement agencies still swear by polygraphs, resulting in their abuse (e.g., wrongful arrests and wrongful convictions), as reported in Holm (2016):

Are polygraph machines credible science as many in law enforcement believe or, as many critics suggest, the modern-day equivalent of reading tea leaves?

Polygraphs, commonly referred to as lie detectors, have been used in law enforcement settings for 80 years, but "no consensus has emerged about the accuracy of polygraph tests," according to a Federation of American Scientists report…

The use of the machines in police investigations has come under increased scrutiny in recent years. In 2014, a federal jury awarded Jeffrey Deskovic more than $40 million after it was determined a polygraph was used to coerce a false confession to the 1989 murder of a high school classmate. Deskovic served 16 years in prison before being exonerated.

Last March in Waukegan, Ill., Juan Rivera was awarded a $20 million settlement for the decades he spent wrongfully imprisoned, largely due to false confessions elicited in part from a polygraph examination Rivera was told he failed.

The use and effectiveness of polygraph testing has also been questioned in the Idaho Falls Police Department's handling of the 1996 Angie Dodge murder case. Polygraph testing was key to the police getting a confession from convicted murderer Christopher Tapp. Judges for Justice, an organization that investigates potential wrongful convictions, last month released a nearly two-hour video detailing why it believes the polygraph tests were used to coerce a false confession from Tapp.

In a recent report, Boise State University professor and polygraph expert Charles Honts concluded Idaho Falls Police officers used the polygraph as a

> *"psychological rubber hose" on Tapp rather than as a tool to detect deceptiveness. The sensors used by the machine are improperly placed, Honts wrote, and the questions aimed at Tapp diverge wildly from accepted procedure.*
>
> *Despite growing concern over the validity of polygraph testing, many in law enforcement believe it to be a valuable investigative tool. The Idaho Falls Police Department recently trained a third officer in its department to administer the tests.*
>
> *The department uses lie detector tests largely for pre-employment purposes and as an investigative tool, not as a sure-fire evidentiary device.*

Ultimately the polygraph enjoys a favored place in the law enforcement tool kit because the results are fuzzy and open to interpretation; and because they can be used, and abused, to whatever ends an investigator desires. This is why polygraph results are not considered reliable forensic evidence.

THE FBI

Consider also the FBI. In the minds of most criminal justice professionals, and the public, the FBI is an organization that sets the standard for investigators and forensic scientists around the world. Often, they are referred to as the gold standard for both.

The FBI's reputation for excellence and integrity is based on assumptions that are simply not true, and often incapable of surviving even the most rudimentary inquiry (see Chapter 1 of this text). This harsh reality was exposed once again in October of 2012. Candice M. Will, then Assistant Director of the FBI's Office of Professional Responsibility, accidentally sent an email intended for a narrow group to all employees. In it, she detailed a litany of ethics violations, incidents of professional misconduct, and criminal violations by its employees (including FBI Special Agents)—the vast majority of whom were disciplined internally and retained. It included cases of FBI agents engaged in sexting (sending nude photos to each other), harassment, unauthorized surveillance, domestic violence (some involving the use of firearms), DUIs, solicitation of sex acts from sex workers, improper handling of evidence, disclosure of confidential internal reports and information outside the Bureau (e.g., to defense attorneys and members of the public), lying to investigators, theft, abuse of authority, and fraud (Will, 2012). The email was leaked to CNN and then published in the free press. As described in Zamost and Griffin (2013): "From 2010 to 2012, the FBI disciplined 1045 employees for a variety of violations …. Eighty-five were fired."

With respect to investigative prowess, the FBI does not have the charter to work sex crimes or homicides; those are municipal responsibilities. Consequently FBI agents do not have a great deal of experience with those kinds of crimes. Though they will not be quick to correct any assumptions that go in their favor during court proceedings, in the authors' experience.

With respect to setting the gold standard in the forensic sciences, the FBI's crime lab has been embroiled in scandal after scandal since at least 1995. As this book goes to press, the public is awaiting the results of yet another quality assurance audit of FBI forensic practices, discussed in Associated Press (2016):

The Justice Department is reviewing forensic sciences practiced by the FBI to ensure that experts are not overstating their findings against criminal defendants, Deputy Attorney General Sally Quillian Yates said Wednesday.

The review will look at whether other scientific disciplines have been tainted by flawed testimony, a problem that surfaced last year when the Justice Department revealed that experts had overstated the strength of their evidence in many older cases dating back decades involving microscopic hair analysis.

Yates said the inquiry wasn't inspired by specific concerns about other disciplines, but described it instead as a "quality assurance review" and general good practice.

The review will focus on disciplines that involve a large degree of human interpretation and are therefore susceptible to different opinions, and will be presented at the March meeting of the National Commission of Forensic Science. The FBI, meanwhile, is in the process of finalizing standards for testimony and reporting.

"We believe that this type of review will help ensure the public's ongoing confidence in the work we do, and put the entire field on stronger footing in the future," Yates said at a Las Vegas meeting hosted by the American Academy of Forensic Science.

The announcement from Yates comes 10 months after the Justice Department and FBI pledged a review of laboratory protocols and procedures following the discovery of flawed forensics testimony in hundreds of older criminal cases involving microscopic hair analysis. That review of lab examiners' testimony found errors relating to hair analysis in at least 90 percent of trial transcripts and covered a period before 2000.

For more information regarding the FBI Crime Lab's documented history of fraud and negligence, refer back to Chapter 1 of this text, as well as to information and case examples provided in Edwards and Gotsonis (2009) and Turvey (2013).

THE PROBLEM

The problem with critical thinking and skepticism is not that it is complicated or otherwise difficult to understand. It is that critical thinking is often inconvenient, and subordinate to other needs or desired outcomes. This is especially problematic in the justice system because it is a strategy that requires full disclosure, hard work, and sometimes leads to uncomfortable confrontations. In many circumstances it is easier, and perhaps more realistic, to accept what others have given us instead of investigating it's providence. There may even be serious consequences for questioning information or findings, especially when it comes from higher up in the chain of command. This is the explicit reality of government service.

Additionally students may be surprised to learn that the justice system is designed not to be transparent. Instead, it has become an information vault. Information is controlled by government agencies authorized to collect it; and their agents are likewise controlled by the will expressed in edicts set forth by superiors, employment contracts, and any related legal rulings. Effectively accessing and disclosing information concealed within this vault is a regular impediment to the interiority of forensic investigations.

The forensic investigator has an obligation to be a critical thinker, embracing related strategies and methods. But there will be times when this is discouraged or even forbidden by those in positions of authority. When that happens, the forensic investigator has an obligation to document it to the point where those applying pressure are compelled to stop or change tactics—in both reports and sworn testimony. This is to preserve the record, and prevent abuse, so that justice may eventually prevail.

THE AVAILABILITY HEURISTIC AND THE PROBLEM WITH EXPERIENCE

The *availability heuristic* is involved when judgments or decisions are made based on what one can immediately remember, rather than complete or accurate information. Sunstein (2005) describes it as the tendency to reach for an explanation that readily comes to mind; this rather than attempting to logically investigate and then determine the origins of a phenomenon. According to Sunstein's research, people are not always that critical, that deliberate, or that bright; many are intellectually lazy, reaching only for the explanations and reasons within their immediate cognitive vicinity. The authors could not agree more.

We tend to use the availability heuristic for judging the frequency or likelihood of events (Crowder & Turvey, 2013). It happens when we reference a recent case, movie, news article, or an anecdote as the basis for a conclusion or a decision. If this habit is not practiced with awareness and humility, the results can be disastrous. Experience teaches us that the availability heuristic is great for theory development, but not so great for reaching conclusions.

On that note, it is common that forensic investigators and examiners of all kinds will offer their years of experience as evidence of reliability and accuracy. The court will even encourage it, as a substitute for demonstrable accomplishment. However, experience, reliability, and accuracy are not necessarily related.

Skill and ability are, of course, potential benefits of age and experience. It does not follow that those with experience will necessarily gain skill or ability, let alone become reliable and accurate in their determinations. Some people are resistant to learning; some people live a life repeating their errors, often unaware of it.

As Thornton (2011) explains, summoning experience instead of logic and reasoning to support a conclusion is an admission to lacking both (p.17):

> *Experience is neither a liability nor an enemy of the truth; it is a valuable commodity, but it should not be used as a mask to deflect legitimate scientific scrutiny, the sort of scrutiny that customarily is leveled at scientific evidence of all sorts. To do so is professionally bankrupt and devoid of scientific legitimacy, and courts would do well to disallow testimony of this sort. Experience ought to be used to enable the expert to remember the when and the how, why, who, and what. Experience should not make the expert less responsible, but rather more responsible for justifying an opinion with defensible scientific facts.*

In other words, the more experience of quality and substance one has, the less one will need to tell people about it to gain their trust and confidence—the quality of one's experience is demonstrated through the inherent quality of one's methods and the temperance of their results.

It has been demonstrated, with respect to the nature of expertize, novice practitioners tend to possess poorer metacognitive skills than do expert practitioners, for lack of experience confronting their own errors or with problem solving particular to the geography of their domain. Kruger and Dunning (1999, p. 1122) argue: "unaccomplished individuals do not possess the degree of metacognitive skills necessary for accurate self-assessment that their more accomplished counterparts possess." This is a reasonable assertion.

Experience and expertize necessarily breed confidence, but they can also breed overconfidence. The experienced can develop an unwillingness to allow for the possibility of their own errors; or a stubbornness against taking the time to follow correct procedures. In other words, they can become complacent, get sloppy, and make mistakes. They become biased in favor of their own thoughts, and start skipping over the methodical processes that their quality experiences, and expertize, have been built upon (Dorner, 1996).

The discipline required during a forensic investigation is to achieve understanding and confidence through the evidence without becoming presumptuous to the point of ignorance.

SCIENCE VERSUS SCIENTIFIC METHOD

The forensic investigator must understand the role of science and the scientific method, demonstrating clear adherence in their casework.

The classic definition of a *science* is provided in Thornton and Peterson (2007; p. 13): "an orderly body of knowledge with principles that are clearly enunciated," as well as being reality oriented and having conclusions susceptible to testing. Giddens (1991) further explains that science involves (p. 20) "the use of systematic methods of investigation, theoretical thinking, and the logical assessment of arguments, to develop a body of knowledge about a particular subject matter." In other words, the development of any field of study as a science requires building a knowledge base that is "accurate and systematized" (Ross, 1964, p. 66).

Scientific knowledge is understanding, enlightenment, or awareness that comes from examining events or problems through the lenses of analytical logic and the scientific method; it is necessarily less fallible than, and distinct from, common knowledge or mere observation (Judson, 2004; Popper, 2002; Ross, 1964). The generation of scientific knowledge in a particular area (e.g., chemistry, biology, psychology, sociology, or criminology) leads to its development as a science. This process is intended to be ongoing and self-correcting (NAS, 2002; Popper, 2002; Ross, 1964).

The scientific method is a systematic way to investigate how or why something works, or how something happened, with the development of hypotheses and subsequent attempts at falsification through testing (Cooley & Turvey, 2014; DiFonzo & Stern, 2007; Giddens, 1991; Kennedy & Kennedy, 1972; Popper, 2002; Thornton and Peterson, 2007).

The scientific method may be regarded as a path to knowledge, involving steps that cannot be skipped. Initially empirical information (e.g., observation and experience) identifies a question or a problem. This is developed into a testable hypothesis for which specific data is identified and then systematically gathered. According to Popper (2002, p. 1): "[a] scientist, whether theorist or experimenter, puts forward statements, or systems of statements, and tests them step by step."

Theory testing is generally accomplished by one of four means: logical comparison of conclusions for internal consistency; investigation of the logical form of a theory; comparison with other theories; and testing empirical applications of the theory with conclusions that can be derived from it (Popper, 2002). With sufficient testing, marked by a consistent failure to falsify, hypotheses can become working scientific theories (Popper, 2002; Raven and Johnson, 1986). Eventually, over time, scientific theories can survive to become scientific principles.

The scientific method is universally accepted as the best approach to knowledge building. As explained in Dewey (1995, p. 397):

> ...is not just a method which it has been found profitable to pursue in this or that abstruse subject for purely technical reasons. It represents the only method of thinking that has proved fruitful in any subject—that is what we mean when we call it scientific. It is not a peculiar development of thinking for highly specialized ends; it is thinking so far as thought has become conscious of its proper ends and of the equipment indispensable for success in their pursuit.

The scientific method is therefore the definitive approach to logical inquiry, knowledge building, and problem solving used by scientists of every kind (DiFonzo & Stern, 2007; Popper, 2002). It must be pointed out that the opposite is also true. Any investigator or examiner who does not understand or use the scientific method as the foundation of their inquiry is not engaging in scientific practice. Moreover, they are shunning the most reliable approach to learning the facts.

SCIENCE AS FALSIFICATION

Subsumed in the previous section, a cornerstone of the scientific method is *falsification*. This is achieved by subjecting a theory to repeated attacks to disprove it, which means testing it against case facts or alternative theories (Popper, 2002). Any study, method, or experiment designed only to confirm a hypothesis or theory is not, by definition, scientific.

The scientific prohibition against seeking only proofs or confirmations was described by Sir Karl Popper (1902–94), the noted Austrian–British psychologist, philosopher, and scientist (Popper, 1963, pp. 33–39):

Science as Falsification

These considerations led me in the winter of 1919–20 to conclusions which I may now reformulate as follows.

1. It is easy to obtain confirmations, or verifications, for nearly every theory—if we look for confirmations.
2. Confirmations should count only if they are the result of risky predictions; that is to say, if, unenlightened by the theory in question, we should have expected an event which was incompatible with the theory—an event which would have refuted the theory.
3. Every "good" scientific theory is a prohibition: It forbids certain things to happen. The more a theory forbids, the better it is.
4. A theory which is not refutable by any conceivable event is nonscientific. Irrefutability is not a virtue of a theory (as people often think) but a vice.
5. Every genuine test of a theory is an attempt to falsify it, or to refute it. Testability is falsifiability; but there are degrees of testability: Some theories are more testable, more exposed to refutation, than others; they take, as it were, greater risks.
6. Confirming evidence should not count except when it is the result of a genuine test of the theory; and this means that it can be presented as a serious but unsuccessful attempt to falsify the theory. (I now speak in such cases of "corroborating evidence.")
7. Some genuinely testable theories, when found to be false, are still upheld by their admirers—for example, by introducing ad hoc some auxiliary assumption, or by reinterpreting the theory ad hoc in such a way that it escapes refutation. Such a procedure is always possible, but it rescues the theory from refutation only at the price of destroying, or at least lowering, its scientific status. (I later described such a rescuing operation as a "conventionalist twist" or a "conventionalist stratagem.")

Falsification being an essential "criterion," scientific inquiry demands objectivity, doubt, and skepticism at every step. Useful stipulations along these lines are found in Kennedy and Kennedy (1972, p. 4):

To be objective, an inquirer should be prepared to accept and record whatever facts he may encounter. He must not let personal feelings affect what he sees or hears. Although he does not need to like the nature of the information, he must be willing to investigate it. When such an investigation is begun, it must be carried through with a degree of skepticism. Skepticism does not imply cynicism or a distrust of the world. It only suggests that the [scientist] must be prepared to distinguish truth from the opinion or inclinations of others.

To succeed at this requires relentless consideration of all available theories against the available facts and evidence. But it also requires that the forensic investigator refrain from becoming personally invested in any preconceived ideas. DeForest (2005, p.115) explains this process, again embracing the scientific method's aim to disprove what is believed and not protect it from scrutiny:

The core of the scientific method is the rigorous testing of hypotheses. Hypotheses that endeavor to explain the event are put forward, and then an earnest attempt is made to disprove each. A hypothesis that fails this testing is discarded. A modified hypotheses or new alternate hypotheses are developed and tested in turn. Only a hypotheses that survives repeated vigorous testing develops into an explanatory theory of the event... The key to the process is the vigorousness and rigorousness of the testing. There is a human tendency to identify with a hypothesis that one has developed and subconsciously overlook observations or data that do not fit the hypothesis. This is antithetical to good science and must be avoided. Scientists must be involved in actively attempting to disprove their own hypotheses.

The scientific method does not seek confirmation of beliefs or ideas; it seeks eradication. Failing at this, hypotheses or theories that survive genuine attempts at falsification are sufficiently "accurate and reliable" to be considered scientific. Those that do not survive are insufficient, no matter what the investigator or their supervisors might desire.

The necessity of forensic endeavors conforming to scientific culture, especially with respect to self-correction, is explored more thoroughly by the National Academy of Sciences (Edwards & Gotsonis, 2009, p. 125):

The methods and culture of scientific research enable it to be a self-correcting enterprise. Because researchers are, by definition, creating new understanding, they must be as cautious as possible before asserting a new "truth." Also, because researchers are working at a frontier, few others may have the knowledge to catch and correct any errors they make. Thus, science has had to develop means of revisiting provisional results and revealing errors before they are widely used. The processes of peer review, publication, collegial interactions (e.g., sharing at conferences), and the involvement of graduate students (who are expected to question as they learn) all support this need. Science is characterized also by a culture that encourages and rewards critical questioning of past results and of colleagues. Most technologies benefit from a solid research foundation in academia and ample opportunity for peer-to-peer stimulation and critical assessment, review and critique through conferences, seminars, publishing, and more. These elements provide a rich set of paths through which new ideas and skepticism can travel and opportunities for scientists to step away from their day-to-day work and take a longer-term view. The scientific culture encourages cautious, precise statements and discourages statements that go beyond established facts; it is acceptable for colleagues to challenge one another, even if the challenger is more junior. The forensic science disciplines will profit enormously by full adoption of this scientific culture.

The forensic investigator has an obligation to embrace a scientific mind-set, and the scientific method, to achieve the reliability that the court demands of its servants. Error, doubt, and uncertainty are integral to scientific practice. Any individual or group that seeks to quell the mandates of scientific practice, seeing it as bad form to doubt or question, works against the essence of truth seeking. Understanding this aspect of scientific inquiry is sometimes difficult for those who have been taught to conform, to follow orders, or who must work within a structured hierarchy that forces unproved theories and assumptions on them.

LOGICAL FALLACIES

One of the fastest ways to determine the reliability of a conclusion is to consider whether it is based on sound logic. That means it must contain deliberate reasoning, free from logical fallacies. Logical fallacies are impermissible in the forensic realm, and can render any related forensic conclusions erroneous. A brief discussion can be found in Bregant (2014, p. 23):

Of course, the path to the truth is full of traps that must be avoided. Unfortunately, there is no other way than knowing the methods and principles through which we distinguish a good from a bad reasoning, and the ability to use it on concrete practical examples. This, however, does not mean that only a person who has dedicated a significant part of her life to the study of logic can reason correctly…

In bad arguments, the premises do not support conclusions and do not justify or prove them even if they are true. It is said that the author committed a fallacy, where the word 'fallacy' is used for typical examples of a poor reasoning… A general rule that we have to take into account when evaluating arguments is that a given argumentative form is not fallacious (is a good argument) when given premises are relevant for conclusions. Recognizing fallacies is difficult for the imperfect argumentation and emotional rhetoric being significant for them. The accurate identification of fallacies is sometimes difficult also because of the violation of several principles of a good reasoning at once.

Binoy (2014) asserts that logical fallacies persist for three central reasons: because of personal and cultural prejudice; because they allow people to avoid answering difficult arguments; and because they are difficult to answer with logic, being of poorly rendered reasoning themselves. Binoy (2014) also makes the observation that logical fallacies enjoy the benefit of raising a new set of issues, potentially sidelining the original arguments or concerns. In other words, logical fallacies are the tools of the inept fraud who is seeking to conceal their weakness with distraction.

It bears mentioning that implicit in these reasons for persistence is the reality that logical fallacies can be effective at the task of convincing those who uninformed, emotional, biased, or otherwise unmindful. Consider the following examples of logical fallacies used by forensic investigators, which are to be avoided by honest forensic investigators[3]:

POISONING THE WELL

This argument involves a preemptory attack, discrediting a potential source before an argument of position is revealed. This is done in anticipation of a contrary report, finding, or view. It generally signals factual weakness on the part of those responsible.

For example, police and prosecutors can often be found holding press conferences prior to suspect arrests, and during criminal investigations, to make their case in the public prior to trial. In doing so they control the facts and narrative, effectively poisoning the well from which the jury is drawn by predisposing them to certain conclusions. These may or may not hold up in court, and in fact the most sensational charges may be dropped. But the jury pool has already been tainted and effectively prejudiced.

This form of logical fallacy is so common that it in some places considered part of the process, despite effectively eradicating the presumption of innocence. When used, it signals that the state lacks confidence in its case; they do not believe they can get everything admitted at trial or they need public support to do something that they probably should not.

SUPPRESSED EVIDENCE OR CARD STACKING

This is a one-sided argument that presents only evidence favoring a particular conclusion and ignores or downplays the evidence against it. It may involve distortions, exaggerations, misstatements of facts, or outright lies. It is, in essence, cherry-picking evidence from that which is available to support a conclusion, while ignoring anything that is contrary.

For example, in a case involving sexual assault, police investigators commonly fail to collect blood samples to test the toxicology of the complainant. This helps avoid questions about reliability related to potential alcohol or drug abuse. They may also neglect to test the sexual assault kit collected from the suspect. This when they suspect additional or contrary male semen donors might be present; or when they suspect the complainant's version of events might not otherwise line up with the physical evidence.

APPEALS TO AUTHORITY

This occurs when someone offers a conclusion based on experience, expertize, or community standing. This kind of reasoning can be fallacious when the authority lacks the expertize suggested; when the authority is an expert in one subject but not the subject at hand; when the subject is contentious and involves multiple interpretations with good arguments on both sides; when the authority is biased; when the area of expertize is fabricated; when the authority is vague or unidentified; and when the authority is offered as evidence in place of defensible scientific fact.

Ultimately the fact that information comes from an authority is not by itself compelling to a critical thinker, because even authorities can get it wrong. Examples of fallacious appeals to authority include the following:

- "…because I've been doing this for 25 years."
- "…because I've been trained and certified."
- "…because I work for the State Police."
- "…because the FBI says so."
- "…because my boss says so."

APPEAL TO FALSE AUTHORITY

This is an appeal to an authority that, in particular, lacks expertize in the relevant subject. It involves either ignorance on the part of the examiner or deliberate misrepresentation. In crime scene examination, a common example would be arguing or assuming that experience in finding, collecting, and/or packaging evidence (aka crime scene processing) is related to experience interpreting the meaning of evidence in its context (aka reconstruction); or that being a law enforcement officer necessarily implies forensic expertize or scientific training. Such faulty assertions and assumptions are common to the admission of "expert" testimony by the courts.

As explained in O'Hara (1970, p. 667), the role of crime scene processing and the role of evidence interpretation do not, and should not, intersect:

> *It is not to be expected that the investigator also play the role of the laboratory expert in relation to the physical evidence found at the scene of the crime… It suffices that the investigator investigate; it is supererogatory that he should perform refined scientific examinations. Any serious effort to accomplish such a conversion would mutilate against the investigator's efficiency.*
>
> *…In general the investigator should know the methods of discovering, "field-testing," preserving, collecting, and transporting evidence. Questions of analysis and comparison should be referred to the laboratory [aka scientific] expert.*

Examples of fallacious appeals to false authority include the following:

- "I work in crime scenes all day picking up evidence in the mud and the blood; of course I know how to interpret what it means."
- "I'm a cop; of course I know how to read a crime scene."
- "I collect fingerprints for a living; therefore I know how to conduct fingerprint comparisons."
- "I have basic firearms training, own many firearms, and shoot firearms all the time; therefore I know how to conduct ballistic comparisons."

APPEAL TO TRADITION

This kind of argument reasons that a conclusion is correct simply because it is older, traditional, or "has always been so." It supports a conclusion by appealing to long-standing, institutional, or cultural opinions, as if the past itself is a form of authority.

Examples of fallacious appeals to tradition experienced by the authors include the following:

- "One swab per hand, front and back, is the correct method for collecting gunshot residue (GSR) because that's that way I was taught and that's the way it's always been done in this department. We've never had to worry about cross-contamination before."[4]
- "When I collect loose shells from a shooting at a crime scene, I put them all in one bag. They don't need individual packaging. That's the way we've always done it and nobody has complained before."
- "We don't talk to victim's more than once; if they give inconsistent statements, the defense will beat them up on the stand. That's the way I've done it for 25 years."

ARGUMENTUM AD HOMINEM, AKA "ARGUMENT TO THE MAN"

This argument attacks an opponent's character rather than an opponent's argument. Because of its effectiveness, it is perhaps the most common logical fallacy. Even if true, it is important to note that arguments against character are not always relevant to the presentation of scientific conclusions, logic, and reasoning.

Examples of fallacious ad hominem attacks experienced by the authors include the following:

- "He's wrong because he's an arrogant jerk."
- "She's a liar because all women lie about who they are sleeping with."
- "He can't be trusted because he's black, and they all hate cops."

EMOTIONAL APPEAL

This is an attempt to gain favor based on arousing emotions and/or sympathy to subvert rational thought. This is used very commonly to sway juries in cases involving traditionally sympathetic victims, such as attractive women or young children.

Examples of fallacious emotional appeals experienced by the authors include the following:

- "You know in your heart the right thing to do."
- "If you work for the defense, then you must hate law enforcement and want to let child killers go free."
- "That was someone daughter; she deserves justice. We need you to help her get it."

CIRCULUS IN PROBANDO, AKA CIRCULAR REASONING

This is an argument that assumes as part of its premises the very conclusion that is supposed to be proven.

Examples of circular reasoning experienced by the authors include:

- At a bail hearing, prior to trial: "He's a danger to society because he killed the victim, and therefore should not be granted bail." violation of the presumption of innocence. The very fact to prove at trial is assumed pretrial.
- At a bail hearing, prior to trial: "She shouldn't be granted bail because she has shown no remorse for her actions." Again, a violation of the presumption of innocence—innocent people cannot be expected to show remorse for crimes that they did not commit.

CUM HOC, ERGO PROPTER HOC, OR "WITH THIS, THEREFORE BECAUSE OF THIS"

This occurs when one jumps to a conclusion about causation based on a correlation between two events, or types of events, that occur simultaneously. The examiner assumes that things found together must be related.

Examples of this fallacy experienced by the authors include the following:

- "We found these knives in the house, so they must be related to the crime that happened in another room—despite the fact that no blood, fingerprints, or other evidence associates it with the crime."
- "We found these condoms at the scene, so they must be related to the rape."
- "We found a gun in the suspects' possession, therefore it must be associated with the shooting."
- "He was the last person to see her alive."

POST HOC, ERGO PROPTER HOC, OR "AFTER THIS, THEREFORE BECAUSE OF THIS"

This kind of argument reasons that a causal conclusion exists based solely on the alleged cause preceding its alleged effect. In other words, the events are linking in time and space, therefore the relationship must be cause and effect.

Examples of this fallacy experienced by the authors include the following:

- "She was killed just after he arrived at the house, so obviously he's involved in her death somehow."
- "He found the body, therefore he must have killed her."
- "He washed his clothes, therefore they must have had blood on them."

HASTY GENERALIZATIONS

This sort of generalization forms a conclusion based on woefully incomplete information or by examining only a few specific cases that are not representative of all possible cases.

Examples of this fallacy experienced by the authors include the following:

- "I don't know all of the facts of the case, and haven't spent more than a few hours examining the evidence, but I can provide a fairly detailed reconstruction of events."
- "I've seen a couple of cases just like this before, so I know exactly what happened."
- "I've read a couple of autopsy reports, so I know what they should look like."

SWEEPING GENERALIZATION

This occurs when one forms a conclusion by examining what occurs in many cases and assuming that it must or will be so in a particular case. This is the opposite of a hasty generalization.

Examples of this fallacy experienced by the authors include the following:

- "All cops are crooked."
- "All scientists do is work with theories; they don't have real-life experience."
- "Books can't teach anyone anything; reading is a waste of time."

FALSE PRECISION

False precision occurs when an argument treats information as more precise or reliable than it really is. This happens when conclusions are based on imprecize information that must be taken as precise to support the conclusion adequately.

Examples of this fallacy experienced by the authors include the following:

- "This method of examination has an error rate of zero."
- "I'm 100% certain of my findings; I've never been wrong."
- "The point of origin of the blood drop is 15.78 inches above the floor and 7.852 inches west of the drop."

It bears mentioning that presenting what appear to be precise statistics or numbers in support of an argument gives the appearance of scientific accuracy when this may not actually be the case. Many people find math and statistics overly impressive and become intimidated by those who wield these numbers with ease. This is especially true with DNA evidence, whose astronomic statistical probabilities are often presented by those without any background in statistics and without full consideration of the databases that such probabilities are being derived from. A specific criticism against those using statistics in forensic interpretations is provided in Moenssens (1993):

Experts use statistics compiled by other experts without any appreciation of whether the database upon which the statistics were formulated fits their own local experience, or how the statistics were compiled. Sometimes these experts, trained in one forensic discipline, have little or no knowledge of the study of probabilities, and never even had a college-level course in statistics.

Recall that this issue was the focal point of the scandal at the Washington DC Department of Forensic Sciences Crime Lab in 2015, discussed in Chapter 1 of this text. The U.S. Attorney's Office argued that forensic personnel suffered from improper training and were using an outdated method for interpreting DNA probabilities. The Lab's Director, Max Houck, argued this was not the case—that these methods were used all over the country, and that methods for interpreting DNA probabilities actually vary. Mr. Houck was forced to resign as were others in the fall-out. The same issue of overly confident and overly precise matching is at issue in the current FBI Crime Lab scandal, which relates to false testimony from hair and fiber analysts (again, discussed in prior chapters). The point being, this is not a remote problem that has been identified and taken care of. Rather, it is one that has yet to be completely understood, let alone resolved, by the forensic science community.

Those using statistics to support their findings have a responsibility to know where they come from, how they were derived, and what they mean to the case at hand. This must happen before they form conclusions, write them up, and certainly before they testify in court. Those using other forms of logic to render investigative or forensic conclusions enjoy a similar responsibility.

CONCLUSION

Dietrich Dorner, a cognitive psychologist and professor of psychology at the University of Bamberg, has conducted extensive research on complex problem solving, and what he refers to as the *logic of failure* (Dorner, 1996). He determined that those who solve complex problems did so by gathering information before acting; thinking systematically; reviewing their progress; and correcting themselves often. Those who made the most errors tended to cling to preconceived theories; did not correct themselves; and blamed others when things went wrong. The errors made in complex situations, Dorner surmised, were not a feature of human capability; rather they were a feature of poorly conceived reasoning and an overall human tendency for laziness.

The authors can only agree, and offer the tools presented in this chapter as the best safeguards against injustice during the comprehensive process of forensic investigation.

Forensic investigators have a duty to use the scientific method because it is the most reliable way to establish the facts and eliminate bias; to consider alternate theories; to avoid becoming invested in a particular theory or outcome; and to be actively involved in the process of testing their theories against any and all new evidence that is uncovered. This means actively seeking out new evidence as opposed to shunning it or shelving it; and this means not failing in their duty to conduct a physical evidence investigation because it is convenient or expedient to do so. Faithfulness to these mental habits preserves justice through evidence; failure ensures something else entirely.

ENDNOTES

1. Portions of this chapter have been adapted from Chisum and Turvey (2012).
2. *Belief* means taking a position on something without evidence or proof; it is a judgment without substantiations or confirmations.
3. This section is adapted from a similar section in Chisum and Turvey (2012).
4. Gunshot residue collection kits generally come with two scanning electron microscope collection tabs per hand (right and left; inside palm and back). Combining inside palm and back of palm transfer evidence onto one tab eliminates the ability to interpret whether the subject had GSR transfer only on the palm, only on the back of the hand, or both. This information can have significant interpretive value.

REFERENCES

Associated Press. (February 24, 2016). *Justice dept. to do 'stress test' of FBI forensic sciences*. Star-Tribune. http://www.startribune.com/justice-dept-to-do-stress-test-of-fbi-forensic-sciences/370031481/.

Binoy, S. (October 4, 2014). Logical fallacies in public discourse and the law. *Economic & Political Weekly, 49*(40), 24–27.

Bregant, J. (2014). Critical thinking in education: Why to avoid logical fallacies. *Problems of Education in the 21st Century, 61*, 18–27.

Chisum, W. J., & Turvey, B. (2012). *Crime reconstruction* (2nd ed.). San Diego, CA: Elsevier Science.

Cooley, C., & Turvey, B. (2014). *Miscarriages of justice*. San Diego, CA: Elsevier Science.

Crowder, W. S., & Turvey, B. (2013). Hypothesis, homology and heuristic: what the H? *International Journal of Arts & Sciences, 6*(3), 627–634.

DeForest, P. (2005). Crime scene investigation. In L. E. Sullivan, & M. S. Rosen (Eds.), *Encyclopedia of law enforcement* (Vol. 1, pp. 111–116). Thousand Oaks, CA: Sage.

Dewey, J. (1995). Science as subject-matter and as method. *Science and Education, 4*, 391–398. Reprint of Dewey, J. (1909). Science as Subject-Matter and as Method. *Science, 31*(787), 121–127.

DiFonzo, J. H., & Stern, R. C. (Spring 2007). Devil in a white coat: The temptation of forensic evidence in the age of CSI. *New England Law Review, 41*, 504–532.

Dorner, D. (1996). *The logic of failure: Recognizing and avoiding error in complex environments*. Cambridge, MA: Perseus Books.

Edwards, H., & Gotsonis, C. (2009). *Strengthening forensic science in the United States: A path forward*. Washington, DC: National Academies Press.

Giddens, A. (1991). *Introduction to sociology*. New York: W.W. Norton and Company.

References

Holm, T. (February 20, 2016). *Despite concerns about accuracy, polygraphs widely used.* The Post-Register. http://www.postregister.com/articles/featured-news-daily-email-todays-headlines/2016/02/20/despite-concerns-about-accuracy.

Judson, H. (2004). *The great betrayal: Fraud in science.* New York: Harcourt.

Kahan, D. M., Peters, E., Dawson, E. C., & Slovic, P. (2013). Motivated numeracy and enlightened self-government. *Yale Law School.* Public Law Working Paper No. 307 http://dx.doi.org/10.2139/ssrn.2319992.

Kennedy, D. B., & Kennedy, B. (1972). *Applied sociology for police.* Springfield, IL: Charles C. Thomas.

Kirk, P. (1953). *Crime investigation.* New York: Interscience.

Kruger, J., & Dunning, D. (1999). Unskilled and unaware of it: How difficulties in recognizing one's own incompetence lead to inflated self-assessments. *Journal of Personality and Social Psychology, 77*(6), 1121–1134.

Miller, W. I. (1993). *Humiliation.* Ithaca, NY: Cornell University Press.

Moenssens, A. (Spring 1993). Novel scientific evidence in criminal cases: Some words of caution. *Journal of Criminal Law and Criminology, 84*(1).

Moreno, J. (2004). What happens when dirty Harry becomes an (expert) witness for the prosecution? *Tulane Law Review, 79*(1), 1–54.

NAS. (2002). *Integrity in scientific research: Creating an environment that promotes responsible conduct, National Academy of Sciences Committee on Assessing Integrity in Research Environments.* Washington, DC: National Academies Press.

Nelson, C. R. (March 2016). Reading: The key to critical thinking. *Army Magazine, 66*(3), 49–51.

O'Hara, C. (1970). *Fundamentals of criminal investigation* (2nd ed.). Springfield, IL: Charles C. Thomas.

Paul, R., & Scriven, M. (2004). *Defining critical thinking. Foundation for critical thinking.* http://www.criticalthinking.org/aboutCT/definingCT.shtml.

People of the Philippines v. Rodrigo Loteyro Aguinaldo. (October 13, 1999) (GR No. 130784).

Popper, K. (1963). *Conjectures and refutations.* London: Routledge and Keagan Paul.

Popper, K. (2002). *The logic of scientific discovery.* New York: Routledge.

Preston, C., Stewart, P., & Moulding, L. (2014). Teaching "thinking like a lawyer": metacognition and law students. *Brigham Young University Law Review, 2014*(5), 1053–1094.

Raven, P., & Johnson, G. (1986). *Biology.* St. Louis, MO: Times Mirror/Mosby College Publishing.

Ross, S. (1964). Scientist: the story of a word. *Annals of Science, 18*(2), 65–85.

Sunstein, C. (June 2005). Group judgments: Statistical means, deliberation, and information markets. *New York University Law Review, 80,* 962–1049.

Thornton, J., & Peterson, J. (2007). The general assumptions and rationale of forensic identification. In D. Faigman, D. Kaye, M. Saks, & J. Sanders (Eds.), *Modern Scientific Evidence: The Law and Science of Expert Testimony* (1). St. Paul, MN: West Publishing Group.

Thornton, J. (2011). Crime reconstruction: ethos and ethics. In W. J. Chisum, & B. Turvey (Eds.), *Crime reconstruction* (2nd ed.). San Diego, CA: Elsevier.

Turvey, B. (2013). *Forensic fraud: Evaluating law enforcement and forensic science cultures in the context of examiner misconduct.* San Diego, CA: Elsevier Science.

Virtanen, M. (February 19, 2016). *Scientists sue state police over 'pro-prosecution' DNA lab.* ABC News. http://abcnews.go.com/US/wireStory/scientists-sue-state-police-pro-prosecution-dna-lab-37063263.

Will, C. (October 1, 2012). FBI Office of Professional Responsibility (Email to "FBI_all_employees," subject line: "oprs quarterly all employee e-mail").

Zamost, S., & Griffin, D. (February 22, 2013). *FBI battling 'rash of sexting' among its employees.* CNN. http://www.cnn.com/2013/02/21/us/fbi-misbehavior.

CHAPTER 5

Crime Scene Investigation and Analysis

Brent E. Turvey[1], Jodi Freeman[2,3]

Forensic Criminology Institute, Sitka, Alaska, United States and Aguascalientes, Mexico[1]; Forensic Solutions, LLC, Sitka, Alaska, United States[2]; University of Western Ontario, London, ON, Canada[3]

CHAPTER OUTLINE

The CSI Effect	92
The FBI Effect	95
Crime Scene Investigation, Reconstruction, and Analysis	**98**
Crime Scene Investigation	98
Crime Reconstruction	99
Crime Scene Analysis	105
Forensic Relevance	**105**
Corpus Delicti	106
Modus Operandi	107
Signature Behavior	108
Linking the Suspect to the Victim	109
Linking a Person to a Crime Scene	109
Disproving or Supporting Witness Testimony	109
Identification of Suspects	110
Providing Investigative Leads	112
Endnotes	**120**
References	**122**

Film and television routinely depict government agents entering crime scenes; taking only a few moments to locate obscure traces of evidence; making quick judgments about what is relevant and what is not; and then deducing a lengthy index of findings with absolute certainty. The product of short viewer attention spans and the need for instant gratification, this style of fast food forensics is a mainstay of the entertainment industry. In keeping with the *CSI effect*, this false image has created the mistaken belief, and expectation, that forensic inquiry can be instant, all knowing, and absolutely certain. In real life, however, forensic inquiry takes time; the more the better. If you can get the results of a forensic examination as quickly as ordering a taco or a cheeseburger at a fast food chain, then those results will have about the same industry quality—that is to say they will be very low.

Forensic Investigations. http://dx.doi.org/10.1016/B978-0-12-800680-1.00005-5
Copyright © 2017 Elsevier Inc. All rights reserved.

In the existing world of legitimate forensic science, speed is an indication of inexperience, incompetence, and inaccuracy. Fast conclusions come at the expense of care and reflection. This is true whether it is a deduction at a crime scene formed without the results of laboratory testing; or a field kit administered and interpreted in the back of a patrol car. If something is done quickly, or before all of the facts and evidence have been evaluated, then the potential for error is increased.

This sounds like common sense, and it is. But common sense has been made uncommon in crime scene investigation work by unrealistic imagery and expectations. And also by an influx of students raised on true crime serials, lacking mentorship from case working scientists. Common sense has further been purged from the professional community by the expectations and pressure that are steadily applied by the justice system. The courts, the police, and the public—they want what they see on TV and in movies. They want instant results; they want absolute certainty, and ultimately they want to be entertained by what they believe to be the theater of criminal investigations and the court.

Too often, those in the profession (or seeking to appear as though they are part of it) are happy to comply. They will play to an image, such as a cartoon character or a caricature, or give results that are too fast or too certain. In some cases, they are more concerned with how they look or appear to others than with the accuracy and reliability of their science, if they are concerned with science at all.

This chapter has been written to alleviate the waves of ignorance that threaten to wash the minds of our students and our colleagues in the justice system. It is intended to provide a conceptual structure for the missions and goals associated with crime scene investigation and analysis. It will do so by establishing the relationship between *crime scene investigation*, *crime scene analysis* (CSA), and the reconstruction of crime.

First, however, it is necessary to deal with myths and establish professional permissions. This requires a brief discussion of the *CSI effect* and the *FBI effect*.

THE CSI EFFECT

CSI, short for Crime Scene Investigation, is a TV show that was produced by the CBS Television Network. It first aired in the year 2000. During its two decade run, *CSI* generated multiple spin-off series. As of this current writing, none of these are in production and exist only in syndication.

Originally, *CSI* was billed as a scientifically accurate program by show-makers and script consultants from the law enforcement community (McKay, 2002). However, under relentless scrutiny from the professional forensic science community, producers were eventually compelled acknowledge the truth to audiences. The show was rife with errors and artistic license taken for purposes of both entertainment and expediency.

Definitions of the associated phenomenon vary, depending upon who is asked. As explained in Dysart (2012): "The now-ubiquitous term the "*CSI* Effect" has been used to describe the phenomenon whereby high-tech, forensic science dramatized in television crime dramas such as *CSI*, *Law & Order*, and *Forensic Files* theoretically promotes unrealistic expectations among jurors of how apparently clearly and definitely forensic evidence can determine innocence or guilt or, from the perspective of the civil litigator, causation or liability".

Other programs that contribute to the phenomenon include *Bones*, *Criminal Minds*, *Dexter*, and *NCIS*—to name but a few. In each of these crime serials, forensic evidence is gathered, examined, and interpreted quickly (sometimes within hours, even minutes) by armed police investigators. Often, they are using technology, or systems, that do not exist. Then they conduct victim and suspect interviews, conveying heavy moral umbrage while directly confronting them with "scientific" findings.

The reality of forensic science, and the impact of these TV shows, is discussed by a practicing forensic scientist in Reavy (2011) (Fig. 5.1).

FIGURE 5.1

Sorenson Forensics Executive Director Tim Kupferschmid has spoken plainly, and on the record about the limitations of TV shows such as CSI. Basically, they do not depict the "real life" of a forensic scientist and can leave a false impression that results in serious misconceptions.

Sorenson Forensics Executive Director Tim Kupferschmid will turn on the TV every once in a while and watch crime shows with forensic labs, like "CSI." But it's not because he expects he'll be inspired with a great new idea or watch something realistic. "I watch them for the entertainment value," he said. "A lot of these things just don't happen in the real world. You don't identify DNA and then get a driver's license pop up (on a computer) and a GPS coordinate leading you to that person."

But because of popularity of shows like "CSI," Kupferschmid said he is asked by members of the public constantly about things that don't happen in real life... The reality is being a forensic scientist can be very tedious and involve long hours of work.

Because of the many misconceptions about forensic scientists and DNA laboratories, Kupferschmid compiled a list of the Top 10 TV Crime Lab Myths. Topping the list is the idea that DNA can be gathered, tested and the results returned in a matter of hours. "When they do their lab analysis, it seems instantaneous," Kupferschmid said.

In reality, the turnaround for analysis on a DNA case is two to five days. And that's if there isn't already a backlog in cases. But crime labs across the country are faced with huge backlogs, he said. Some labs have a 30- to 60-day waiting period before a case will even be looked at. For cases that aren't high profile or don't involve crimes against a person, the waiting list at some labs in the U.S. can be years, he said.

Another CSI myth is that the person who conducts the lab work also interrogates suspects, makes arrests and does police work. "We don't go driving around in new Hummers and cruise the beaches in Miami," Kupferschmid said of his real life job.

Very rarely do you find forensic scientists today who are also certified law enforcers, he said. "You wouldn't send someone to the police academy and then stick them in a lab. It would be a waste of their training. Just like you wouldn't send someone to be a scientist and then put them on the street for patrol," he said.

Another misconception: forensic scientists don't keep track of all their cases once they finish testing evidence. "We do so many cases, we just can't possibly follow them all. We may follow some of them. Very rarely do we find out the final disposition of the case," Kupferschmid said. Because only about 10 percent of the cases Salt Lake-based Sorenson Forensics handles come from Utah, Kupferschmid said most of the time his scientists have no idea if the case they're working on is high profile…

Top 10 TV crime lab myths [a list of thing that ARE NOT true]

1. Crime labs can gather, prepare, test, and have results from DNA and other forensic tests within a few hours.
2. A suspect will sit in an interrogation room wearing the same clothes he wore during the crime — and conclusive test results arrive just as you sit down to question him.
3. Crime scene investigators follow cases from start to finish and conclude investigations within a few days.
4. Crime scene investigators are directly involved with the investigation, raids, and arrests.
5. Crime scene investigators can get DNA evidence from any surface.
6. DNA analyses provide two results: Yes, he did it, or no, he didn't do it.
7. Crime scene investigators can not only pull up DNA, but they can tell whether it came from tears, saliva, and sweat or cremated remains.
8. Everyone is in a DNA database.

9. When a DNA match is indicated, crime lab computers flash big red letters declaring a "99 percent match," and a driver's license photo for good measure.
10. Crime scene investigators conduct DNA testing while munching snacks or joking with colleagues.

As further explained in Cooley (2007), religious viewers of such programs (p. 471) "come to believe or blindly assume three broad themes regarding the forensic science community: (1) crime labs are pristine scientific sanctuaries, which always have the most up-to-date forensic technology; (2) crime labs only employ the most skilled and imaginative "scientists" who make few, if any, errors; and (3) forensic scientists are actually practicing and engaging in legitimate science."

The reality is that forensic evidence examination, testing, and interpretation are lengthy processes involving scientists, not police officers, many of whom work in less than ideal conditions with limited budgets and training, surrounded by many biasing influences—to say nothing of error rates for evidence testing being generally unknown. This means that, too often, there is no science in forensic science (see generally Edwards & Gotsonis, 2009). For those that have already forgotten, please review the long history problems with the FBI crime lab, and others, presented in the early chapters of this text (see also Turvey, 2013).

The CSI effect can impact the justice system in two ways. First, it can create unreasonable expectations for the prosecution—that physical evidence will always be collected, tested, and examined in every case, even when available resources do not permit it, or the facts of the case do not require it. Second, it can create an unreasonable bias against the defense, as the evidence presented by the state's forensic examiners may be presumed infallible or more certain than it actually is. This is even more problematic when attorneys and forensic scientists intentionally distort their legal arguments and testimony to meet the expectations created by the CSI effect, in essence leaving false impressions behind in the minds of jurors about their abilities and the certainty of the evidence.

In plain language, the writers and producers of crime shows and movies make up a lot of stuff because real technology is not as advanced or flashy; real scientific investigation takes weeks, even months—not hours; and real forensic scientists should not have guns, badges, or scores to settle (see generally Cooley, 2007; Smith, 2014; Turvey, 2013). Nor should they have some of the personal problems that are added in as story lines for dramatic effect (e.g., alcoholism, drug problems, gambling addictions, mental disorders). Real forensic scientists do their casework objectively; and if they commit crimes, take psychotropic medication, or suffer from addictions, they are very likely to become unemployed.

THE FBI EFFECT

The *FBI effect* refers to the series of myths, perpetuated by the media and popular culture, which reinforce the erroneous notion that the FBI sets the gold standard for all manner of criminal investigation and forensic analysis. A corollary being that all FBI agents are uber experts in criminal investigation and evidence interpretation. Again, this series of related beliefs is false.

These widely held fictions allow FBI agents to portray themselves as super cops, with unsurpassed knowledge, skill, and ability—whether they are dealing with the public or others within the justice system. This phenomenon is at the core of most crime fiction. It is also the basis for the misplaced faith that many citizens have in the security, and reliability, of the criminal justice system as a whole.

The myths that comprise the *FBI effect* include the following:

Myth #1: *FBI agents are experts in the areas of both murder and sex crimes investigation.*

The Facts: The FBI is a federal agency with jurisdiction over federal crimes. Murder and rape are most commonly state crimes and are lawfully the jurisdiction of local or state law enforcement agencies. Therefore, it does not have jurisdiction over most of these cases, unless they occur on federal land or in federal buildings. Even then the FBI is very likely to hand these few case over to local authorities. Local agencies (e.g., city, county, and state) may ask for assistance from the FBI, with respect to evidence collection, testing, or manpower—but the FBI is not able to simply step in and take charge whenever they want.

To be clear, the FBI has jurisdiction over the following types of violent crime, and only when federal law is suspected of being violated: some gang-related crime, cybercrime, bank robbery, kidnapping, terrorism, and "Indian Country Crime" (FBI, 2016).[1] Consequently, the image of FBI agents working homicides, investigating rapes, ordering the local police around, or taking over murder investigations from local authorities is almost pure fantasy. It is also a convenient writer's device, because it creates drama and people want to believe that is how the justice system works.

Further still, unless an FBI agent received experience working such cases during employment with another agency, they are unlikely to have it at all. In other words, FBI agents do not generally have experience working homicides or sex crimes unless they got it working somewhere else. This reality is not something that FBI agents prefer to acknowledge, and in most instances they will be happy to leave anyone with the opposite impression.[2]

Myth #2: *FBI agents receive special training, unavailable to anyone else in the world.*

The Facts: The training available to the FBI is the same as is available to anyone else in law enforcement. When dealing with specialized subjects, they actually bring in civilian instructors to augment and enhance their knowledge. There are no secret techniques or unique abilities being conveyed at any level.[3] Moreover, the reality is that any training received by an FBI agent can be disclosed during the voir dire process, when the agent is under oath and being screened as a witness by the court. It will also be on their professional resume. The suggestion that there is unique training, or access to secret knowledge, is again pure fantasy. If it exists, it must be disclosed or it is a violation of the rules of discovery in court.

Myth #3: *FBI agents have special access to secret, high-tech databases and are able to search complex strings of information in real time.*

The Facts: There are no secret databases in use by the FBI for criminal investigation. Any databases that are used in the identification and apprehension of criminal suspects must be revealed as part of the discovery process in the subsequent criminal trial. What these proceedings have collectively revealed is that federal databases do not communicate with each other (meaning that agencies are digitally blind to each other's files and information); that they are full of incomplete and even false information; and in many cases the technology involved is quite antiquated (e.g., many federal agencies still use out of date paper-based systems; old style CRT green-screen computers; floppy disks; or Windows 3.11).[4] There is also no national repository of fingerprints or DNA. There are state-level databases, regional databases, and FBI databases. But none of these contain all available fingerprints or DNA. And they certainly are not linked (e.g., networked), such that they can be searched in tandem or cross-referenced. Again, if such databases existed and were being used in criminal casework, they would need to be disclosed or it would be a violation of the rules of discovery in court.

Myth #4: *All FBI agents are experts at interview and interrogation.*

The Facts: FBI agents are among the poorest trained interview and interrogators in law enforcement. They rely heavily on the unfounded reputation of the FBI to get people to make statements out of fear of the FBI. When that does not work, they resort to scientifically disproved technology such as the polygraph and voice stress analysis. Moreover, they are among the many federal agencies that do not record their interviews of witnesses or suspects. This substandard practice has cost them a number of high profile cases, both in the United States and abroad.[5]

Myth #5: *The FBI Crime Lab sets the gold standard for scientific practice and evidence examination in the world.*

The Facts: The FBI's crime lab has suffered and continuous string of scandals since the mid-1990s related to phony areas of unfounded practice (e.g., hair and fiber analysis; and Comparative Bullet Lead Metal Analysis); examiner bias (e.g., fingerprinting); examiner fraud (e.g., DNA); and examiner incompetence (e.g., all of the above). They have also been caught hiding evidence of these realities, demonstrating a culture obsessed with its image over accuracy and reliability. These revelations have been public, they have been acknowledged by the FBI (eventually, and under great pressure), and then they have been just as quickly forgotten.[6]

Myth #6: *When all other investigative avenues fail, the FBI is a professional law enforcement agency that will step in and make sure that no crime goes unsolved.*

The Facts: See Myths #1–#5.

The recognition and discussion of these myths is not intended to diminish the work of those currently employed by the FBI, or their potential value to criminal investigations. For instance, they have an amazing Evidence Response Team available to law enforcement with limited resources in major cases. They can have been known to provide manpower to agencies that need it. They partner with other agencies on various organized crime task forces to good effect (e.g., human trafficking; Medicaid/Medicare fraud; and health clinics selling illegal prescriptions for painkillers and anabolic steroids). And they have done some excellent work in the area of public corruption (e.g., arresting corrupt law enforcement officers).

Rather, identifying these myths it is intended to bring the institution, and its employees, back to reality. It is a law enforcement agency run by normal people, just like any other, equally capable of dishonesty, error, and ability.[7] It is in the best interests of the public, and the justice system, to understand its strengths as well as its limitations. This is the only way to prevent misrepresentations by those who are less than honest, and thereby avoid future injustice.

CRIME SCENE INVESTIGATION, RECONSTRUCTION, AND ANALYSIS

In this section, we will define and discuss the relationship between crime scene investigation, crime reconstruction, and CSA. These terms are used a great deal in forensic investigation, and often inappropriately. When this is allowed to happen, roles are confused and expectations can be misplaced.

CRIME SCENE INVESTIGATION

Crime scene investigation refers to the entire process of establishing the scientific facts of a case using the physical evidence that is produced in relation to suspected criminal activity, including its component parts (see generally DeForest, 2005; Chisum & Turvey, 2012; Lee, Palmbach, & Miller, 2001). An emphasis must be placed on the investigation component, as we are required to acknowledge that until crime scene investigation efforts bear fruit, the facts of a case are unknown or uncorroborated. We investigate to establish facts and understand them and to determine whether or not actions and events genuinely occurred. We investigate not knowing the outcome, and not toward predetermined findings.

Although often confused with crime scene processing efforts (discussed in the next chapter), crime scene investigation is actually more comprehensive. As explained in DeForest (2005; p.113):

The stages of the crime scene investigation extend beyond the work at the scene. Once the evidence has been analyzed in the laboratory, the scientific interpretation of the laboratory results may lead to a reconstruction of the event.

Crime scene investigation, it is understood, does not occur *only* within the confines of yellow police barrier tape. It is a broad inquiry that seeks to establish the record of physical evidence during an event or a series of related events. It is ultimately the unified result of aggregated crime scene examination and processing efforts; forensic laboratory examinations and analyses; digital and social media evidence; medicolegal examinations and analyses; and collateral victim—suspect evidence and history.

As this implies, crime scene investigation efforts must always be conducted in such a fashion, and with sufficient attention to detail, as to ensure that results are reliable enough for use by other forensic professionals, as well as attorneys, judges, and juries. Crime scene investigation is not a secret process; it must be transparent, with step by step documentation. Otherwise, there is little point to it, as the resulting evidence may have adequate providence for courtroom admissibility.

The goal of crime scene investigation is to provide for scientific crime reconstruction and CSA efforts. As will be discussed, these are separate and ongoing analyses necessarily conducted at a later point. The scope of crime scene investigation must therefore be as broad and formulated as possible. This is because the truth of a case is not known at the outset. It can only be guessed at. Crime scene investigation must be conducted in such a fashion that it does not blindly follow a single path; but rather in such a way that it will reveal the facts. Each case, it must be remembered, has its own issues and eventual twists that cannot be predicted. They can only be uncovered, and that takes an investigative mindset as opposed to a biased or political one. This reality demands a thorough and inclusive crime scene investigation effort at the outset, with protocols that are carefully followed each time, to allow for the most complete retrospective inquiry of any evidence that comes to light.

CRIME RECONSTRUCTION

Scientific crime reconstruction is the ultimate goal of all crime scene investigation efforts.[8] *Crime reconstruction* is the determination of the actions and events surrounding the commission of a crime. Crime reconstruction is further defined in DeForest (2005; p.115):

> *Reconstruction is the culmination of the scientific work on the physical evidence in a case. It is at this stage where the information gleaned from the examination of all the evidence is integrated and interpreted to yield an objective understanding of the event. In most jurisdictions, this activity is given insufficient scientific attention.*

Crime reconstruction can be accomplished by examining the statements of witnesses, the confessions of suspects, the statements of living victims, or by examining and interpreting physical evidence. However, the physical evidence is the most objective record of the crime and must therefore be given the most weight by the forensic examiner (Kirk, 1974).[9]

Crime reconstruction is best practiced as the work of forensic generalists generating theories of the crime based on the consideration of aggregated results from a variety of forensic disciplines (e.g., ballistics reports; DNA reports; toxicology reports; medicolegal reports). Integration of findings is a key because crime is best reconstructed when forged by a collaboration of the forensic evidence, not by a reliance on one single examination or discipline. Even DNA findings cannot be given meaning in a particular case absent a reconstruction of the conditions of transfer. Relying on one piece of evidence, or one theory, without placing it in context with other physical evidence and thus reconciling it, is highly misleading.

DIGITAL EVIDENCE AND CRIME RECONSTRUCTION: *BY JODI FREEMAN*

With advances in technology, the boundaries of crime scenes have been expanding to include forms of digital evidence.[10] While cell phone records, text messages, and email correspondences have all become acceptable evidence gathering tools used in crime scene investigations, modern technological advances, such as social networking websites, which have gained enormous popularity in recent years (e.g., Facebook, Youtube, MySpace). As these websites and associated technology become more a part of our lives, and the volume of shared information grows, it is becoming obvious that data posted to and extracted by the cyberverse has tremendous and often untapped investigative value. As an extension of the physical crime scene, these threads of digital evidence have the potential to support or refute investigative theories and provide crucial details necessary for the reconstruction of crime.

Specifically, digital evidence gained from social networking websites has the potential to influence the following aspects of crime reconstruction:

Timeline

Online communication and Internet postings provide a date and time stamp of online activity. This digital evidence is useful not only in determining when an individual was accessing an online Website, but the nature of the communication may also establish an individual's behavioral timeline that may support or refute reconstructive information.

For example, photographs posted online may document the activities of a suspect (or victim) before, during, and after the commission of a crime. This may allow examiners to piece together a timeline of events. Photographs not only offer a snapshot of a specific point in time, but also provide investigatively useful information. This includes evidence of specific friends or associates, and locations visited.

Victimological Information

Forensic victimology[11] is an important aspect of crime reconstruction that is often overlooked. Without an understanding of the victim as a person, it is difficult to reconstruct victim behavior. Social networking websites may contain victimological information that provides a more complete understanding of victim risk, victim exposure, and past behavior. Victimological information that can be gained from social networking sites includes, but is not limited to, the following:

- friends and acquaintances;
- enemies or history of conflict;
- relationship status;
- history of drug/alcohol use or abuse;
- prior criminal activity;
- educational and employment history;
- locations routinely visited;
- daily schedule or routine activities.

The level of online privacy or security set by the victim will indicate who had access to this information. Detailed victim information that is publicly available and easily searchable will ultimately influence an investigation by drastically increasing the suspect pool.

Suspect Information

Similar to victimological information, suspect information relevant to crime reconstruction can be gained from social networking Websites. This includes photographs and online communication, posted by the suspect or others, that establishes a timeline of behavior prior to crime commission, or evidences a prior association with the victim and/or the location of the crime scene. It can also provide alibi evidence.

While digital evidence may be useful to develop a reconstruction, there are limitations associated with this form of evidence. Digital evidence must not be taken at face value. Without further investigation, it is insufficient to assume ownership or that information posted online is correct or authentic, without digital alteration. Furthermore, without laws in place to govern the obtainment of information from social networking sites, a fine line is drawn between the retrieval of publicly available information and the privacy infringement of individual users.

Scientific crime reconstruction is distinct in process and reliability from reconstruction efforts attempted by nonscientists; by those in law enforcement; or by those with a vested interest in the outcome of findings. Pretending that physical evidence is best interpreted by the police, or that it is selectively irrelevant, is a common practice among law enforcement, attorneys, and even judges. In reality, this is what happens when physical evidence runs contrary to prevailing case theories: it is dismissed as unimportant so that the facts can be kept from the record to facilitate a conviction.[12] The ethical forensic investigator does not participate in such obfuscations; they follow the evidence where it leads, and they are disinterested in what those around them might prefer.

As previously explained, the reconstructionist should attend the crime scene if possible. However, this effort should be forensic science oriented and entirely detached from the police investigation with respect to roles and responsibilities. This approach will help preserve the reconstructionist's objectivity and avoid role strain.

Unfortunately, crime reconstruction is an afterthought in most police investigations—engaged primarily when there are no witnesses, or after it is announced that the defense has hired an independent forensic examiner to assess some or all of the physical evidence. In most cases, including homicides, crime reconstruction simply does not happen. This makes no practical sense, as the only reason to collect evidence is to examine and interpret it. In fact, law enforcement agencies have a clear duty of care to ensure that this occurs. However, more and more agencies seem to be collecting and testing less and less physical evidence out of ignorance, shrinking budgets, or a combination of both. The victims, the accused, and the courts deserve much better.

CASE EXAMPLE: *KANSAS V. ARTIS COBB*

According to the appellate brief, and consistent with the observations of this examiner, the following is a summary of some of the facts in the 1994 murder of Kasey (19-year-old black female) and Alannah (1-year-old black infant) Blount (*Kansas v. Artis Cobb, 2002*) (Fig. 5.2).

FIGURE 5.2

Kasey Blount was found dead in her apartment in Junction City by her husband when he returned home from military exercises. The crime scene presented as an apparent sexual homicide, given the strangulation and nudity. She had semen in vagina from multiple men, all of whom admitted to sex with her in the same time frame. None of the DNA, fingerprints, or other evidence at the scene matched Artis Cobb, who was convicted of her murder.

Kasey Blount was found dead in her apartment in Junction City by her husband when he returned home from military exercises. Her decomposing body was on its back on the living room floor, naked below the waist. Kasey had a baby's sock in her throat and a pillow under her leg. A cushion was off of the nearby loveseat, and a knife was on the floor. An autopsy determined that Kasey had been asphyxiated.

Alannah's body was in an upstairs crib. She died of dehydration, apparently after her dead mother could no longer respond to quench her thirst.

Physical evidence at the crime scene included semen from Keith Jones, semen from Javis Devore, and a fingerprint from James Battle. All three men admitted to having sex with Kasey in her apartment during her husband's absence. Jones eventually directed the attention of authorities to "Scoop," whom he later identified as Cobb. No physical evidence ever tied Cobb to the crime scene.

The author examined the case for reconstruction purposes and gave expert testimony in front of the jury in May of 2000. The author was qualified as a forensic expert; however, his testimony was limited to some victimology and general reconstruction theory. Bizarrely, the judge decided the reconstruction opinions were compound to testimony from state experts. This ruling made little sense to the author then, and upon reflection it makes no sense now. The only purpose it served was to prevent the defense from developing a theory of innocence, which the judge clearly did not accept.

The author's forensic examination report was submitted to the court as follows:

April 3, 2000
Mr. Mark Dinkel
Salina Regional Public Defender.
234 N. 7th, Suite A.

Salina, KS 67401
Ph# (785) 827-9961.

Re: State of Kansas v. Artis T. Cobb

This examiner, Brent E. Turvey of Knowledge Solutions LLC of Watsonville, California was asked by Mark Dinkel, an attorney representing Artis T. Cobb, to review case material related to the asphyxial death of Casey Blount and the subsequent "dehydration" death of her one-year-old daughter, Alannah. This examiner was further asked to provide an opinion on the accuracy and veracity of statements made by Artis Cobb relating to the known forensic evidence in these related cases.

In order to complete this task, this examiner made a review of related case material including, but not limited to, the following documentation:

1. *Crime scene photos of both victims;*
2. *Autopsy photos of both victims;*
3. *Various Junction City Police Department investigative and forensic reports;*
4. *Various Kansas Bureau of Investigation (KBI) investigative reports;*
5. *Various Kansas Bureau of Investigation (KBI) crime lab reports;*
6. *Autopsy report of Casey Blount, dated July 25, 1994;*
7. *Autopsy report of Alannah Blount, dated July 25, 1994;*
8. *Pattern Analysis report by Norm Reeves of BPA Consulting, undated;*
9. *Historical information and records relating to Casey Blount and her husband, Jade Blount;*
10. *Various financial information and records relating to Casey Blount and her husband, Jade Blount;*
11. *Transcript of interview with Artis Cobb by FDLE Agent William Pheil and KBI Agent Ray Lundin dated July 26, 1997;*
12. *Statement of Artis Cobb dated August 6th, 1997;*
13. *Investigation Report by Agent Ray Lundin dated August 6th, 1997;*
14. *Retraction of statement by Artis Cobb dated August 7th, 1997;*
15. *Investigation Report by Agent Ray Lundin dated August 8th, 1997.*

Conclusions

This examiner found major discrepancies between the two descriptive statements given to authorities by Artis Cobb (July 26 and August 6, 1997) and the known forensic evidence relating to the deaths of Casey and Alannah Blount. This conclusion is based primarily on the consideration of the following issues together in context:

1. The statements made by Artis Cobb describe the victim being held down by the arms and struggling. However, according to the autopsy report and visible in the autopsy photos, there is no evidence of injury to the victim's arms or trunk to support the conclusion that this occurred.
2. The statements made by Artis Cobb describe his ejaculation into the victim. He does not describe the use of a condom. However, no sperm evidence related to Artis Cobb was found to support the conclusion that this actually occurred. This would be expected, as sperm evidence relating to other individuals was found.
3. The statements made by Artis Cobb describe forced sexual intercourse between himself and Casey Blount. She is described as resistant and requiring restraint. However, there is no evidence in the autopsy report or photos to suggest forced vaginal or anal penetration. This type of corroborating evidence would include bruising to the thighs, and anal/vaginal tearing, lacerations, bruising, or ecchymosis. While this issue by itself is not conclusive, it becomes of interest when considered in the context of the other issues in this section.
4. None of the statements made by Artis Cobb account for the kitchen knife, evident in the crime scene photos, which is on the carpeted floor in the living room. If the knife was involved in any part of the crime, this would represent a significant discrepancy (it is unlikely, though

not impossible, that a mother with a small child would leave a kitchen knife on the floor in such a manner).
5. The statements made by Artis Cobb suggest that he touched the top of the television when standing up after having intercourse with Casey Blount. However, according to a KBI Laboratory Report dated September 11, 1997, comparison of Artis Cobb's fingerprints with unknown impressions at the scene achieved a negative result.
6. The statements made by Artis Cobb suggest that Andrew Jones was with him in the victim's home that evening. However, according to the KBI Laboratory, none of the unknown impressions at the scene match Andrew Jones.
7. None of the statements made by Artis Cobb account for the internal and external evidence of manual strangulation/neck injuries to Casey Blount. This evidence is detailed in the autopsy report (*Evidence of Injury*, pp. 2–3) and visible in both the crime scene and autopsy photos.
8. The statements made by Artis Cobb describe the suffocation of Casey Blount with a pillow from the couch. However, there is no evidence to support the conclusion that this occurred. In point of fact, it would be redundant to the manual strangulation and the placement of the sock.
9. None of the statements made by Artis Cobb account for the placement of a baby's sock in Casey Blount's throat. According to the autopsy report (*Evidence of Injury*, p. 3), and visible in autopsy photos, a baby's sock was found in Casey Blount's throat, completely occluding her airway.
10. The match to the sock described in item #7 was found at the base of the stairs, the sock was baby sized, and the baby's high chair was downstairs in plain view. Therefore, a rational argument may be made that the killing of Casey Blount necessarily involved knowledge, direct or indirect, of the baby. None of the statements made by Artis Cobb refer to the presence of, or contact with, the baby, Alannah Blount.
11. There are no witnesses or alleged participants that corroborate the crime-related activity described by Artis Cobb.
12. The autopsy report of one-year-old Alannah Blount states that she died of dehydration. This opinion is argued by virtue of the overall dryness of the victim's various tissues and the lack of other anatomic defect. However, a review of the relevant literature suggests that this may be insufficient reason for such a finding. According to *Bourne* et al. (1996):

Because the clinical history and postmortem markers in cases of dehydration may be unreliable, careful biochemical assessment is required in each case. Postmortem serum sodium, potassium and chloride levels are much less reliable markers of antemortem fluid and electrolyte status than samples taken from the vitreous humor.

Kirschner & Wilson (1996) agree with this assertion, stating also:

…the ability to evaluate the state of hydration at autopsy is limited… Sunken eyes, depressed fontanelle, and serosal membranes may be indicators of moderate to sever dehydration. Skin turgor is generally not a good indicator in the dead child. Refrigerated bodies develop significant postmortem drying artifact, which may mimic dehydration when a small infant is left refrigerated overnight.

Of further significance on the issue in this case are the following facts. (1) According to the autopsy report (*External Examination*, p.2), Alannah Blount showed no signs of "chronic rash in the diaper area." A diaper rash would be expected if a child wore the same diaper for more than a day. (2) According to the autopsy report (*Internal Examination*, p.3), and evident in the autopsy photographs, Alannah Blount still had chyme particles (partly digested food passed from the stomach into the duodenum) as well as fecal material in her digestive tract. If the child was alive for more than a day, this food should have been completely digested and the diaper subsequently soiled in less than a day's time. (3) Dehydration from neglect would have taken more than one day after the death of Casey Blount, unless that neglect began prior to her death.

Given these facts in combination with the limited reliability of the methods used to determine dehydration, and the apparent absence of tests on the victim's vitreous fluids, this examiner is unable to accept the cause of death given in the autopsy report of Alannah Blount at face value. This examiner makes no claims as an expert in the area of forensic pathology. Having said that, the issues above described, unless otherwise cited, clearly fall into the realm of general knowledge. As such, the evidence relating to the facts and circumstances in this case begs certain questions that apparently were not addressed at the time of autopsy, and certainly were not addressed in the autopsy report.

The possibilities raised by these facts could be used to suggest a more direct involvement of the offender in this case with the death of Alannah Blount. This could tend to increase the significance of issue #10 described in this report.

I swear and affirm to the best of my knowledge that the above statements are true under penalty of perjury.

Brent E. Turvey, MS
Forensic Scientist

References

Bourne, A.J., Byard, R.W., Cooper, R.T.L., Moore, L., and Whitehead, E.J., "Dehydration Deaths in Infants and Young Children," *The American Journal of Forensic Medicine and Pathology*, 1996, 17 (1); pp. 73–78.

Kirschner, R.H. & Wilson, H.L., "Fatal Child Abuse: The Pathologist's Perspective," pp. 325–357 from Reece, R.M., *Child Abuse: Medical Diagnosis and Management*, (Williams and Wilkins, 1996)

In sentencing, the judge openly speculated that the crime may have involved alcohol or drugs, despite no direct evidence of such. He then gave Mr. Cobb 8 years in prison. This sentence makes no sense if one truly believes that Artis Cobb, on his own, raped and murder Kasey Blount, resulting in the death of her infant child.

CRIME SCENE ANALYSIS

Crime scene analysis is the analytical process of interpreting the specific features of a crime and related crime scenes. It involves an integrated assessment of the forensic evidence, forensic victimology, and crime scene characteristics. It is an interpretive stage of crime scene investigation efforts, subsequent to crime reconstruction efforts, and provides a language for categorizing, explaining, and comparing victim and offender behavior.[13]

The results of CSA may be used to determine the limits of the available evidence and the need for additional investigative and forensic efforts, as in a threshold assessment (discussed shortly). When sufficient behavioral evidence is available, these same results may also be used to infer offender modus operandi (MO) and signature behaviors, evidence of crime scene staging, crime scene motive, and offender characteristics, or to assist with linkage analysis efforts.

See *Chapter 14: Oklahoma v. Elver Thacker* for an example of an integrated crime scene analysis.

FORENSIC RELEVANCE

The relevance of crime scene investigation, and subsequent reconstructions and scene analyses, is often forgotten, ignored, or even denied in legal venues. This is problematic.

The only reason for the collection of evidence is its examination and interpretation by forensic scientists. Otherwise, why bother to collect it, or to submit it for forensic examinations of any kind? For that matter, why have publicly funded crime labs? The answer is that there is broad agreement by the courts, and the legal system they are meant to serve, that physical evidence has value to legal proceedings with respect to establishing scientific facts. It can aid the trier of fact in the resolution of issues that arise, or with respect to establishing the occurrence of events that may be disputed.

This includes the following.[14]

CORPUS DELICTI

The corpus delicti, literally translated as the "body of the crime," refers to those essential facts that show a crime has taken place. Without the corpus delicti there is no evidence of a crime, and there can be no criminal proceedings.

To establish the crime of burglary, for instance, a forensic analysis of the crime scene for physical evidence could include searching for items of evidence such as, but not limited to, the following:

- tool marks and fingerprints at the point of entry;
- broken doors or windows;
- glass lodged in the suspect's shoes tread matching broken glass at the scene;
- ransacked rooms with valuables missing;
- missing valuables found in the suspect possession;
- footwear impressions on the ground outside of the residence.

To establish a rape or sexual assault, however, a forensic analysis of the crime scene for physical evidence could include searching for items of evidence such as, but not limited to, the following:

- the victim's blood at the crime scene;
- the suspect's semen/sperm in the victim's body cavities, or on their clothing;
- a bloody knife;
- wound patterns on the victim;
- Torn items of victim clothing
- fibers from ligatures used by the suspect to bind the victim;
- DNA from pulled victim hair in the suspect's vehicle;
- the suspect's pubic hair on the victim's genitals, or vice versa.

While none of the above prove that sexual assault must have occurred, they may be used to disprove the suspect's version of events, or to find inconsistencies in the victim's complaint. They are given weight in court to support the victim's testimony or the people's case.

To establish the crime of homicide, a forensic analysis of the crime scene for physical evidence could include searching for items of evidence such as, but not limited to, the following:

- the murder weapon;
- suspect computer browser history evidencing searches for the method of killing used;

- suspect social media evidence evidencing a motive for killing the victim;
- a receipt for specific items purchased and used in the commission of the murder (e.g., ligatures, ammunition, a mask, and tools).

MODUS OPERANDI

All criminals have a *modus operandi* (or method of operation) that consists of their habits, techniques, and peculiarities of behavior. Sometimes this MO is somewhat consistent, but often it grows and changes over time as the offender becomes more skillful, including what has been successful, excluding what has been unsuccessful (O'Hara, 1970). Physical evidence can help establish that MO.

To establish the MO in the crime of burglary, for instance, a forensic analysis of the crime scene for physical evidence could include searching for items of evidence such as, but not limited to, the following:

- tools used to gain entry (e.g., screwdriver, pry bar, keys to the front door);
- types of items taken (e.g., cash, jewelry, credit cards, sport memorabilia, clothing, lingerie, personal toiletries);
- lack of fingerprints at the established point of entry, suggesting a gloved offender;
- avoidance of security cameras, suggesting presurveillance or foreknowledge.

To establish the MO in the crime of rape, a forensic analysis of the crime scene for physical evidence could include searching for items of evidence such as, but not limited to, the following:

- the types of restraints used on the victim (e.g., handcuffs, rope, duct tape, victim clothing), if any;
- tire marks nearby suggesting the type of vehicle used, if any;
- wound patterns on the victim indicating a type of weapon used (e.g., incision marks from a knife; bite marks on the victim's back; fingermark contusions on the victim's neck and arms; cylindrical bruises from a baton);
- tape found on the victim's body, used to cover the eyes or the mouth;
- victim's cell phone with text messages, photos, and social media history—to connect with other potential victim's and shared victim activity.
- The suspect's cell phone with text messages, photos, and social media history—to evidence GPS locations, and times, associated with victim activity and attacks.

To establish the MO in the crime of homicide, a forensic analysis of the crime scene for physical evidence could include searching for items of evidence such as, but not limited to, the following:

- location of the attack/use of multiple scenes;
- use of a weapon/weapon type;
- use of a vehicle;
- use of restraints;
- use of gloves/mask (precautionary acts);
- use of force.

SIGNATURE BEHAVIOR

Some criminals repeatedly commit the same or thematically similar acts during their crimes that may be referred to as *signature behaviors*. As described in California v. Odell Clarence Haston (1968):

> *Professor McCormick states: "Here [i.e., in the matter of proving identity by means of other-offenses modus operandi evidence] much more is demanded than the mere repeated commission of crimes of the same class, such as repeated burglaries or thefts. The device used must be so unusual and distinctive as to be like a signature."*
>
> **McCormick, Evidence (1954, 157, p. 328).**

McCormick is cited again on the subject of signature behaviors in California v. Rhonda Denise Erving (1998), stating that they must be:

> *...sufficiently distinctive so as to support the inference that the same person committed both acts. The pattern and characteristics of the crimes must be so unusual and distinctive as to be like a signature.*
>
> **1 McCormick [on Evidence (fourth ed., 1992)], § 190, pp. 801–803.**

Signature behaviors establish the theme of the crime; they are committed to satisfy psychological and emotional needs. Physical evidence can be used to help establish signature behaviors and their context.

To establish signature behaviors in the crime of burglary, for instance, a forensic analysis of the crime scene for physical evidence could include searching for items of evidence such as, but not limited to, the following:

- slashing the clothing in the closets;
- ejaculating, urinating, or defecating in specific locations;
- stealing female undergarments;
- destroying furniture;
- vandalizing vehicles in the garage.

To establish the signature behaviors in the crime of rape and/or homicide, a forensic analysis of the crime scene for physical evidence could include searching for items of evidence such as, but not limited to, the following:

- type of ligature used;
- specific sequences of sexual acts;
- level of injury to the victim (from minimal to brutal);
- specific type of weapon used;
- specific injuries to specific locations (e.g., headshot, nipples removed, genitals removed or otherwise mutilated);
- personal items taken from the victim not related to theft, such as identification, clothing, or inexpensive jewelry.

LINKING THE SUSPECT TO THE VICTIM

Blood, tissue, hair, fibers, and cosmetics may be transferred from a victim to an offender. Furthermore, items found in the possession of the suspect can be linked back to the victim. Examples include the following:

- the victim's vaginal epithelial cells dried onto an offender's penis or clothing;
- the victim's skin cells and hairs on a piece of rope in an offender's vehicle;
- the victim's blood on an offender's knife;
- the victim's artificial nails broken off during a struggle and left in an offender's vehicle.

It is also possible that trace evidence can be transferred from a perpetrator onto a victim. Suspect's belongings and clothing should be examined thoroughly for this type of trace evidence. Victims and their belongings, of course, should be similarly examined.

LINKING A PERSON TO A CRIME SCENE

This linkage is a common and significant one provided by physical evidence analysis. Fingerprints and glove prints, blood, semen, hairs, fibers, soil, bullets, cartridge cases, tool marks, footprints or shoe prints, tire tracks, and objects that belonged to the criminal are examples of deposited evidence (Lee, 1994). Depending on the type of crime, various kinds of evidence from the scene may be carried away. Stolen property is the most obvious example, but two-way transfers of trace evidence can be used to link a suspect, a victim, or even a witness to a crime scene.

DISPROVING OR SUPPORTING WITNESS TESTIMONY

While consideration of witness and victim statements is necessary, physical evidence is considered a more objective and reliable source of information regarding offense activity. More to the point, the forensic examiner has a duty to compare any statement regarding crime-related events against the physical evidence to test its veracity, when possible. Though an established pillar of courtroom proceedings, witness testimony has a terrible capacity for unreliability, as discussed in Miller (2008, p. 143):

> The use of eyewitnesses in criminal investigations and courtroom testimony has been well established in the United States (Becker, 2000). Their usefulness for the gathering of information is often the first step in any criminal investigation when looking for who, what, when, where, and even the how and why of a crime. Their reliability, however, is often called into question (Lyman, 2008). The Innocence Project has estimated that almost 75% of the over 200 wrongful convictions in the United States have been due to mistaken identification by eyewitnesses (Innocence Project, n.d.)…

> *Physical evidence found at any crime scene can be used to corroborate the statements of witnesses, to assist investigators in determining the credibility of eyewitnesses, and to assist in the reconstruction of the events leading to the crime including the way in which the crime itself was committed.*
>
> **Gaensslen, Harris, & Lee (2008).**

Physical evidence analysis can indicate conclusively whether a witnesses' version of events is credible, or whether they are in error or even being deceptive. A simple example would be a driver whose car matches the description of a hit-and-run vehicle. An examination of the car may reveal blood and other tissue on the underside of the bumper. The driver may explain the findings by claiming to have hit a dog. A simple species test on the blood could reveal whether the blood was from a human, dog, or some other animal. If it is found to be human blood, a DNA test can be used to confirm the identity of its source.

IDENTIFICATION OF SUSPECTS

The most conclusive evidence for individuating and identifying a suspect includes fingerprints and some kinds of DNA evidence. A relevant fingerprint can be found at a crime scene, on a victim's skin or possessions, or on the murder weapon. Later, if it is identified as belonging to a particular person, this result can be strong identification. Similarly, if a suspect's DNA is found on a murder weapon, at the crime scene, or associated with the victim's body, this can have probative value. However, the conditions of transfer must be reconstructed such that the evidence is firmly associated with the crime. Absent that context, the evidence has limited value.

For example, the author worked a serial murder case involving the murder of a prostitute. These cases often involve multiple used suspect condoms filled with semen and sperm found at the scene; and victims with semen and sperm from multiple donors in their orifices. Consequently, that DNA evidence has limited value without further reconstruction efforts. In one such case, the author wrote the following limitation regarding the DNA evidence found in the body of the report:

A sexual act is any offender behavior involving sexual organs, sexual apparatus, or sexualized objects (Turvey, 2011). *The physical evidence in this case (e.g., DNA) does not confirm sexual activity in direct association with the death of the victim. Such an assumption would in fact be a fallacy of logic that is referred to as "Cum hoc, ergo propter hoc," or "with this, therefore because of this"* (Chisum *and* Turvey, 2011, p. 622). *This occurs when one jumps to a conclusion about causation based on a correlation between two events, or types of event, that occur simultaneously. In other words: just because two things are found together at a crime scene does not mean that they must be the result of the same actions and events or that they must have occurred at the same time. This is especially true of evidence of sexual activity found in association with sex workers, such as prostitutes. Any evidence of sexual activity found (e.g., DNA) must therefore be independently linked in some fashion to the homicide via a proper reconstruction of the crime, and not assumed; the mere presence of such evidence is not sufficient basis in this context. The sexual acts in this case, as directly related to the homicide, are therefore unknown* (Fig. 5.3).

The Latin referenced in this explanation is among the most common fallacies of logic found in forensic science opinions—either as an assumption or a direct

FIGURE 5.3

The author has worked hundreds of cases in which prostitutes have been killed. Often they were the ones working busy street corners, out of hotel rooms, or on "the stroll" in general. Sex workers under these circumstances see many clients in a day—sometimes 40 or more. Those working outside tend to use the same secluded locations. Those working inside are not known for their hygiene or housekeeping abilities. In any case, the result is the same: dozens, if not hundreds, of condoms accumulating around them each day. Consequently, when a prostitute is killed under such circumstances, DNA identification of potential suspects with sperm or semen becomes problematic. If they use condoms, there are dozens in the environment associated with them. If they do not, their body cavities and clothing can reveal a host of donors. All are potential suspects.

argument. Failure to grasp and accept that this is a logical fallacy, and therefore impermissible, evidences a lack of science and potential bias.

In rape and homicide cases, DNA can be used to make identifications from the following sources (not by any means an exclusive list):

- sperm left behind at the scene or on the victim;
- epithelial cells left behind with urine collected from the toilet;
- blood left behind at the scene from injuries inflicted by the victim;
- tissue collected beneath the victim's fingernails during defensive activity;
- pubic hair left behind at the scene or on the victim.

In rape/sexual assault cases, bite mark evidence can sometimes be used to make identifications from the following sources (not by any means an exclusive list):

- bite marks inflicted on the victim's back during the victim's struggle to make the victim compliant;
- bite marks made to victim's genital areas as part of the sexual attack;
- bite marks made to the victim's face and extremities as a part of a punishment (child abuse).

Bite mark evidence is best used to source suspect DNA during the creation of the suspected injury. This is because the identification and interpretation of bite mark patterns has a long history of creating wrongful convictions. Generally, this has been due to the lack of science employed by many forensic bite mark experts, and the bias they have shown with respect to an improper alliance with the prosecution. Collecting DNA transferred from saliva at these sites is therefore a much more reliable forensic practice.

PROVIDING INVESTIGATIVE LEADS

Physical evidence analysis can be helpful in directing an investigation along a productive path. In a hit-and-run case, for example, a chip of paint from the vehicle can be used to narrow down the number and kinds of different cars that may have been involved. In a rape/sexual assault case, DNA evidence can be used to quickly exclude suspects as they are generated—even when the actual offender remains elusive. In a homicide, fingerprints found on a weapon can establish association with a suspect or a group of suspects. And in a shooting case, the directionality of shots and number of different weapons used can be used to suggest multiple shooters.

CASE EXAMPLE: *TENNESSEE V. RALPH O'NEAL*

Consider *Tennessee v. Ralph O'Neal*. The author's report in this case was used to demonstrate that multiple shooters may have been involved (not just one) and that statements made by the state's only witness in the case were not substantiated. Moreover, there was no direct physical evidence associating the suspect with the murder, when there should have been given the nature of the crime.

FORENSIC RECONSTRUCTION REPORT

Forensic Solutions, LLC
P.O. Box 2175
Sitka, Alaska 99835
Ph: (907) 738-5121

For: Robert Vogel, Attorney
               The Vogel Law Firm
               101 Sherlake Lane, Suite 106
               P.O. Box 31464
               Knoxville TN 37930
               Ph. (865) 357-1949

Examiner: Brent E. Turvey, MS, PhD

Date: March 31, 2014

Case: *Tennessee v. Ralph O'Neal*, Case No. 14164

Victim: Ronnie Dean "Boone" Cofer

PURPOSE
The purpose of this report is to provide forensic opinions resulting from an examination of crime scene and physical evidence related variables in the shooting death of 59 year old Ronnie Cofer.

BACKGROUND
Mr. Cofer's body was discovered in a ditch along Clax Gap Road, near Harriman, on the morning of August 6, 2007. He was found face up, wearing a buttoned shirt, pajama bottoms, and sandals. His wooden walking cane was also found at this location, underneath his body. At autopsy, it was determined that Mr. Cofer died as the result of multiple gunshot wounds to the head.

It is the state's position that Mr. O'Neal was, at the time, a drug dealer. At the same time, Mr. Cofer was known as a drug dealer to law enforcement. Mr. Cofer also had a pending drug charge in Roane County. It is further the state's position that Mr. O'Neal killed Mr. Cofer in order to protect his illegal enterprise. This out of fear that Mr. Cofer had been or intended to become a law enforcement informant.

MATERIALS
The examiner was provided with, and relied upon, at least the following materials relating to the shooting death of Ronnie Cofer (case material provided to this examiner's officer between October 25, 2013 and March 22, 2014):

1. Various Investigative Reports prepared by the Roane County Sheriff's Department;
2. Various Evidence Collection Reports prepared by the Roane County Sheriff's Department;
3. Crime Scene Diagram reportedly prepared by Det. Greg Scalf of the Roane County Sheriff's Department, undated and unsigned;
4. Autopsy report of Ronnie Cofer by Dynacare Tennessee, August 7, 2007;
5. Tennessee Bureau of Investigation, Official Firearms Report by analyst Alex Brodhag, August 9, 2007;
6. Tennessee Bureau of Investigation, Official Firearms Report by Criminalist Robert Royce, November 19, 2007;
7. Various Investigative Reports and prepared by the Tennessee Bureau of Investigation;
8. Various Interviews and Interview Summaries by the Tennessee Bureau of Investigation;
9. Summary of the DEA interview with Jaclyn Miller by Agent James Blanton (December 4, 2008);
10. Transcript of recorded conversation between Jaclyn Miller and Michael Currier (January 11, 2008);
11. Summary of the interview with Michael Jackson by Det. Kris Mynatt of the Roane County Sheriff's Department (August 20, 2008);
12. Summary of FBI interview with Cornelius Jennings, August 20, 2008;
13. Summary of the interview with James Murray by Det. Greg Scalf of the Roane County Sheriff's Department (May 20, 2009);

FINDINGS

The findings in this case have been made in comportment with the literature on proper scientific methodology (see generally Edwards and Gotsonis, 2009; NAS, 2002; NAS, 2009) as well as being in agreement with the education, training, research, publications, and experience of this examiner (see Chisum and Turvey, 2012).

Note: While it is acceptable to use eyewitness statements to assist with a forensic reconstruction of the physical evidence, these statements must be deemed sufficiently reliable. This requires corroboration with objective evidentiary findings. In other words, the statement must be confirmed in part by the physical or documentary evidence that it necessarily leads to (e.g., security video, blood evidence in a vehicle, a hidden murder weapon, or passive documentation of activities by digital evidence). The statements made by the police informants in this case have not been corroborated by the physical evidence, are in conflict with each other, and are therefore not considered a reliable source of information by this examiner.

1. **The victim in this case, Ronnie Cofer, was shot to death at the location where he was found - in the ditch along Clax Gap Road. This finding is based on at least the following:**

    A. Crime scene photographs document medium and high velocity blood spatter on the leaves of bushes adjacent to the victims body, next to the telephone pole. This evidence, and it's general height, is consistent with a gunshot wound delivered while the victim was standing very near where his body was found.

    B. Crime scene photographs document medium and high velocity blood spatter evidence on the ground around to the victim's head, along with an unknown volume of pooled blood. This evidence, and it's orientation, is consistent with at least a second gunshot wound delivered while the victim was laying on his back in the ditch as he was found.

    C. The blood evidence associated with the victim's face and body, documented at the time of discovery at the scene, is pooled and dried in accordance with gravity. There is no evidence of blood drying while the body was in another position. There is no evidence of blood smeared as the result of the body being moved.

    D. This examiner is unaware of any other physical evidence consistent with the victim's gunshot injury associated with any other scene or vehicle investigated in this case.

2. **The victim was likely shot at a muzzle distance of approximately 3-8 inches, both times. This estimate is based on at least the following:**

    A. As explained in Moran (2012; p.412): "When a firearm is discharged, a variety of materials are expelled from the barrel in addition to the bullet. Such firearm discharge products include fine carbonaceous particles or soot from incomplete combustion of the propellant; unburned and partially burned powder particles; metal particles stripped from the bullet; bullet lubricant; and inorganic elements from the cartridge primer, such as lead, barium, and antimony in traditional U.S. center-fire ammunition and possibly other elements in some of the recently developed lead-free ammunition formulations. The heavier materials are propelled from the muzzle as a very fine spray within the gas cloud of lighter materials emerging from the firearm." This description is generally consistent with the forensic science literature.

B. As explained in Moran (2012; p.414), there are five "Zones" used to characterize the distance between the end of the muzzle and the target in shooting incident reconstruction efforts. Zone I: Contact; Zone II: Near Contact (1-4 inches); Zone III (3-8 inches); Zone IV: (6-36 inches - no visible sooting; chemical testing required to raise latent powder or gunshot residue patterns); Zone V (3-4 ft. or greater) No discernible firearm discharge products present.

C. Moran's classification system and descriptions are based on a combination of examiner experience and repeated testing with various firearms and ammunitions.

D. Moran's classification system and descriptions were developed using the Zone system in Haag (2004) as a general guideline.

E. Moran's classification system and descriptions comport's with this examiner's experience with firearms, and with testing conducted by this examiner of various firearms with various ammunitions unrelated to the case at hand.

F. There is a wide dispersion of powder burns and unburned powder around two of the projectile entry sites in this case. This is documented by the Medical Examiner and the photographs provided in this case.

G. These findings comport with Moran's description of Zone III (3-8 inches). As provided in Moran (2012, p.414), Zone III "Causes some medium to light gray sooting with a roughly circular "shotgun" pattern of powder particles around the bullet hole."

H. Note: The most accurate method to determine distance of muzzle to target in a particular case is to perform documented distance tests with the actual firearm involved, using similar ammunition. The result would be a record of visible and latent gunpowder patterns from multiple distances. As the weapon or weapons involved in this crime have not been found or identified, this level of testing is not possible in this case.

3. **The firearms evidence in this case can be used to support a theory of either one or two shooters. This finding is based on at least the following:**

    A. The victim was shot with a firearm at least twice from radically different angles - once to the top of the head, and once to the left side of his face.

    B. The ballistic evidence in this case includes a fired, jacketed bullet (Ex. 13-a) that is consistent with either a .38 cal or a .357 cal handgun. This means that it was fired from either a .38 cal or a .357 cal handgun. It is not known for certain which is the case. This bullet was recovered from the body of Ronnie Cofer.

    C. The ballistic evidence in this case includes a bullet jacket (Ex. 01-a) that is consistent with either a .38 cal or a .357 cal handgun. This means that it was fired from either a .38 cal or a .357 cal handgun. It is not known for certain which is the case. This jacket was recovered near the victim's head.

    D. Either GSW could be the result of a .38 cal or a .357 cal handgun: The totality of the ballistic evidence in this case (i.e., gunshot wound size and recovered projectile) is consistent with being inflicted by either a .38 cal or a .357 cal handgun. Neither gunshot wound is definitively associated with one caliber or the other.

    E. The murder weapon or weapons are unknown: The ballistic evidence recovered in this case cannot be associated with a single firearm to the exclusion of all other firearms.

    F. As mentioned previously, none of the firearms collected in this case have been associated with the injuries inflicted on Mr. Cofer. The firearm or firearms used to kill Mr. Cofer are currently unknown and unidentified.

4. **There is no physical evidence connecting Mr. O'Neal to the crime scene, which is significant. This finding is based on at least the following:**

A. *Locard's Exchange Principle* is a cornerstone of forensic science and crime reconstruction (see Chisum and Turvey, 2012; and Thornton, 1997)[1].

B. Given the violent interaction between the victim and the offender in this case, and the resulting physical evidence (e.g., blood evidence, ballistics evidence, and gunshot residue), an exchange of this evidence is expected between the suspect, the suspect's vehicle, the victim, and the crime scene.

C. No physical evidence associating the crime scene with the suspect, or the suspect's vehicle, is evident in the materials provided to this examiner.

Brent E. Turvey
MS - Forensic Science
PhD - Criminology

---

[1] Thornton (1997) explains "Forensic scientists have almost universally accepted the *Locard Exchange Principle*. This doctrine was enunciated early in the 20th Century by Edmund Locard, the director of the first [police] crime laboratory, in Lyon, France. Locard's Exchange Principle states that with contact between two items, there will be an exchange of microscopic material."

REFERENCES

Chisum, W.J. and Turvey, B. (2012) *Crime Reconstruction*, 2nd Ed., San Diego: Elsevier Science.

Edwards, H. and Gotsonis, C. (2009) *Strengthening Forensic Science in the United States: A Path Forward*, National Academies Press, Washington, DC.

Haag, L. (2004) *Shooting Incident Reconstruction*, Boston: Academic Press.

Chisum, W.J. and Turvey, B. (2012) *Crime Reconstruction*, 2nd Ed., San Diego: Elsevier Science.

NAS (2002) *Integrity in Scientific Research: Creating an Environment that Promotes Responsible Conduct*, National Academy of Sciences Committee on Assessing Integrity in Research Environments. National Academies Press, Washington, DC.

NAS (2009) *On Being a Scientist: A Guide to Responsible Conduct in Research*, third ed., National Academy of Sciences Committee on Science, Engineering, and Public Policy. National Academies Press, Washington, DC.

Saferstein, R. (2010) *Criminalistics: An Introduction to Forensic Science, 10th Ed.*, Upper Saddle River, NJ: Prentice Hall.

Thornton, J. I. (1997) "*The General Assumptions and Rationale of Forensic Identification*," in D.L. Faigman, D. H. Kaye, M. J. Saks, & J. Sanders (Eds.) *Modern Scientific Evidence: The Law and Science of Expert Testimony*, vol. 2, West Publishing.

Subsequent to the receipt of this author's forensic report in April of 2014, the state's case essentially fell apart. The late Defense Attorney Robert Vogel (d2016) filed a motion to dismiss citing the report and other factors. He went into court for a hearing on the case a couple of months later. Surprisingly, the prosecution did not fight his motion. As reported in Lawrence (2014):

> "We would ask that you allow us to enter a dismissal," Assistant District Attorney General Alyson Kennedy told Criminal Court Judge E. Eugene Eblen. Eblen, who appeared surprised, granted the request.
>
> "We have no objection," O'Neal attorney Bob Vogel said. And with that, the case was over.
>
> O'Neal was charged in Roane County Criminal Court with first-degree murder in the death of Ronnie Dean "Boone" Cofer... "I think it's the right thing to do," Vogel said after the hearing. "I applaud the state for their decision."
>
> O'Neal will not be a free man, however. In 2011 he was sentenced to life in federal prison for his conviction on drug charges. He'll be heading back to federal prison now that the state case is over...
>
> O'Neal was indicted in the case on June 8, 2009. He was scheduled to stand trial this past April, but the trial was postponed because Pamela Smith, the key witness,

couldn't be found. Authorities have continued to search for her with no success. "Numerous law enforcement agencies have scoured the earth essentially looking for Ms. Smith," Kennedy said. "We've had local law enforcement, out-of-county law enforcement, TBI and the U.S. Marshals. As of this morning, no one has found her."

The hearing was a lot easier than O'Neal's lawyer had anticipated. Vogel said he was surprised the state didn't argue against his motion to dismiss. "I had come here expecting we would argue the motions," he said. "It was a welcome surprise."

Vogel disputed the notion that O'Neal got off on a technicality. "You know better than to ask me that question," he said. "I do believe he's innocent of this charge, and that's why I applaud the state because I think justice was done today… I do hope that they find the killer of Boone Cofer, because it's not right for the family that they have this open," he said.

The loss of the state's main witness, in combination with the mountain of physical evidence which contradicted their theory of guilt, essentially forced the prosecution to drop the charges and avoid potential embarrassment at trial, a trial that they had every right to fear losing. However, this author has seen no shortage of prosecutors willing to take weak cases with no direct physical evidence to trial; and no shortage of judges willing to let them do it, even when the physical evidence contradicts the state's theory. This is because in court, in front of jury, just about anything can happen if a lawyer is willing to roll the dice. Each time, and under these circumstances, they gamble on whether anyone will understand how physical evidence works. The truth is that most do not, and the theater of court is made more theatrical because of it.

ENDNOTES

1. This refers to crime that occurs on Native American Reservations or in those respective communities. However, they collaborate and generally defer to Native law enforcement, as reservations are sovereign soil.
2. Retired FBI agents can often be found forming private investigation or consulting firms where they offer expertise in the area of "violent crime" and even murder. Most would assume this includes rape and homicide. In reality, this has caused private clients of such firms to dump a great deal of money into obtaining presumed expertise for results that are inept at best. At worst, FBI agents can be found giving expert testimony in which they falsify their education; testify falsely about their case experience; and pretend to be experts in areas where they have no education, training, or experience (see Turvey, Petherick, & Ferguson, 2010, in re: retired FBI Agent Gregg O. McCrary providing false testimony about his education and experience; and Turvey, 2011, in re: retired FBI Agent Mark Safarik providing false informing about his education and experience to multiple courts).
3. For example, the training regimen for FBI profilers includes watching videos from the Discovery Channel, publicly available textbooks, and lectures from various university professors. This was revealed after one of those in law enforcement who received that training, Steve Longford of the Queensland Police Service in Australia, was compelled to disclose the year-long training regimen. He initially claimed it was comprised of classified material, but eventually admitted that it contained material available to the general public. Sadly, much of the regimen was superficial and more than a little outdated.
4. See Alonso-Saldivar (2016): "They're still using floppy disks at the Pentagon."; Mangan (2016): "US military uses 8-inch floppy disks to coordinate nuclear force operations"; and Ryan (2010): "Secret Service Computers Only Work at 60 Percent Capacity; Agency Uses 1980s Mainframe."
5. See the murder of Jamie Penich, discussed in Kirk (2001) and Jae-Suk (2003).

6. The FBI crime laboratory holds itself out as the premier forensic laboratory in the United States, offering services of every kind to domestic law enforcement agencies and others around the world. It is also the largest crime laboratory in the United States, "with some 500 scientific experts and special agents working in a state-of-the-art facility in rural Virginia, traveling the world over on assignment and providing forensic exams, technical support, expert witness testimony, and advanced training to Bureau personnel and partners around the globe" (FBI, 2012). Furthermore, it is responsible for maintaining a number of national forensic databases, including those related to fingerprints and DNA. For details regarding the long list of FBI-related scandals in forensic science alone, review the beginning of this text, as well as Hsu, Jenkins, and Mellnick (2012); Crowder and Turvey (2013, 2013).
7. For example, Candice M. Will, Assistant Director of the FBI-OPR, sent an email to all employees in October 2012 that detailed extensive ethics violations, professional misconduct, and criminal violations by its employees (including FBI Special Agents)—the vast majority of whom were disciplined internally and retained. It included cases of FBI agents engaged in sexting (sending nude photos to each other), harassment, unauthorized surveillance, domestic violence (some involving the use of firearms), Driving Under the Influence (DUIs), solicitation of sex acts from sex workers, improper handling of evidence, disclosure of confidential internal reports and information outside the Bureau (e.g., to defense attorneys and members of the public), lying to investigators, theft, abuse of authority, and fraud (Will, 2012). The email was leaked to CNN and then published in the free press. As described in Zamost and Griffin (2013): "From 2010 to 2012, the FBI disciplined 1045 employees for a variety of violations… Eighty-five were fired."
8. Portions of this section have been adapted from more comprehensive material presented in Chisum and Turvey (2012).
9. One of the most pervasive fictions in the justice system has been that suspect statements, witness statements, and physical evidence should each have equal value as evidence in court. This has been the origin of much apathy, abuse, and coercion with respect to law enforcement and prosecutorial effort in criminal casework. Slowly, the courts are being compelled by an endless river of overturned convictions; perjury from jailhouse informants; and eyewitness research on unreliability to change their views. Once this is accomplished, law enforcement will be required to become better trained with respect to physical evidence. Until then, there is no need for them to do so, and they will continue to coerce confessions or enlist reliable liars (see Cooley & Turvey, 2014).
10. See Chapter 17: Reconstructing Digital Evidence.
11. See Turvey (2012).
12. The author has worked dozens of cases where law enforcement, attorneys, and judges have intentionally subverted the physical evidence when it did not fit their beliefs or wishes about a case—and the guilt of a defendant. This has even happened in cases with DNA. Too often, the source of pertinent DNA evidence is not investigated or ignored, for fear that it will result in the identification of alternate suspects and case theories. In this way, and around the nation, scientific evidence is routinely given a back seat to the preferences of the prosecution team. For those who would doubt the occurrence of such blatant subversions, note that this is why Innocence Projects exist. Also, "Google" the following cases, all part of the casework and/or expert testimony of the author: *Alaska v. Richard Bingham* (1997; sexual homicide of a teenage girl; defendant charged and tried despite vaginal sperm DNA that did not match him; defendant acquitted by jury); *Kansas v. Artis Cobb* (2000; man tried and convicted of manslaughter in the rape homicide of a woman, and with the incidental death of her infant child—despite vaginal DNA belonging to a third party that served as a police witness; charges reduced from first degree murder by judge); *Kentucky v. Donald Southworth* [2012; sexual homicide of an adult female; defendant (husband) charged and tried despite vaginal sperm DNA that matched an unidentified male; defendant convicted by jury; case overturned; defendant took an Alford Plea in 2016]; *Oklahoma v. Kevin Sweat* (2014; sexual homicides of two teenage females; defendant charged and tried despite sperm DNA on both victims that did not match him; defendant convicted by jury; case pending appeal). These are but a few, and each involves the collusion of less than ethical state employed forensic investigators and personnel.

13. For a thorough exploration of the nature and importance of forensic victimology, see *Chapter 9*: *Medicolegal Death Investigation: Protocols and Practice*, which delineates specific requirements for the collection of various victim histories.
14. Adapted from Turvey (2011).

REFERENCES

Alonso-Saldivar, R. (May 25, 2016). *Government wastes billions of dollars on old computers, GAO report says*. PBS Newshour. url: http://www.pbs.org/newshour/rundown/government-wastes-billions-of-dollars-on-old-computers-report-says/.

Bourne, A. J., Byard, R. W., Cooper, R. T. L., Moore, L., & Whitehead, E. J. (1996). Dehydration Deaths in Infants and Young Children. *The American Journal of Forensic Medicine and Pathology, 17*(1), 73–78.

California v. Odell Clarence Haston. (August 19, 1968). *No. 11710, Supreme court of California*. En Bank.

California v. Rhonda Denise Erving. (April 29, 1998). *No. B111324* [73 Cal. Rptr. 2d 815].

Chisum, W. J., & Turvey, B. (2012). *Crime reconstruction*. San Diego: Elsevier Science.

Cooley, C. (2007). The CSI effect: its impact and potential concerns. *New England Law Review, 41*, 471–501. Spring.

Cooley, C., & Turvey, B. (2014). *Miscarriages of justice*. San Diego: Elsevier Science.

Crowder, W. S., & Turvey, B. (2013). *Ethical justice*. San Diego: Elsevier Science.

DeForest, P. R. (2005). Crime scene investigation. In L. E. Sullivan, & M. S. Rosen (Eds.), *Encyclopedia of law enforcement* (pp. 111–116). New York: Sage Publications.

Dysart, K. (May 28, 2012). *Managing the CSI effect in jurors*. American Bar Association, Trial Evidence Committee. url: http://apps.americanbar.org/litigation/committees/trialevidence/articles/winterspring2012-0512-csi-effect-jurors.html.

Edwards, H., & Gotsonis, C. (2009). *Strengthening forensic science in the United States: A path forward*. Washington, DC: National Academies Press.

FBI. (2012). *Laboratory services*. U.S. Department of Justice, Federal Bureau of Investigation. url: http://www.fbi.gov/about-us/lab.

FBI. (2016). *Violent crime*. FBI Website. url: https://www.fbi.gov/investigate/violent-crime.

Hsu, S., Jenkins, J., & Mellnick, T. (April 17, 2012). *DOJ review of flawed FBI forensics processes lacked transparency*. Washington Post. http://www.washingtonpost.com/local/crime/dojreview-of-flawed-fbi-forensics-processes-lacked-transparency/2012/04/17/gIQAFegIPT_print.html.

Jae-Suk, Y. (June 19, 2003). *Kenzi Snider acquitted in murder of Jamie Lynn Penich*. Associated Press.

Kansas v. Artis Cobb. (April 12, 2002). *Court of appeals of Kansas*. Nos. 85,309, 85,445, Decided.

Kirk, P. (1974). *Crime investigation* (2nd ed.). New York: John Wiley & Sons.

Kirk, J. (May 24, 2001). *U.S. forensic scientist says investigation of student's murder was flawed*. Stars and Stripes.

Kirschner, R. H., & Wilson, H. L. (1996). Fatal child abuse: the pathologist's perspective. In R. M. Reece (Ed.), *Child abuse: Medical diagnosis and management* (pp. 325–357). Williams and Wilkins.

Lawrence, D. (July 1, 2014). *Murder charge dropped.* Roane County News. url: http://www.roanecounty.com/content/murder-charge-dropped.

Lee, H. (1994). *Crime scene investigation.* Taoyuan, Taiwan: Central Police University.

Lee, H., Palmbach, T., & Miller, M. (2001). *Henry Lee's crime scene handbook.* Boston: Academic Press.

Mangan, D. (May 25, 2016). *GAO: US military uses 8-inch floppy disks to coordinate nuclear force operations.* CNBC. url: http://www.cnbc.com/2016/05/25/us-military-uses-8-inch-floppy-disks-to-coordinate-nuclear-force-operations.html.

McKay, M. (October 25, 2002). *Investigators: The real CSI.* CBS News. url: http://www.cbsnews.com/stories/2002/10/25/48hours/main526983.shtml.

Miller, M. (2008). Eyewitnesses, physical evidence, and forensic science: a case study of state of North Carolina v. James alan Gell. *Victims and Offenders, 3*, 142—149.

O'Hara, C. (1970). *Fundamentals of criminal investigation* (2nd ed.). Springfield, IL: Charles C. Thomas.

Reavy, P. (November 30, 2011). *Real forensic scientists shake their heads at TV 'CSI' counterparts.* Deseret News. url: http://www.deseretnews.com/article/705395141/Real-forensic-scientists-shake-their-heads-at-TV-CSI-counterparts.html.

Ryan, J. (February 26, 2010). *Secret service computers only work at 60 percent capacity; agency uses 1980s mainframe.* ABC News. url: http://abcnews.go.com/Politics/us-secret-service-outdated-computer-mainframe-system-1980s/story?id=9945663.

Smith, J. (April 30, 2014). *FORGET CSI: A disaster is happening in America's crime labs.* Business Insider. url: http://www.businessinsider.com/forensic-csi-crime-labs-disaster-2014-4.

Turvey, B. (2011). *Criminal profiling: An introduction to behavioral evidence analysis* (4th ed.). San Diego: Elsevier Science.

Turvey, B. (2012). *Forensic victimology* (2nd ed.). San Diego: Elsevier Science.

Turvey, B. (2013). *Forensic fraud.* San Diego: Elsevier Science.

Turvey, B., Petherick, W., & Ferguson, C. (2010). *Forensic criminology.* San Diego: Elsevier Science.

Will, C. (October 1, 2012). *Email to "FBI_ALL_EMPLOYEES," subject line: "OPRS QUARTERLY all EMPLOYEE e-mail" FBI office of professional responsibility.*

Zamost, S., & Griffin, D. (February 22, 2013). *FBI battling 'rash of sexting' among its employees.* CNN. url: http://www.cnn.com/2013/02/21/us/fbi-misbehavior.

CHAPTER 6

Crime Scene Processing

Brent E. Turvey[1], W. Jerry Chisum[2]

Forensic Criminology Institute, Sitka, Alaska, United States and Aguascalientes, Mexico[1];
California Department of Justice (ret.), Elk Grove, CA, United States[2]

CHAPTER OUTLINE

Crime Scenes 126
    Primary Crime Scene 127
    Secondary Crime Scene 129
    Intermediate Crime Scene 129
    Dumpsite/Disposal site 129
    Tertiary Crime Scene 131
Crime Scene Processing 131
Crime Scene Processing: A Descriptive Tiered System 133
    Police: Level 1 134
    Scientist: Level 1 135
    Police: Level 2 135
    Scientist: Level 2 135
    Police: Level 3 136
    Scientist: Level 3 136
Crime Scene Processing Protocols 140
    Checklists 140
    Inside the Tape 140
    National Institute of Justice Guidelines 141
        National Institute of Justice Protocols 142
    Evidence Recognition 146
        Macroscopic, Latent, and Microscopic Evidence 147
    Evidence Documentation 148
        Photography 148
        Videography 149
        Sketching 150
    Evidence Collection and Preservation 151
        Evidence Technicians and Training 152
        Cross-Contamination 152

Biological Material 153
Evidence Storage 154
Evidence Transportation 154
Conclusion 154
Endnotes 155
References 155

In 2009, the Congressionally funded inquiry into the forensic science community nationwide conducted by the National Academy of Science (NAS; Edwards & Gotsonis, 2009), concluded that there was no science in forensic science. This was, they wrote, in no small part because of the improper alignment of forensic science with law enforcement. In other words, law enforcement officers and representatives tend to populate or control forensic science community. This was, they made clear, a conflict of interest with substantial implications for objectivity, science, and the needs of justice.

This improper alignment comes about almost too naturally, as law enforcement is responsible for responding to reported crime. They are also subsequently responsible for decisions related to the identification, collection, preservation, and testing of physical evidence.[1] In these obligations, which are a matter of legal authority, we find the heart of problem. Law enforcement, and by extension prosecutorial agencies, are solely responsible for determining what is going to be evidence, whether or not it is collected, and whether or not it is going to get tested during the initial stages of crime scene investigation. The partiality exercised in this regard, and the implications for truth seeking, are profound. Especially given that *Brady violations* (illegally withholding evidence; see Chapter 2) and *biased forensic testimony* from government experts are two leading causes of wrongful convictions (Cooley & Turvey, 2014; Turvey, 2013).[2]

This improper alignment and control over the physical evidence has confused law enforcement and their prosecutorial counterparts into believing that they alone are capable of interpreting the meaning of physical evidence. Even more disturbing, they tend to believe that they conduct the ONLY crime scene investigation related to criminal investigations. The courts, whether out of ignorance or bias, tend to accept this false narrative as reality—reinforcing it with prejudiced funding and admissibility rulings against the defense.

The purpose of this chapter is to present a more complete view of crime scene processing than students and professionals have generally been allowed to conceive in their work. It will be inclusive of major crime scene processing efforts at every stage of the forensic process, without being narrowed by intuitional or courtroom biases. It will also help dispel any related myths as they naturally arise—of which there are many.

CRIME SCENES

Before we can discuss the requirements of crime scene processing, it is first necessary to define what they are. A *crime scene* is defined as any area where a crime has taken place (Chisum & Turvey, 2012). In many cases, a crime scene is discovered because of violence that is witnessed or inferred from some fact or evidence. Others are happened on by accident or routine—such as those found by hunters outdoors; or those found by housekeeping in hotels. There are also those that remain undiscovered for lack of obvious signs or traces, either due to offender precaution, remoteness and lack of access, or a lack of evident foul play in the crime itself. As explained in O'Hara (1970, p. 47):

> *Obviously, many kinds of crime do not have a "scene" in the sense of an area where traces are usually found. Offenses such as forgery and embezzlement require no vigorous or exceptional physical activity in their commission. There is no impact of the criminal on his surroundings. Crimes of violence, however, involve a struggle, a break, the use of weapons, and the element of unpredictability. In homicide, assaults, and burglary, the criminal is in contact with the physical surroundings in a forceful manner.*

However, crime does not always limit itself to a single location as this definition might imply. It is best for the forensic investigator to conceive of a given case as consisting of multiple connected scenes where different events and activities occurred related to victims and suspects alike. With this mind-set, it becomes easier to grasp the necessity for comprehensive investigation of different areas as one works to establish a timeline of events. To that end, it is also useful to understand that there are different types of crime scenes.

One of the most important considerations of crime scene investigation, reconstruction, and analysis is determining what type of crime scene has been discovered. By this, we are referring to establishing the relationship of the crime scene to the offense behavior, in the context of the offense. When determining the *crime scene type* in a particular case, the reconstructionist is warned not to use intuition or experience as a primary guide. Let the physical evidence tell the story. Work from the physical evidence out to a sound reconstruction, not from biased theories into a corner.

Consider the following types of crime scenes. These are not mutually exclusive categories (taken from Chisum & Turvey, 2012).

PRIMARY CRIME SCENE

The *primary crime scene* is the location where the offender engaged in the majority of his or her principle offense behavior. Principle offense behavior is determined by motive and/or criminal statute, such as homicide, sexual assault, or theft. In many instances, it is the location where the offender spent the most time—whether by virtue of criminal behavior or cleanup. It is also likely to be where the most physical evidence was created during the offense.

In more complex, involved, or prolonged criminal offenses, the concept of a primary scene may still be applied, but not without care. If attacks on multiple victims occur within a single offense at separate locations, it is most useful to separate out these offenses with one primary scene for each victim. Similarly, if a single victim suffers multiple types of harm within a single offense, it is most useful to separate out incidents of attack with one primary scene for each.

For example, in a sexual homicide there may be a primary sexual assault scene and a primary homicide scene. If multiple victims are involved, each victim may have their own primary sexual assault scene and a primary homicide scene. Or they may be sexually assaulted and killed at the same location. This must be determined by a careful reconstruction of each crime, and the appropriate classification applied (Fig. 6.1).

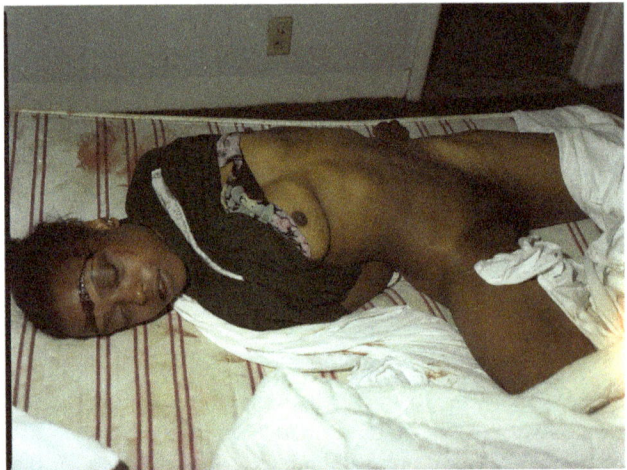

FIGURE 6.1

From the Author's Case Files: On May 24, 1996, the Partially Nude Body of Kimberly Moore Was Found by a Housekeeper at the Trade Winds Motel in Yonkers, NY. She Was Bound, Killed by Ligature Strangulation, and Covered With a Blanket on the Bed. She and Other Prostitutes Worked Out of This Same Motel, and This Was the Room That She Had Rented. She Saw Multiple Clients That Day. This Is the Primary Scene, and No Other Crime Scenes Are Known to Be Associated With Her Death. In 2011, Francis Acevedo Was Convicted of Killing Her and Two Other Known Prostitutes.

Classifying the primary scene in a given case as merely the location where the offense begins misses the point of this effort and prevents meaningful investigative and forensic comparison to other offenses. It also ignores the complexity of criminal behavior. Not all offenders do just one thing with one victim at one place; some are much more developed and complex. We must acknowledge this in our classifications.

SECONDARY CRIME SCENE

A *secondary crime scene* is a location where some of the victim–offender interaction occurred, but not the majority of it. Also a secondary scene does not involve principle offense behavior, but rather supporting behavior. There can be several *secondary crime scenes* associated with a single crime.

For example, if the victim is abducted from one location and taken to another to be raped of killed, the located where they are abducted from is a secondary scene.

If the scene is the location where the body is found, a secondary scene is also the *disposal site*.

INTERMEDIATE CRIME SCENE

An *intermediate crime scene* is any crime scene between the primary crime scene and a *disposal site*, where there may be transfer evidence. This includes vehicles used to transport a body to a disposal site after a homicide and locations where a body has been stored before final disposal. It also includes ground that has sustained drag marks of any kind. *Intermediate crime scenes* are a type of *secondary crime scene*.

DUMPSITE/DISPOSAL SITE

Dumpsite, or *disposal site*, is a rough term used to describe a crime scene where a body is found. This may be the primary scene or it may be a secondary scene.

More often than not, the use of this term implies that the victim was assaulted somewhere else and transported to this location after or just before death. This is an unfortunate and very dangerous investigative assumption to make. A disposal site may also be the primary crime scene; this possibility must not be excluded by virtue of an investigator's subjective experience. It must be investigated and confirmed by the physical evidence (Fig. 6.2).

FIGURE 6.2

From the Author's Case Files: The Naked Body of Maria Ramos Was Found in an Industrial Area on the Sidewalk, Across the Street From the Westchester Co. Waste Treatment Plant on February 5, 1989. She Had Been Strangled and Stabbed to Death. This Is a Dumpsite Only. The Primary Scene for This Crime Was Never Located, but It Is Reasonable to Presume That She Was Transported to This Location in a Vehicle (an Intermediate Scene) due to Geographical and Logistical Variables. Ms. Ramos Had a History of Arrests for Prostitution in Area Multiple Precincts; for Grand Larceny; and Was Reported by Other Prostitutes to Regularly Rip-off Her "johns." In 2011, Francis Acevedo Was Convicted of Killing Her and Two Other Known Prostitutes.

Many crime scene efforts encountered by the author seem actively disinterested in interpreting the relationship of outdoor locations to the bodies of victims found within them. Often, it will be assumed that an outdoor crime scene is both a primary scene and a disposal site, ignoring other nearby potential underwater, indoor, or vehicle locations. They will also fail to consider that the victim's home might be related to the crime, and miss the opportunity to include related evidence in their investigation.

Once it has been established that the crime scene at hand is a secondary disposal site, certain questions must be answered:

- How was the body transported there—was dragging, carrying, containers, wraps, or vehicles involved?

- What route was taken during transportation—direct, indirect, public, or private?
- Why was the disposal site chosen—convenience, crime concealment, evidence destruction, or emotion/fantasy?
- Why was the transportation away from the primary scene necessary?

Transporting a body under any circumstance is a cumbersome and risky proposition. The body itself is heavy, unwieldy, and in some cases may even need to be dismembered. Just getting it out of, or away from, the primary scene under good conditions exposes the offender to innumerable risks. Consequently there is often a good reason for moving the body—namely, that the offender is somehow associated with the primary scene and would be a logical suspect if the body had been found there.

TERTIARY CRIME SCENE

A *tertiary crime scene* is any location where physical evidence is present but there is no evidence of victim–offender interaction. This includes locations where *evidentiary items* (e.g., a used weapon, bloody clothing) are stored after a crime has been committed. It can also include transfer of evidence resulting from victim movement after the offense such as vaginal purge subsequent to a sexual assault or bloody-hand transfer to areas and objects that are reached outside of the primary or secondary scenes while escaping or seeking help.

Investigating and establishing the crime scene types that present in a given case, and evaluating the nature of any evidence that has been found there, will reveal the existence of other potentially related crime scenes. Failure to accurately determine the crime scene type, or to ask this question at all, can therefore result in the loss of physical evidence. It can also prevent the forensic investigator from understanding what actually happened.

CRIME SCENE PROCESSING

Crime scene processing refers to the function of recognizing, documenting, collecting, preserving, and transporting physical evidence for the purposes of subsequent storage, examination, and testing. It is not the same as crime reconstruction, which can only be conducted when the results of forensic examinations and testing are complete. Those results are generally available until weeks, or even months, after scene processing efforts have concluded. DeForest explains further (2005; pp. 112):

> The term crime scene processing is commonly used as a synonym for crime scene investigation. This is unfortunate and betrays an ignorance about the nature of crime scenes and what is necessary to extract the relevant information from them. Crime scene investigation should not be perceived as a mechanical process, carried out in a rote fashion. Too commonly, this is the way it is viewed by law

enforcement policy makers; administrators; supervisors; and perhaps, surprisingly, those who actually "process" the crime scene. Change is necessary...

In many jurisdictions, specially designated law enforcement evidence technicians (aka crime scene investigators or CSIs) are charged with initial crime scene processing duties (*Level 1*; see the next section). They are expected to *locate and protect* physical evidence without damaging it; without causing potentially misleading transfers; and without adding artifact evidence to the scene. They are expected to *document and preserve*, as much as possible, the overall scene and all the physical items present. They are also required to document any pattern evidence. They are further expected to *collect and package* the evidence in a manner that preserves it for subsequent *transportation*, *analysis*, and *interpretation*. In smaller departments, or when evidence technicians are otherwise unavailable, police officers will perform these processing tasks themselves.

DeForest (2005) explains one cause of the problem and suggests a solution that the authors completely agree with (pp. 112):

In most law enforcement jurisdictions in the United States, scientific expertise is absent from the initial crime scene investigation. This is true for many other parts of the world as well, and it is a situation that needs to be rectified. An argument can be made that crime scene investigation should be carried out exclusively by forensic scientists, but at the very least, experienced forensic scientists should form part of the crime scene investigation team.

The NAS report also offers some insight regarding the need for crime scene investigation reform (Edwards & Gotsonis, 2009, pp. 56–57):

Evidence recovery and interpretation at the crime scene is the essential first step in forensic investigations. Several organizational approaches to crime scene investigation and subsequent forensic laboratory activity exist, sometimes involving a large number of personnel with varied educational backgrounds. Conversely, in some jurisdictions, a single forensic examiner might also be the same investigator who goes to the crime scene, collects evidence, processes the evidence, conducts the analyses, interprets the evidence, and testifies in court. In other jurisdictions, the investigators submit the evidence to a laboratory where scientists conduct the analyses and prepare the reports. Crime scene evidence collectors can include uniformed officers, detectives, crime scene investigators, criminalists, forensic scientists, coroners, medical examiners, hospital personnel, photographers, and arson investigators. Thus, the nature and process of crime scene investigation varies dramatically across jurisdictions, with the potential for inconsistent policies and procedures and bias. Some analysts say that the lack of standards and oversight can result in deliberate deception of suspects, witnesses, and the courts; fraud; and "honest mistakes" made because of haste, inexperience, or lack of a scientific background.

Our position on the subject remains the same as published in the first edition of our text on Crime Reconstruction (Chisum & Turvey, 2007): to be blunt, modern-day crime scene processing efforts are entirely inadequate and in need of major reform. There are some notable and even exceptions, but few if any agencies regularly employ and subsequently require qualified personnel at the crime scene. Rather, it is commonly believed, and generally practiced, that new personnel can and should learn scene-processing duties on the job from other police officers, all with little or no scientific background. Because many in law enforcement perceive that crime scene processing is a simple task that anyone can learn and perform by rote, literally anyone is doing so. This cannot be allowed to continue, as the results are often not amenable to providing objective or reliable scientific findings.

The purpose of crime scene processing, it bears repeating, is to provide the basis for secondary review, analysis, and reconstruction by qualified personnel. The results will be utilized by investigators, attorneys, judges, and forensic scientists. Crime scene processing efforts are either sufficient and competent for use by all of them or none of them. In other words, forensic reconstructionists need not attend crime scenes to reconstruct the crime so long as scene processing efforts are sufficiently competent.

Too often, the argument is made by clever attorneys that crime reconstruction requires direct knowledge of the scene, and that processing efforts do not provide sufficient details on their own. In other words, they argue that one must attend the scene, and even process the evidence, to reconstruct the crime. They argue, incorrectly, that these are somehow related tasks.

This is a specious and uniformed line of thinking. If this were the case, then the results of crime scene processing would not be sufficient for any conclusions to be drawn by anyone. Consider that reconstructionists are meant to be highly educated and trained forensic professionals. If they cannot interpret evidence from processing efforts, then certainly layperson, attorneys, and investigators must be barred as well. Again crime scene processing is entirely intended to provide for crime reconstruction efforts, which cannot take place until after the evidence is examined and tested. This will necessarily occur only weeks after the fact, requiring thorough documentation of the scene.

Forensic investigators understand that the important questions regarding any case, and related physical evidence, are not really known until well AFTER the crime scene has been released. Crime scene processing efforts must therefore be comprehensive and systematic—the same way every time. In this way, there will always be enough documentation to allow investigators to go back and ask questions of the scene; even after it has been released and perhaps lost or destroyed.

CRIME SCENE PROCESSING: A DESCRIPTIVE TIERED SYSTEM

The authors recommend using the descriptive tiered classification system in this section to describe scene processing efforts in reports and testimony. This system is meant to convey that crime scene processing efforts take place at different times throughout the legal process, and by differently qualified individuals. It is suggested to avoid confusion regarding roles; the potential scope, quality and reliability of evidence that has been collected; and the subsequent competence or certainty that may be associated with related findings.

The development of this classification system has become necessary due to three convergent factors:

1. Law enforcement agencies control access to the initial crime scene. As a consequence, they control the initial evidentiary narrative. They also tend to believe this threshold contact is the only relevant processing effort (ignoring the defense investigation, the appellate process, and the rate at which wrongful convictions have been overturned nationwide by newly discovered physical evidence);
2. Prosecutors control access to the evidence collected by law enforcement and represent to the justice system that no other relevant evidence exists in their zeal to make legal arguments favoring their case theories[3];
3. Too many judges, in their zeal to shield law enforcement from criticism, have joined in promoting the false notion that crime scene processing is only ever done by law enforcement; and that their work serves as the only genuine basis for experience relating to crime reconstruction efforts. This allows for the illegitimate suggestion that law enforcement experience, wandering around inside of a crime scene without adherence to scientific protocols, is the best foundation for rendering opinions about what the evidence means. In other words, it enables a court with preexisting disdain for scientific inquiry to block or minimize testimony from actual scientists in favor of police experience; experience that is uniformed by methodology and tainted by the "improper alignment" mentioned at the beginning of this chapter.

A further cautionary regarding evidence complexity, and the persistent reality of failure in crime scene efforts, is offered in DeForest (2005, p. 111):

It would not be an exaggeration to assert that crime scene investigation ranks with the most intellectually challenging and difficult of human activities. It is also one of the most misunderstood. In practice, crime scene investigation is rarely carried out efficiently or effectively. Successful outcomes, when and where they occur, are often fortuitous rather than following from intelligently adaptive plans or designs…

Bearing this in mind, consider the following classifications and inherent limitations.

POLICE: LEVEL 1

Police: Level 1 crime scene processing efforts are those conducted in response to reported crime,[4] by nonscientist law enforcement employees. Under these circumstances, there is a high degree of bias and potential evidentiary neglect due to lack of proper scientific training and institutional bias. Evidence is often collected as a reflection of prevailing case theory; and alternate theories (and related evidence) are commonly missed or ignored. Responders tend to lack training, essential equipment, and basic scientific protocols (e.g., failure to document collection efforts; failure to collect substratum, etc.). These processing efforts create an inherently unreliable record of events, and should be viewed with skepticism.

SCIENTIST: LEVEL 1

Scientist: Level 1 crime scene processing efforts are those conducted in response to reported crime by forensic scientists (e.g., those educated and trained in the forensic sciences, with a four year degree in a related scientific subject). Evidence is collected in a comprehensive and systematic fashion in accordance with clearly established (and written) scientific protocols (e.g., NIJ, 2013). It is also done without concern for prevailing case theories or interference from detectives. Under these circumstances, there is reduced potential for institutional bias and potential evidentiary neglect. These processing efforts have the potential to create the most reliable initial record of events, and should be the goal of any professional responding agency.

POLICE: LEVEL 2

Police: Level 2 crime scene processing efforts are those conducted during the pretrial and trial phase, AFTER the development and arrest of criminal suspects, by nonscientist law enforcement employees. At this level, the crime scene has been released at least once and law enforcement is revisiting items of evidence and additional locations in search of support for prevailing case theories. In other words, they are still building their case against a particular suspect and have identified weaknesses or questions that need to be addressed. Their work is focused on that goal, and not on revealing or investigating other possible suspects or case theories.

SCIENTIST: LEVEL 2

Scientist: Level 2 crime scene processing efforts are those conducted during the pretrial and trial phase, AFTER the development and arrest of criminal suspects, by forensic scientists. At this level, the crime scene has been released at least once and there is the open consideration, and exploration, of alternate case theories. There is also recognition and collection of evidence initially missed by crime scene processing efforts during Level 1 efforts. This effort can be a comprehensive review of first level efforts; or it can be the first time that certain evidence or crime scene locations are recognized, collected, and examined because of first-level failures.

During *Scientist: Level 2* efforts, the authors have identified and/or collected the following items of evidence suitable for forensic testing—within the crime scene itself, and initially missed by *Police: Level 1–2* efforts:

- Bloodstain patterns on floors and walls.
- Suspect glasses and cell phones dropped in the crime scene.
- A projectile recovered from the wall with the victim's blood on it.
- A blanket, with a stab wound and a related bloodstain from the victim, on a neatly made bed.
- The suspect's bloody clothing.
- DNA evidence from blood and semen on a victim's clothing, associated with a sexual homicide.
- The defendant's wallet.
- Footwear patterns.

An exhaustive list of such evidence need not be rendered to make the point that it is easy to miss pertinent evidence in a crime scene, and transfer evidence on related collected items, when one is operating without proper protocols or when one is operating with a particular bias. Hence there is a need for a secondary or scientific review.

POLICE: LEVEL 3

Police: Level 3 crime scene processing efforts are those conducted during the post-conviction phase, AFTER the prosecution of criminal defendants, by nonscientist law enforcement employees. This is, in short, the reexamination of a case after a trial has concluded. In some cases, the defendant will have been convicted; in others they will have been acquitted; or there has been a mistrial.

Level 3 processing efforts can be a legitimate review of a case with fresh eyes and open minds; or they can be an attempt to further build a case against a particular defendant that has received a mistrial or an overturned conviction.

SCIENTIST: LEVEL 3

Scientist: Level 3 crime scene processing efforts are those conducted during the posttrial phase, AFTER the prosecution of criminal defendants, by forensic scientists. They typically involve a comprehensive examination and review of all physical evidence related efforts (Levels 1 and 2), to ensure adherence to scientific protocols and integrity. They also involve a hands on inventory of the physical evidence to conduct examinations in light any newly developed cases theories. These reviews are commonly done at the request of defense attorneys and state agencies as a matter of routine in the appellate process. They are also a common mechanism by which new evidence is discovered; fraudulent evidence and testimony are identified; and wrongful convictions are identified and overturned.

Each of these *levels* is a part of the overall crime scene processing effort; and each contributes to crime scene analysis and reconstruction efforts. When conducted by law enforcement, in accordance with the NAS report, it is important to view findings with skepticism and demand proofs (e.g., proper chain of custody and written evidentiary protocols). When conducted by actual forensic scientists, there will be no need to demand proofs or protocols, as they will be readily apparent and noted.

FORENSIC FIELD TESTS

Field tests related to forensic evidence are meant to provide a quick preliminary forensic results for law enforcement officers working on the street. Field tests, also known as color tests, are used to make presumptive identifications of unknown liquids, powders crystals, and other substances suspected of having evidentiary value. Field tests conducted on unknown substances by law enforcement officers are not confirmatory; in other words, all results must be confirmed by a laboratory test. The problem is, law enforcement officers and prosecutors do not practice this level of care, and it is too often not a part of their objectives or training. This is true whether they are field testing for suspected blood or suspected drugs. They want a confirmation so they can make an arrest. Period. Then that arrest becomes leverage, improperly gained in the name of science.

Consider the recent scandal regarding field drug tests and the thousands of related wrongful convictions; the issue is reviewed thoroughly in Gabrielson and Sanders (2016) (Fig. 6.3):

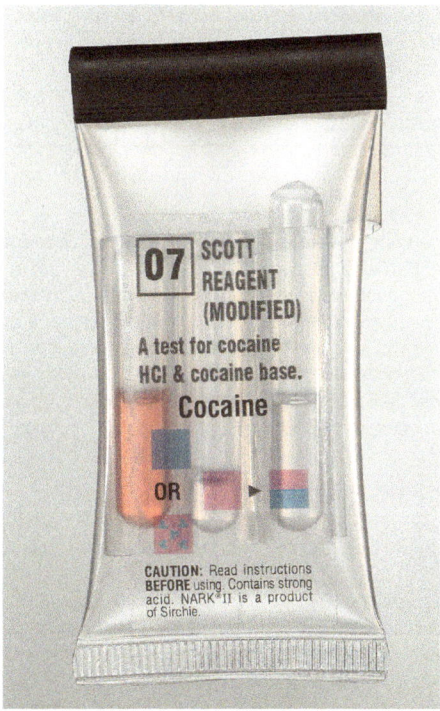

FIGURE 6.3

Field Test for Drugs, Intended for Use by Law Enforcement, Manufactured and Distributed by Sirchie. The Label Only Hints at the Limitations of Results Stating That "Read Instructions BEFORE Using." It Should Read "Presumptive Results" and "Results Must Be Confirmed With Laboratory Findings".

At the police academy four years earlier, [Officer David] Helms was taught that to make a drug arrest on the street, an officer needed to conduct an elementary chemical test, right then and there. It's what cops routinely do across the country every day while making thousands upon thousands of drug arrests. Helms popped the trunk of his patrol car, pulled out a small plastic pouch that contained a vial of pink liquid and returned to Albritton. He opened the lid on the vial and dropped a tiny piece of the crumb into the liquid. If the liquid remained pink, that would rule out the presence of cocaine. If it turned blue, then Albritton, as the owner of the car, could become a felony defendant...

Police officers arrest more than 1.2 million people a year in the United States on charges of illegal drug possession. Field tests like the one Officer Helms used in front of Amy Albritton help them move quickly from suspicion to conviction. But the kits — which cost about $2 each and have changed little since 1973 — are far from reliable.

The field tests seem simple, but a lot can go wrong. Some tests, including the one the Houston police officers used to analyze the crumb on the floor of Albritton's car, use a single tube of a chemical called cobalt thiocyanate, which turns blue when it is exposed to cocaine. But cobalt thiocyanate also turns blue when it is exposed to more than 80 other compounds, including methadone, certain acne medications and several common household cleaners. Other tests use three tubes, which the officer can break in a specific order to rule out everything but the drug in question — but if the officer breaks the tubes in the wrong order, that, too, can invalidate the results. The environment can also present problems. Cold weather slows the color development; heat speeds it up, or sometimes prevents a color reaction from taking place at all. Poor lighting on the street — flashing police lights, sun glare, street lamps — often prevents officers from making the fine distinctions that could make the difference between an arrest and a release.

There are no established error rates for the field tests, in part because their accuracy varies so widely depending on who is using them and how. Data from the Florida Department of Law Enforcement lab system show that 21 percent of evidence that the police listed as methamphetamine after identifying it was not methamphetamine, and half of those false positives were not any kind of illegal drug at all. In one notable Florida episode, Hillsborough County sheriff's deputies produced 15 false positives for methamphetamine in the first seven months of 2014. When we examined the department's records, they showed that officers, faced with somewhat ambiguous directions on the pouches, had simply misunderstood which colors indicated a positive result.

No central agency regulates the manufacture or sale of the tests, and no comprehensive records are kept about their use. In the late 1960s, crime labs outfitted investigators with mobile chemistry sets, including small plastic test tubes and bottles of chemical reagents that reacted with certain drugs by changing colors, more or less on the same principle as a home pregnancy test. But the reagents contained strong acids that leaked and burned the investigators. In 1973, the same year that Richard Nixon formally established the Drug Enforcement Administration, declaring "an all-out global war on the drug menace," a pair of California inventors patented a "disposable comparison detector kit." It was far simpler, just a glass vial or vials inside a plastic pouch. Open the pouch, add the compound to be tested, seal the pouch, break open the vials and watch the colors change. The field tests, convenient and imbued with an aura of scientific infallibility, were ordered by police departments across the country. In a 1974 study, however, the National Bureau of Standards warned that the kits "should not be used as sole evidence for the identification of a narcotic or drug of abuse." Police officers were not chemists, and chemists themselves had long ago stopped relying on color tests, preferring more reliable mass spectrographs. By 1978, the Department of Justice had determined that field tests "should not be used for evidential purposes," and the field tests in use today remain inadmissible at trial in nearly every jurisdiction; instead, prosecutors must present a secondary lab test using more reliable methods.

But this has proved to be a meaningless prohibition. Most drug cases in the United States are decided well before they reach trial, by the far more informal process of plea bargaining. In 2011, RTI International, a nonprofit research group based in North Carolina, found that prosecutors in nine of 10 jurisdictions it surveyed nationwide accepted guilty pleas based solely on the results of field tests, and in our own reporting, we confirmed that prosecutors or judges accept plea deals on that same basis in Atlanta, Boston, Dallas, Jacksonville, Las Vegas, Los Angeles, Newark, Philadelphia, Phoenix, Salt Lake City, San Diego, Seattle and Tampa.

This puts field tests at the center of any discussion about the justice of plea bargains in general. The federal government does not keep a comprehensive database of prosecutions in county and state criminal courts, but the National Archive of Criminal Justice Data at the University of Michigan maintains an extensive sampling of court records from the 40 largest jurisdictions. Based on this data, we found that more than 10 percent of all county and state felony convictions are for drug charges, and at least 90 percent of those convictions come by way of plea deals. In Tennessee, guilty pleas produce 94 percent of all convictions. In Kansas, they make up more than 97 percent. In Harris County, Tex., where the judiciary makes detailed criminal caseload information public, 99.5 percent of drug-possession convictions are the result of a guilty plea. A majority of those are felony convictions, which restrict employment, housing and — in many states — the right to vote.

Demand for the field tests is strong enough to sustain the business of at least nine different companies that sell tests to identify cocaine, heroin, marijuana, methamphetamine, LSD, MDMA and more than two dozen other drugs. The Justice Department issued guidelines in 2000 calling for test-kit packaging to carry warning labels, including "a statement that users of the kit should receive appropriate training in its use and should be taught that the reagents can give false-positive as well as false-negative results," but when we checked, three of the largest manufacturers — Lynn Peavey Company, the Safariland Group and Sirchie — had not printed such a warning on their tests. (Lynn Peavey Company did not respond to our request for comment. A spokesman for the Safariland Group said the company provides law-enforcement agencies with extensive training materials that are separate from the tests and their packaging. We asked John Roby, Sirchie's chief executive, about the missing warnings and requested an interview in May. He responded in writing a month later saying that the boxes carrying Sirchie's cocaine tests had been updated and now display a warning that reactions may occur with both "legal and illegal substances." After our inquiry, Sirchie added another warning to its packaging, listing at the bottom of its printed instructions: "ALL TEST RESULTS MUST BE CONFIRMED BY AN APPROVED ANALYTICAL LABORATORY!")

Even trained lab scientists struggle with confirmation bias — the tendency to take any new evidence as confirmation of expectations — and police officers can see the tests as affirming their decisions to stop and search a person. Labs rarely notify officers when a false positive is found, so they have little experience to prompt skepticism. As far as they know, the system works. By our estimate, though, every year at least 100,000 people nationwide plead guilty to drug-possession charges that rely on field-

test results as evidence. At that volume, even the most modest of error rates could produce thousands of wrongful convictions.

A good rule of thumb is this: unless there is an actual forensic scientist testifying about the reliability of forensic testing, the results must be viewed with skepticism. Law enforcement officers are not experts in chemistry, and therefore not a reliable source when interpreting the results of any chemical test—whether it is Luminol, Blue Star, a breathalyzer result, or any field drug test. In fact, the presence of a law enforcement officer in court, testifying on these issues, is a red flag; it can suggest that perhaps crime lab personnel were not amenable to the state's theories, or that they were unwilling to testify in a manner that prosecutors preferred.

In short, all field tests must be confirmed by the crime lab. No field tests should be allowed as evidence at trial on its own, as interpretive abuses by nonscientists have become far too common. And these limitations must be made clear to defense attorneys during any plea negotiations, otherwise continued use in this fashion is an abuse of authority.

CRIME SCENE PROCESSING PROTOCOLS

In this section, we will present and discuss scientific crime scene processing protocols. These guidelines have been aggregated from those developed by the National Institute of Justice, as well as other learned sources.[5] References are provided as needed.

CHECKLISTS

A brief note on crime scene checklists is warranted, as many authors have a great fondness for presenting them in their written works (including this one). A checklist is useful tool for initial instruction, but blind adherence to checklists is a vice that telegraphs ignorance and pedantic understanding of what is essentially a dynamic process. Checklists are a temporary stand-in prepared by someone with knowledge for someone without—to help jump-start the learning process.

The protocols in the section are the least that is required for good science; and good scientists come to understand when they must be ignored and how to explain why. If a CSI must rely on a checklist to do their job, this is a clear indication that they have no idea what their job is and what it means to the case. Conversely a CSI cannot simply ignore these protocols without good reason. And when they do it must be spelled out and integrated into the certainty of their findings.

To be clear, crime scene processing efforts that do not embrace the dynamic nature of physical evidence will most certainly misunderstand its complexity and eventual meaning. This will result in inaccurate reporting and testimony. And this in turn will lead to injustice. Consequently oversimplification must be avoided when dealing with the physical evidence and deliberate thought must be given to any report of findings.

INSIDE THE TAPE

Crime scene barrier tape symbolizes the forbidden and the unknown. And in accordance with forbidden fruit logic, everyone wants inside of it—either out of morbid curiosity; to demonstrate professional power; or to suggest special knowledge to others. The reality is that crime scenes are often attended by those with very little education and training; and they are meant to be processed in such a way as to make it unnecessary for others to enter at all (e.g., by preventing unnecessary evidence destruction and transfer). This mystique crushing reality is not good news for the many crime scene phonies in the forensic community who rely on associated myths to defraud others with false bravado and expertise.

The barrier tape exists to ensure the security and integrity of the physical evidence in the scene, not only from the public but also from nonessential personnel. As explained in Snyder (1944, p. 12) "The first concern of the trained observer is to exclude everyone from the immediate area who does not have some duty to perform in carrying out the investigation." This is consistent with NIJ (2013, p. 4), which instructs:

> *Exclude unauthorized and nonessential personnel from the scene (e.g., law enforcement officials not working the case, politicians, media)... Controlling the movement of persons at the crime scene and limiting the number of persons who enter the crime scene is essential to maintaining scene integrity, safeguarding evidence and minimizing contamination.*

In other words, unless you have a specific task to perform, there is no reason to be inside the crime scene tape.

Moreover being inside the tape should not result in special knowledge. Rather, it should result in documentation that allows everyone to see and understand everything that was there. That it is the point of processing the crime scene.

Pretending otherwise has long been a habit within the cult of law enforcement that must be put to rest in the name of objective scientific practice. If one is a competent CSI, then one is creating fully processed scenes with complete documentation available to all in the discovery process. If one is suggesting that CSI's divine special knowledge is unavailable to the rest of the forensic community, then this can only be the result of incompetence or willfully negligence.

NATIONAL INSTITUTE OF JUSTICE GUIDELINES

The *National Institute of Justice*'s Technical Working Group on Crime Scene Investigation first published their guidelines for crime scene investigation in Rau (2000).[6] These guidelines have been reviewed and updated since then, with the most recent protocols divided into the following topics (NIJ, 2013):

- Section A: Arriving at the Scene: Initial Response/Prioritization of Efforts
- Section B: Preliminary Documentation and Evaluation of the Scene
- Section C: Processing the Scene
- Section D: Completing and Recording the Crime Scene Investigation
- Section E: Crime Scene Equipment

In this section, we will present and discuss excerpts from the NIJ protocols most relevant to scientific crime scene processing efforts. However, we recommended that readers download and review the complete protocols on their own. They are freely available in pdf form at: http://www.nfstc.org/bja-programs/crime-scene-investigation-guide/.

National Institute of Justice Protocols
Section A: Arriving at the Scene

The initial policies and procedures for first responders are provided in NIJ (2013, p. 1), Section 1, as follows:

1. Initial Response/Receipt of Information

Principle: One of the most important aspects of securing the crime scene is to preserve the scene with minimal contamination and disturbance of physical evidence. The initial response to an incident should be expeditious and methodical.

Policy: The initial responding officer (s), upon arrival, shall assess the scene and treat the incident as a crime scene. They shall promptly, yet cautiously, approach and enter the crime scene, remaining observant of any persons, vehicles, events, potential evidence, and environmental conditions.

Procedure: The initial responding officer(s) should:

  a. *Note or log dispatch information (e.g., address/location, time, date, type of call, parties involved).*
  b. *Be aware of any persons or vehicles leaving the crime scene.*
  c. *Approach the scene cautiously, scan the entire area to thoroughly assess the scene, and note any possible secondary crime scenes.*
  d. *Be aware of any persons and vehicles in the vicinity that may be related to the crime.*
  e. *Make initial observations (look, listen, smell) to assess the scene and ensure officer safety before proceeding.*
  f. *Remain alert and attentive. Assume the crime is ongoing until determined to be otherwise.*
  g. *Treat the location as a crime scene until assessed and determined to be otherwise.*
  h. *Safely direct additional responding units into the area.*

The authors wholeheartedly agree with these initial protocols and the mind-set they require. Basically, assume nothing; stay alert; consider the possibility that the crime is not over yet; and consider the possibility of other related crime scenes, while logging relevant documentary information.

Section 2 details protocols related to "Safety Procedures"; and Section 3 relates to "Emergency Care." While not unimportant, they need not be discussed here as they are separate from the investigative effort.

Section 4 is "Secure and Control Persons at the Scene," and provides the following essential investigative and forensic protocols (NIJ, 2013, p. 4):

The initial responding officer(s) should:

  a. *Control all individuals at the scene—prevent individuals from altering/destroying physical evidence by restricting movement, location and activity while ensuring and maintaining safety at the scene.*

b. Identify all individuals at the scene, such as:
   - *Suspects: Secure and separate.*
   - *Witnesses: Secure and separate.*
   - *Bystanders: Determine whether witness, if so treat as above; if not, remove from the scene.*
   - *Victims/family/friends: Control while showing compassion.*
   - *Law Enforcement, Medical and other assisting personnel.*

In other words, find out who everyone is; keep them separated so that they can be interviewed separately to avoid "getting their stories straight" and evidence contamination; and do not let anyone go anywhere or touch anything for the same reason. This is among the biggest problems at crime scenes, as untrained or unprofessional officers allow friends and family into the scene to get things; or to sit together and share details; and thereby contaminate the investigation at every level.

Section 5 is "Boundaries: Identify, Establish, Protect and Secure" and provides the following essential investigative and forensic protocols (NIJ, 2013, p. 4–5):

Principle: Defining and controlling boundaries provide a means for protecting and securing the crime scene(s). The number of crime scenes and their boundaries are determined by their location(s) and the type of crime. Boundaries are established beyond the initial scope of the crime scene(s) with the understanding that the boundaries can be reduced in size if necessary but cannot be as easily expanded…

Procedure: The initial responding officer(s) should:

a. *Establish boundaries of the scene(s), starting at the focal point and extending outward to include:*
   - *Where the crime occurred.*
   - *Potential points and paths of exit and entry of suspects and witnesses.*
   - *Places where the victim/evidence may have been moved (be aware of trace and impression evidence while assessing the scene).*
b. *Secure the scene. Set up physical barriers (e.g., ropes, cones, crime scene barrier tape, available vehicles, personnel, other equipment) or use existing boundaries (e.g., doors, walls, gates).*
c. *Document the entry/exit of all people entering and leaving the scene, once boundaries have been established.*
d. *Protect the scene. Control the flow of personnel and animals entering and leaving the scene to maintain integrity of the scene.*
e. *Institute measures to preserve/protect evidence that may be lost or compromised (e.g., protect from the elements (rain, snow, wind) and from footsteps, tire tracks, sprinklers).*
f. *Document the original location of the victim or any objects that you observe being moved.*

> g. *Consider search and seizure issues to determine the necessity of obtaining consent to search and/or obtaining a search warrant.*
>
> *Note: Persons should NOT smoke, chew tobacco, use the telephone or bathroom, eat or drink, move any items from the scene including weapons (unless necessary for the safety and well-being of persons at the scene), adjust the thermostat or open windows or doors (maintain scene as found), touch anything unnecessarily (note and document any items moved), reposition moved items, litter, or spit within the established boundaries of the scene. Do not allow suspect to use bathroom facilities, or to alter his/her appearance, including brushing hair or washing hands.*

Section 6 is "Turn Over Control of the Scene and Brief Investigator(s) in Charge," which should be self-explanatory.

Section 7 is "Document Actions and Observations" and provides the following essential investigative and forensic protocols (NIJ, 2013, p. 6–7)

> *Principle: All activities conducted and observations made at the crime scene must be documented as soon as possible after the event to preserve information…*
>
> *Procedure: The initial responding officer(s) should document:*
>
> a. *Observations of the crime scene, including the location of persons and items within the crime scene and the appearance and condition of the scene upon arrival.*
> b. *Conditions upon arrival (e.g., lights on/off; shades up/down, open/closed; doors and windows open/closed; smells; ice, liquids; movable furniture; weather; temperature; and personal items.).*
> c. *Personal information from witnesses, victims, suspects and any statements or comments made.*
> d. *Their own actions and actions of others.*
>
> *Summary: The initial responding officer(s) at the crime scene must produce clear, concise, documented information encompassing his or her observations and actions. This documentation is vital in providing information to substantiate investigative considerations.*

Rarely, if ever, does one find this level of documentation made by first responders. If it does happen, it will be a rookie officer, who is fresh out of training. More seasoned officers document far less for a variety of reasons. The first is apathy. The second is intentional, to allow for theory vacillation by detectives and prosecutors. When this level of documentation is absent, it generally speaks to one of these two things and should raise concern either way.

Section 8 is "Establish a Command Post (Incident Command System) and Make Notifications," which is self-explanatory; and Section 9 is "Manage Witnesses," which basically states keep witnesses separate, transport them separately, interview them separately, and establish activity timelines for each.

Section B: Preliminary Documentation and Evaluation of the Scene

The policies and procedures for preliminary documentation and evaluation of the scene are divided into three sections: Conduct Scene Assessment, Conduct Scene "Walk-Through" and Initial Documentation, and Note Taking and Logs. These are responsibilities to be managed by trained investigators and not first responders.

The policies and procedures for conducting a scene assessment are provided in NIJ (2013, pp. 10–11), Section 1, as follows:

Procedure: The investigator(s) in charge should:

a. *Converse with the first responder(s) regarding observations/activities.*
b. *Evaluate safety issues that may affect all personnel entering the scene(s) (e.g., blood-borne pathogens, hazards).*
c. *Evaluate search and seizure issues to determine the necessity of obtaining consent to search and/or obtain a search warrant.*
d. *Evaluate and establish a path of entry/exit to the scene to be utilized by authorized personnel.*
e. *Evaluate initial scene boundaries.*
f. *Determine the number/size of scene(s) and prioritize.*
g. *Establish a secure area within close proximity to the scene(s) for the purpose of consultation and equipment staging.*
h. *If multiple scenes exist, establish and maintain communication with personnel at those locations.*
i. *Establish a secure area for temporary evidence storage in accordance with rules of evidence/chain of custody.*
j. *Determine and request additional investigative resources as required (e.g., personnel/specialized units, legal consultation/prosecutors, equipment).*
k. *Ensure continued scene integrity (e.g., document entry/exit of authorized personnel, prevent unauthorized access to the scene).*
l. *Ensure that witnesses to the incident are identified and separated (e.g., obtain valid ID).*
m. *Ensure the surrounding area is canvassed and the results are documented.*
n. *Ensure preliminary documentation/photography of the scene, injured persons and vehicles.*

Summary: Scene assessment allows for the development of a plan for the coordinated identification, collection, and preservation of physical evidence and identification of witnesses. It also allows for the exchange of information among law enforcement personnel and the development of investigative strategies.

Of note is that these protocols make clear the relationship between physical evidence and the rest of the investigation, as both a driving force and a foundation for further inquiry. The evidence is necessary to find witness and to conduct helpful suspect interviews; and it is also necessary to help dictate the extent of additional canvassing and documentation. They also make clear the limited role that prosecutors should serve, to prevent bias from influencing the process.

Section 2 is "Conduct Scene Walk-Through"; it asserts (NIJ, 2013, p. 12):

Conducting a scene walk-through provides the investigator(s) in charge with an overview of the entire scene. The walk-through provides the first opportunity to identify valuable and/or fragile evidence and determine initial investigative procedures, providing for a systematic examination and documentation of the scene. Written and photographic documentation records the condition of the scene as first observed, providing a permanent record.

This effort is a more formal and structured procedure than conducted by first responders, with more care taken in creating a record of the evidence. It also may help to establish whether any evidence has been lost, moved, or otherwise disturbed.

This section dovetails nicely into Section 3, "Note-Taking and Logs." Here the protocols require that investigators take notes of their activities and create logs documenting the entry, exit, and responsibilities of others inside of the crime scene. In this way, there is a clear record of every professional who worked inside of the tape, the agency they were working for, and when. It is quite common for such a log to be either absent or incomplete, with no definitive record of who had access or who had control of the scene. This speaks to a lack of training, leadership, and professionalism across the board—as such conditions are only allowed to persist when agencies want to the ability to have individuals move in and out of their crime scenes undocumented. There can be no legitimate reason for this.

The remaining sections detail specific protocols for processing all manner of physical evidence, including firearms and related evidence; pattern evidence; biological material and fluids; and digital evidence. They also dictate that crimes scenes must be documented with sufficiently detailed sketches, photos, and video of good quality. These protocols are extensive, and deserve to be referenced separately from this chapter.

What follows are discussions of crime scene processing topics drawn from the author's experiences.

EVIDENCE RECOGNITION

As we have stated many times, a competent reconstruction of the crime is not possible until all of the physical evidence from the scene has been recognized, collected, examined, and identified. As suggested by the protocols already presented, a great deal of vital information can be established at the scene through careful observations. According to Kirk (1974), the most important things to observe at the scene are (p. 34) as follows:

(1) Displaced objects or objects in unusual locations or attitudes.
(2) Distribution, indications of direction, and character of all blood traces, whether they be spots, stains, pools, or smears.
(3) Presence of objects which appear foreign to the environment, e.g., weapons as well as objects, traces, or materials not suitable as weapons but apparently involved with the criminal activity.

Each of these occurrences must be documented with photos and sketches to preserve them for later interpretation in the light of other facts revealed during the investigation.

The key is a thorough, planned, practiced execution of duties. That is to say, it is not a good idea to walk into a new scene and start collecting evidence as it is found, jumping from one place to the next as someone shouts "Over here! Look what I found!" Investigators are better served by a deliberate, patient, and systematic approach. As provided in DeForest (2005, p. 113): "Recognizing significant items among a much larger number that are ultimately irrelevant is a very challenging task. It takes time… There is no need to rush into action. Observation and thought should precede action." Moreover, DeForest explains that it is not possible to find every relevant item of evidence; things will be missed in the hard work that is assessing relevance.

The best advice is to go slow and be deliberate. Do not release the scene until the physical evidence has been thoroughly documented, collected, and packaged. Keep it secure to consider all findings of evidence in context that may suggest further items for collection.

Macroscopic, Latent, and Microscopic Evidence

In terms of what we search for, consider, and ultimately visualize, there are three kinds of physical evidence in a crime scene: *macroscopic*, *latent*, and *microscopic*.

Macroscopic evidence refers to that which may be viewed with the naked eye and photographed with limited technical assistance. This would include firearms, knives, blunt objects covered with biological materials, bodies, clothing, shell casings, and large bloodstain patterns—to name just a few.

Latent evidence refers to evidence that cannot be seen with the naked eye, and it is best visualized and then photographed with technical assistance (e.g., powders, chemical reagents, alternative light sources such as UV or infrared). This includes blood that has been washed away; blood dried on dark porous surfaces; many types of fingerprints; and dried biological fluid such as urine, mucous, and semen.

It is common for crime scene investigators to understand macroscopic and latent forms of evidence and incorporate them into their processing efforts, as they are among the more traditional and often require limited training to realize.

Most crime scene investigators are not, however, trained to think microscopically. *Microscopic evidence* refers to trace amounts of evidence that cannot be visualized and discriminated with the naked eye. This kind of evidence includes soil, pollen, hairs, fibers, gunshot residue, and trace amounts of biological transfer evidence. Thorough crime scene investigation will involve consideration of the microscopic evidence that may be present related to the crime. We must consider it light of what actions are evident; what traces may be present; and where we should take greater care, and also a closer look, so as not to disturb or miss what could be a crucial bit of evidence.

EVIDENCE DOCUMENTATION

Once an item of evidence has been recognized, and before collection efforts can begin, its location in the crime scene must be thoroughly documented. As explained in Snyder (1944, p. 17): "Never touch, change or alter anything until identified, measured and photographed." The purpose of documenting an item of evidence prior to collection is to assist with establishing a chain of custody, as well as its relationship to other objects taken from and remaining in the scene. To be useful for reconstruction purposes, documentation methods should provide anyone with the ability to return to the crime scene and place the item in the same location and orientation that it was originally discovered.

For the best results, it would be ideal for the forensic investigator to be present at the crime scene as early as possible. This would allow them to view all the evidence, including the body, in position. This makes the task of reconstruction far easier than working from the cherry-picked observations of someone else. However, this ideal is seldom obtained. Frequently the reconstructionist is not called on until the case is going to court, and the observations of others must be relied on. The more complete the documentation of those observations, the more reliable the reconstruction.

The person assigned to document the evidence at the crime scene must include documentation of all observations; not only that which supports the theories of investigating officers, but also that which shows why other theories are unsupported or eliminated.

The principal means of crime scene documentation include note taking, photography, videography, and sketching.

Photography

Photographs are one of the best ways to quickly and accurately document evidence. Ideally, this would be the duty of personnel trained in the techniques of forensic photography. Consider these following basic guidelines, consistent with, but not limited to, Rau (2000, pp. 24–260) and NIJ (2013):

1. Start each roll of film (or digital photo series) with a written placard that provides date, time, location, agency, case number, and the name of the photographer.
2. Keep a log of persons and agencies taking photographs, and note any specific items of evidence being photographed.
3. Be certain to take overall shots of the scene and associated areas; put the crime scene in a context regarding the area and its relationship to other nearby areas.
4. Take photographs of any crowds, victims, witnesses, or suspects for later identification purposes.
5. Take photographs of any associated parking areas for vehicle identification purposes. Try to get discernible plate numbers.
6. Photograph the perspective of any witness from their height and angle.
7. Take long-, medium-, and close-range photographs of each item of evidence. This will begin to provide the necessary context for reconstruction efforts.

8. Take relational photos to show the relationship between an item of evidence and other items in the scene.
9. Work with those measuring evidence and sketching the scene. Get additional shots after a scale and evidence number have been placed with an item, prior to its collection.
10. Use side lighting to bring out texture, damage, tool marks, and any other irregularities on a surface.
11. Too many pictures are better than too few. Take lots.

There is a particular limitation to photographs that is all too often ignored by those examining them, especially when pattern evidence is involved. Photographs provide only a two-dimensional likeness. This limitation is important to remember because a photograph is a flattened representation of evidence on sometimes uneven, curved, or even jagged surfaces. As a surface changes, so does the pattern that was left behind. Two-dimensional photographs may also misrepresent spatial relationships; they can distort objects and make them appear closer or farther apart than they actually are. Taking photos from multiple angles, employing detailed sketches, and video documentation may work to alleviate this particular limitation.

It bears repeating that using crime scene photographs and other documentation it should be possible for anyone to return to the crime scene and place the item in the same position when it was originally discovered. If the original location of an item of evidence cannot be ascertained from the photo record, then it is inadequate at best.

The authors frequently encounter cases where the photo record is inadequate, disjointed, and without a clear sense of purpose. This to say nothing of cases where there are only a few photographs taken. This should not be tolerated, and signals an utter lack of appreciation for documenting the physical evidence as well as a lack of professionalism and leadership.

Videography

Video is a useful way to document crime scene elements that involve time and motion—how long something takes or how something moves. It can also be used, with photos, to get an overall perspective of the spatial relationships between objects. It also provides a means of showing the relationship to, and nature of, other areas associated with or adjacent to the scene that may be missed by the person in charge of still photos that is focusing on the scene and not around it (geographical features, buildings, streets, parking lots, etc.).

Many law enforcement agencies currently shy away from taking video of anything, let alone crime scenes and the activity that goes on within, for fear that this documentation will be used against the prosecution in court by defense counsel. Given the duty of care regarding crime scene investigation, such considerations are inappropriate. Investigators should want the truth on the record, with all of its frailty intact. If their complete crime scene investigation efforts can survive the crucible of court, then there is some indication that a level of professionalism was achieved. If they cannot, then it should identify a training need.

However, if still photography is thorough, and time and motion are not factors at the scene, then video may not be necessary. This should not be taken as an excuse to avoid videography as many agencies are known to do. Rather, video should be seen as an important augmentation to the record, to capture things that might be otherwise missed outside of a frame. So the agency's default should be to take video unless there is nothing to be gained by, which is generally not going to be the case.

Sketching

The sketch is an integral part of crime scene investigation. Photography, both still and moving, is insufficient to make a complete record of the crime scene. The crime scene sketch supplements these, clarifying the location of the evidence and the relationships between items. It may be a rough drawing made at the scene with a pencil, or it can be a polished (aka "smooth" or professional) document prepared for court using a CAD program.

Essentially, the crime scene sketch is a method of documentation that is a shortcut for descriptive text. The crime scene sketch isolates the items of evidence from the background. The sketch at the scene is not made to scale, however, the items should be in their relative positions and relatively proportional in size. These are your notes; make them so that you can understand them. Neatness and artistic ability does not count, accuracy does.

When measurements are made by a novice, they appear directly on the sketch. This soon develops into a confusion of lines and numbers that makes the sketch incomprehensible to anyone other than the sketch artist. Scene measurements should always be placed in a table on a separate page in the investigators notebook.

Most sketches are *overviews*, that is, they are drawn as if looking down on the scene. This is essentially a map of the scene. They are easily understood and they show the positions and relationships of objects well.

For complete understanding of the crime scene, the overview sketch may not be adequate. A side view, sometimes called an *elevation or projected cross section* view is needed to show relative heights.

Visualizing a room as a box, then cutting the sides of the box and laying it flat makes a combination of overview with side-view sketch called an *exploded sketch*.

Drawings made to show three dimensions and perspectives are rare. One, they require a high skill level; two, they are imitations of photographs. The *perspective sketch* is the least useful sketch for most purposes.

A *finished sketch* is one that is prepared for court; it is drawn accurately and to scale. To be able to draw to scale, the locations of all items at the scene must be documented by measuring. A clear presentation of these measurements is essential to communicate what was done at the scene to those using the sketch and the documented relationships. A sketch that is not to scale is not useful for visualizing the crime scene and may be kept out of evidence in court. To-scale sketches are now made using CAD programs. A measured line should be included at the bottom of the sketch defining the scale. The phrase "approximate scale" should be associated with the line. Due to inherent measurement limitations, a drawing should never give an exact scale.

The sketch has two basic uses. First, it is used to *rebuild* the crime scene. That is, it allows persons who have not been at the scene to visualize the location and relationships. The investigator who uses the sketch to familiarize his or her fellow officers with the relationships between items at the crime scene and the attorney who uses the sketch to show a jury are rebuilding the crime scene. While photographs show the detail of the scene, the sketch eliminates the clutter showing only the important items. The sketch ties the photos together allowing the jurors to understand where items are within the location.

The second function of the sketch is for *reconstruction* of the crime. Reconstruction of actions or positions of the participants within the scene and the relationships of evidence requires accurate measurements and a clear sketch. The reconstruction analyst must understand the size limitations at the scene to interpret bloodstain patterns. The measurements relating to bullet holes and/or powder patterns must be accurate for the trajectory analyses to be correct. The actions of the participants in a crime are frequently illustrated on the sketch. An example would be the location and movements of the shooter based on the trajectories of multiple shots.

To be accepted in court, the sketch should meet certain legal requirements, the same as any other piece of evidence[7]. First, someone must be available to authenticate the sketch. If it is not the original, they must testify that it truly and accurately represents the original. The witness must know the circumstances under which the sketch was produced and that it is an accurate representation of what it purports to be. To ensure the admissibility of the sketch into a court of law the following notations need to be present (Chisum, 2000):

- The name and agency of the person doing the original sketch
- The name and agency of the person preparing the final sketch
- Case identifiers
- Date of original sketch
- Location or address
- Appropriate scale

As already mentioned, the key and the legend to the items of evidence in the sketch and their respective orienting measurements should be prepared and kept as a separate document.

The authors frequently encounter cases where the crime scene sketch is either illegible, erroneous (e.g., evidence missing, in the wrong location, or present in the sketch but not in photos), or simply absent. This should not be tolerated, and signals an utter lack of appreciation for the physical evidence as well as a lack of professionalism and leadership.

EVIDENCE COLLECTION AND PRESERVATION

Once an item of evidence has been thoroughly documented, it may be collected and hopefully preserved for examination and testing. Proper evidence collection techniques for everything from DNA swabs to fingerprints to arson debris are dictated by laboratory protocol. All physical evidence is not equal; therefore proper methods for preserving it depend on the nature of the evidence (DeForest, 2005).

There are simple concepts to begin with. Volatile material (e.g., arson debris, drug lab chemicals, accelerants) should be packaged into airtight containers to prevent evaporation and spillage. Biological material should be dried and packaged in paper. Firearms, explosives, and drug evidence should be packaged safely. And every single item of evidence should be packaged separately—no big bags of clothing, even if taken from the same person. Every shoe, every belt, every item of jewelry should be packaged separately and identified with its own unique evidence number.

A complete reference for scene processing efforts is not intended here. However, some specific issues of concern to the authors are discussed, as they have been a regular feature in casework. In short, we keep seeing the same kinds of basic evidence-related problems and misinterpretations.

Evidence Technicians and Training

As discussed in Lee, Palmbach, and Miller (2001), one person should be assigned to the task of evidence collection per scene to maintain accountability for the chain of evidence and limit the potential for contamination. This individual should seek training from crime lab personnel in the proper methods of collecting, marking, preserving, and packaging the wide variety of physical evidence that will be encountered at crime scenes. If they do not have training or cannot get training, they must seek the assistance of those who do.

Crime scene personnel should not be allowed to use evidence-related technology unless they are proficient with it. This includes everything from fuming wands, to presumptive blood tests and enhancement reagents, to alternative light sources. If someone needs to read the instructions at the scene before using any piece of technology, then they probably should not. This basic policy will prevent much evidence destruction, as well as potential misinterpretations by forensic scientists during reconstruction efforts.

Cross-Contamination

In general, it is best for all crime scene personnel to wear nitrile gloves[8] to prevent transfer from the investigator to the evidence. The forensic investigator must change gloves after handling each item of evidence to prevent cross-transfer from one item to the next. This is the most basic of forensic procedures, yet crime scene photos commonly show scene personnel handing all manner of items within the barrier tape without any gloves at all.

Also each item of evidence must be collected into a separate bag or container to prevent cross-contamination during transportation and storage. This cannot be stressed enough. Though it seems obvious, there is no shortage of investigators who bag entire areas instead of individual items, and then claim under oath that this is acceptable from a forensic or reconstruction standpoint. This evidences either a lack of training or a bias to prevent criticism of the evidence and by extending the prosecution.

Biological Material

Items of suspected biological and botanical materials should not be collected into plastic or airtight containers, as these can breed bacteria and destroy the sample. They should be collected into paper packaging. Separately, and when applicable, an undisturbed or unstained sample of the surface where the material landed should also be collected. This is necessary for crime lab personnel seeking to resolve unknown or unclear results and to help identify potential contaminants. This is why it is best to collect entire objects when possible. As discussed in Spear (2003, p. 1):

> *The standard recommendation for collecting biological evidence is* not *to remove the stain from an object but rather to collect the object with the stain. The advantages of this strategy are that the entire stain is obtained, it is not necessary to collect an "unstained control" sample and there are no further manipulations required that might negatively impact the sample. If the stain is on a smooth, non-porous surface (i.e. it can be easily "flaked" off), it will be necessary to protect the stain from contact with other objects.*

When collecting wet or only partially dry items, roll or wrap them first in clean paper. Then use paper bags, not plastic, for packaging as they allow the evidence to breathe. Plastic enclosures will cause condensation of moisture and promote bacterial and fungal growth. Items of evidence not completely dry should be allowed to air-dry in a well-ventilated room prior to packaging when possible. Do not use a fan to move the air as it can blow dried blood, fibers, and other trace items away. It can also spread pathogens.

Never dry two persons' clothing in the same area; it is not possible to guarantee the prevention of cross-contamination under this circumstance.

When collecting dry items containing potential biological evidence, wrap the item in clean paper first, and then place inside of a paper bag. In the case of biological stains on pliable surfaces (cloth, rubber, paper, etc.), it may be necessary to fold the item in some way for packaging purposes. Do not fold through visible stains, as this may damage existing biological material and hamper DNA testing efforts. And more importantly, it can cause the cover-up of small stains or create new and modified patterns. In the case of solid objects with potential biological transfer, cover the stained area with clean paper and seal the edges down with tape to prevent loss or contamination.

In the case of immovable items or surfaces, there are three approaches: cutting, swabbing, and scraping. As discussed in Spear (2003), cutting is preferable (p. 1):

> *Some samples will need to be collected in the field. If the entire object cannot be collected then* the next best way to collect biological evidence is to remove the stain by cutting it out (e.g. from a piece of carpet). *Remember to use clean scissors and to cut out an "unstained" control. Scissors or tweezers can be cleaned by rinsing with clean water and then drying with tissue. Repeat this cleaning process twice prior to each sampling.*

Cutting is especially important when dealing with pattern evidence, such as bloody fingerprints or bloody footwear impressions. It is preferable to preserve the entire pattern, as it was found, whenever possible.

Sometimes it is not possible to collect a stain by cutting it from an item or surface. This can include biological transfer onto items of great strength or mass, and certain types of walls, floors, or supporting structures. This leaves the remaining options of swabbing and scraping. When swabbing or scraping, it will be necessary to take unstained control samples and package them separately (Spear, 2003, p. 2). It will also be necessary to thoroughly document the stain with photos and sketch work, as either process will destroy it and any evident patterns.

The authors do not recommend scraping, as it causes blood dust that leads to contamination in the sensitive DNA arena. Stick to swabs, and always use a swab protector.

Evidence Storage

Physical evidence should generally be stored in a dry, cool environment. Preferably this will be a secure evidence room or facility that has a controlled environment with limited access. The authors are aware of numerous agencies that store evidence in uncontrolled environments susceptible to heat and other damaging influences. They are also aware that some agencies store their biological samples in the same refrigerators as their staff meals. This is not acceptable!

EVIDENCE TRANSPORTATION

Eventually after packaging, evidence will be transported from the scene to either a law enforcement storage facility or a crime laboratory. Transportation can change the evidence by shaking it up, knocking things loose, and moving it all around. This is true of bullets, bodies, and blood alike. Bloodstains continue to soak and transfer on clothing; trace evidence dries up and falls off; blood purges from wounds and orifices; and there can even be continued injury and bruising.

Crime scene documentation efforts should be sufficient to compare the state of evidence collected at the scene with that which is under examination, to note any artifacts of transportation that might interfere with an accurate reconstruction. If they are not, this needs to be noted in related findings.

It should also be clear who transported what evidence where and when. This will be part of any legitimate chain of custody, and attempts to alter that information are considered as a serious form of scientific fraud (see generally Turvey, 2013).

CONCLUSION

Crime scene processing is a term that refers to the recognition, documentation, preservation, collection, and transportation of physical evidence for examination and testing. There are different kinds of crime scenes, and different levels of processing, each with its own limitations and considerations. These efforts must be consistent, comprehensive, and objective to provide a scientific record that may be questioned by case developments, and questions, that arise well after the crime scene has been released. Crime scene processing is not the sole realm of law enforcement investigators with special knowledge; but a responsibility that requires transparency to provide a reliable foundation for all future crime reconstruction and analysis efforts.

ENDNOTES

1. Law enforcement agencies are responsible for deciding whether evidence gets tested. Forensic scientists are responsible for the actual testing and scientific interpretation of physical evidence as discussed in the prior chapter.
2. Brady violations are at epidemic levels in the United States, with the majority of prosecutors essentially unwilling to police themselves or those in their employ. That is why many states are considering legislation that goes beyond the Brady rule. For example, in California there is draft legislation for a bill that would make it a felony for prosecutors to withhold evidence in a criminal matter (Ciaramella, 2016). This would make it easier to arrest prosecutors, hold them civilly liable, and even put them in jail as has occurred in a small number of exceptional cases nationwide (e.g., Johnson, 2013; re: Ken Anderson; and Dewan, September 8, 2007; re: Mike NiFong).
3. To be clear, lawyers should not be allowed to discuss physical evidence or what it means from a scientific standpoint without referencing an actual scientist's findings. Otherwise, the potential for abuse of science and actual findings is high (Thornton, 1994).
4. It should not need to be mentioned that all reported crime is only potential crime; and that the occurrence of a crime must be established by an investigation of the evidence. Until that investigation is concluded, it is not known whether a crime has occurred. This demonstrates a key difference between a purely law enforcement mind-set and a scientific one.
5. While police agencies often have their own protocols, these should be reviewed and approved by an actual forensic scientist for overall integrity. The reality is, too many of these protocols are the result of law enforcement response to, or collaboration with, prosecutorial agencies. Prosecutors and police officers are not scientists, and therefore have only a limited role to play in the development of scientific protocols. This becomes important because they may go into court and present themselves as scientific, and the court may mistakenly believe them.
6. Various guidelines have been around for more than 100 years, but these represent a national effort to render best practice in accordance with scientific principles such as objectivity and transparency.
7. This is an ideal, as some courts will allow sketches into evidence that do not meet these standards, in an effort to assist the prosecution and prevent criticism of law enforcement.
8. Too many people are allergic to latex, and fingerprints can be transferred through latex gloves.

REFERENCES

Chisum, W. J., & Turvey, B. (2007). *Crime reconstruction.* Boston: Elsevier Science.
Chisum, W. J., & Turvey, B. (2012). *Crime reconstruction* (2nd ed.). San Diego, CA: Elsevier Science.
Chisum, W. J. (2000). Crime scene sketch. In L. S. Turnbull, E. H. Hendrix, & B. D. Dent (Eds.), *Atlas of crime: Mapping the criminal landscape* (pp. 229–235). Phoenix, AZ: Oryx Press.

Ciaramella, C. J. (August 16, 2016). *California bill would make it a felony for prosecutors to withhold evidence: Spurred by a series of botched murder cases and little accountability, a California lawmaker wants to rein in prosecutorial misconduct*. Reason Magazine. http://reason.com/blog/2016/08/16/california-bill-would-make-it-a-felony-f.

Cooley, C., & Turvey, B. (2014). *Miscarriages of justice*. San Diego, CA: Elsevier Science.

DeForest, P. R. (2005). Crime scene investigation. In L. E. Sullivan, & M. S. Rosen (Eds.), *Encyclopedia of law enforcement* (pp. 111–116). New York: Sage Publications.

Dewan, S. (September 8, 2007). *Duke prosecutor [Mike NiFong] jailed; students seek settlement*. New York Times. http://www.nytimes.com/2007/09/08/us/08duke.html.

Edwards, H., & Gotsonis, C. (2009). *Strengthening forensic science in the United States: A path forward*. Washington, DC: National Academies Press.

Gabrielson, R., & Sanders, T. (July 7, 2016). *How a $2 roadside drug test sends innocent people to jail: Widespread evidence shows that these tests routinely produce false positives. Why are police departments and prosecutors across the country still using them?* New York Times Magazine. http://www.nytimes.com/2016/07/10/magazine/how-a-2-roadside-drug-test-sends-innocent-people-to-jail.html.

Johnson, A. (November 8, 2013). *Ex-Texas prosecutor [Ken Anderson] first in history to be jailed for withholding evidence*. NBC News. http://www.nbcnews.com/news/other/ex-texas-prosecutor-first-history-be-jailed-withholding-evidence-f8C11566289.

Kirk, P. (1974). *Crime investigation* (2nd ed.). New York: John Wiley & Sons.

Lee, H., Palmbach, T., & Miller, M. (2001). *Henry Lee's crime scene handbook*. Boston: Academic Press.

NIJ. (June 2013). *Crime scene investigation: A guide for law enforcement*. Washington, DC.: National Institute of Justice. Research Report NCJ 234457 http://www.nfstc.org/bja-programs/crime-scene-investigation-guide/.

O'Hara, C. (1970). *Fundamentals of criminal investigation* (2nd ed.). Springfield, IL: Charles C. Thomas.

Rau, R. (January 2000). *Crime scene investigation: A guide for law enforcement*. National Institute of Justice, Technical Working Group on Crime Scene Investigation, NCJ 178280.

Snyder, L. (1944). *Homicide investigation*. Illinois: Charles C. Thomas.

Spear, T. (June 16, 2003). *Sample handling considerations for biological evidence and DNA extracts*. California Department of Justice, California Criminalistics Institute.

Thornton, J. I. (1994). Courts of law v. Courts of science: a forensic Scientist's reaction to Daubert. *Shepard's Scientific and Evidence Quarterly, 1*(3), 475–485.

Turvey, B. (2013). *Forensic fraud: Evaluating law enforcement and forensic science cultures in the context of examiner misconduct*. San Diego, CA: Elsevier Science.

CHAPTER 7

Forensic Victimology[1]

Brent E. Turvey[1,2]**, Jodi Freeman**[2,3]

Forensic Criminology Institute, Sitka, Alaska, United States and Aguascalientes, Mexico[1]*; Forensic Solutions, LLC, Sitka, Alaska, United States*[2]*; University of Western Ontario, London, ON, Canada*[3]

CHAPTER OUTLINE

Forensic Victimology: Evidence of Context 159
Goals 161
Victim Exposure Analysis 164
    Categorizing Victim Exposure 164
    Lifestyle Exposure 165
        Careers 165
        Afflictions 166
        Personal Traits 166
        Assessing Lifestyle Exposure 167
    Situational/Incident Exposure 168
        Assessing Situational Exposure 170
Victimology Guidelines 174
    Creating a Timeline: The Last 24 h 178
Conclusion 179
Endnotes 179
References 179

Latin America has among the highest documented rates of female homicide in the world. This is due to a number of convergent factors. First, Latin America is a primary source of human trafficking victims, with thousands of women and children abducted or sold into prostitution each year. Second, Latin America is a major source of immigrant trafficking into North America. Third, organized crime cartels are well established in Latin America, and sex trafficking has become a means by which they can augment their cash flow when the war on drugs ramps up in their regions of operation. Fourth, there are the joined issues of male machismo and high rates of domestic violence.[2] And finally, there is chronic poverty throughout many parts of Latin America, limiting choices and opportunities in a way that it is difficult for most of the North Americans to comprehend. All of these circumstances constitute a terrible storm within which female murder becomes an inevitability, for what are obvious reasons. They reflect pervasive social and cultural belief systems that marginalize females and treat them as a disposable commodity rather than people.

To address this problem, and the pathological failure of law enforcement to competently resolve the vast majority of these murder cases, the United Nations has taken some initiative. They explain (UN, 2014, p. 4):

Impunity for violence against women compounds the effects of such violence as a mechanism of male control over women. When the State fails to hold the perpetrators of violence accountable and society explicitly or tacitly condones such violence, impunity not only encourages further abuses, it also gives the message that male violence against women is acceptable or normal. The result of such impunity is not solely the denial of justice to the individual victims/survivors, but also the reinforcement of prevailing gender relations and replicate inequalities that affect other women and girls as well.

Consequently, the United Nations, through their Regional Office for Central America of the United Nations High Commissioner for Human Rights (OHCHR), have developed much needed protocols for the investigation and resolution of femicides in Latin America. This publication is freely available online and is titled: *Latin American Model Protocol for the Investigation of Gender-Related Killings of Women (Femicide/Feminicide)* (UN, 2014). This historic project references a number of key texts on the subjects of sex crimes, homicide, criminology, and gender issues. It also references the foundational work on criminal profiling and forensic victimology published by the primary author of this chapter (Turvey)—often using it as a verbatim guideline for thorough and competent investigative practice.

Partly as a consequence of inclusion in these international protocols, and partly because of the sheer volume of unavoidable casework, the authors have spent the past 5 years traveling back and forth Latin America. This has included teaching, publishing, and consulting on femicide cases with law enforcement agencies, universities, and the courts throughout in multiple countries. By invitation, our team of international experts has worked in Juarez (Mexico); Mexico City (Mexico); Aguascalientes (Mexico); Guatemala City (Guatemala); Bogota (Colombia); and Guayaquil (Ecuador), all places where the homicide rate, and female homicides in specific, is at epidemic proportions.

What we have learned through our work is that, wherever we go, the root causes are the same and that the most effective investigative and forensic response is universally the same, starting with forensic victimology.

The purpose of this chapter is to present the essential protocols of forensic victimology. They exist in agreement with, and even rely upon, the National Institute of Justice (NIJ) protocols developed along the same lines for sexual assault investigations and medicolegal death investigation. They also have the support of the United Nations, having been incorporated into their femicide investigation guidelines.

FORENSIC VICTIMOLOGY: EVIDENCE OF CONTEXT

The forensic victimologist seeks to examine, consider, and interpret particular victim evidence in a scientific fashion to answer investigative and forensic (i.e., legal) questions. The philosophy of forensic victimology is that victim facts are preferable to victim fictions; that victim evidence must be gathered and examined in a consistent, thorough, and objective fashion as with any other form of evidence; and that interpretations of any victim evidence must comport with the tenets of the scientific method.

The guiding principle for studying victims in investigative and forensic contexts is this: a comprehensive understanding of victims and their circumstances will allow for an accurate interpretation of the facts of a case, which will allow for an accurate interpretation of the nature of their harm or loss, and subsequently tell us about the offender. The less we know about the victim, the less we know about the crime and the criminal. Consequently, the way we collect and develop victim evidence is just as important as our eventual interpretations: they must not be weak, narrow, or based on unproved assumptions.

Developing a clear and factually complete victim history as part of a thorough case examination is universally understood as best practice for just about any of the helping professions, as it provides a baseline against which to compare current circumstances, behavior, illness, or injury. This includes medical and mental health specialists of every kind, who accept that what presents in a given case is a reflection of, and can be affected by, past events. Moreover, they are mindful that any diagnosis or treatment must take into account the changes brought about by past treatment efforts. In addition, both medical and mental health professionals are trained to recognize behavioral indicators of those presenting false symptoms (e.g., drug-seeking behavior and malingering). Consequently, the failure of medical and mental health practitioners to take an adequate history prior to diagnosis and treatment efforts is generally considered an unacceptable practice.

The importance of gathering victim background information is understood within the forensic professions as well. For example, medical examiners, coroners, and their respective death investigators understand this, as reflected in the NIJ manual, *Death Investigation: A Guide for the Scene Investigator* (1999, p. 39):

> *Establishing a decedent profile includes documenting a discovery history and circumstances surrounding the discovery. The basic profile will dictate subsequent levels of investigation, jurisdiction, and authority. The focus (breadth/depth) of further investigation is dependent on this information.*

Sex crime investigators understand this as well, as reflected in the importance of gathering information related to complainant criminal, medical, and mental health background prior to conducting formal interviews, as provided in Savino and Turvey (2012). This is because sex crimes investigators are solely responsible for investigating and determining the veracity of the complaints they receive. Without victim history, they have no context for investigating allegations of sex crimes and the forensic evidence (or lack thereof) that presents.

Victim history is also a required component of sexual assault examinations, performed by medical specialists as part of their dual treatment and evidence-gathering mission. As explained in Jamerson (2009, p. 114):

> ...intake and history information is necessary to competently inform and prioritize the physical examination... Each patient is unique; any treatment and forensic efforts should be individually crafted to his or her particular condition and history.
>
> Medical history[2] *is a significant component of the evaluation in the context of any suspected sexual assault, child molestation, or domestic assault. It provides a baseline of information for the examiner so that recent trauma and injury can be discriminated from past conditions and events. Therefore, it must cover all body systems. In this way, the examiner can identify any acute or chronic problems, as well as any history of past injury or surgeries. It also informs the nature, extent, and sequence of the forensic medical exam. A failure to document and report medical background information prevents informed medical treatment and leaves the forensic examiner without the proper context for accurate interpretations. Ultimately, conducting an accurate forensic medical examination in the absence of a patient medical history is not possible.*
>
> *Fn.2* Medical history *is the information about a patient gathered by a health care professional for the purposes of making examinations, providing treatment, and rendering a diagnosis. It commonly involves asking patients questions regarding the current and former state of their physical and mental health. Without this background information, examinations, treatments, and diagnoses are at best uninformed, and at worst potentially lethal.*

This also specifically includes (p. 117—120) "recent consensual sexual activity," "postassault activities," "history of drug abuse," history of mental health and behavioral problems, and history of STDs—as these can be instrumental in determining whether sexual activity occurred, the type of sexual activity, the parties involved, and the reliability of the account provided.

The forensic necessity of this extensive history-gathering effort is affirmed in the NIJ guidelines, *A National Protocol for Sexual Assault Medical Forensic Examinations* (2004), which provides that informed sexual assault examinations require a complete victim history (p. 81):

> **Coordinate medical forensic history taking and investigative interviewing.** *Examiners typically ask patients to provide a medical forensic history after initial medical care for acute problems and before the examination and evidence collection. This history, obtained by asking patients detailed forensic and medical questions related to the assault, is intended to guide the exam, evidence collection, and crime lab analysis of findings.*

Inherent in the scientific method and the professional guidelines mentioned is the understanding that evidence observed in relation to an alleged victim or crime scene may not be the result of the criminal activity being reported. Such evidence may in fact be the result of some previous and unrelated activity or event. In fact, sex crime investigators and forensic examiners will not necessarily know what features of complainant or victim history are relevant to a forensic assessment until well after they have begun their work.

Because it is not always possible to know which factors of victim history are going to be relevant, professional guidelines, as well as the scientific method, require that a broad net be cast at the outset of every case. In one case the primary issue may become a question of toxicology (e.g., how many drinks and how intoxicated was the reporting party). In another it may be a question of where an alleged murder occurred (e.g., which room did the victim normally occupy, where is it in relation to location where the body was found, and could they physically occupy that space). In yet another there may be a question of sexual habits or preferences (e.g., were they virgin, did they engage in sadomasochistic activity resulting in frequent bodily injury of a sexual nature, did they often have more than one sexual partner on the day of the alleged sexual assault). All of these issues and related details have been a deciding factor in criminal cases. Each victim is different, each case is different, and therefore less victim history is not better.

GOALS

Forensic victimology is an essential component of crime scene analysis and therefore an unavoidable feature of any criminal profile. The information gathered from a thorough victimology has the potential to impact each stage of a criminal profile, from crime reconstruction to establishing offender motivation. The goals of forensic victimology include, but are not limited to, the following:

- **Assist in understanding elements of the crime**. By studying the victim, the examiner is better able to understand the relationship between a victim to his or her lifestyle and environment, and subsequently of a given offender to that victim. Victimology provides the context for the victim—crime scene interaction, the offender—crime scene interaction, and the victim—offender interaction.
- **Assist in developing a timeline**. Retracing a victim's last known actions and creating a timeline are critical to understanding the victim as a person, understanding the victim's relationship to the environment, understanding the victim's relationship to other events, and understanding how the victim came to be acquired by an offender. The timeline will be further discussed later in the chapter.
- **Define the suspect pool**. In an unsolved case, where the offender is unknown, a thorough victimology defines the suspect pool. Their lifestyle in general and their activities in particular must be scrutinized to determine who had access to

them, what they had access to, how and when they gained and maintained access, and where the access occurred. If we can understand how and why an offender has selected known victims, then we may also be able to establish a relational link of some kind between the victim and that offender. These links may be geographic, work related, schedule oriented, school related, hobby related, or they may be otherwise connected. These connections provide a suspect pool that includes those with knowledge of or access to the related area.
- **Provide investigative suggestions**. A thorough victimology compiled in the investigative stage will offer suggestions and provide direction to the investigation. Such suggestions may include interviewing those in the defined suspect pool, interviewing witnesses about discrepancies in their statements or contradictions with timeline information, and examining any physical evidence that may have been overlooked during the initial investigation.
- **Assist with crime reconstruction**. By understanding the victim's behavior patterns, the examiner is better equipped to complete a thorough crime reconstruction. Knowing why a victim was in the location where they were acquired or what the victim was doing in that location will provide the examiner with information that may be necessary when inferring the most reasonable behavior of that victim.
- **Assist with contextualizing allegations of victimization**. Developing a clear and factually complete victim history will provide context to the allegations of victimization. Victimological information may also support or refute the allegations of victimization.
- **Assist with the development of offender modus operandi**. Knowledge of the victim's pattern of behavior in relation to the location where the victim was acquired may assist with the development of the offender's modus operandi (MO), specifically in regards to victim selection. For example, an offender who is trolling for victims may choose to acquire an opportunistic victim at a location with increased victim availability and vulnerability, such as a busy pub with intoxicated patrons. This tells us about the offender's MO or the choices made during the commission of the crime.
- **Assist with the development of offender motive**. Without a thorough examination of victim history, the examiner may overlook important victimological information that may reflect the offender's motivation. For example, an examiner can only appropriately establish a list of items missing from a crime scene if it is known what the victim had in his or her possession at the time of victimization. Without this information, a profit-oriented motivation may be disregarded in such a case.
- **Assist with establishing the offender's exposure level**. *Offender exposure* is the general amount of exposure to discovery, identification, or apprehension experienced by the offender. The context surrounding the point at which the offender acquired the victim may assist with establishing the offender's level of exposure. For example, an offender who acquires a victim in broad daylight is at

an increased risk of detection and apprehension, which may suggest an increased level of confidence or skill.
- **Assist with case linkage**. When determining whether or not a series of crimes can be behaviorally linked, victim selection is an important behavioral factor that cannot be ignored during a linkage analysis. A study of the victims across a series of cases may reveal a unique connection between the victims, or the exposure levels of the victims may allow the examiner may support or refute a linkage.
- **Assist with public safety response**. If we can understand how and why offenders have selected their previous victims, then we have a better chance of predicting the type of victim they may select in the future. This will allow the appropriate public safety messages to be delivered to the public that aim to reduce the exposure levels of those affected individuals. For example, an offender who enters multiple residences through unlocked windows may prompt a public safety message to be delivered to affected communities warning them to lock their windows and doors.
- **Reduce victim deification and vilification**. The objective, scientific, and thorough examination of victims assists in reducing victim deification and vilification. *Deification* involves idealizing victims based on who or what they are, without consideration of the facts (e.g., young schoolchildren, missing adolescents, and others who are favored in the press or by public opinion). Because of the political or public culture of a certain area or region, certain victim populations tend to be more politically or publicly sympathetic. This view facilitates rationalizations about time expended on the deified case while other investigations suffer, and it does not allow for an unbiased victimology by virtue of depriving the crime and the investigation of true victim context. Deification has the capacity to accomplish the following:
  - Remove good suspects from the suspect pool
  - Provide coverage for the false reporter
  - Provide coverage for suspects who are family or household members

  Vilification involved viewing a victim as worthless or disposable by virtue of who or what they are, without consideration of the facts (e.g., the homeless, the poor, minority groups, and prostitutes). This view presumes that it is okay, or not as bad, to commit crimes against people of certain lifestyle, races, religions, or creeds. Ultimately, this tends to be guided by an investigator's subjective sense of personal morality—or that of a like-minded community. Ultimately, it facilitates investigative apathy. Examples of vilified groups, or groups toward which there is no lack of apathy, commonly include the following:
  - The homeless/mentally ill
  - Homosexuals
  - Minority populations within particular regions, such as immigrants and Native Americans
  - Prostitutes
  - Drug dealers
  - Drug addicts

- Teen runaways who becomes prostitutes or drug addicts
- Individuals of particular religious beliefs

If we idealize victims, or vilify them, we will not learn who they were. Forensic victimology reduces victim bias by examining the victim through an objective and scientific lens.

- **Help establish the nature of victim exposure to harm or loss**. An examination of the harmful elements experienced by a victim, throughout his or her life and at the time of crime commission, will allow the examiner to determine the victim's level of exposure to suffering harm or loss. Victim exposures are discussed in the following section.

VICTIM EXPOSURE ANALYSIS

Victim exposure is the amount of contact or vulnerability to harmful elements experienced by the victim. It is not necessarily from the victim's perspective, but what we as criminal profilers perceive for a given victim.

Victim risk has been defined as victim exposure. However, the concept of *victim risk* refers to the possibility of suffering harm or loss and is associated with predictions about potential harm—what might happen. By utilizing the concept of victim risk, one may infer a conclusion based on a statistical analysis of the potential to be harmed as being part of a demographic group. However, these conclusions often do not account for the victim's particular characteristics and context or how they interact with the offender. Making conclusions about the victim's level of harm based on statistical analyses or probability estimates of risk do not accurately reflect how a specific victim's lifestyle contributed to his or her harm, nor does it necessarily provide investigative relevance. Exposure analysis, on the other hand, is concerned with examining harmful elements that are actually present. This concept examines how an environmental factor or personal trait of the victim specifically increased their contact with harm.

It is important to remember that the victims are not responsible for the predatory acts of offenders. This may seem like an obvious concept, but unfortunately, many people do blame the victim as being partially or wholly responsible for certain crimes committed against them. Detectives might blame a prostitute, in whole or in part, for being the victim of a violent crime. The same detective might view a student in a similar situation as being an unfortunate victim of circumstance. However, establishing victim "blame" does not add anything to the investigative effort. All citizens have moments of vulnerability, no matter what level of harm their lifestyle and circumstances expose them to. Criminals are not entitled to commit crimes just because citizens have these moments of vulnerability. As we will discuss, this begs understanding the difference between *lifestyle exposure* and *situational exposure*.

CATEGORIZING VICTIM EXPOSURE

Ultimately, the aim is to arrive at an understanding of victims in the context of their lifestyle and conditions, in order for exposure to be fully understood and described to others. The question to be investigated and answered here is this: *what is a particular victim exposed to*? Ask when and how a particular victim's lifestyle places the individual in harm way, if at all. For example, a teen male may have a high victim exposure to domestic violence by virtue of living with a parent who is an abusive alcoholic. At the same time, the teen may have a low exposure to being abducted, raped, and killed by a stranger, by virtue of a fixed schedule with a great deal of group activity and adult supervision.

Victim exposure can, and should, be categorized further in terms of *lifestyle exposure* and *situational exposure*.

LIFESTYLE EXPOSURE

Victim *lifestyle exposure* is concerned with studying the *frequency* of potentially harmful elements experienced by the victim and resulting from the victim's usual environment and personal traits, as well as past choices. It requires an investigation and assessment of the victim's personality and his or her personal, professional, and social environment.

Generally, lifestyle factors can influence harm to the victim in three ways:

1. By creating a perceived conflict with an offender
2. By increasing the victim's presence around offenders or those predisposed toward criminality
3. By enhancing an offender's perception of victim vulnerability

There are many lifestyle factors that are commonly known to increase victim exposure and vulnerability to harm. However, we find even the most experienced investigators and examiners can fail to consider them in their individual assessments—especially when it suits their purposes. It should also be noted that, generally speaking, not all lifestyle factors can be said to have the potential to increase harm to a victim. Thus, to argue that a lifestyle factor influences victim–offender dynamics, it needs to be both potentially harmful, in the sense that its presence could be argued to influence opportunity for harm to occur, and also relevant, within the context of who the particular victim was and the criminal behavior that occurred.

Notable lifestyle factors include, but are not limited to, the following examples:

Careers

- **Attorneys**. It is true that attorneys do have regular contact with criminals, which provides an increased lifestyle exposure to violence and the possibility of retaliation. However, these crimes tend to be underreported by attorneys and the media, leading to a lack of general awareness outside of the legal community.
- **Law enforcement**. Law enforcement officers have regular contact with a wide variety of criminals and controlled substances. This results in an increased lifestyle exposure to violence and the possibility of retaliation for simply showing up to work on any given day. They also suffer higher rates of divorce, depression, alcoholism, domestic violence, and suicide than regular citizens. Law enforcement officers are therefore exposed to dangers on the job, at home, and at every place in between, from themselves, their cases, and those they love.

- **Prostitutes**. A *prostitute* is any person who engages in sexual activity for payment. Because prostitution is often illegal and therefore unregulated, prostitutes are often defined by their willingness to get into vehicles or go into hotel rooms with men they do not know, to perform sex acts without being seen by others. This increases their exposure to potential assault, rape, robbery, kidnapping, and even homicide, to say nothing about the risks related to drug abuse and venereal disease, both of which form a crime and criminal nexus with prostitution.
- **Drug dealers**. Drug dealing is among the most violent and dangerous criminal occupations that exist, no matter the community or the culture. It commonly involves the presence of drugs, cash, and firearms—each of which attracts crime and may be used in the perpetuation of violence of just about every kind. It creates, as with prostitution, a nexus of crime and criminals.

Afflictions

- **Drug addiction**. Drug addiction involves a steady progression of drug use, increased dosages, and decreased dosage intervals. Each drug affects the addict differently, depending upon the amount taken, personal chemistry, and the other drugs in the system. The one universal consequence of drug use is the inability to think rationally.

  Drug addiction can also be associated with progressively violent and criminal drug-seeking behavior. This behavior is characterized by an intense focus on supporting a drug habit regardless of the cost or consequences. Drug addicts engage in drug-seeking behavior exist on a continuum that includes falsifying the symptoms of illness to get prescription medications; stealing medication from neighbors under a false pretext; stealing items of value for cash to buy drugs; engaging in prostitution to support a drug habit; robbing a pharmacy. Whatever they believe will get them their drug is what they do. Period. This essentially completed the nexus of crime and criminals associated with drugs and prostitution.

- **Alcoholism**. *Alcoholism* is a particular kind of drug addiction that is not necessarily illegal—though it can result in illegal activity because of the lack of inhibition and absence of rational thought that necessarily results. Additionally, alcoholics may be very difficult to identify if they develop high functioning, coping, rationalization, and concealment skills. These combine to increase their vulnerability to harm from themselves and others with respect to a persistent lack of judgment, memory, and dexterity.
- **Mental disease/defect**: A mental illness or disorder is a health problem that significantly affects how a person feels, thinks, behaves, and interacts with other people.

Personal Traits

- **Aggressiveness**. People who are more aggressive and confrontational in their behavior are more likely to evoke aggressive behavior in others (see Singer, 1981).

- **Impulsivity**. Impulsive behavior is done without planning or forethought. As a consequence, impulsive individuals are generally unprepared to meet the challenges that they face, as well as fail to consider the actual consequences of their actions.
- **Self-destructive behavior**. Some individuals engage in reckless or self-destructive behavior that routinely puts them in harm way. Such behaviors exist on a continuum from reckless to overtly self-destructive. They can include driving too fast, binge drinking or eating, overmedicating, and spending beyond one's means.
- **Passivity**. Passive individuals are those who allow or accept the actions and choices of others without question or defiance. This can remain true even when they are put in situations that expose them to harm or loss and is especially problematic if they are known to be passive, as others might see them as excellent targets.
- **Low self-esteem**. Those with low self-esteem are more apt to be depressed, to engage in self-destructive behaviors, and to be taken advantage of or otherwise victimized. Depression can create a strong desire to gain and maintain the approval of others—a tendency that is ripe for abuse by those with bad intentions. Low self-esteem can also foster the belief that one deserves to be victimized.
- **Aberrant sexual behavior**. Sexual promiscuity can lead to increased exposure to sexually transmitted disease and jealous or possessive lovers. Extreme sexual behavior can actually be physically dangerous, depending upon the types of behaviors involved.

It should be noted that any combination of these elements could have a synergistic effect. In other words, two or more of these or similar circumstances are likely to enhance the frequency and impact of others. Chronic drug abuse can enhance chronic drug abuse; mental illness can lead to and exacerbate abusive relationships. These types of self-destructive behaviors and circumstances do not typically occur in a vacuum, and those afflicted are not always able to self-correct.

Assessing Lifestyle Exposure

The authors have developed a more objective method of classifying the lifestyle exposure level of victims. These categories of exposure have been adapted from Turvey (2012) and influenced by similar classifications from Hazelwood (1995).

With respect to lifestyle exposure:

Extreme-exposure victims are those who are exposed to the possibility of suffering harm or loss everyday (7 days a week). The following examples illustrate extreme-exposure victims:

- A prostitute who is engaged in sexual activity for money on a daily basis.
- An alcoholic who is constantly intoxicated.
- A prisoner who lives in a confined environment with constant exposure to criminals.

High-exposure victims are those who are exposed to the possibility of suffering harm or loss more often than not (4—6 days a week). These victims are frequently exposed to harmful elements; however, the exposure is not constant. For example, a child who lives in an abusive and neglectful environment during the week with his mother but lives in a healthy environment with his father on weekends. This child is exposed to harm or loss during the week, but is removed from the harmful environment on the weekend.

Medium-exposure victims are those who are exposed to the possibility of suffering harm or loss less often than not (1—3 days a week). For example, a college student who engages in excessive drinking to the point of intoxication every weekend.

Low-exposure victims are those who are rarely exposed to the possibility of suffering harm or loss (less than once a week). These victims rarely engage in behaviors, or put themselves in positions, that increase their exposure or vulnerability to experiencing harm or loss.

Because lifestyle exposure refers to the *frequency* of exposure, the above categories of victim exposure have been broken down into timeframes. The examiner must acknowledge that not every victim trait or characteristic can be perfectly slotted into one of the above categories. For example, a child who accesses the Internet unsupervised on a daily basis is at an increased risk of communicating with online predators. However, daily-unsupervised Internet or chat room usage will not necessarily elevate the child's lifestyle exposure to extreme. These categories are merely a guideline to establishing victim lifestyle exposure and must be evaluated in the context of the specific victim's lifestyle, personal traits, and choices.

SITUATIONAL/INCIDENT EXPOSURE

Victim *situational* or *incident exposure* refers to the amount of actual exposure or vulnerability experienced by the victim to harm, resulting from the environment and personal traits *at the time of victimization.* This is distinct from lifestyle exposure, which again refers to harmful elements that exist, generally, in a victim's everyday life. A few useful analogies are in order.

Consider the issue of alcohol. Being a person who routinely becomes intoxicated increases one's lifestyle exposure to the many harmful effects of alcohol. However, unless a victim is actually intoxicated at the time of victimization, it does not necessarily raise situational exposure. It is possible to have a high lifestyle exposure related to alcohol abuse, but a low situational exposure from lack of alcohol use or abuse at the time of victimization. The opposite is also true.

Consider also the use of firearms. Being a person who does not own a firearm, use a firearm, have one in one's home, or live with or interact with those that do decreases one's overall lifestyle exposure to the harmful effects of firearms. However, if a victim is at a shooting range for the first time with a new friend or romantic interest and is accidentally shot, it must be recognized that his situational exposure to harm from firearms was quite high at the time of victimization. This is true even if he was not participating or holding a gun, given his situational proximity to multiple loaded firearms being discharged by multiple persons of varying skill.

However, not all immediately harmful exposures are as transparent and easy to recognize from the victim's perspective as these basic examples might suggest. Harmful exposure may not even be apparent to investigators, owing to investigative apathy, or the reliance on false investigative assumptions about who and what was present during the crime. The situational harm coming from persons, environments, and circumstances related to a particular crime must be thoroughly investigated, carefully established, and never assumed.

Notable situational factors include, but are not limited to, the following:

- **Time of occurrence**. Certain times of day can result in more exposure to various kinds of harm than others. However, any interpretation of the impact of this factor is highly dependent on the location of occurrence as well as other converging circumstances. Time of day cannot be considered in a vacuum. Time of day is a factor heavily influenced by the regular activities of the victim, their proximity to abusers, and subsequent supervision—all of which is very often a function of age.
- **Location of occurrence**. Location is one of the most important factors to consider in terms of victim situational exposure. Certain environments contain a great deal of criminal activity; others may place a victim outside the immediate reach of assistance; and still others may physically isolate or confine the victim.
- **Proximity to criminal activity**. Nearness in space, time, or relationship to criminal activity increases one's incident exposure. This can include victim nearness to crime and criminals or direct victim participation and involvement in criminal activity. The more violence associated with a proximal crime, the greater subsequent victim exposure to harm.
- **Number of potential victims**. It is generally true that there is safety in numbers; in other words, the buddy system can remove one from the path of harm or speed one from harmful circumstances. This is true as long as the people one is with are not at an increased lifestyle or situational exposure. If your buddy is intoxicated, rather than being an asset he becomes a liability. The same is true if your buddy has a temper, just got in a fight with his significant other and is distressed, or has a mental illness and is not taking medication.

    Also, some more competent and confident offenders prefer to select victims in pairs to use one to control the other, such as a mother and a child. This situation is one of the exceptions that proves the rule. Examples include an abusive parents who threaten the life of other family members should anyone tell the police, or the rapist who selects mothers with small children to gain total compliance by threatening to harm the child.
- **Availability of weapons**. The availability of any weapon or material in a given environment increases the likelihood that it will be used in a physical altercation, should one ensure, or that someone will accidentally injure himself or herself or others while handling it for any number of legitimate or illegitimate

purposes. The availability of a shotgun in an environment increases victim exposure to shotgun injury or fatality; the availability of knives in an environment increases victim exposure to sharp force injury or fatality; the availability of coat hangers in an environment increases victim exposure to related ligature injury or fatality. However, a weapon's availability does not cause its use.
- **Care and supervision**. Individuals become more willing to engage in criminal activity when they are not being watched. That is to say, criminal propensity can increase as supervision and accountability decrease.
- **Victim state of mind or perception**. This factor refers to the victim's emotional state before, during, and following an attack as evidenced by convergent patterns of behavior and any reliable witness accounts. An agitated or distressed emotional state, for example, may increase victim incident exposure. Additionally, a victim who feels safe in a particular environment or situational will act differently from a victim who does not. Many variables, including the presence of drugs, alcohol, mental illness, or a heightened emotional state such as anger or sadness, affect this directly.
- **Drug and alcohol use**. The use of mind-altering substances may decrease physical reaction time, impair judgment, and alter one's perception of reality. In either drug or alcohol use, victim situational exposure is increased dramatically, even for otherwise low-exposure victims. One thing that a person cannot do under the influence of drugs or alcohol is to think rationally.

The existence of any one circumstance is not necessarily enough to cause the tipping point of victim harm, unless direct harm is inherent (such as with drug and alcohol use). Having a gun in the home will not cause someone to use it for violence; having drugs in the home will not make someone use them; leaving a child unsupervised at school will not cause the child to be raped. It is the synergy of corresponding factors and circumstances that exposes victims to ever-increasing levels of harm until their demise becomes almost unavoidable.

Assessing Situational Exposure

The authors have developed a more transparent method of classifying the situational exposure level of victims. These categories of exposure have been adapted from Turvey (2012) and influenced by similar classifications from Hazelwood (1995).

With respect to situational exposure:

High-exposure victims are those who are exposed to harm or loss immediately prior to victimization. These victims are already suffering actual harm or loss prior to the point of victimization. Take for example, a young child who is abducted while home alone in an unsafe environment. This child was already suffering harm and neglect by their primary caregiver prior to the point of victimization.

Medium-exposure victims are those who are vulnerable to harm or loss immediately prior to victimization. These victims are not suffering actual harm or loss prior to victimization, but the environment or personal traits of the victim increase their vulnerability or susceptibility to experiencing harm. Take for example, a female victim who is walking alone late at night. The time of day and victim's environment increase his/her vulnerability to suffering harm, as it provides the offender with an available and vulnerable victim and reduces the offender's exposure level.

Low-exposure victims are those who are exposed to little contact or vulnerability to harm or loss immediately prior to victimization. The environment and personal traits of these victims do not expose them to harmful elements or increase their vulnerability to harmful elements prior to victimization. It is important to note here that we are generally exposed to at least some level of vulnerability to harm or loss at any point in time, whether within our immediate environment or reflective of our personal traits.

CASE EXAMPLES: *MARIA RAMOS, TAWANDA HODGES, AND KIMBERLY MOORE*

In 2011, the examiner (Turvey) evaluated the crime scene behavior, and victimology, related to a serial murder trial in New York. This is for the specific purpose of conducting a linkage analysis to determine whether the defendant should be tried jointly for the crimes.[a] The examiner was hired by the defense and gave expert testimony at an admissibility hearing. The case was New York v. Francisco Acevedo.

The examiner gave expert testimony on a number of areas. Of note, the victimology in the case was roughly consistent across all three cases.

1) Maria L. Ramos (1989)

Victim last seen: Last seen by Migdalia Nunez on Friday, February 3, 1989 at approximately 10 p.m., entering a burgundy Thunderbird owned by Willie Rodriguez in front of the Olympic Restaurant on Jerome Avenue.

Body found: Reported February 5, 1989 at 0852 h; found at 78 Fernbrook St., Yonkers, nude on the sidewalk across the street from the Westchester Co. Waste Treatment Plant.

1.1) Victimology
   Race: Hispanic
   Sex: Female
   D.O.B: February 5, 1962
   Age: 26
   Height: 5'4"
   Weight: 117 lbs
   Hair color: Black

A. Residence type and description
   At the time of the homicide, Maria Ramos' last known address was 228 West Tremont Ave, #9A, Bronx, NY.

B. Employment history
   Maria Ramos earned money as a prostitute and thief.

C. Social history
   Born in Puerto Rico, Maria Ramos was known by other prostitutes and was reported to be best friends with a prostitute named Migdalia Nunez (they often worked together). She was also reported to be regularly seeing a steady "john": a married Dominican man named Willie Rodriguez (aka Raul), in his 50s, for the past 3–4 months. Normally picked up by Raul on Friday afternoons and dropped off Sunday afternoons or evenings via private care service; spent time with him at an apartment in Yonkers; and always came back with a few hundred dollars.

D. Criminal history
   Maria Ramos had a history of arrests for prostitution in multiple precincts, for grand larceny, and was reported by other prostitutes to regularly rip-off her "johns."

E. Drug and alcohol use
Maria Ramos was an I.V. drug user as indicated by track marks on her arms and was reported to abuse cocaine and heroine.

F. Medical and mental health history
Maria Ramos was suspected of having AIDS and suffered from heroine addiction.

1.2) Victim Exposure

Victim exposure is the amount of contact or vulnerability to harmful elements experienced by the victim. It is a function of both lifestyle and situational exposure.

A. Lifestyle exposure

A victim's lifestyle exposure is related to the frequency of potentially harmful elements experienced by the victim and resulting from the victim's usual environment and personal traits, as well as past choices (Turvey, 2011).

Mario Ramos was an extreme-exposure victim [exposed to the possibility of suffering harm or loss everyday (7 days a week)]. This is supported by the fact that she was a prostitute working the streets, was regularly seeing a married man, was regularly engaged in criminal enterprise including theft, and was also a drug addict.

B. Situational exposure

A victim's situational or incident exposure refers to the amount of actual exposure or vulnerability to harm resulting from the environment and the victim's personal traits at the time of victimization. This is distinct from lifestyle exposure, which again refers to harmful elements that exist, generally, in a victim's everyday life (Turvey, 2011).

Mario Ramos was a high situational exposure victim, in that she was exposed to harm or loss immediately prior to victimization. This is supported by the fact that she was a prostitute, a drug addict, and last seen in a vehicle with one of her regular "johns."

The victim exposure in this case dramatically increases the possibility of suffering violence, sexual violence, and homicide. It also dramatically increases the suspect pool as opposed to narrowing it.

2) Tawanda Hodges (1991)

Victim last seen: Last seen by mother, Devon Hodges, on Tuesday, March 26, 1991 at 7 p.m. at her apartment. Left on a "date." Called an hour later looking for her keys. Never seen or heard from again.

Body found: Reported March 28, 1991 at 1103 h; found at the Dead End of 1 Federal St., Yonkers, nude except for two layers of socks (gray and red) on a pile of gravel in an enclosed area.

2.1) Victimology

Race: Black
Sex: Female
D.O.B: February 18, 1963.
Age: 28
Height: 5'2"
Weight: 126 lbs
Hair color: Black

A. Residence type and description
At the time of the homicide, Tawanda Hodges' last known address was 2690 Valentine Ave., Apt. 2A, Bronx, NY.

B. Employment history
Tawanda Hodges earned money as a prostitute and thief (stealing from cabbies and "johns").

C. Social history
Tawanda Hodges lived with her mother, Devon Hodges, and her two daughters (LaTiesha Hodges, B/F/5; Tara Lothian, B/F/4). Her son (Lameek Hodges, B/M/9) lives with her great-grandmother Lucille Hunter at 420 W. 130 St., Apt. 17. Dating a man named Rodney Rodgers

for 2–3 years, with whom she had been arrested for armed robbery of a cab driver. Ron was incarcerated at Riker's Island at the time of her murder.

Previously, Tawanda Hodges had lived with Clive Lothian for about 4 years. He is the father of her children LaTiesha and Tara. At the time, he was a cab driver. Tawanda Hodges was engaged in drug use and prostitution while they were together. He reported last seeing Tawanda Hodges 1 month prior to her murder.

D. Criminal history

Tawanda Hodges had a history of arrest for robbery. She was also engaged in prostitution, crack cocaine use, and had a history robbing her "johns."

E. Drug and alcohol use

Tawanda Hodges had a long history of crack cocaine abuse and was found to have cocaine in her system at the time of her death.

F. Medical and mental health history

Unknown.

2.2) Victim Exposure

Victim exposure is the amount of contact or vulnerability to harmful elements experienced by the victim. It is a function of both lifestyle and situational exposure.

A. Lifestyle exposure

A victim's lifestyle exposure is related to the frequency of potentially harmful elements experienced by the victim and resulting from the victim's usual environment and personal traits, as well as past choices (Turvey, 2011).

Tawanda Hodges was an extreme-exposure victim [exposed to the possibility of suffering harm or loss everyday (7 days a week)] This is supported by the fact that she was a prostitute, was regularly engaged in criminal enterprise including theft, and was also a drug addict.

B. Situational exposure

A victim's situational or incident exposure refers to the amount of actual exposure or vulnerability to harm resulting from the environment and the victim's personal traits at the time of victimization. This is distinct from lifestyle exposure, which again refers to harmful elements that exist, generally, in a victim's everyday life (Turvey, 2011).

Tawanda Hodges was a high situational exposure victim, in that she was exposed to harm or loss immediately prior to victimization. This is supported by the fact that she was a prostitute, a drug addict, and last known to be going out to meet one of her "johns." The victim exposure in this case dramatically increases the possibility of suffering violence, sexual violence, and homicide. It also dramatically increases the suspect pool as opposed to narrowing it.

3) Kimberly Moore (1996)

Victim last seen: Last seen on May 24, 1996 by the Trade Winds Motel manager (Carlos Gonzalez) at approximately 2:30 p.m., entering room #45 with an unknown white male.

Body found: Found by Trade Winds Motel housekeeper (Katrina Fadda) and on May 24, 1996 at approximately 6:45 p.m. in Trade Winds Motel, room #45, Yonkers, NY.

3.1) Victimology

Race: Black
Sex: Female
D.O.B: unknown
Age: 30
Height: 5'5"
Weight: 110 lbs
Hair color: Black

A. Residence type and description

At the time of the homicide, Kimberly Moore's last known residence was 13 Beach St., Mt. Vernon, NY. No further information was provided.

B. Employment history
Kimberly Moore earned money as a prostitute.

C. Social history
On the morning of the day of her murder, Kimberly Moore had an argument with her boyfriend/pimp. She left him in the Bronx and was working the street on Yonkers Ave. in front of the Trade Winds Motel late that morning and throughout the afternoon. No further information was provided.

D. Criminal history
Kimberly Moore had a history of prostitution and drug addiction. Her criminal history was not provided to this examiner and is therefore unknown.

E. Drug and alcohol use
Kimberly Moore was found in a motel room with empty alcohol bottles and drug paraphernalia. She was also known to be a crack cocaine addict. Cocaine was found to be in her system at the time of her death, but not alcohol.

F. Medical and mental health history
Drug addict; otherwise unknown.

3.2) Victim Exposure

Victim exposure is the amount of contact or vulnerability to harmful elements experienced by the victim. It is a function of both lifestyle and situational exposure.

A. Lifestyle exposure
A victim's lifestyle exposure is related to the frequency of potentially harmful elements experienced by the victim and resulting from the victim's usual environment and personal traits, as well as past choices (Turvey, 2011).

Kimberly Moore was an extreme-exposure victim [exposed to the possibility of suffering harm or loss everyday (7 days a week)]. This is supported by the fact that she was a prostitute working the streets and was also a drug addict.

B. Situational exposure
A victim's situational or incident exposure refers to the amount of actual exposure or vulnerability to harm resulting from the environment and the victim's personal traits at the time of victimization. This is distinct from lifestyle exposure, which again refers to harmful elements that exist, generally, in a victim's everyday life (Turvey, 2011).

Kimberly Moore was a high situational exposure victim, in that she was exposed to harm or loss immediately prior to victimization. This is supported by the fact that she was a prostitute, a drug addict, and last known to be entering her motel room with one of her "johns."

The victim exposure in this case dramatically increases the possibility of suffering violence, sexual violence, and homicide. It also dramatically increases the suspect pool as opposed to narrowing it.

[a]Linkage analysis refers to the process of determining whether or not there are discrete connections, or behavioral commonalities, between two or more previously unrelated cases through crime analysis (a.k.a., crime scene analysis) (Turvey, 2011). As explained in Turvey (2011), it is most often employed to serve one of two purposes: (1) to assist law enforcement with the application of its resources by helping to direct investigative efforts and (2) to assist the court in determining whether or not there is sufficient behavioral evidence to suggest a common scheme or plan to address forensic issues, such as whether similar crimes may be tried together or whether other crimes may be brought in as evidence.

VICTIMOLOGY GUIDELINES

Weston and Wells (1975, p. 97) provide a quick checklist of preliminary victimological queries that have been proven to be most useful in eliciting investigative information. This is the kind of information that should be gathered immediately, ideally before the investigator arrives at a given crime scene.

- Did the victim know the perpetrator?
- Does the victim suspect any person? Why?
- Had the victim a history of crime? A history of reporting crimes?
- Did the victim have a weapon?
- Had the victim an aggressive personality?
- Has the victim been the subject of any field [police] reports?

The problem with this checklist is that it may require some misleading assumptions and interpretations prior to the start of the investigation. For example, unless there is no doubt about the identity of the offender, this is a question to be answered by virtue of an investigation. Also, it presumes that there was actually a crime committed. Not all complaints are founded; not all deaths are homicides. Again, this is something that can only be established by a thorough investigation. The lesson here is that victim information, and victim history, has long been considered essential to professional investigators of fact, to the point of developing these kinds of conceptual checklists.

Turvey (2012) also provides basic victimological inquires that have been useful when applied to actual casework. Gathering this information, along with the careful examination of physical evidence, provides the starting point for investigative activity. Again, no one checklist can suffice; the victimologist must be willing to sift through each victim's history carefully, with no preconceived theories. When compiling a forensic victimology, it is important to reference the case material that each piece of information was taken from, ensuring the reader can locate the original document.

The following adapts those victim guidelines into a more cohesive set of objective packages that must be gathered and assessed by the criminal investigator and profiler alike, as with any intelligence. There can be no mistake as to the importance of this effort and the investigative clarity it will provide. Conversely, the failure to collect these data packages leaves gaping holes in the investigation through which unexamined theories of the crime will most certainly escape.

Again, the gathering and assessment of these packages provide context and should lead to additional information and evidence. They are not the end of the inquiry but rather the beginning. Moreover, this kind of information is required to be collected by medicolegal personnel—either by forensic nurses in cases of sexual assault or by forensic pathologists in cases of homicide.

Personal package:

1. Sex
2. Race
3. Height
4. Weight
5. Hair color/length/dyed
6. Eyes: color/glasses/contacts

7. Clothing/jewelry
8. Personal items: contents of wallet, purse, handbag, backpack, briefcase, suitcase, or medicine bag
9. Grooming/manner of dress
10. Smoker or nonsmoker
11. Hobbies/skills
12. Routine daily activities and commitments
13. Recently scheduled events
14. Upcoming scheduled events

Digital package

1. Cell phone: calls, chats, address book, GPS, photos, video.
2. Laptop/desktop: email, calls, chats, documents, address books, browser history, photos, video.
3. Personal websites: recent browser history, social network activity (e.g., Facebook, Twitter), blogs, dating websites, and other personal subscription websites.
4. Financial websites/payment history: stocks, mutual funds/401k, credit cards, and online banking.
5. Personal GPS device: recent trips, destinations, book-marked points of interest.

Residence package

1. Physical home address
2. .Location/condition of bedroom
3. Evidence of music/literature/personal interests
4. Personal correspondence
5. Personal sexual items/explicit material
6. Missing items
7. Signs of violence
8. Location/condition of personal vehicle
9. Hard-line phone calls (incoming and outgoing)
10. 911 calls and criminal history of residence

The investigator or profiler should spend time, when possible, with the victim's personal items, in the personal environments (hangouts, work, school, home/bedroom, etc.). Examine any available photo albums, diaries, or journals. Make note of music and literature preferences. Do this to find out who the victims seemed to believe they were, what they wanted everyone to perceived, and how they seemed to feel about their life in general.

Relationship package

1. Current and previous intimate or marital partner(s)
2. Current and previous family members
3. Current and previous household members
4. Current and previous friends

5. Current and previous coworkers/classmates
6. History of relationship counseling

Employment package

1. Educational background and history
2. Current occupations/job titles (many people have multiple employers)
3. Place of employment/work schedule/supervisor
4. Employment history
5. Work phone: calls, chats, address book, GPS, photos, video
6. Laptop/desktop: email, calls, chats, documents, address books, browser history, photos, video
7. Business GPS device: recent trips, destinations, book-marked points of interest
8. Business vehicle: logs, travel (times/destinations), GPS device
9. Business insurance policies

This list can be adapted for students, with the school as the employer, class schedule as work schedule, and teachers as supervisor, and so forth.

Financial package

1. Wallet/purse: contents, cards, personal items
2. Credit cards/history
3. Bank accounts/history
4. Property ownership (residences and vehicles)
5. Stocks/mutual funds/401k/retirement benefits
6. Insurance policies

Medical package

1. Current state of intoxication (alcohol and drug levels)
2. Current medical conditions (physical and mental)
3. History of serious medical conditions
4. Current medications (see purse, desk drawers, and medicine cabinets)
5. Current treatment regimes
6. Current treatment professionals
7. Recent medical appointments
8. Addictions (drugs, alcohol, or obsessive behavior)

Court package

1. Criminal history (active investigations, protection orders, arrests, warrants, convictions)
2. Civil court history (lawsuits, judgments, and role)
3. Witness history (previous depositions or testimony given in legal proceedings)
4. In-state and out-of-state records
5. Evidence of victim criminal activity during the crime
6. Evidence of ongoing victim criminal activity unrelated to the crime

These packages should be used to:

1. Compile a list of the victim's daily routines, habits, and activities.
2. Compile a complete list of victim family members with contact information.
3. Compile a complete list of victim family with contact information.
4. Compile a complete list of victim friends with contact information.
5. Compile a complete list of victim coworkers/schoolmates with contact information.
6. Create a timeline of events using witness statements, digital evidence, and physical evidence.

Everyone should be interviewed, as people with important information often do not come forward. Many well-meaning witnesses wait for someone to approach them out of ignorance with respect to how the investigative process works. Investigators must be proactive in this regard.

CREATING A TIMELINE: THE LAST 24 H

The general purpose here is to familiarize the forensic victimologist with the last known activities of the victim and subsequently determine, if possible, how a given victim got to a place and time where an offender was able to access him or her. The picture needs to be built from the ground up. It is a rewarding and illuminating process that should not be overlooked.

A good approach to creating this timeline of locations and events includes at least the following steps:

- Compile all witness data.
- Compile all available forensic evidence.
- Compile all of the police/media crime scene photographs and video.
- Compile all security stills and video covering the crime scene and any paths taken by the victim or offender to or from it.
- Create a linear timeline of events and locations.
- Create a map of the victim's route for the 24 h before the attack, as detailed as possible.
- Physically walk through the victim's last 24 h using the map and forensic evidence as a guide.
- Document expected background elements of the route in terms of vehicles, people, activities, professionals, and so on for the time leading up to, during and after the victim was acquired. It is possible that the offender is, or was masquerading as, one of those expected elements.

Attempt to determine the following:

- The point at which the offender acquired the victim.
- The place where the offender attacked the victim.
- How well the attack location can be seen from any surrounding locations.
- Whether or not the offender would need to be familiar with the area to know of this specific location or get to it.

- Whether or not knowledge of the route would require or indicate presurveillance.
- Whether or not this route placed the victim at higher or lower exposure to an attack.
- Whether or not the acquisition of the victim on that route placed the offender at higher or lower exposure to identification or apprehension.

CONCLUSION

Forensic victimology is concerned with the investigation and examination of particular victims alleged to have suffered specific crimes, which is an idiographic form of knowledge building. It is intended to serve both investigative and forensic goals, which are very different in scope and reliability with respect to findings. To reduce bias and achieve a minimum threshold of reliability, the forensic victimologist must request a sufficient amount of victim information, determine its reliability, and perform examinations in accordance with the practice standards provided. A key feature of this is an applied understanding of the scientific method and an emphasis on theory falsification.

Forensic victimology assists in establishing the nature of victim exposure to harm or loss. Victim exposure can be categorized in terms of *lifestyle exposure* and *situational exposure*. Victim *lifestyle exposure* is concerned with studying the *frequency* of potentially harmful elements experienced by the victim and resulting from the victim's usual environment and personal traits, as well as past choices. Victim *situational* or *incident exposure* refers to the amount of actual exposure or vulnerability experienced by the victim to harm, resulting from the environment and personal traits *at the time of victimization*.

To use victimology effectively in the course of an investigation, a complete picture of the victim history is required. Ignoring victim history, in part or whole, creates gaps in the investigative and factual record that will make victim-related interpretation incomplete, if not inaccurate.

ENDNOTES

1. This chapter has been adapted from material originally published in *Criminal Profiling: An Introduction to Behavioral Evidence Analysis, fourth Ed* (Turvey, 2011).
2. See generally Yagoub (2016).

REFERENCES

Hazelwood, R. (1995). Analyzing rape and profiling the offender. In R. R. Hazelwood, & A. W. Burgess (Eds.), *Practical aspects of rape investigation: A multidisciplinary approach* (2nd ed.). New York: CRC Press.

Jamerson, C. (2009). Forensic nursing: approaching the victim as a crime scene. In W. Petherick, & B. Turvey (Eds.), *Forensic victimology*. San Diego: Elsevier Science.

National Institute of Justice. (September 2004). *A national protocol for sexual assault medical forensic examinations*. Washington, DC: U.S. Department of Justice, Office on Violence Against Women. NCJ 206554.

NIJ (National Institute of Justice). (1999). *Death investigation: A guide for the scene investigator. Research Report NCJ 167568*. Washington, DC: NIJ.

Savino, J., & Turvey, B. (2012). *Rape investigation handbook* (2nd ed.). Boston: Elsevier Science.

Singer, S. (1981). Homogenous victim-offender population: a review and some research implications. *Journal of Criminal Law and Criminology, 72*, 779–788.

Turvey, B. (2011). *Criminal profiling: An introduction to behavioral evidence analysis* (4th ed.). San Diego: Elsevier Science.

Turvey, B. (2012). *Forensic victimology* (2nd ed.). San Diego: Elsevier Science.

UN. (2014). *Latin American model protocol for the investigation of gender-related killings of women (femicide/feminicide), United Nations high commissioner for human rights, United Nations entity for gender equality and the empowerment of women (UN women)*. http://lac.unwomen.org/en/digiteca/publicaciones/2014/10/modelo-de-protocolo.

Weston, P., & Wells, K. (1974). *Criminal investigation: basic perspectives* (2nd ed.). Englewood Cliffs, NJ: Prentice-Hall.

Yagoub, M. (February 11, 2016). *Why does Latin America have the world's highest female murder rates?* Insight Crime. http://www.insightcrime.org/news-analysis/why-does-latin-america-have-the-world-s-highest-female-murder-rates.

CHAPTER 8

The Sexual Assault Examination

Brent E. Turvey[1], Charla Jamerson[2]
Forensic Criminology Institute, Sitka, Alaska, United States and Aguascalientes, Mexico[1];
Forensic Nurse, Fayetteville, AR, United States[2]

CHAPTER OUTLINE

The Role of Reconstruction	182
The "Team"	183
Forensic Nursing	187
Time Constraints	188
Consent Forms	189
The Intake Form	191
Sexual Assault Examination Protocols	192
History	193
Rationale	193
Collecting History	195
Physical Examination: Head to Toe	197
NIJ Guidelines: Forensic Medical Examination and Evidence Collection Procedures	197
Full Body Photos	204
Physical Injuries	204
Bruise and Other Injury Patterns	205
Inner Thighs	206
Physical Restraint and Bindings	206
Hands and Forearms	206
Neck	207
Knees	209
Breasts	209
Aging Bruises	210
Genital Examination	210
Evidence of Sexual Activity	211
Semen and Sperm	212
Saliva	213
Fecal Matter	213
Condoms	213

Clothing 214
False Positives: Conditions That Mimic Abuse 215
Toxicology 216
    Mental Incapacity 216
    Substance Abuse 217
Presentation of Findings 217
Endnotes 218
References 218

> *A lot people when they hear 'rape' they think gruesome and lots of injuries. And it's not always like that. In fact it is common to not find any injuries. So just because there are no physical injuries does not mean it didn't happen.*
> **Dr. Lorna Bell, MCG Health, Georgia (Coyle, 2011)**

In cases of sexual assault, law enforcement investigators are responsible for conducting the criminal investigation, gathering evidence, and developing suspects. However, forensic examiners are responsible for conducting the scientific investigation into the physical evidence. What they find, and are willing to document, shapes the foundation of law enforcement and prosecutorial efforts.

However, because of the sensitive and often political nature of sexual assault casework, roles are often confused; political pressure increases; and evidence can go uncollected or ignored.

The purpose of this chapter is to provide the forensic investigator with an applied understanding of the variety of physical evidence that must be collected from the bodies of complainants and suspects in cases of alleged sexual assault, to ensure the most objective and comprehensive investigative and forensic results effort. This will provide them with the necessary background to be comfortable discussing the examination with victims when questions arise. It will further help them to understand how this kind of evidence is collected, evaluated, and interpreted by forensic scientists,[1] to utilize it more effectively in their investigations.

THE ROLE OF RECONSTRUCTION

Crime reconstruction is determination of the actions and events involved in the commission of a crime by forensic scientists (Chisum & Turvey, 2011). It is an objective process that requires a formal scientific background, an education in the forensic sciences, and specialized training in various forensic techniques. Reconstructionists are subsequently required to demonstrate the scientific basis for their findings in written reports and then be capable of explaining what they mean under oath in a court of law.

The purpose of crime reconstruction is to establish what did and did not happen during an event by virtue of an impartial examination of the physical evidence. This can aid the efforts of law enforcement, and the courts, tremendously. As explained in Boland, McDermott, and Ryan (2007, p. 110):

The fundamental role of a forensic scientist is to help those who address the burdensome issue of guilt or innocence in a court of law…

A large percentage of crimes against the person, dealt with by forensic science laboratories, are crimes of sexual assault… In these cases, finding semen and in fact getting a matching DNA profile, may offer no additional evidential value to the case. Other examinations, such as damage interpretation, possibly indicating a struggle or that force was used, may be critical. This analysis may be used to corroborate or refute a particular scenario and indeed, in a small, but significant number of cases, damage interpretation may be critical in preventing false allegations proceeding to prosecution.

Forensic scientists are not allowed to assume facts for the purposes of a reconstruction: facts must be established. This may seem redundant, as *facts* are generally defined as verifiable and undisputable circumstances or information. However, it is not uncommon for the investigative assumptions and theories generated in early in a case to be treated as facts and remain uninvestigated or unexamined. This is particularly true of witness statements that favor prevailing or expedient investigative theories—such as the complaint of a sexual assault. The uncritical acceptance of any statement, without an assessment of its internal integrity or evidentiary corroboration, provides an insufficient basis for the reliable reconstruction of events. A scientific examination investigates the evidence to learn the facts, seeking to support or refute the elements of crime related behavior. It does not assume them.

The reconstruction of a sexual assault is accomplished by a comprehensive assessment of the crime scene investigation; interviews with complainants, the accused, and any witnesses; and the results of victim and suspect sexual assault examination protocols. It is not accomplished by uncritically accepting the statements of any one party over another.

THE "TEAM"

Many states have come to recognize that sexual assault cases are distinct enough to warrant suggesting, or mandating, the organization of response teams. This is typically in the form of an edict from the State Department of Public Safety or the State Attorney General's Office. These guidelines dictate the duties befalling distinct team members, with clear tasks that are deliberately assigned. The hope being that everyone will understand what they are supposed to do and that evidence is less likely to be missed.

These different "team members," joined by state funding but separated by leadership, training, and mandate, are meant to work together toward a common goal. They are meant to share information, ensure professionalism, and facilitate criminal prosecutions. The team concept associated with state mandates is associated with the investigation and prosecution of sex crimes by state and local employees. It does not mention the work of private forensic examiners, investigators, or attorneys, all of which are necessary for achieving justice in an adversarial system. As explained in NIJ (2013), the state mandated roles are as follows (pp. 2–3):

Advocates may be involved in initial victim contact (via 24-hour hotline or face-to-face meetings); offer victims advocacy, support, crisis intervention, information, language assistance services, including interpreters, and referrals before, during, and after the exam process; and help ensure that victims have transportation to and from the exam site. They often provide comprehensive, longer term services designed to aid victims in addressing any needs related to the assault, including but not limited to counseling, legal (civil, criminal, and immigration), and medical system advocacy.

Law enforcement representatives (e.g., 911 dispatchers, patrol officers, officers who process crime scene evidence, detectives, and investigators) respond to initial complaints, work to enhance victims' safety, arrange for victims' transportation to and from the exam site as needed, interview victims in a language they understand, collect evidence from the scene, coordinate collection and delivery of evidence to designated labs or law enforcement facilities, interview suspects, and conduct other investigative activities (such as interviewing suspects and witnesses in a language they understand, requesting crime lab analyses, reviewing medical and lab reports, preparing and executing search and arrest warrants, writing reports, and presenting the case to a prosecutor).

Health care providers assess patients for acute medical needs and provide stabilization, treatment, and/or consultation. Ideally, sexual assault forensic examiners perform the medical forensic exam, gather information for the medical forensic history, collect and document forensic evidence, and document pertinent physical findings from patients. They offer information, treatment, and referrals for sexually transmitted infections (STIs), and other nonacute medical concerns; assess pregnancy risk and discuss treatment options with the patient, including reproductive health services; and testify in court if needed. They coordinate with advocates to ensure patients are offered crisis intervention, support, and advocacy before, during, and after the exam process and encourage use of other victim services. They may follow up with patients for medical and forensic purposes. Other health care personnel who may be involved include, but are not limited to, emergency medical technicians, staff at hospital emergency departments, gynecologists, surgeons, private physicians, health care interpreters, and/or local, tribal, campus, or military health services personnel.

Forensic scientists analyze forensic evidence and provide results of the analysis to investigators and/or prosecutors. They also may testify at trial regarding the results of their analysis.

Prosecutors determine if there is sufficient evidence for prosecution and, if so, prosecute the case. They should be available to consult with first responders as needed. A few jurisdictions involve prosecutors more actively, paging them after initial contact and having them respond to the exam site so that they can become familiar with the case and help guide the investigation.

The presentation of these roles by National Institute of Justice (NIJ) makes clear, and necessarily so, that investigators collect and document evidence, while forensic scientists examine and interpret it. Otherwise there is role confusion, and even the potential for bias.

The *Alaska Council on Domestic Violence and Sexual Assault*, for example, offers the following guidelines with respect to "team" structure, to include separation of advocacy, law enforcement, and health-care roles (CDVSA, 2011, pp. 1–4)[2]:

Team Structure

A. Roles of team members:

Each team member has a unique role. However, circumstances may require flexibility in serving the needs of a victim beyond those suggested below.

1. Victim advocate (hereafter referred to as "advocate")

   Advocates provide immediate and ongoing support to the victim such as:
   - listening to the victim
   - informing the victim of her or his rights including confidentiality and payment
   - answering questions about the SART process
   - being present for the victim
   - identifying resources and options for immediate needs and long-term support (i.e., child care, food, transportation, safe shelter, and medical and court accompaniment)
   - assisting with creating a safety plan
   - assisting with all other duties normally associated with victim advocacy

   Advocates do not:
   - participate in the gathering of evidence, fact-finding, or investigating of the assault
   - provide an opinion on the merits of the case
   - conduct the medical forensic or law enforcement interviews
   - generally testify in court

2. Law enforcement: Law enforcement officers generally perform the following functions:
   - being responsible for the immediate safety needs of the victim
   - interviewing the victim
   - investigating the crime
   - conducting or arranging for a forensic exam of the suspect when necessary
   - collecting and preserving evidence
   - identifying, arresting, and/or referring charges on the suspect
   - writing a report

- participating in court proceedings
  Law enforcement officers do not:
- conduct a complete victim medical forensic exam
- actively advocate on behalf of the victim

3. Health-care provider: Health-care providers generally perform the following services:
   - assessing, diagnosing, and treating injuries and conditions related to the assault
   - offering health-care information and referrals as needed
   - identifying, documenting, collecting, and preserving forensic evidence during the medical forensic exam in a way to ensure the chain of custody
   - testifying in court as needed
   Health-care providers do not:
   - investigate the crime
   - provide victim advocacy services

B. Training recommendations.

Each team member is expected to have training in their field. It is also recommended that each team member receives general team training, specialized instruction, and practical experience responding to sexual assault.

1. General team training

   It is strongly recommended that team members share information regarding their respective roles and responsibilities to ensure a victim-centered, multidisciplinary team approach. The roles and responsibilities include:
   - confidentiality as it applies to each team member
   - victim-centered advocacy
   - use of the Sexual Assault Evidence Collection Kit (see description below)
   - the forensic interview
   - investigation by law enforcement
   - evidence collection
   - the medical forensic exam

   It is also recommended that each team member learns about the following topics as related to sexual assault:
   - the criminal/civil legal process
   - responses to impact of trauma on victim
   - diversity and cultural awareness
   - disabilities
   - substance abuse
   - mental health
   - sexually transmitted infections
   - pregnancy
   - self-care for team members

   For further information about training or assistance in creating your community's Sexual Assault Response Team, contact the Council on Domestic Violence and Sexual Assault (CDVSA) at (907) 465-4356.

2. Suggested specialized training
   Advocates: Familiarity with Alaska sexual assault statutes and civil legal options, support groups, long-term follow-up and support, special populations, and ways of providing services without revictimization
   Law enforcement officers: Familiarity with Alaska sexual assault statutes, sexual assault evidence collection, interview/interrogation techniques specific to sexual assault, and preplanned recorded conversations (Glass warrants)
   Health-care providers: Minimum of 40 h sexual assault nurse examiner (SANE)/sexual assault forensic examiner (SAFE) training and familiarity with standards of practice

The recommended levels of training here would barely qualify anyone as an expert in these areas, so this must be acknowledged at the outset. Advocates are not necessarily experts in mental health; law enforcement agents are not necessarily experts in sex crimes investigation; and health-care providers do not generally specialize in sexual assault cases. Basic training is required to respond with some level of competence, but experts and specialists must be used to facilitate forensic interpretations.

In fact, these guidelines are written precisely because they are violated so often by agencies, and individuals, that are poorly trained. Advocates can often be found improperly interfering with investigations and victim access; investigators improperly advocate for, and even protect, the victims they are sympathetic toward; and health-care providers see themselves as investigators and advocates in almost the same breath, interfering as they can to manipulate results toward a preferred outcome (e.g., failing to take a history; failing to take a victim toxicology; or editing medical information from reports). This kind of cross-contamination of roles and responsibilities is avoided by forensic professionals and guarded against at every possible turn. This is to avoid the ethical conflicts of interest which are obvious to even the most junior professional—yet relied upon as the basis for all too many criminal prosecutions.

FORENSIC NURSING

In cases of alleged sexual assault, each reporting victim must be given a sexual examination to identify, document, and collect any physical evidence related to their attack. This effort is intended to help corroborate their version of events and to assist with the identification of potential suspects. Should they refuse, the opportunity to collect this evidence will be lost.

Suspects should be given a sexual assault examination as well; however, their circumstances are much different. In any case, the professionals charged with conducting these examinations are forensic nurses, attached to either a hospital emergency room or specialized clinic.

Forensic nursing is a subspecialty of forensic science where the science of nursing is applied to the resolution of legal matters. It involves patient care in the context of evidence documentation, collection, and preservation efforts. Consequently, *forensic nurses* are registered nurses with additional education and training in forensic science and evidence collection.

The role of the forensic nurse is to function as an objective and scientific finder of fact and to utilize scientific principles and methodology in the recognition, documentation, collection, and interpretation of physical evidence related to diseases, injuries, and crimes that may be suffered by victims. In doing so, the forensic nurse operates with the understanding that those examined in a forensic context are the potential extension of a crime scene. Subsequently, the forensic nurse must serve as a forensic investigator; as an educator to victims and the community; and as an expert witness within the legal system.

TIME CONSTRAINTS

Because time, the environment, and individual body chemistry all conspire to degrade the physical evidence, the sooner that a forensic examination can be performed on the victim the better. In fact, most jurisdictions allow no more than 72 hours between the alleged crime and any evidence collection efforts performed. Consequently, forensic nurses must be available to work when crime occurs and to respond to a case within approximately an hour. This means being on call essentially 24 hours a day, 7 days a week. Occasionally there will be extenuating circumstances—such as a victim being held in captivity by a perpetrator or delayed reporting under some circumstances—that make a longer interval between crime and examination acceptable. These time constraints vary from state to state and are often determined by the state office of the attorney general.

These concerns are echoed in the NIJ published guidelines, *A National Protocol for Sexual Assault Medical Forensic Examinations* (2004, p. 67; consistent with NIJ, 2013, pp. 73–74) which offers the following recommendations regarding evidence collection and its context:

> *Recognize the importance of gathering information for the medical forensic history, examining patients, and documenting exam findings, separate from collecting evidence. Examiners should obtain the medical forensic history as appropriate, examine patients, and document findings when patients are willing, whether or not evidence is gathered for the sexual assault evidence collection kit. The history and documentation of exam findings can help in determining if and where there may be evidence to collect and in addressing patients' medical needs. In addition, they can be invaluable in and of themselves to an investigation and prosecution if a report is made. It is also important to document patients' demeanor during the exam process (e.g., crying, shaking, or showing signs of*

upset) and their statements made related to the assault, because if the case is reported, this information could be admitted as evidence at trial.

Examine patients promptly to minimize the loss of evidence.

Evidence can be lost from the body and clothing through a number of mechanisms. For example, degradation of some seminal fluid components can occur within body orifices, semen can drain from the vagina or wash from the mouth, sperm can lose motility, bodily fluids can get washed away, and dried secretions and foreign materials can fall from the body and clothing. Prompt examination also helps to quickly identify patients' medical needs and concerns.

Recognize that evidence may be available beyond 72 hours after the assault. *In recent history, 72 hours after a sexual assault has been considered a guideline to use as an outside limit for obtaining evidence for the evidence collection kit. Research and evidence analyses indicate that some evidence may be available beyond this time period. For instance, sperm might be found inside the cervix after 72 hours and urine may reveal traces of certain drugs up to 96 hours after ingestion. Some examples of situations where evidence may be found even after considerable periods of time include when patients complain of pain or bleeding, have visible injuries, or have not washed themselves since the assault, or where there is a history of significant trauma from the assault. Some jurisdictions have extended their standard cutoff time beyond 72 hours (e.g., to 5 days or 1 week).*

Due to the stability of DNA and sensitivity of tests, advancing DNA technologies also continue to extend time limits. These technologies are even enabling forensic scientists to analyze stored evidence from crimes that occurred years before. Such breakthroughs demonstrate the importance of collecting all possible evidence.

As suggested, forensic nurses are often a "frontline" professional with respect to making victim contact subsequent to the commission of a violent crime. This is primarily because of how victims enter the justice system. In many cases, victims will report their assault directly to the police. Or they may show up at a local emergency room or medical clinic seeking treatment for their injuries.

Once the report to the police has been made and the alleged victim arrives, the forensic nurse should begin the examination. It starts with obtaining consents, biographical intake information, a medical history, and finally a history of events leading up to and surrounding the crime. The same protocol must be followed in every case to avoid missed background information and potential evidence.

CONSENT FORMS

Once the complainant arrives at the exam location and the forensic nurse has made their introductions, it is necessary to obtain informed consent. Then they can become a patient. Forensic examiners are best off if they begin by explaining the entire forensic medical examination procedure, along with the necessity of evidence collection, to patients, no matter what their age. This will empower patients, involve them in the process, and give them an opportunity to think of and ask questions.

Consent to treat must be obtained before any evidence collection or treatment takes place. This is in keeping with NIJ (2004, p. 4); also consistent with NIJ (2013), which stipulates:

> *Prior to starting the exam and before each procedure, describe what is entailed and its purpose to patients. Be sure that communication/language needs are met and information is conveyed in a manner that patients will understand. After providing this information, seek patients' permission to proceed and respect their right to decline any part of the exam. However, follow exam facility and jurisdictional policy regarding minors and adults who are incompetent to give consent…*
>
> *Patients should understand the full nature of their consent to each exam procedure. By presenting them with relevant information, they are in a position to make an informed decision about whether to accept or decline a procedure. However, they should be aware of the impact of declining a particular procedure, as it may negatively affect the quality of care, the usefulness of evidence collection, and, ultimately, any criminal investigation and/or prosecution. They should understand that declining a particular procedure might also be used to discredit them in court. If a procedure is declined, reasons why should be documented if the patient provides such information.*

Consent forms may vary from one institution to another, but often include consent to conduct a forensic medical examination, including the collection of evidence, urine specimen with drug testing as needed, collection of blood for lab work as needed, use of a colposcope to assist with injury identification, forensic photography (colposcope and digital photography), use of recording equipment, and consent for emergency contraception. If the victim is a minor, then the parent or guardian will need to sign in his or her place.

This is a good time to take stock of the fact that not every victim will react the same way to the procedures involved in the forensic medical exam, let alone the prospect. As explained in the NIJ (2004, p. 28); consistent with NIJ (2013, p. 30), victims' perceptions and reactions may be influenced by a variety of circumstances:

> *Recognize that the medical forensic exam is an interactive process that must be adapted to the needs and circumstances of each patient. Patients' experiences during the crime and the exam process, as well as their postassault needs, may be affected by multiple factors, such as:*

- Age;
- Gender and/or gender identity;
- Physical health history and current status;
- Mental health history and current status;
- Disability;
- Language needs and communication modalities;
- Ethnic and cultural beliefs and practices;

- Religious and spiritual beliefs and practices;
- Economic status, including homelessness;
- Immigration and refugee status;
- Sexual orientation;
- Military status;
- History of previous victimization;
- Past experience with the criminal justice system;
- Whether the assault involved drugs and/or alcohol;
- Prior relationship with the suspect, if any;
- Whether they were assaulted by an assailant who was in an authority position over them;
- Whether the assault was part of a broader continuum of violence and/or oppression (e.g., intimate partner and family violence, gang violence, hate crimes, war crimes, and trafficking);
- Where the assault occurred;
- Whether they sustained physical injuries from the assault and the severity of the injuries;
- Whether they were engaged in illegal activities at the time of the assault (e.g., voluntary use of illegal drugs or underage drinking) or have outstanding criminal charges;
- Whether they were involved in activities prior to the assault that traditionally generate victim blaming or self-blaming (e.g., drinking alcohol prior to the assault or agreeing to go to the assailant's home);
- Whether birth control was used during the assault (e.g., victims may already have been on a form of birth control or the assailant may have used a condom);
- Capacity to cope with trauma and the level of support available from families and friends;
- The importance they place on the needs of their extended families in the aftermath of the assault;
- Whether they have dependents who require care during the exam, were traumatized by the assault, or who may be affected by decisions patients make during the exam process;
- Community/cultural attitudes about sexual assault, its victims, and offenders; and
- Frequency of sexual assault and other violence in the community and historical responsiveness of the local justice system, health care systems, and community service agencies.

Forensic nurses and other assisting staff are admonished to be sensitive about these factors in the process of obtaining consent, as well as during the exam itself. A judgmental, coercive, or inflexible approach is not advised, nor is it professional.

THE INTAKE FORM

The intake form establishes the informational foundation upon which to start prioritizing different aspects of an eventual forensic medical exam. It also acts as a valuable face sheet, giving case basics at a glance for future reference. Intake information includes biographical data about the patient, those involved in the case, and a thumbnail sketch of the crime and the alleged perpetrator. Additional in-depth information is gathered during the forensic interview process or during the medicolegal examination.

Specifically, the intake form establishes the following baseline information:

1. The time and date of the exam.
2. The name of the forensic nurse examiner and anyone who assisted.
3. The patient's name and other identifying information.
4. How to reach the patient if needed, including contact numbers and mailing address.
5. The patient's family and/or guardian information.
6. The patient's insurance information.
7. Date of referral and referral source (hospital, clinic, law enforcement, department of health, etc.).
8. Collaborating law enforcement agencies responsible for investigating the case.
9. Suspect information; this may or may not be available.
10. Brief history of sexual assault exams; some victims receive more than one medical examination related to their injuries, the forensic medical exam being secondary.

It is also necessary that the intake form documents the name of the person providing the patient's history to the examiner and his or her relationship to the patient (such as a mother or father if the patient is a minor). With this information documented, anyone reviewing the file at a later time will be aware of whether the history came directly from the victim. This may go to the credibility of the information provided at some later date.

These guidelines are consistent with the NIJ (2004, 2013).

Once these intake issues have been addressed or attended, the sexual assault examination can begin.

SEXUAL ASSAULT EXAMINATION PROTOCOLS

This section will discuss the purpose, procedures, and evidence interpretations involved in a sexual assault examination. In general, the guidelines provided in NIJ (2004, 2013), regarding "Forensic Medical Examination and Evidence Collection Procedures," should be followed. Reconstructionists should read these and become familiar with them. It should not need to be explained that both the complainant and the suspect must undergo the same level of forensic sexual assault examination. It is, after all, an investigation to determine the facts, and not a one-sided procedure intended to screen only for evidence that supports the complainant's version of events.

HISTORY

When a patient (a.k.a. complainant) presents for a sexual assault examination, documenting the history of the event as well as any medical/surgical history is the first step of the evidentiary process. Taking a good history is probably the single most important task in the work-up. Reliable patient information lays the foundation for a thorough physical exam and subsequent evidence collection.

Components of the history assist the examiner in reaching a differential diagnosis or otherwise distinguishing one finding from another. For example, a patient may present stating that he or she was sexually assaulted. They may also have a history of illness or an injury that is present but unrelated to the sexual assault. Differentiating and documenting those kinds of findings are significant to the case and to the patient's continuum of care and referral for additional medical services.

Rationale

The importance of taking a history as part of a patient examination is universally understood as best practice for just about any of the helping professions. This includes medical and mental health specialists of every kind, who accept that what presents in a given case is a reflection of, and can be affected by, past events. Moreover, they are mindful that any diagnosis or treatment must take into account the changes brought about by past treatment efforts. In addition, both medical and mental health professionals are trained to recognize behavioral indicators of those presenting false symptoms (e.g., drug-seeking behavior and malingering). Consequently, the failure of medical and mental health practitioners to take an adequate history prior to diagnosis and treatment efforts is generally considered a form of malpractice.

The importance of gathering victim background information is understood within the forensic professions as well. Without it, there is no context for criminal complaints or for the interpretation of the evidence gathered in relation to them. For example, medical examiners, coroners, and their respective death investigators are meant to understand this, as reflected in the NIJ manual, *Death Investigation: A Guide for the Scene Investigator* (NIJ, 1999, p. 39):

> *Establishing a decedent profile includes documenting a discovery history and circumstances surrounding the discovery. The basic profile will dictate subsequent levels of investigation, jurisdiction, and authority. The focus (breadth/depth) of further investigation is dependent on this information.*

Sex crimes investigators agree, as reflected in the importance of gathering information related to complainant criminal, medical, and mental health background prior to conducting formal interviews provided in Chapter 7.

Patient history is also a required component of sexual assault examinations, performed by medical specialists as part of their dual treatment and evidence-gathering mission. As explained in Jamerson (2009, p. 114):

> ...intake and history information is necessary to competently inform and prioritize the physical examination... Each patient is unique; any treatment and forensic efforts should be individually crafted to his or her particular condition and history.
>
> Medical history[a] is a significant component of the evaluation in the context of any suspected sexual assault, child molestation, or domestic assault. It provides a baseline of information for the examiner so that recent trauma and injury can be discriminated from past conditions and events. Therefore, it must cover all body systems. In this way, the examiner can identify any acute or chronic problems, as well as any history of past injury or surgeries. It also informs the nature, extent, and sequence of the forensic medical exam. A failure to document and report medical background information prevents informed medical treatment and leaves the forensic examiner without the proper context for accurate interpretations. Ultimately, conducting an accurate forensic medical examination in the absence of a patient medical history is not possible.

This also specifically includes (p. 117–120) "recent consensual sexual activity," "postassault activities," "history of drug abuse," history of mental health and behavioral problems, and history of STDs.

Inherent in these guidelines is the understanding that evidence and injury observed in relation to the alleged victim or crime scene may not be the result of criminal activity. Such evidence or injury may in fact be the result of some previous and unrelated activity or event. For example, a complainant may present with extensive bruising of the shins and may not clearly recall their origins. Such injuries might be related to a sexual assault, depending on the events described. Or, upon conducting a history, the forensic examiner may learn that the complainant played a soccer game in the days preceding the alleged attack, in which her shins were repeatedly kicked. The forensic examiner interpreting these injuries without the relevant history could improperly make the assumption that they must be related to a sexual assault.

It is also important to note that investigators and forensic examiners will not know what features of complainant history are relevant to an examination until well after they have begun their work. In one case it may be a question of toxicology. In another it may be which bedroom of the home they occupied. In yet another there may be a question of sexual habits, preferences, or diseases. All of these issues and related details have turned into cases, despite seeming irrelevant or minor at the outset. Each victim is different, each case is different, and, therefore less victim history is not better.

---

[a]*Medical history* is the information about a patient gathered by a health care professional for the purposes of making examinations, providing treatment, and rendering a diagnosis. It commonly involves asking patients questions regarding the current and former state of their physical and mental health. Without this background information, examinations, treatments, and diagnoses are at best uninformed, and at worst potentially lethal.

Collecting History

Collecting history from the complainant, as well as collateral sources (e.g., friends, family members, other witnesses), is necessary to ensure that the most complete and accurate information is relied upon during forensic examinations. As provided in NIJ (2004, pp. 83–84); consistent with NIJ (2013):

> The specific questions asked of patients by examiners for the medical forensic history vary from one jurisdiction to the next, as do forms used to record the history. However, the following information should be sought routinely from patients:
>
> 1. *Date and time of the sexual assault(s):* It is essential to know the period of time that has elapsed between the assault and the collection of evidence. Evidence collection may be directed by the time interval since the assault. Interpretation of both the physical exam and evidence analysis may be influenced by the time interval between the assault and the exam.
> 2. *Pertinent patient medical history:* The interpretation of physical findings may be affected by medical data related to menstruation, recent anal–genital injuries, surgeries, or diagnostic procedures, blood-clotting history, and other pertinent medical conditions or treatment.
> 3. *Recent consensual sexual activity:* The sensitivity of DNA analysis makes it important to gather information about recent consensual intercourse, whether it was anal, vaginal, and/or oral and whether a condom was used. A trace amount of semen or other bodily fluid may be identified that is not associated with the crime. Once identified, it may need to be associated with a consensual partner, and then used for elimination purposes to aid in interpreting evidence.
> 4. *Postassault activities of patients:* The quality of evidence is affected both by actions taken by patients and the passage of time. It is critical to know what, if any, activities were performed prior to the examination (e.g., have patients urinated, defecated, wiped genitals or the body, douched, removed/inserted a tampon/sanitary pad/diaphragm, used oral rinse/gargled, washed, brushed teeth, ate or drank, smoked, used drugs, or changed clothing?).
> 5. *Assault-related patient history:* Information such as whether there was memory loss, lapse of consciousness, vomiting, nongenital injury, pain and/or bleeding, and anal-genital injury, pain, and/or bleeding can direct evidence collection and medical care. Collecting toxicology samples is recommended if there was either loss of memory or lapse of consciousness, according to jurisdictional policy.
> 6. *Suspect information (if known):* Forensic scientists seek evidence on crosstransfer of evidence among patients, suspects, and crime scenes. The gender and number of suspects may offer guidance to types and amounts of foreign materials that might be found on patients' bodies and clothing. Suspect information gathered during this history should be limited to that which will guide the

exam and forensic evidence collection. Detailed questions about suspects are asked during the investigative interview.
7. *Nature of the physical assault(s):* Information about the physical surroundings of the assault(s) (e.g., indoors, outdoors, car, alley, room, rug, dirt, mud, or grass) and methods employed by suspects is crucial to the detection, collection, and analysis of physical evidence. Methods may include, but are not limited to, use of weapons (threatened and/or injuries inflicted), physical blows, grabbing, holding, pinching, biting, using physical restraints, strangulation, burns (thermal and/or chemical), threat(s) of harm, and involuntary ingestion of alcohol/drugs. Knowing whether suspects may have been injured during the assault may be useful when recovering evidence from patients (e.g., blood) or from suspects (e.g., bruising, fingernail marks, or bite marks).
8. *Description of the sexual assault(s):* An accurate but brief description is crucial to detecting, collecting, and analyzing physical evidence. The description should include any:
   - Penetration of genitalia (e.g., vulva, hymen, and/or vagina of female patient), however slight;
   - Penetration of the anal opening, however slight;
   - Oral contact with genitals (of patients by suspects or of suspects by patients);
   - Other contact with genitals (of patients by suspects or of suspects by patients);
   - Oral contact with the anus (of patients by suspects or of suspects by patients);
   - Nongenital act(s) (e.g., licking, kissing, suction injury, and biting);
   - Other act(s) including use of objects;
   - If known, whether ejaculation occurred and location(s) of ejaculation (e.g., mouth, vagina, genitals, anus/rectum, body surface, on clothing, on bedding, or other); and
   - Use of contraception or lubricants.

These questions require specific and sometimes detailed answers. Some may be difficult for patients to answer. Examiners should explain that these questions are asked during every sexual assault medical forensic exam. They should also explain why each question is being asked. This information is essential for the forensic nurse to gather before starting the forensic medical examination, as some preexisting conditions can mimic or be confused for abuse (i.e., skin conditions, nonviolent or sports-related injuries unrelated to assault, etc.) and will need to be clearly differentiated. Also, having an awareness of the medical history guides the clinician in making necessary referrals for other problems that may be assessed during the examination.

This information is essential for the forensic examiner to gather before starting any examination, as some preexisting conditions mimic or be confused for abuse (e.g., skin conditions, allergic reactions, medical conditions, nonviolent or sports-related injuries unrelated to assault) and will need to be clearly differentiated. Also, having an awareness of the medical history guides the clinician in making necessary referrals for other problems that may be assessed during the examination.

Ultimately, the purpose of taking a history is to inform collection efforts and eventual interpretations of findings. As stated in the NIJ (2004, p. 8), forensic examiners must "avoid basing decisions about whether to collect evidence on a patient's characteristics or circumstances (e.g., the patient has used illegal drugs)." Too often, there is a failure to document evidence, including areas of noninjury and history, because the examiner is either uncomfortable, or preferential, with respect to their patient. In cases of extreme bias, there may even be attempts to suppress or conceal such evidence. This is professionally unacceptable. Each patient must undergo the same level of examination and documentation—there can be no exceptions. In particular, the forensic examiner must comprehend and acknowledge importance of history to the integrity of their examinations, interpretations, and subsequent court testimony.

PHYSICAL EXAMINATION: HEAD TO TOE

A head-to-toe physical exam is the next step in the process. This allows the examiner to conduct a general survey of the patient's body and assess normal versus abnormal findings, as well as inflicted versus accidental injuries the patient may have sustained. During this assessment, the examiner should take scrupulous notes of where injury is found and where it is not. They must pay particular attention to the locations and orientation of injuries, injury patterns, and any plausible injury mechanisms. Concurrently, the examiner needs to maintain clinical awareness of whether a given injury, or its absence, is consistent with the stated history of events (Giardino & Giardino, 2003).

NIJ GUIDELINES: FORENSIC MEDICAL EXAMINATION AND EVIDENCE COLLECTION PROCEDURES

The NIJ (2004, 2013) guidelines regarding the Forensic Medical Examination and Evidence Collection Procedures should be learned by every sex crimes investigator.[3] This will help them understand what must be done to complete a thorough and investigatively useful sexual assault examination. It will also provide them with a guide to what must be requested from those who are less than experienced or knowledgeable about the actual scope of these exams. They are as follows (NIJ, 2004, pp. 89–99):

> 6. Exam and Evidence Collection Procedures
>
> *Recommendations at a glance for health care providers to facilitate the exam and evidence collection: ...*
>
> **Recognize the forensic purpose of the exam.** *During the exam, examiners methodically document physical findings and facilitate the collection of evidence from patients' bodies and clothing. The findings in the exam and collected evidence often provide information to help reconstruct the details about the events in question in an objective and scientific manner. Of course, health care needs and*

concerns of patients may be presented in the course of the exam that should be addressed prior to discharge. However, patients must understand that the exam does not provide routine medical care. For example, a pap smear will not be done during the female pelvic exam. (This chapter focuses on forensic components of the exam. Other chapters in the protocol discuss more fully medical and other related needs and concerns of patients.)

Collect as much evidence from patients as possible, guided by the scope of informed consent, the medical forensic history, exam findings, and instructions in the evidence collection kit. *Evidence collected during the exam mainly includes biological and trace evidence. To reconstruct the events in question, evidence collected is used in two potential ways in sexual assault cases:*

- Transfer or associative evidence can provide information about contact between patients and suspects, patients and crime scenes, and suspects and crime scenes. The type of evidence recovered and its location can provide details about the nature of the contact.
- Identification evidence can give scientific data about the source of a specific piece of evidence.

Be aware of evidence that may be pertinent to the issue of whether the patient consented to the sexual contact with the suspect. *In the majority of sexual assaults, patients know the suspects. For example, according to the National Crime Victimization Survey, in 2002, 66.1 percent of rapes/sexual assaults involved offenders who were nonstrangers. Most nonstranger suspects and many stranger suspects (if confronted by the criminal justice system) will claim that the patient consented to the sexual contact. Consent claims typically stem from a lack of evidence and documentation concerning force and coercion.*

Thus, evidence and documentation of physical findings related to whether force or coercion was used against patients (e.g., findings that reveal injuries, drugs taken involuntarily, or signs of a struggle) are important in these types of cases. However, the absence of physical trauma does not mean that coercion/force was not used or prove that patients consented to sexual contact. Also, some physical findings that suggest force are not necessarily indicative of a sexual assault. It is important to remember that if an investigation takes place, law enforcement officials will look for additional crime scene evidence that may help to overcome a claim of consent.

Understand how biological evidence is tested. *Semen, blood, vaginal secretions, saliva, vaginal epithelial cells, and other biological evidence may be identified and genetically typed by a crime lab. The information derived from the analysis can often help determine whether sexual contact occurred, provide information regarding the circumstances of the incident, and be compared to reference samples collected from patients and suspects. A primary method used by crime labs for testing biological evidence is DNA (deoxyribonucleic acid) analysis…*

Distinguish patients' DNA from suspects' DNA. *Blood, buccal (inner cheek) swabbings, or saliva should be collected from patients for DNA analysis to distinguish their DNA from that of suspects... If the case is reported, patients' biological samples and DNA profiles should be used only for investigation of the sexual assault, and their DNA profiles should not be inputted into CODIS [Combined DNA Index System].*

Neither biological samples nor DNA profiles should be provided to law enforcement or prosecution for another case in which patients may be suspects, inadvertently given to health insurance carriers, or used for research purposes without patients' consent. Criminal justice agency policies should be in place and followed for the secure storage of biological samples and appropriate disposal of these samples and DNA profiles.

Reduce exposure to infectious materials and risk of contamination of evidence. *Examiners should take precautions during the exam to prevent exposure (to both patients and health care staff) to blood-born pathogens and other potentially infectious materials. For example, it is important to follow facility policies on washing hands, handling contaminated needles and other contaminated sharps, wearing protective equipment, and minimizing splashing, spraying, and spattering of these materials...*

With the ever-increasing sensitivity of DNA analysis, there is a greater chance that accidental contamination can be detected. Forensic evidence, which is usually small in volume, can be contaminated and diluted by foreign DNA. Every precaution should be taken by all first responders to reduce outside contamination and dilution of evidence...

Understand the importance of semen evidence. *The relevance of semen evidence in cases involving male suspects covers the spectrum, depending upon case facts. Semen is composed of cellular and liquid components known as spermatozoa (sperm) and seminal fluid. Semen evidence can be useful because it is positive identification that ejaculation occurred, and it can be used to positively identify suspects.*

However, it is critical to note that failure to recover semen is not an indication that a sexual assault did not occur. There are a number of reasons why semen might not be recovered in these cases: Assailants may have used condoms, ejaculated somewhere other than in an orifice or on patients' clothes or bodies, or not ejaculated at all. Semen may have been depleted by frequent ejaculation prior to the sample in question. Chronic alcohol or drug abuse, chemotherapy, cancer, infection (e.g., mumps or tuberculosis), or congenital abnormalities also may suppress semen production.

Other factors may contribute to the absence of detectable amounts of semen evidence. For example, significant time delays between the assault and collection of evidence may cause loss of semen evidence, semen may be washed away prior to the exam or improperly collected, and an object other than a penis may have been used for penetration.

Modify the exam and evidence collection to address patients' needs and concerns… *In addition, examiners should be aware that patients' beliefs might affect whether and how certain evidence is collected. For example, patients from certain cultures or religious backgrounds may view hair as sacred and decline collection of hair evidence.*

Explain exam and evidence collection procedures to patients. *Whatever the methods used for seeking informed consent from patients for the exam and evidence collection, the full nature of procedures and options should be explained. Examiners may provide some basic information prior to starting the exam and additional information as the exam proceeds. For example, if the colposcope is used, examiners can explain to patients, at some point prior to its use, what the colposcope is, how it will be used, for what purpose, and how long the procedure will take. Encourage patients to ask questions and to inform examiners if they need a break or do not want a particular part of the exam or evidence collection done…*

Conduct the exam*. In addition to instructions included in the evidence collection kit, the exam should be guided by the scope of informed consent and the medical forensic history. In the course of the exam, examiners may question patients about trauma related to the assault. These questions should be specific enough to yield clinically relevant information. For example, simply asking if patients are injured or hurt anywhere is not focused enough—they may not know where they are injured until examined or asked questions such as if they hurt in specific body locations.*

General physical examination. *Obtain patients' vital signs, note the date and time of the exam, physical appearance, general demeanor, behavior, and orientation, and condition of clothing on arrival. Record all physical findings (which include observable or palpable tissue injuries; physiologic changes; and foreign materials such as grass, sand, stains, dried or moist secretions, or positive fluorescence) on body diagram forms. Use an alternate light source to assist in identifying findings. Be observant for redness, abrasions, bruises, swelling, lacerations, fractures, bites, burns, and other forms of physical trauma…*

Anogenital examination. *During the female genital exam, examine the external genitalia and perineal area for injury, foreign materials, and other findings in the following areas: abdomen, thighs, perineum, labia majora, labia minora, clitoral hood and surrounding area, periurethral tissue/urethral meatus, hymen, fossa navicularis, and posterior fourchette. The use of a colposcope during the external genital exam enhances viewing microscopic trauma and may provide photographic documentation.*

Then examine the vagina and cervix for injury, foreign materials, and foreign bodies. Use a colposcope or other magnifying device if available. In some jurisdictions, toluidine blue dye may be used to detect trauma, either with or without the use of a colposcope. Examine the buttocks, perianal skin, and anal folds for injury, foreign materials, and other findings. If rectal injury is suspected, an anoscope can be used as a tool to identify and evaluate trauma (it may also be used to help obtain anal swabs and trace evidence).

For male patients, examine the external and perineal area for injury, foreign materials, and other findings, including from the abdomen, buttocks, thighs, foreskin, urethral meatus, shaft, scrotum, perineum, glans, and testes. Document whether patients are circumcised.

Documentation of findings. *Record findings from the general physical and anogenital exam on appropriate body diagram forms. Detailed descriptions of findings should be provided as required. During the exam, collect evidence as specified in the evidence collection kit and photograph anatomy involved in the assault according to jurisdictional policy. Follow jurisdictional policy regarding documentation, photography, and collection of bite mark evidence.*

Collect evidence to submit to the crime lab for analysis, according to jurisdictional policy. *The following evidence from patients, along with completed documentation forms, typically is submitted to the crime lab designated by the jurisdiction. Jurisdictions may require collection of additional or different specimens. Instructions on evidence collection are usually contained in the evidence collection kit. If any requested evidence is not collected, examiners should note reasons on documentation forms.*

Collect clothing evidence. *Clothing frequently contains important evidence in sexual assault cases. It provides a surface upon which traces of foreign materials, such as semen, saliva, blood, hairs, fibers, and debris from the crime scene, may be found. While foreign matter can be washed off or worn off the body, the same substances often can be found intact on clothing for a considerable length of time following an assault. Damaged or torn clothing may be significant, as damage may be evidence of force (do not cut through any existing holes, rips, or stains on clothing). Evidence on patients' clothing can be compared with evidence collected from suspects and crime scenes. Common items collected from patients include underwear, hosiery, blouses, shirts, and pants…*

Collect debris.

- *Collect obvious debris on patients' bodies (e.g., dirt, leaves, fibers, and hair) on a collection sheet—package, label, seal, and initial seal.*
- *Fingernail evidence: ask patients whether or not they scratched the suspects' face, body, or clothing. If so, or if fibers of other materials are observed under patients' fingernails, collect fingernail clippings, scrapings, and/or swabbings, according to jurisdictional policy. If fingernail scrapings are collected, package fingernail scrapings and tools used to obtain the sample, label, seal, and initial seal. Cut broken fingernails at the remaining jagged edge for later comparison.*

Collect a fake nail as a known sample if one is missing. Package, label, seal, and initial the seals.

- *If requested, assist patients in putting on exam gowns after clothing and debris are collected.*

Collect foreign materials and swabs from the surface of the body.

Carefully inspect the body, including head, hair, and scalp, for dried or moist secretions and stains (e.g., blood, seminal fluid, sweat, and saliva) and other foreign material. Use an alternate light source to assist in identifying evidence. Obtain swabs from any suspicious area that may be a dry secretion or stain, any moist secretion, any area that fluoresces with longwave ultraviolet light, and any area for which patients relate a history or suspicion of bodily fluid transfer (e.g., licking, kissing, biting, splashed semen, or suction injury). Also collect swabs from potentially high-yield areas (e.g., neck, breasts, or external genitalia) if the history is absent or incomplete…

Collect hair combings. *Follow jurisdictional policy for collecting hair combings. The purpose of this procedure is to collect hair shed by suspects that may have been transferred to patients' hair. Hair combings may also reveal other foreign materials. Some jurisdictions collect head hair combings only if indicated. Whether or not head combings are collected, it is important to examine head, facial, and pubic hair for secretions, foreign materials, and/or debris and collect as appropriate (see above for collection of debris and foreign materials). Pubic hair combings are typically collected if the assault involved the genital area of patients…*

Collect hair reference samples as needed. *Follow jurisdictional policy for collection of hair reference samples. Many jurisdictions do not collect pubic hair reference samples routinely and some do not collect head hair reference samples routinely during the exam. In other jurisdictions, both samples are collected routinely unless otherwise indicated or declined by patients. Whatever the jurisdictional policy, patients should always be informed about the purpose of collection, procedures used to collect samples, discomfort that may be involved, and how these samples may be used during the investigation and prosecution. If hair reference samples are not collected at the initial exam, it is important to inform patients that there might be a need to collect these samples for crime lab analysis at a later date. They should be aware that hair evidence collected at a later date may not be as conclusive as if it is collected at the time of the initial exam (e.g., due to the fact that hair characteristics can change over time).*

When these samples are collected, the indications, timing, and techniques vary. Jurisdictional policies should be in place and followed. Give patients the option of collecting samples themselves.

Collect oral and anogenital swabs and smears. *Patients' consent, the medical forensic history, and exam findings should guide collection of oral and anogenital specimens. In general, specimens should be collected only from orifices and areas surrounding the orifices that patients report to be involved in the assault. Keep in mind that some patients may be vague about the type(s) of sexual contact that occurred. Examiners can help clarify which orifices were involved by asking appropriate questions. If there is uncertainty about involved orifices (e.g., because patients have little memory of the assault, were unconscious or incoherent, or do not understand what occurred), collection from oral, vaginal, and anal orifices (with patients' permission) may be appropriate. In some jurisdictions, policy calls for collection from all three orifices. Again, patients' consent is needed to collect these samples…*

Wet-mount evaluation. *Some jurisdictions require examiners to conduct wet-mount examinations of vaginal/cervical secretions for motile and nonmotile sperm in cases in which a male suspect may have ejaculated in a patient's vagina. Because sperm motility decreases quickly with time and removal from the vagina/cervix, wet-mount evaluation during the exam can provide the only opportunity to see sperm motility. The presence of motile sperm may help narrow the timeframe that the crime could have occurred. In other jurisdictions, however, the crime lab is responsible for all analysis of evidence and examiners do not do the wet-mount evaluation for sperm. Follow jurisdictional policy on whether wet-mount evaluation for sperm is needed and methods of evaluation. If it is required, examiners should be educated on use of the microscope, identification of sperm, and reporting their findings…*

Known blood or saliva sample or buccal swab for DNA analysis and comparison. *Many samples collected during the exam contain a mixture of secretions. To interpret genetic typing results obtained from these swabs, it is essential to know the genetic profile of patients. Patients' DNA reference samples are used for this purpose. Follow jurisdictional policy regarding the type of samples accepted by the crime lab.*

Collection of a buccal swab or saliva sample is encouraged unless it is medically or forensically necessary to take blood. If a blood sample is collected, the most noninvasive method of collection should be used. Buccal swabs: Decide on a case-by-case basis whether it is appropriate to collect a buccal (inner cheek) swab reference sample for DNA typing rather than a blood sample. For example, a blood sample may not be needed or patients might not allow blood to be drawn. A saliva sample is an alternative to the buccal swab. (Note that buccal swabs and saliva samples are not suitable for blood typing and serology.) If oral copulation is asserted or suspected, a buccal swab or saliva sample for patients' DNA reference may be contaminated. In those cases, blood is usually the better reference sample.

Collect other evidence. *Other evidence may be collected beyond what is needed for the sexual assault evidence collection kit.*

Toxicology samples. Make the decision about whether to collect toxicology samples for forensic purposes, what to collect, and collection methods according to jurisdictional policy. Do not put toxicology samples in the sexual assault evidence collection kit, unless otherwise indicated. Identify which forensic labs the jurisdiction has selected to analyze these samples, choose a lab, and follow transfer policies…

It is important to bear in mind that while these guidelines are thorough (although presented in an abbreviated form here for investigators), they cannot and will not apply in every case. Forensic examiners must know them well enough to know when they do not apply, and why. It is the spirit of these guidelines, and not the pedantic letter, that matters.

FULL BODY PHOTOS

Full body photos should be taken of the patient, including individual stills of the front, back, and sides of their head, torso, arms, hands, legs, and feet. Such documentation is very helpful to have in the patient's chart, or in the patient database, as it provides a pictorial view of their presentation at the time of assessment such questions arise at a later time. It also provides for *negative documentation*—recording of areas of the body where there is no evidence of defect, disease, injury, or potential transfer. As explained in Dolinak, Matshes, and Lew (2005), "negative examination" is often useful for exonerating alleged suspects. The forensic examiner must refrain from becoming a tool of either the prosecution or the defense and simply document what they find as completely as possible. The absence of findings is, in fact, a significant forensic finding.

In any case, all areas of injury must be photo-documented contextually and with close-ups, both with and without a measuring scale. The orientation of injuries must be made clear, as well as their size. Notes should also be taken as to their color, given that what is seen by the eye and recorded by the camera are not always in synch.

PHYSICAL INJURIES

Injuries resulting from sexual assault can occur on multiple sites on the patient's body. They can also occur from differing levels of force, varying with respect to disease, diet, medication, and age. Again, without a complete history, it is not always possible to assess etiology with accuracy. Common injuries to assess for include:

Abrasions: A scraping away of a portion of skin or mucous membrane, resulting when the skin contacts a rough object with sufficient force.
Bruises: An injury producing a hematoma or diffuse extraversion of blood without rupture of the skin.
Chop wounds: These injuries are the result of heavy instruments with a sharp edge. They go deep into the tissue, can be associated with bone fractures, and

can have a combination of incised and lacerated characteristics. Examples include injuries inflicted by axes, hatchets, machetes, swords, and meat cleavers.
Contusions: These are injuries (usually caused by a blow of some kind) in which blood vessels are broken, but the skin is not. They can be patterned (imprinted, not directional) and nonpatterned. They include bruises and hemorrhages, which can often be aged based on color. Differentiating postmortem and antemortem contusions is also an important consideration in reconstruction (Adelson, 1974).
Ecchymosis: An irregularly formed hemorrhagic area of the skin (i.e., a bruise); the color is blue-black, changing over time to shades of greenish brown or yellow.
Edema: A local or generalized condition in which the body tissues contain an excessive amount of tissue fluid.
Erythema diffused: A redness caused by capillary dilation.
Hematoma: A solid swelling of clotted blood within the tissues.
Hymenal transaction: A complete or partial tear or laceration through the width of the hymenal membrane extending to (partial) or through (complete) its attachment to the vaginal wall; if the transaction is nonacute and does not extend to the vaginal wall, it is called a cleft; hymenal transections may be associated with acute and nonacute injuries.
Incise wounds (cuts): These injuries are the result of sharp instruments being drawn across the surface of the skin, even into the tissue, and are generally longer than they are deep.
Lacerations: An injury resulting from ripping, crushing, overstretching, pulling apart, bending, and shearing; lacerations result from blunt force. These are torn or jagged wounds that tend to have abraded and contused edges. They can be differentiated from sharp force injuries by the recognition of tissue bridging from one side of the laceration to the other (indicating shearing or crushing force). Adelson (1974) warns examiners to beware that bullets striking the skin tangentially, without penetrating, can mimic lacerations and incise wounds.
Stab wounds: These injuries are the result of being pierced with a pointed instrument. The depth of the injury into the tissue is usually greater than its width in the skin.

Some of these will be discussed further in this chapter, as they relate to specific kinds of attacks and wound patterns.

BRUISE AND OTHER INJURY PATTERNS

As previously mentioned, a bruise is an injury producing a hematoma or diffuse extraversion of blood without rupture of the skin; it appears as an area of discolored skin on the body. Bruises are caused by a blunt force blow or impact that ruptures underlying blood vessels. This impact can result in a distinctive pattern of bruising and/or lacerations that reflect the type of object used because of its shape or the position of the victim and/or the attacker because of its location.

While there are an infinite number of possibilities with respect to potential bruise and injury patterns in cases of sexual assault, there are characteristic patterns that tend to repeat, and even some "unique identifiers of the particular event" (Dolinak et al., 2005, p. 480).

Inner Thighs
Forcible penetration of the vagina from the front, with the victim on her back, can result in a characteristic bruise pattern to either side of the inner thighs. Redness and some bruising are expected to result from consensual sexual encounters. However, forced sex may be determined by evidence of repeated injury that breaks the skin, even to the point of bleeding.

Physical Restraint and Bindings
The offender may physically restrain the victim during the assault. This is most often accomplished manually. However, it may also involve the victim's jewelry or clothing being grabbed, or some kind of ligature.

Manual restraint most often results in bruising to the inner aspect of the victim's arms, resulting from a violent grab (Dolinak et al., 2005). The authors have observed that such "grab" injuries are often characterized by two, three, or four contusions visible on one side of the victim's arm, and one on the other, corresponding with the offender's fingers and thumb.

Binding materials, or ligatures, commonly include rope, twine, electrical wire, electrical cords, shoelaces, wire coat hangers, telephone cords, and even handcuffs. Each leaves behind a patterned ligature furrow in the skin, characteristic of its shape and any surface patterns. Often, the victim's jewelry or clothing is used as a ligature because of its availability (e.g., necklace, shirt, bra, underwear, belt, necktie, stockings). In these cases, the distinctive pattern of the material (e.g., the weave of the cloth or the marks on metal) is often left behind on the skin. Bunched material leaves behind an irregular pattern. Restraints are most commonly placed on the wrists and/ or ankles. The victim may be restrained to himself or herself or to an object such as a bed or chair.

In living victims, tight restraints result not only in redness and patterned furrows, but also abrasions and contusions at the same location. These are a result of the victim's struggle. This is especially true when victims are restrained and sexually assaulted during the same interval, as physical pain, along with efforts to recoil and break free, may intensify. The absence of such injury associated with binding suggests a lack of physical resistance, binding after the loss of consciousness, or binding after death as in cases of sexual homicide.

Hands and Forearms
Victims use their hands and forearms defensively, to ward off physical attacks or to protect their heads from physical blows. Evidence of sharp force injury to the fingers, palms, and forearms are the common result of a knife attack. As the offender moves in for a sharp force attack, the victim may react by putting up their hand, arms, or even grabbing at the blade of the sharp force weapon. Similarly, blunt force trauma and

broken fingers, hands, or forearms are commonly the result of repeated blows with a blunt object (e.g., fist, baseball bat). In either case, this type of defensive injury is an indication that the victim's hands/arms were not restrained during this part of the attack, if at all. It also indicates that they were conscious, facing their attacker, and aware of the attack.

Neck

There are a variety of injuries that a victim may suffer to their neck. They include manual strangulation, ligature strangulation, and self-inflicted defensive abrasions and contusions. Symptoms and physical signs of strangulation are detailed in Stapczynski (2010):

With strangulation, the initial presenting symptoms and physical signs may be deceptively minimal. It takes time for hemorrhage and edema to develop after compressive injuries, and the full clinical manifestations may not occur for 36 hours after the event.

The following specific clinical manifestations are possible in strangulation victims:

• Voice changes are reported in up to 50% of manual strangulation victims and may range from a raspy or hoarse voice to complete inability to talk.

• Swallowing abnormality is not a common symptom on initial emergency department assessment, but is reported during the subsequent two weeks in 44% of women who survive a domestic violence strangulation episode. Swallowing may be painful (odynophagia) or difficult (dysphagia).

• Breathing difficulties are common, seen in up to 85% of women during the initial two weeks after a strangulation event. The dyspnea can be psychogenic in origin and may be due to anxiety, fear, depression, or hyperventilation. Difficulty breathing can also be due to laryngeal edema or hemorrhage, although those injuries are less common in surviving victims.

• Pain in the throat or neck is common after strangulation. The patient may be able to localize it to a specific area of injury, or it may be diffuse and poorly localized.

• Mental status changes can be due to the occurrence of cerebral hypoxia or from concomitant intracranial injury or ingestion of drugs or ethanol.

• Neurologic symptoms are frequently reported in victims of strangulation and include changes in vision, tinnitus, eyelid droop, facial droop, or unilateral weakness. While common, many of these reported symptoms may not be detectable or confirmed by neurologic testing.

• Injury to the soft tissues in the neck may manifest with edema, hyperemia, ecchymoses, abrasions, or scratches. Abrasions and scratches may be defensive

in nature, as the victim has tried to remove the assailant's from his or her neck. The hyperemia may be transient and not visible by the time of assessment. Ecchymoses and swelling may take time to develop and may not be visible on initial assessment. Ligature marks can be hidden within the natural skin folds of the neck and potentially missed on cursory examination, especially if the cervical collar is not removed and good lighting is not used. Chin abrasions have been reported to occur from the defensive actions of the victims as they flex their cervical spines forward and bring their chins down in an effort to protect their necks from the manual strangulation of the assailant.

- *Petechiae can occur at or above the area of compression and are most frequently reported on the face and conjunctiva. More extensive cutaneous and mucosal bleeding, such as a subconjunctival hemorrhage, is generally seen only after a particularly vigorous struggle between the victim and the assailant.*

- *Laryngeal injuries can manifest with focal tenderness of the laryngeal cartilage or subcutaneous emphysema over or around the laryngeal cartilage.*

- *Pulmonary findings can be due to aspiration pneumonitis if the victim vomits and then inhales during the strangulation event. As noted above, pulmonary edema can occur, but this is generally only seen in hanging victims who remain comatose after emergency department arrival.*

- *Neurologic findings can include ptosis, facial droop, and unilateral weakness. In many patients, the findings are transient and believed to be incited by focal cerebral ischemia produced by the strangulation process that resolves with time. In rare cases, damage to the internal carotid artery may induce thrombosis with a delayed neurologic presentation.*

The authors have observed that manual strangulation injuries, when visible, are often characterized by two, three, or four contusions visible on one side of the victim's neck, and one on the other, corresponding with the offender's fingers and thumb. As described in Downing (2006; p. 9):

Circular or oval contusions on the neck caused by the fingertips of the assailant's grasp may be visible. Singular thumb impressions are more commonly found, as the thumb cause more pressure than other fingers.

These contusions may also be characterized or interrupted by characteristic crescent-shaped lacerations and abrasions from the offender's fingernails.

When ligature strangulation is suspected or alleged, a careful examination of the neck is required. A ligature pattern is generally going to be located at the level of the victim's larynx or lower. In homicide cases it is generally going to be a uniform and horizontal mark encircling the neck completely. But it can also be a partially circling mark, visible only in the front, the assailant having pulled the ligature tightly from behind. This is in keeping with a homicidal strangulation rather than suicidal or homicidal hanging. In either case, the ligature pattern will mark the skin of the neck generally the same way all around and will not rise sharply to a suspension point.

The ligature pattern should be documented (photos and measurements) as soon as possible, as it may disappear in short period of time. It can also be used to determine whether suspected ligatures could have caused the patterned injury. In severe cases, the ligature pattern may become more pronounced as bruising develops and healing occurs, in which case follow-up photos may be required.

If the ligature is not immediately present (i.e., around the victim's neck or found at the scene), the pattern and furrow left behind should evidence the kind of ligature to search for at the scene or during the subsequent investigation.

As mentioned in Stapczynski (2010), defensive abrasions and contusions may also appear on the victim's neck and chin in association with both manual and ligature strangulation. These injuries may also be self-inflicted, observed in cases where the victim scratches at their neck and anything that is compressing their airway. As described in Downing (2006; p. 9): "Superficial curvilinear abrasions are usually the result of the victim's struggle to pry the assailant's hands off his or her neck." These are the result of victim struggle and resistance, indicating consciousness and the absence of restraint. Such defensive resistance can cause injury to the offender's hands and forearms as well and result in DNA transfer beneath the fingernails of the victim.

Knees

Injury to the victim's knees suggests their direct contact with a hard surface. This generally requires them to be bent, unless it is an artifact or dragging. It can also be an indication of forced oral sex. Although certainly oral sex may be forced without resulting in knee injuries, their presence is consistent with it. The type of injury will depend on the surface that the victim kneels on, any clothing that might be covering the area, and any additional force applied by the offender. The authors have seen a wide range of such knee injuries, from mild redness and swelling, to bruising, to bleeding lacerations. When confronted with injuries to the knees (one or both) in a sexual assault, this line of inquiry is suggested.

Breasts

Common injuries to the victim's breasts associated with sexual assault include forceful sucking, pinching, slapping, and biting. In extreme cases, violent acts of tearing and cutting have been known to occur, up to and including the removal of the entire breast (such destructive acts are referred to as *defeminization*). Injury to the breast may be accomplished through the clothing, resulting in injury patterns on the skin from clothing material and corresponding damage to the clothing itself. Injury to the breast may also be accomplished after the clothing has been removed.

If any injury to the victim results in blood flow, it is useful to examine the corresponding site on all items of clothing that might have covered the area for blood patterns and damage (often multiple layers of clothing are involved). This will indicate what the victim was wearing, or not, when attacked.

Aging Bruises

It can be difficult to determine the age of a single bruise and associate it with a particular event. As bruises heal, they change color; this is the primary means of determining when bruising occurred. Of the five different classification schemes for aging bruises reviewed in Bialas and Stephenson (1996), all of them provide that yellowing associated with a bruise-type injury (blunt force trauma) is an artifact of healing and is evident only 1–2 weeks after the injury. Their own research found that green and yellow coloring in a bruise suggests that the injury is at least 24–48 h old.

Therefore, if presented with a yellowing bruise, it is not reasonable to associate it with a sexual assault that is reported to have occurred within 24 h. However, different people bruise differently, and their bruises age differently, owing to many factors such as diet, medication, illness, and substance abuse. A patient history on this issue is necessary for the most informed opinions.

However, most cases do not involve the evaluation of one bruise, but rather multiple bruises and bruise patterns. If the patient presents with multiple bruises in the same general location, in radically different stages of healing, this suggests that they are the result of injuries inflicted at different times.

The important thing to note here is that aging bruises is not impossible, and their association with a sexual assault must be investigated and confirmed or refuted—not assumed.

GENITAL EXAMINATION

After a thorough head-to-toe physical exam, with corresponding documentation, the next component is the general survey of the patient's genitalia, both macroscopically and with colposcope (as already mentioned in the NIJ guidelines provided). A colposcope is a lighted magnifying instrument used by a gynecologist to examine the tissues of the vagina and the cervix. The process of using a colposcope during a vaginal and cervical examination is called *colposcopy*.

A colposcope allows the forensic examiner to assess for, and record, the presence or absence of genital injury. It is like a camera, flashlight, and microscope all in one. It allows visualization of genital tissue areas that may be missed with the naked eye or poor lighting. As explained by Finkel (2002), the colposcope provides not only excellent magnification of the genital tissue, but also an excellent light source that identifies and captures any potential injury or abnormalities on tape or film. Furthermore, it provides a noninvasive method for examining the genitalia—and because the examination is on a screen or monitor, it actually makes the process less intimidating. A genital examination conducted macroscopically, without a colposcope and corresponding documentary photos, is essentially incomplete.

In terms of the sexual assault examination, injuries if present vary according to force of the penetrating object, the object itself, time elapsed between assault and examination, position of victim, and/or use of lubrication. The most common site of female genital injury is the posterior fourchette, the labia minora, hymen, and fossa navicularis (Giardino & Giardino, 2003). The examiner must have a strong foundational knowledge of normal genital anatomy, and normal anatomical and cultural variations, to competently assess genital abnormality. Identification and interpretation of abnormal findings evolve from there.

During the genital exam, the forensic examiner must also pay close attention to injury, and the absence of injury, in the anal and perianal regions. As explained in Dolinak et al. (2005), finding injury here is not necessarily evidence of sexual penetration, unless the proper context is present (p. 475):

The passage of feces could result in rectal bleeding. However, radiating perianal lacerations seen around the anus without trauma to the rectal mucosa rule out the passage of hard feces as an etiology. The mechanism of such radiating tears is an object pushed from outside in and not an object from within coming out.

It is also relevant to note that injury to the anogenital region can occur during consensual sexual activity and that many cases of rape do not involve visible trauma. Cybulska and Forster (2010) reports that (p. 235) "Genital injuries are found in 24—53% of cases; most require no treatment. About 20% of women have no injuries following rape." As explained in Keller and Nelson (2008), there are many factors to consider (p. 135): "genital tissues are vulnerable to tearing, bruising, scraping, irritation, and swelling during sexual contact, whether it is consensual or nonconsensual. Additionally, trauma from consensual or forced sexual intercourse varies depending on the female's age and sexual experience." In other words, the absence of genital trauma does not invalidate a claim of rape, and the presence of trauma does not prove it (DiMaio & DiMaio, 2001). Injury must be assessed in its context and informed by sufficient history to screen for confounding or misleading artifacts.

EVIDENCE OF SEXUAL ACTIVITY

Although there is no proof of rape or sexual assault on its own, establishing evidence of sexual activity (or its absence) is a key issue in the reconstruction of any suspected sex crime. Evidence of recent sexual activity can include, under the proper circumstances, the presence of condoms and/or lubricant; the presence of semen and/or sperm; evidence of saliva; and even evidence of fecal matter. However, positive findings related to sexual activity must not be interpreted out of context. Victim history must be collected and investigated to establish whether artifacts from prior, recent, and consensual sexual activity are being confused for, or blended with, evidence of sexual assault.

Evidence of sexual activity cannot be understood, let alone ascribed to criminal intent, outside of its context. It also must not be interpreted as an isolated behavior. When placed in the context of victim history, physical evidence, and other reconstructed events, the meaning of any established sexual activity is more completely understood.

SEMEN AND SPERM

Semen is the fluid mixture of male bodily secretions that contains the sperm. There are certain secretions in semen that are considered to be reliable markers for confirming the presence of semen, due to either uniqueness or quantity. These markers are categorized by the results of the tests performed to assay them as either presumptive or conclusive. Using these markers, forensic examiners are able to make reasonable statements about the presence of semen in a sample of evidence.

Acid phosphatase—The acid phosphatase (AP) test is a well-documented *presumptive* test for the presence of semen. There is generally a large amount of the enzyme AP in human semen. If the amount assayed in a sample of evidence is large enough (there is no consistent agreement as to how much is enough), then it can be said that semen could be present, that is, a finding consistent with the presence of semen. For example, if the examiner achieves this result on an oral swab, a nasal swab, or from clothing stains up near the head or shoulders, then this result is consistent with oral sex. But it is not confirmed.

P30—P30 is a protein specific to semen; it has not been found in any other body fluids or organs. It is easily detectable at even the lowest average levels in the semen of the average male, making it an excellent marker when examining very small amounts of trace evidence. A positive result for P30 is also a strong confirmatory result for semen, even without the presence of sperm. This becomes important given the large number of males in the general population who have undergone vasectomy operations and who subsequently have ejaculate that contains no sperm. If the examiner achieves a confirmatory result for P30 antigen, then semen is present.

Sperm—The microscopic identification of sperm cells is the most reliable and widely used forensic technique for confirming the presence of semen (Virkler & Lednev, 2009). As argued in DiMaio and DiMaio (2001):

> *In living individuals, motile sperm are usually seen only up to 6 h, occasionally 12 h, and, very rarely, up to 24 h. In the latter case, it is probable that the sperm was obtained from cervical mucus. Thus, it is important when searching for motile sperm in an individual alleged to have been raped only a few hours before to obtain this material from the vaginal pool and not from the cervix.*

> *Non-motile sperm with tails in the living individual are usually seen up to 26 h, with occasional reports of 2 to 3 days. In the latter cases, these are probably sperm trapped in cervical mucus. The identification of only a single sperm on one or two slides should make the examiner wary that he may have one of those cases in which there is unusual prolonged survival of the sperm, that is, sperm from cervical mucus. In most rape cases, numerous sperm will be seen on each smear. The presence of several sperm on a slide, with a history of the last voluntary intercourse 2 or 3 days before, would be inconsistent with the sperm's originating at that time, but would be consistent with a recent rape.*

Any sperm identified should be collected and DNA-tested for suspect comparisons and eliminations. Semen may also contain epithelial cells from the male urethra and can therefore also be submitted for DNA testing.

DNA—DNA testing may be used to confirm the ownership of cells collected from swabs taken during the sexual assault examination, but it does not discriminate the type of cell tested. This must be accomplished visually or by other means of testing. The presence of suspect DNA indicates only that contact, or penetration, occurred. Its meaning in a given case cannot be interpreted unless the conditions of that contact and evidence transfer have been carefully reconstructed using other physical evidence.

SALIVA

Saliva is transferred in association with a broad range of sexual activity, including oral sex (mouth to genitals), and the kissing or licking of eroticized objects and body parts (e.g., sex toys, lips, breasts, buttocks). It is also transferred in association with bite mark evidence. While there are no confirmatory tests for saliva, suspected transfer sites can be swabbed and tested for the epithelial DNA that it carries.

FECAL MATTER

The presence of fecal matter (excrement) on an object, on a victim's body or clothing, or simply in a crime scene, can indicate anal penetration or activity. As a result of anal penetration, it is often found smeared on the victim's buttocks, legs, clothing, or on towels found nearby. This transfer evidence is found in association with an attacker withdrawing his penis, or an object, from the victim's rectum, and then wiping it off with whatever is available.

While fecal matter does not have DNA of its own, as it is digested material, it is coated with trace amounts of bodily mucous and often blood that contains its owner's DNA. This can be tested and its ownership established.

CONDOMS

Condoms are often reported and collected in association with rape. The use of a condom, and any associated spermicidal lubricants, does not imply victim consent. Nor does it necessarily imply offender precaution—to avoid evidence transfer that might leave behind physical evidence of identity. Rather it may suggest offender concern for contracting sexually transmitted diseases.

When a condom is found at a crime scene, it can be DNA-tested both internally and externally: internally for ejaculate (semen and/or sperm) and epithelial cells from the male's penis and externally for epithelial cells sloughed off from the complainant's mouth, vagina, or anus. This is done to establish the identity of those who used the condom, as well as allowing the ability to make a clear inference that sexual penetration of some form took place. To determine whether the penetration was oral, vaginal, or anal, an external examination of the condom for saliva, fecal matter, or lubrication associated with a particular orifice, for contrast with the results of the physical examination, is necessary.

CLOTHING

As already suggested, complainant and suspect clothing must be collected and examined carefully for any evidence of injury or force, such as biological material, rips, tears, and cuts. However, clothing damage from an attack should not be confused with regular garment wear and tear. Again, the complainant interview should act as a guide, establishing whether clothing was reported to be forcibly removed or whether injuries were reported to be inflicted through the clothing. As explained in Boland et al. (2007, p. 110):

> *Clothing damage analysis is an integral part of the examinations carried out in sexual assault type cases. This analysis can be used to corroborate different versions of events and is at its most powerful in elucidating false allegation cases and consent cases.*

The forensic examiner must therefore note whether injuries to the clothing match the complainant's report or line up with corresponding injuries to their body.

The complainant's underwear and bra are of particular forensic value. If either are cut or torn, this may indicate force unless there is an established history of consensual activity that involves this behavior as part of fantasy sex play. Again, this determination requires a complete and honest history from the complainant or collateral history from other evidence sources or witnesses. Further, as discussed in DiMaio and DiMaio (2001):

> *The victim is asked whether she douched, bathed, showered, defecated, or urinated prior to the examination. All the aforementioned factors can influence whether the physical evidence needed to document sexual intercourse is present. Vertical drainage from the vagina is the worst enemy to the collection of evidence. Because of this, it is recommended that the examiner retain the [undergarment] the victim was wearing. Thus, any drainage of semen into the [undergarment] can be documented.*

Drainage can occur on any surface where the complainant sits or lies after being attacked, not just their underwear: a coat, a sanitary napkin or tampon, a bedsheet, a blanket, or a vehicle seat—all have been on the receiving end of such material. Developing the timeline of activities, and actively searching for drainage material to potential transfer sites, should be a forensic priority.

FALSE POSITIVES: CONDITIONS THAT MIMIC ABUSE

There are numerous conditions and circumstances that can cause injury consistent with assault or abuse. Therefore, the forensic nurse must be fully aware of the *differential diagnosis*[4] for any finding before making firm conclusions about its origins. As explained in Pfitzer (2009, p. 88):

> *Often numerous other conditions mimic sexual abuse. It is important for the individuals who take care of [victims] to become familiar with such conditions, as well as the variations of normal [patient] genital exam that can be particularly confusing for non-medical professions.*

This involves taking into account the possibility that injuries and symptoms may have more than one cause or a cause unrelated to an assault.

Unfortunately, this fundamental diagnostic concept can be lost or ignored in a forensic context, where examiners are presented with law enforcement officers or sympathetic complainants insisting that injuries are indeed the result of an assault. The forensic nurse may not make this assumption. Absence of differential diagnosis considerations in any forensic medical exam is the absence of science and the scientific method.

Specific to eliminating false positives in child abuse, but just as important in all other patient examinations, is the advice provided in Burns and Mayer (2000):

> *When assessing injuries, the clinician must obtain a complete history, including present illness, review of systems, past medical and psychosocial history, family history (particularly bleeding disorders), and history of injury-related disorders. The caregiver should be permitted to lead the interview with a narrative of the injury.*

Apart from misleading injuries, such as old bruises, unintentional burns, and broken bones from known accidents, there are also misleading infections and skin conditions. For example, an adult female patient may reveal during her history that she has suffered from chronic urinary tract infections since the age of 5, due to the fact that she was born with an anatomical abnormality of the *urethral meatus*.[5] A female with a shorter than normal urethral meatus may be prone to a higher incidence of urinary tract infections. This is because when the tube leading from the bladder to the opening where urine exits the body (also known as the "pee hole," urethral meatus, urethral opening) is short, general bacteria and bacteria from poor hygiene practices, improper wiping, and feces are more likely to migrate up the tube and cause bladder infections. On the other hand, if the patient reports that she has been experiencing burning upon urination, itching, and discharge only since the alleged assault, then these symptoms are more likely related to it.

Differential diagnosis considers the possibility that there is more than one cause for any set of injuries, conditions, or symptoms presented by a patient. The objective forensic examiner embraces this medical reality and works to eliminate causes rather than to prove a relationship between injuries, conditions, and crime. At the very least, this requires the forensic examiner to document each symptom, condition, and injury present with the patient, as well as to establish any specific history that is relevant.

TOXICOLOGY

Drug use, most commonly alcohol, is a vital consideration in the reconstruction of an alleged sexual assault. As such, it is a standard forensic protocol to collect blood and/or urine from both complainants and suspects during the investigation. The failure to collect and test toxicological samples is substandard and in some cases may indicate a desire to protect the complainant from the outcome.

MENTAL INCAPACITY

As already explained, the use of drugs and alcohol in sufficient quantities prevents the user from thinking rationally and subsequently from being able to form any kind of rational intent (victims and offenders alike). This bears directly on cases of rape involving drug and alcohol use, described in Cowan (2008, pp. 900–901):

> *A complainant's intoxication can impact consent in a rape trial in two possible ways. First, the complainant and the defendant could disagree about the fact or level of intoxication - i.e., capacity, so that the defendant claims either that the complainant was not drunk at all, or that she was not drunk to the degree that she was incapable of consenting but merely was disinhibited, and therefore she was in fact capable of, and did, consent. Second, there could be disagreement about whether or not there was consent - i.e., the defendant claims that the complainant gave consent, albeit drunken, and that she was capable even though intoxicated, whereas the complainant states that she cannot remember what happened because she was extremely drunk but that she knows that she did not want to have sex with the defendant (and she may also claim that she was too drunk to resist). The claim then could be either that she was not intoxicated (enough) and capable, or, that despite a high level of intoxication, she did consent.*

Though referring specifically to alcohol intoxication, the issues discussed in Cowan (2008) remain the same with other drugs that cause similar mental defects. This temporary state of being incapable of rationally appraising the nature of one's own conduct is referred to as *mental incapacity*.

Significantly, research of published in Boykins (2005) found that half of the sexual assault victims in her study reported current use of prescription medication, primarily for mental health problems such as depression. This becomes more significant with respect to perception and memory if such medications are mixed with alcohol.

SUBSTANCE ABUSE

It is important to ask the patient if he or she has a history of substance abuse. If the answer is yes, then immediate follow-up questions must include which substances, when was the last use, and how much was taken. Here, it is critical for the forensic examiner to explain the patient the importance of being honest.

The patient needs to fully understand that if he or she has recently ingested a substance such as alcohol, marijuana, cocaine, heroin, methamphetamine—or any other illicit drug—that it will likely show up on the lab tests submitted for analysis. Therefore it is better for patients' health and overall credibility to be up front about drug use. Patients need to know that if they deny drug use and test "hot" for the presence of something illicit, this will make them look intentionally deceitful, as though they are trying to hide information. The forensic examiner should explain that it is better to establish a pattern of honesty during the forensic medical examination, so that any other information provided may be trusted if trust is required.

Ultimately, victim toxicology will be used to inform estimates of the patient's physical and mental capabilities, as well as to assist with addressing the issue of consent (see discussion in Chapter 13: Drug Facilitated Sexual Assault). In cases involving recreational use or abuse of drugs and alcohol by the patient, it may be necessary to obtain collateral descriptions of the patient's typical behavior while under the influence from friends and family members. In this way, the forensic examiner will have a more complete understanding of how particular drugs affect a particular patient to inform subsequent interpretations—though not necessarily his or her own. That is to say, there are happy drunks, loud drunks, "amorous" drunks, forgetful drunks, and angry drunks. It helps to know who the patient is.

PRESENTATION OF FINDINGS

As explained in the NIJ (2004, 2013) guidelines, forensic nurses must conduct and document every examination they perform thoroughly, as though it will go to trial, even though many will not. This is part of maintaining a forensic mindset.

The purpose of any forensic examination is to educate the court system. Examination reports that do not provide interpretations about whether and how findings may be consistent with forcible sexual activity or the patient's account as provided in the forensic interview (with the appropriate caveats) are unfortunately common. Such reports are also unprofessional—they allow forensic examiners to vacillate in their ultimate interpretations; they leave a false or confused impression in the minds of those who read them; and they allow investigators and attorneys to characterize findings with their own adventitious interpretations.

However, forensic examiners must not invade the province of the jury by addressing the issue of guilt or innocence. As explained in DiMaio and DiMaio (2001):

In court, the physician or forensic nurse is never expected to state whether the crime of rape has occurred. Rape is not a diagnosis, it is a matter of jurisprudence. All that the examiner can do is document any evidence of trauma, determine, if possible, whether there has been recent sexual intercourse, and collect trace evidence.

Forensic interpretations of exam findings must be made in light of the known victim history and the most current advances in relevant research, methods, and other developments in the field. This places the burden of thorough forensic interviewing squarely on the forensic examiner, as well as the requirement of continuing education. The court, and criminal investigators, should treat forensic interpretations made in the absence of these considerations with skepticism.

To be clear, all forensic reports should say what the examiner did, what they found, and what it means—not in general, not in part, and not in collusion with a particular side.

ENDNOTES

1. This chapter has been adapted and updated from material published in Jamerson (2009); Turvey and Jamerson (2011, 2012).
2. The State of Alaska enjoys the highest per capita rate of rape in the United States.
3. A free copy of the complete guidelines may be acquired online at http://www.ncjrs.gov/pdffiles1/ovw/206554.pdf.
4. *Differential diagnosis* is strictly defined as the process of weighing the probability of one disease versus that of other diseases possibly accounting for a patient's condition. It considers that symptoms can have multiple causes.
5. The urethra is the tube leading from the bladder that discharges urine outside of the body. In females the urethra is significantly shorter than in males. The female urethral meatus (i.e., opening) is above the vaginal opening.

REFERENCES

Adelson, L. (1974). *The Pathology of homicide*. Springfield, IL: Charles C Thomas.

Bialas, Y., & Stephenson, T. (1996). Estimation of the age of bruising. *Archives of Disease in Childhood, 74*, 53–55.

Boland, C. A., McDermott, S. C., & Ryan, J. (2007). Clothing damage analysis in alleged sexual assaults—the need for a systematic approach. *Forensic Science International, 167*, 110–115.

Boykins, A. (2005). "The forensic exam: assessing health characteristics of adult female victims of recent sexual assault,". *Journal of Forensic Nursing, 1*(4), 166–171.

Burns, P., & Mayer, B. (2000). Differential diagnosis of abuse injuries in infants and young children. *Nurse Practitioner, 25*, 15–37.

CDVSA. (2011). *CDVSA guidelines for response to sexual assault*. The Alaska Council on Domestic Violence and Sexual Assault, Alaska Department of Public Safety. http://www.dps.state.ak.us/ast/docs/SARTProtocols.pdf.

Chisum, W. J., & Turvey, B. (2011). *Crime reconstruction* (2nd ed.). San Diego: Elsevier Science.

Cowan, S. (2008). The trouble with drink: intoxication, (In)capacity, and the evaporation of consent to sex. *Akron Law Review, 41*, 899–922.

Coyle, C. (2011). *"Local nurses training to help sexual assault survivors,"* WRDW-TV.com, February 22.

Cybulska, B., & Forster, G. (2010). Sexual assault: examination of the victim. *Medicine, 38*(5), 235–238.

DiMaio, D., & DiMaio, V. (2001). *Forensic pathology* (2nd ed.). Boca Raton: CRC Press.

Dolinak, D., Matshes, E., & Lew, E. (2005). *Forensic pathology: Principles and practice*. Boston: Elsevier Science.

Downing, R. (2006). Manual and ligature strangulation. *On the Edge, 12*(2), 9–13, 1.

Finkel, M. (2002). The evaluation. In M. Finkel, & A. Giardino (Eds.), *Medical evaluation of child sexual abuse: A practical guide* (2nd ed.). Thousand Oaks, CA: Sage Publications.

Giardino, E. R., & Giardino, A. P. (2003). *Nursing approach to the evaluation of child maltreatment*. Maryland Heights, MO: G.W. Medical Publisher.

Jamerson, C. (2009). Forensic nursing: approaching the victim as a crime scene. In W. Petherick, & B. Turvey (Eds.), *Forensic victimology*. San Diego: Elsevier Science.

Keller, P., & Nelson, J. (2008). Injuries to the cervix in sexual trauma. *Journal of Forensic Nursing, 4*, 130–137.

NIJ. (1999). *Death investigation: A guide for the scene investigator, Research Report NCJ 167568*. Washington, DC: National Institute of Justice.

NIJ. (2013). *A National protocol for sexual assault medical forensic examinations* (2nd ed.). Washington, DC: U.S. Department of Justice, National Institute of Justice, Office on Violence Against Women https://www.ncjrs.gov/pdffiles1/ovw/241903.pdf.

NIJ. (September 2004). *A National protocol for sexual assault medical forensic examinations, Research Report NCJ 206554*. Washington, DC: U.S. Department of Justice, National Institute of Justice, Office on Violence Against Women.

Pfitzer, L. (2009). Sexual abuse mimics. *Pedijatrija Danas, 5*(1), 88–93.

Stapczynski, J. S. (August 2, 2010). Strangulation injuries. *Emergency Medicine Reports*.

Turvey, B., & Jamerson, C. (2011). Sexual assault: issues in evidence examination and interpretation. In W. J. Chisum, & B. Turvey (Eds.), *Crime reconstruction* (2nd ed.). San Diego: Elsevier Science.

Turvey, B., & Jamerson, C. (2012). Sexual assault examination and reconstruction. In B. Turvey (Ed.), *Forensic victimology* (2nd ed.). San Diego: Elsevier Science.

Virkler, K., & Lednev, I. (2009). Analysis of body fluids for forensic purposes: from laboratory testing to non-destructive rapid confirmatory identification at a crime scene. *Forensic Science International, 188*, 1–17.

CHAPTER 9

Medicolegal Death Investigation: Protocols and Practice

Stan Crowder[1], Brent E. Turvey[2]

Kennesaw State University, Georgia, GA, United States[1]*; Forensic Criminology Institute, Sitka, Alaska, United States and Aguascalientes, Mexico*[2]

CHAPTER OUTLINE

Terms and Definitions 223
    Medicolegal 223
    Medicolegal Death Investigator 225
    Medical Doctor 225
    Medical Opinions 225
    Forensic Pathology 225
    Medical Examiner 226
    Coroner 226
    Autopsy 227
        Logical and Comprehensible 227
        Statutory Authority 228
        The Autopsy as Medical Practice 228
        Investigate, Examine, Then Opine 229
    Cause of Death 230
    Manner of Death 231
        Natural 231
        Accidental 231
        Homicide 231
        Suicide 232
        Undetermined 232
Protocols for Medicolegal Death Investigators 233
    Chain of Custody 233
    Death Investigation Protocols 236
Autopsy Protocols 249
    The National Academy of Sciences Report 249
The National Association of Medical Examiners Standards 250
    Contents 255

Medicolegal Failures: A Top 10 List 256
Conclusion 258
Endnotes 258
References 259

In every case of violent or unattended death, a comprehensive medicolegal investigation is required to establish the facts and circumstances surrounding it. As explained in *Death Investigation*, a forensic guide published by the National Institute of Justice (NIJ, 1999), this notion is not best practice (e.g., a cadillac investigation, or gold standard). It is the minimum that may be done to satisfy a basic duty of care. It is also a scientific requirement for competency and forensic accuracy, without which results may not be considered scientifically reliable.

This is not new information. Objective scientists and competent investigators nationwide agree that comprehensive death scene protocols must be followed at "every scene," and "every time"—as though each case is a potential homicide (NIJ, 1999). Otherwise, the truth about a victim's death can be missed, lost, or intentionally concealed by those who wish it.

Finding good information with respect to comprehensive death scene and autopsy protocols is not difficult. In truth, a number of excellent references on the subject have been written. These include the following texts, some of which will be referenced in this chapter:

- Adelson, L. (1974) *The Pathology of Homicide*, Springfield, IL: Charles C. Thomas.
- DiMaio, D. & DiMaio, V. (2001) *Forensic Pathology, 2nd Ed*, Boca Raton: CRC Press.
- Dix, J. (2000) *Color Atlas of Forensic Pathology*, Boca Raton: CRC Press.
- Dolinak, D., Matshes, E. & Lew, E. (2005) *Forensic Pathology: Principles and Practice*, Boston: Elsevier Science.
- Spitz, W. & Fisher (1993) *Medicolegal* Investigation *of Death, 3rd Ed*, Springfield, IL: Charles C. Thomas Publisher.

It is fair to say that if a forensic student or professional does not possess at least three of these texts, then they are not serious about their work. They are also dangerously underinformed on the subjects of medicolegal death investigation and forensic pathology. It is, in all seriousness, difficult to imagine how any forensic professional could make it through a case involving death investigation without reaching for at least one of these texts for a refresher, for clarification, or for a citation in their own report.

The problem with these works is not related to their existing content. The information contained within their pages is generally good, with only minor concerns of note to the advanced professional. These volumes are, collectively, essential to forensic science practice and worthy of careful study.

However, these works fail on a practical level. While being accurate, they present the suggestion of uniform processes under ideal conditions. That is to say, they presume the honesty, integrity, and competence of not only fellow medicolegal professionals, but the entire law enforcement, prosecutorial, and courtroom apparatus. Death investigation is presented in a nearly blinding white light, as a discipline immune to obfuscation or agendas. In other words, these works do not account for the intrusion of personal bias, incompetency, and political scheming. To anyone that operates in the criminal justice system, this consistent omission is immediately apparent. For students who are on the cusp of entering the working world of criminal justice agencies and agendas, such a consistent omission leaves them unprepared for what is coming.

The purpose of this chapter is to provide students and professionals with an unfiltered look at how death investigations are conducted in the real world, contrasted against essential protocols for competent scientific practice. By identifying the weakness that is known to exist, we will be better prepared to negotiate them when they are encountered in casework. Awareness allows for preparedness.

Additionally, by providing protocols that are multi-referenced, we will be better prepared to defend their existence and acceptance when confronted by those in the criminal justice system who would rather pretend that they do not exist at all. This is the constant burden of professional forensic operative. Each day is battle against the ignorance of those who are looking to avoid responsibility and explain things away.

We will begin with basic terms and definitions; discuss the state of the science; identify common myths; provide essential roles, duties and protocols; and conclude with a list of common medicolegal failures.

TERMS AND DEFINITIONS

The terms and definitions associated with medicolegal death investigation are among the least understood in all of forensic science. Therefore, they are also among the most commonly misused, and abused, by those in the criminal justice system, the media, and the general public. Investigators get them wrong; attorneys get them wrong; and judges get them wrong. Sometimes misuse of terms is an honest mistake; sometimes it is an intentional distortion.

The honest forensic investigator seeks to avoid imprecise language whenever possible and endeavors to use terms appropriately to the extent that it is possible. This is because the use of single word out of place can bar evidence that is vital; admit evidence that is improper; and enhance evidence that is weak. The following definitions must therefore be kept handy and operationalized in reports, research, and testimony whenever necessary.

MEDICOLEGAL

Medicolegal is one of those terms that is used all of the time by people that never have to define it, nor could they if pressed. It may generally be defined as "relating to the law concerning medical questions" (Black, 1990, p. 982). In essence, it is an intentionally broad term used to describe those disciplines or activities that exist at the intersection of medicine and law, such as those practiced by medicolegal death investigators, forensic nurses, coroners, or medical examiners.

The state of the medicolegal death investigation system in the United States is explained in a congressionally funded report prepared by the National Academy of Sciences (NAS; Edwards & Gotsonis, 2009, p. 243):

Individual state statutes determine whether a medical examiner or coroner delivers death investigation services, which include death scene investigations, medical investigations, reviews of medical records, medicolegal autopsies, determination of the cause and manner of death, and completion of the certificate of death.

The NAS determined that this is a deeply troubled and even broken system, stating (p. 49): "The medicolegal death investigation system is a fragmented organization of state and local entities called upon to investigate deaths and to certify the cause and manner of unnatural and unexplained deaths." This fragmentation is characterized by high variability across the board in terms of structure, function, organizational accreditation, and individual credentials (Edwards & Gotsonis, 2009, p. 50):

Currently, 11 states have coroner-only systems, 22 states have medical examiner systems, and 18 states have mixed systems—in which some counties have coroners and others have medical examiners. Some of these states have a referral system, in which the coroner refers cases to medical examiners for autopsy…

Variability also is evident in terms of accreditation of death investigation systems. As of August 2008, 54 of the medical examiner offices in the United States (serving 23 percent of the population) have been accredited by the National Association of Medical Examiners, the professional organization of physician medical examiners. Most of the country is served by offices lacking accreditation. Similarly, requirements for training are not mandatory. About 36 percent of the population lives where minimal or no special training is required to conduct death investigations. Recently, an 18-year-old high school student was elected a deputy coroner in Indiana after completing a short training course.

To sum, the NAS Report confirms what those of us working in the criminal justice system already know: that death investigation is managed differently in each state and that the requirements and qualifications for those legally responsible for such investigations vary. Many, in fact, are dangerously underqualified. This is as much a funding issue as it is an issue of ignorance, as many jurisdictions simply cannot afford to pay for competent death investigations.

This reality creates confusion for everyone. It also cannot help but facilitates erroneous medicolegal conclusions and subsequent wrongful convictions. To be blunt, many crimes are missed, while others are fabricated from whole cloth, by death investigators who are by and large unqualified to do the job that they have been elected, appointed, or hired to do, with no hope or mandate for change any time in the near future.

MEDICOLEGAL DEATH INVESTIGATOR

As defined by the National Association of Medical Examiners (NAME), a medicolegal death investigator is (Peterson & Clark, 2006, p. 20): "An individual who is employed by a medicolegal death investigation system to conduct investigations into the circumstances of deaths in a jurisdiction."

MEDICAL DOCTOR

A *medical doctor* is a professional licensed to practice medicine in the state within which they are working. They must hold a doctorate in medicine from an accredited institution. Moreover, their licensure must be both regionally appropriate and current. Someone with a medical degree and licensure in the state of New York, for example, may not be lawfully entitled to practice medicine, or give medical opinions, in the state of Georgia, that is, until they have obtained the proper lawful permissions from that state's medical board. At the same time, a medical doctor may lose their license to practice in one state and then simply move to another where they can continue to practice once they have satisfied local state medical board requirements. This is not much different from the requirements and restrictions placed on attorneys and the practice of law.

This reality should place unequivocal restrictions on the testimony of any forensic pathologist. Legally, and ethically, they should not be allowed to give medical opinions outside of their state(s) of licensure. However, they are rarely called out for this in court, owing to the ignorance of attorneys and owing to a general lack of due diligence when checking resumes. In the experience of the authors, when most legal professionals hear that a witness holds a medical degree, they let them testify to whatever they want or need without objection.

MEDICAL OPINIONS

A *medical opinion* is any opinion given by a medical professional that is based on their medical education, training, and experience. A broad definition is provided in *Hunter v. Astrue* (2009), in which medical opinions are defined as "statements from physicians and psychologists or other acceptable medical sources." This definition narrows the field to those professionals that provide medical treatment. It could potentially include psychologists, medical doctors, nurses, and others holding some kind of medical background (e.g., education, training, and experience with the prevention, cure, and alleviation of diseases).

As this may suggest, not all medical professionals have the same medical background and expertise, therefore they may not opine equally on all areas of medicine. Professional testifying or opining beyond their area of expertise is generally violating their professional code of ethics. If they have no code of ethics governing them, then they are not a professional.

FORENSIC PATHOLOGY

Forensic pathology refers to an area of study; not an individual. It can be defined as "a branch of medicine that applies the principles and knowledge of the medical sciences to problems in the field of law," (DiMaio & DiMaio, 2001, p. 1). Consequently, to be a practicing forensic pathologist, one must also be a medical doctor. If one refers to oneself as a forensic pathologist without holding a medical degree, and a board certification in forensic pathology, this could be considered fraud, if not perjury when done under oath (e.g., affidavits and sworn testimony).

MEDICAL EXAMINER

The term *medical examiner* refers to a physician who is usually appointed or hired to public office and charged with the duties associated with medicolegal death investigation. They necessarily hold a medical degree and are likely to have a board certification in pathology or forensic pathology (note: pathology and forensic pathology are not the same thing). When a medical examiner gives opinion in relation to their medicolegal findings, it may properly be referred to as a *medical opinion*.

CORONER

The term *coroner* refers to a public official, usually elected to office, also charged with duties associated with medicolegal death investigation. As an elected official, they may need to only satisfy the most basic requirements to take public office. As explained in the NAS Report (Edwards & Gotsonis, 2009, p. 247):

> *Coroners as elected officials fulfill requirements for residency, minimum age, and any other qualifications required by statute. They may or may not be physicians, may or may not have medical training, and may or may not perform autopsies… Some serve as administrators of death investigation systems, while others are responsible solely for decisions regarding the cause and manner of death. Typical qualifications for election as a coroner include being a registered voter, attaining a minimum age requirement ranging from 18 to 25 years, being free of felony convictions, and completing a training program, which can be of varying length. The selection pool is local and small (because work is inconvenient and pay is relatively low), and medical training is not always a requirement. Coroners are independent of law enforcement and other agencies, but as elected officials they must be responsive to the public, and this may lead to difficulty in making unpopular determinations of the cause and manner of death.*

It should be noted that some states elect sheriff coroners, meaning that the office of coroner and the office of sheriff are held by the same person—which eradicates any notion of independent investigation. It should also be noted that despite the existence of separated agencies, some coroners are quite cozy with law enforcement. To the point of outright collusion, every relationship is different.

When a coroner gives opinion in relation to medicolegal findings, it may or may not be properly referred to as a *medical opinion*. Coroners and medical examiners are intended to conduct the same examinations and render the same medicolegal findings. When a coroner does it, however, it might not be a medical opinion because they might not be a medical doctor or have sufficient medical training. In other words, the determinations made during a death investigation are not by themselves medical opinions; they only become medical opinions when a medical professional gives them.

What this means is that the determinations made during a death investigation apparently need not be medical opinions. This is because many of those giving such opinions in courtrooms around the United States are not medical professionals, having no medical training or degrees, let alone board certifications. This reality is something that law enforcement, prosecutors, and even some judges work hard to conceal from juries—though only when it suits them.

AUTOPSY

The term autopsy refers to "the systematic external and internal examination of a body to establish the presence or absence of disease by gross and microscopic examination of body tissues" (Edwards & Gotsonis, 2009, p. 248). An autopsy is part of the overall medicolegal death investigation, not the whole thing. Its conclusions rely heavily on other information that is collected in relation to the death scene and the forensic evidence.

As explained in DiMaio and DiMaio (2001), the forensic autopsy includes the following investigative and forensic responsibilities (p. 1):

- To determine the cause and manner of death
- To identify the deceased if unknown
- To determine the time of death and injury
- To collect evidence from the body that can be used to prove or disprove an individual's guilt or innocence and to confirm or deny the account of how the death occurred.
- To document injuries or lack of them
- To deduce how the injuries occurred
- To document any natural disease present
- To determine or exclude other contributory or causative factors to the death
- To provide expert testimony if the case goes to trial

Logical and Comprehensible

Dolinak, Matshes, and Lew (2005) offer perhaps one of the most important notes on the autopsy report: that it be written logically and in a fashion that is easy to understand. Autopsy reports are not for medical professionals but law enforcement, attorneys, jurors, and other forensic professionals. That is to say, they must be written "for the benefit of the reader. The report should be comprehensible on first reading" (p. 3).

Too often, autopsy reports are written with unnecessarily complex terminology and without any meaningful sequence. Moreover, they tend to be written in such a fashion as to require multiple readings of a single sentence just to get the meaning (if it can be understood at all). Such practice suggests either an insecure mind, attempting to obfuscate inability; or an inexpert mind, lacking the ability to communicate with nonmedical personnel. Worse, it allows forensic opinions to be flexible during testimony, as the original findings are buried with equivocal or incomprehensible language.

Statutory Authority

The legal authority to document a death scene, take custody of a decedent's remains, and conduct a subsequent autopsy is delegated by regional statute to the coroner or medical examiner's office. This means that they do not need the permission of the police or the family to do their job. The results of the death scene investigation, combined with the results of the autopsy, are used to determine the cause and manner of death. Specific autopsy protocols will be discussed in a later section.

As proscribed by the National Association of Medical Examiners, there are a number or conditions when an autopsy is warranted, and perhaps even mandated. They offer the following list (Peterson & Clark, 2006, p. 3–4):

The forensic pathologist shall perform a forensic autopsy when:

B3.1 the death is known or suspected to have been caused by apparent criminal violence.
B3.2 the death is unexpected and unexplained in an infant or child.
B3.3 the death is associated with police action.
B3.4 the death is apparently nonnatural and in custody of a local, state, or federal institution.
B3.5 the death is due to acute workplace injury.
B3.6 the death is caused by apparent electrocution.
B3.7 the death is by apparent intoxication by alcohol, drugs, or poison.
B3.8 the death is caused by unwitnessed or suspected drowning.
B3.9 the body is unidentified and the autopsy may aid in identification.
B3.10 the body is skeletonized.
B3.11 the body is charred.
B3.12 the forensic pathologist deems a forensic autopsy is necessary to determine cause or manner of death or collect evidence.

Failure to conduct an autopsy when these circumstances are present is an abrogation of professional responsibility and should be viewed as an act of ignorance or apathy. It may also be a violation of law, depending on the jurisdiction.

The Autopsy as Medical Practice

The NAME explains that conducting an autopsy is a medical procedure to be carried out by exclusively by licensed physicians. They offer the following series of warnings (Peterson & Clark, 2006, p. 4):

Performance of a forensic autopsy is the practice of medicine. Forensic autopsy performance includes the discretion to determine the need for additional dissection and laboratory tests. A forensic autopsy must be conducted by a licensed physician who is a forensic pathologist or by a physician who is a forensic pathologist-in-training (resident/fellow). Responsibility for forensic autopsy quality must rest with the forensic pathologist, who must directly supervise support staff. Allowing non-forensic pathologists to conduct forensic autopsy procedures without direct supervision and guidance is fraught with the potential for serious errors and omissions.

This directly suggests that any autopsy, or related medicolegal death investigation, performed by a "nonforensic pathologist" (e.g., someone without a medical degree, and without board certification in forensic pathology), is necessarily substandard and likely to be full of error. The authors tend to agree, however, the absence of a prevailing federal statute makes it clear that the courts do not.

Investigate, Examine, Then Opine

The NAME guidelines stress the importance of formulating opinions and rendering findings only after the medicolegal death investigation has been completed. This means that forensic interpretations and opinions may not be given at the scene, and certainly not prior to establishing autopsy or toxicology results. Of course, this is inconsistent with every film and TV show that exists, wherein fictional medical examiners render fast findings at the scene, without the benefit of reflection or the results of forensic testing.

The authors could not agree more and would add that all information provided to the medical examiner or coroner must be validated. The theories of law enforcement and other first responders are not facts. They must be checked against the evidence established during forensic examinations of the evidence. They are not to be assumed valid and allowed to languish within, or otherwise taint, the medicolegal investigation. Unchecked theories and assumptions have no place in forensic findings, let alone providing their foundation.

CASE EXAMPLE: *ST. LOUIS COUNTY MEDICAL EXAMINER THOMAS UNCINI*

Consider the case of Thomas Uncini, MD, the former Medical Examiner of St. Louis County in Minnesota. He was, by all indications, forced to resign from his position under tremendous political pressure. As reported in Kraker (2015):

> Uncini pushed to perform autopsies on Native Americans who died in car accidents in Carlton County. Mushkoob Aubid, a 65-year-old member of the Mille Lacs Band of Ojibwe, died Feb. 7, a day after his car veered off a northern Minnesota highway and struck a utility pole. Autumn Martineau, a 24-year-old member of the Fond du Lac Band of Lake Superior Chippewa, died Feb. 10 in another crash.

> Both families were incensed. They practice a traditional form of Ojibwe religion known as Midewiwin, in which the cutting of a body is considered desecration and interferes with a four-day ritual performed when someone dies. The families obtained last-minute emergency orders from a Carlton County judge to have the bodies returned without autopsies...

> Uncini, who operates Lakeland Pathology, has contracts with St. Louis County and three other northern Minnesota counties to serve as medical examiner. There's no word yet whether Uncini also plans to resign as medical examiner there, Carlton County Attorney Thom Pertler said...
>
> Under state law, medical examiners have sole discretion to determine whether it is in the public interest to perform an autopsy when a death occurs from unnatural causes. St. Louis County Commissioner Keith Nelson said he supports the effort to change the law. But he worries that a family's choice to decline an autopsy could potentially "get in the way of justice."

What this case serves to demonstrate is that for all of independence and statutory authority enjoyed by a medical examiner—it is only theoretical. It is only as real and strong as the resolve of the politicians in charge, which is to say that, under the right conditions, independence and authority may not exist at all.

CAUSE OF DEATH

Determining the cause of death is a primary goal of any medicolegal death investigation. DiMaio and DiMaio (2001) define the *cause of death* as "any injury or disease that produces a physiological derangement in the body that results in the death of the individual." According to the Centers for Disease Control (CDC), the top 10 leading causes of death in the United States are, in order or greatest to least (CDC, 2016; total number of deaths in 2015 provided):

- Heart disease: 614,348
- Cancer: 591,699
- Chronic lower respiratory diseases: 147,101
- Accidents (unintentional injuries): 136,053
- Stroke (cerebrovascular diseases): 133,103
- Alzheimer's disease: 93,541
- Diabetes: 76,488
- Influenza and pneumonia: 55,227
- Nephritis, nephrotic syndrome, and nephrosis: 48,146
- Intentional self-harm (suicide): 42,773

Consistent with the experience of the authors, common causes of homicidal death include gunshot wounds; sharp force wounds (e.g., cuts and stabs); vehicles; asphyxia (e.g., manual and ligature strangulation; plastic bag over the head); blunt force trauma (e.g., struck by objects such as hammers, fists, boots, or baseball bats). Less common causes of homicidal death include poisoning; arson; and forcible drowning.

It is not always possible to establish a precise cause of death. This occurs for a variety of reasons. Sometimes the body is unavailable, or badly decomposed. Sometimes the medicolegal death investigation is insufficient. Regardless, cause of death must not be called without all evidence, and certainly not until a thorough medicolegal death investigation has been completed. As explained in the guidelines set forth by the NIJ (1999, p. xvii): "Elimination of unanswered questions, confusion, sloppiness, and the lack of attention to detail all can contribute to the genuine acceptance that the cause of death has been properly determined."

MANNER OF DEATH

Establishing the manner of death is another primary goal of any medicolegal death investigation. *Manner of death* refers to how the cause of death came about, generally. Put another way—it refers to classifying the nature of the interaction between an individual and his/her environment, such that it resulted in his/her death. The acceptable classifications for manner of death are limited to the following: *natural, accidental, homicide, suicide,* and *undetermined* (see generally DiMaio & DiMaio, 2001; Dolinak et al., 2005).

Natural

The CDC explains that *natural deaths* are those "due solely or nearly totally to disease and/or the aging process" (CDC, 2003, p. 21). In other words, the body stops functioning on its own, without intervening variables. Black (1990), however, reveals a common pathway to determining a natural death, defining it as "Death from causes other than accident or violence" (p. 1026). This would tend to suggest that *natural causes* might be improperly used as a default finding when other possibilities have been excluded. The authors would hold that unless a precise cause of death can be established, labeling a death *natural* is at best ill advised. This is, after all, intended to be a certain forensic finding and not a best guess.

Accidental

The CDC explains that *accidental deaths* are those where "there is little or no evidence that the injury or poisoning occurred with intent to harm or cause death. In essence, the fatal outcome was unintentional" (CDC, 2003, p. 21). Black (1990) offers that accidental deaths are those "caused by unexpected or unintended means" (p. 16). In these cases, it is important to understand that the individual unintentionally causes his/her own demise, and there are no other parties directly involved or responsible.

If someone else kills an individual, whether they meant to or not, that is classified as a *homicide*. No exceptions.

Homicide

Homicide is death at the hands of another. It has nothing to do with intent or state of mind (CDC, 2003; DiMaio & DiMaio, 2001; Dolinak et al., 2005). It is a neutral term without legal implication. Illegal homicide is referred to as *murder*.

Black (1990) goes further, explaining that homicide is not necessarily a criminal act. Rather "it is a necessary ingredient of the crimes of murder and manslaughter, but there are cases in which homicide may be committed without criminal intent and without criminal consequences," (p. 734). These include state sanctioned executions and cases of self-defense. This is also discussed in Melinak (2015):

> *Homicide means "death at the hand of another." Intent is not a factor—only a volitional act is required. It's up to the district attorney to determine whether it is in the state's interest to charge the defendant with murder or manslaughter, or not press any charge at all. Even if the DA does not press charges, or the defendant is prosecuted but acquitted, that fatal event is still a homicide. But it is not a murder. Calling a homicide a murder does not fall within the purview of the agency performing the forensic death investigation.*

Therefore, even when someone accidentally kills an individual, it is still classified as a *homicide*. This is often misunderstood and misapplied in police shootings, or in custody death cases, where law enforcement wishes to argue that a suspect death is accidental because officers did not intend to kill anyone. Again, death at the hands of another is still a homicide, no matter the intent, and it must be investigated as such. Arguing against this classification is generally the point, because all deaths classified as homicide must endure a criminal investigation. The result of that investigation determines whether or not the homicide was in fact murder.

Suicide

The CDC (2015) explains that *suicide* is "when people direct violence at themselves with the intent to end their lives, and they die as a result of their actions." In these cases, the individual intentionally causes their own demise, without the direct assistance or intervention of any other parties. As already mentioned, suicide is one of the leading causes of death in the United States.

If an individual unintentionally causes his/her own death, this must be classified as an accident. This is an important notion, as many cases involving autoerotic death are improperly classified as *suicide*. An autoerotic death is one that occurs during autoerotic behavior (e.g., masturbation) in which a device, apparatus, prop, chemical, or behavior that is engaged to enhance sexual stimulation actually causes death.

Autoerotic death scenes are often mistaken for either a *homicide* or a *suicide*.[1] They are in fact largely accidental in nature, resulting from behavior that is repeated and which the decedent expected to survive. There are certainly some cases in which the victim intended to commit suicide by autoerotic means, but these cases are few. When an autoerotic fatality is identified, it should be presumed accidental in manner unless there is strong evidence to the contrary. Furthermore, autoerotic fatalities are not the result of criminal behavior and should not be treated as crimes. Once a determination of autoerotic fatality is made, law enforcement may no longer be required to investigate the matter further (for thorough discussions, see Turvey, 2011; Turvey, 2013a).

Undetermined

Undetermined means there is not enough information to render a classification, or that multiple classifications cannot be eliminated. As explained in DiMaio and DiMaio (2001, p. 5):

> *A manner of death is ruled undetermined when there is insufficient information about the circumstances surrounding the death to make a ruling, or, in some*

instances, when the cause of death is unknown. Thus, if one finds the skeletonized remains of a young adult male without evidence of trauma, one cannot say whether the manner of death was accident, homicide, or suicide, because the cause of death is not known. In other instances, there may be insufficient information concerning the circumstances surrounding the death to explain the manner of death.

The authors have witnessed this classification levied in many instances. Sometimes it is the result of an incomplete or incompetent investigation. Sometimes it is impossible to know the precise manner of death because the body is not available or has been utterly destroyed (e.g., fire, decomposition). Suffice it to say that when the manner of death is *undetermined*, charging someone with homicide is not supported by the scientific evidence.[2]

PROTOCOLS FOR MEDICOLEGAL DEATH INVESTIGATORS

The NIJ has set forth and exceptional set of protocols in their collaborative work *Death Investigation: A Guide for the Scene Investigator* (NIJ, 1999). Developed and approved by the National Medicolegal Review Panel, with dozens of consulting experts from all over the United States, this free handbook provides anyone with the knowledge required to properly process a death scene so as to preserve the evidence for medicolegal purposes. It is not complicated nor is it expensive.

It consists of Sections A—F. The first sections, A and B, are set forth as follows in the table of contents:

Section A: Investigative Tools and Equipment
Section B: Arriving at the Scene
1. Introduce and Identify Self and Role
2. Exercise Scene Safety
3. Confirm or Pronounce Death
4. Participate in Scene Briefing (With Attending Agency Representatives)
5. Conduct Scene "Walk Through"
6. Establish Chain of Custody
7. Follow Laws (Related to the Collection of Evidence)

These are self-explanatory, save item *6B—Chain of Custody*.

CHAIN OF CUSTODY

A *chain of custody* (a.k.a. chain of evidence) is the record of each person, and agency, who has controlled, taken custody of, examined, tested, or had any other kind of contact with a particular item of evidence, from its discovery to the present day. It has tremendous importance with respect to providing the context for, and a record of, any scientific examinations. It also has considerable value with respect to establishing the origins of evidence when it is presented in court.

As explained in the NAS Report (Edwards & Gotsonis, 2009), the chain of custody is created and exists as a forensic pathway along which evidence examination, testing, and interpretation are meant to occur (p. 36):

Crime scene evidence moves through a chain of custody in which, depending on their physical characteristics (e.g., blood, fiber, handwriting), samples are analyzed according to any of a number of analytical protocols, and results are reported to law enforcement and court officials. When evidence is analyzed, typically forensic science "attempts to uncover the actions or happenings of an event… by way of (1) identification (categorization), (2) individualization, (3) association, and (4) reconstruction." Evidence also is analyzed for the purpose of excluding individuals or sources.

Without a chain of sufficient strength, reliable interpretations about the evidence and its role in a given crime cannot be made. Challenges to its integrity will follow, as they should. However, breaks in the chain do not necessarily make an item of evidence inadmissible. When evidence is admitted into court without a sufficient chain of evidence, forensic scientists must be able and willing to explain how this may influence the certainty, accuracy, or relevance of their findings.

Moreover, misconduct, incompetence and even forensic fraud related to falsifying chain of custody documents are not uncommon (Turvey, 2013b). For this reason and others, *chain of custody* is glossed over by attorneys, and courts, seeking to ignore the persistent failure of law enforcement investigators in this regard. The authors have even seen attorneys stoop so low as to suggest that chain of custody is an academic concern of the high-minded, and not a real concern for police investigators who cannot be bothered with paperwork when hot on the trail—or nonsensical explanations when the chain is absent or violated.

In any case, if there is no chain, there is no evidence integrity or no trust. Taken from *Death Investigation* (NIJ, 1999, p. 20), it is incumbent upon all forensic investigators to establish and attend chain of custody for all items of evidence:

6. Establish Chain of Custody

Principle: Ensuring the integrity of the evidence by establishing and maintaining a chain of custody is vital to an investigation. This will safeguard against subsequent allegations of tampering, theft, planting, and contamination of evidence…

Policy: Prior to the removal of any evidence, the custodian(s) of evidence shall be designated and shall generate and maintain a chain of custody for all evidence collected.

Procedure: Throughout the investigation, those responsible for preserving the chain of custody should:

A. Document location of the scene and time of arrival of the death investigator at the scene.

B. Determine custodian(s) of evidence, determine which agency(ies) is/are responsible for collection of specific types of evidence, and determine evidence collection priority for fragile/fleeting evidence.
C. Identify, secure, and preserve evidence with proper containers, labels, and preservatives
D. Document the collection of evidence by recording its location at the scene, time of collection, and time and location of disposition.
E. Develop personnel lists, witness lists, and documentation of times of arrival and departure of personnel.

Summary: It is essential to maintain a proper chain of custody for evidence. Through proper documentation, collection, and preservation, the integrity of the evidence can be assured. A properly maintained chain of custody and prompt transfer will reduce the likelihood of a challenge to the integrity of the evidence.

CASE EXAMPLE: *RICHMOND COUNTY CORONER GROVER TUTEN, JR.*

Consider the case of Grover F. Tuten, former Coroner of Richmond County, Georgia (Fig. 9.1). He was sentenced to 3 years in prison for stealing a dead person's debit card and illegally withdrawing almost $10,000 from various ATM machines around greater Augusta. As reported in FBI (2015):

> Grover F. Tuten, Jr., 72, the former Coroner for Richmond County, Georgia, was sentenced today to 36 months in prison by United States District Court Judge J. Randal Hall after pleading guilty to his repeated use of a deceased person's debit card without authorization.
>
> According to evidence presented at the guilty plea and sentencing hearings, the victim passed away on August 24, 2012. Afterwards, and while he was the Richmond County Coroner, Tuten obtained the victim's bank card from the victim's caretaker. Tuten proceeded to unlawfully make 33 ATM withdrawals in the Augusta area. Many of these withdrawals were captured on bank surveillance video. Tuten unlawfully received $9800 in cash as a result of his theft...
>
> Tuten still faces state charges of theft by taking and violation of oath by a public officer and is being prosecuted by District Attorney Ashley Wright of the Augusta Judicial Circuit.

Further details are provided in Hodsen (2015):

> On Wednesday, FBI Special Agent Charges McKee testified that after the news of Tuten's arrest broke, a tip led to Patricia Williams, who was Coleman's caregiver for several years until he died on Aug. 24, 2012. Williams told McKee that she turned over Coleman's personal property to Tuten, including an ATM card for Coleman's bank account that held $20,000, McKee testified. She said she refused Tuten's requests to withdraw money for him and provide the PIN number.
>
> McKee obtained Coleman's bank records and found calls from Tuten's private work number to the bank requesting that Coleman's PIN number be reset, the agent testified. As coroner, Tuten had access to all of Coleman's personal identification such as date of birth and Social Security number...

FIGURE 9.1

Grover F. Tuten, Jr., 72, the Former Coroner for Richmond County.

Questioned by Tuten's attorney, McKee said there was no record of Tuten using the money from Coleman's account to pay for the burial. A $3000 check from Richmond County paid for the funeral expenses, McKee testified. Tuten told the judge Wednesday that Coleman's caretaker refused to pay for the funeral and that was why he withdrew the money.

Tuten worked for the coroner's office for 26 years. He was first elected coroner in 2004. He resigned from office Feb. 20, 2014.

Mr. Tuten's crimes exemplify a recurring problem within medical examiner and coroner offices nationwide: theft of property. Medicolegal death investigators, especially coroners, can too often be found stealing personal items from the deceased individuals they are investigating. This includes cash, jewelry, checkbooks, credit cards, debit cards, and prescription medication.

DEATH INVESTIGATION PROTOCOLS

What follows are the remaining essential protocols mandated by Death Investigation (NIJ, 1999), to include Sections C—F: Documenting and Evaluating the Scene; Documenting and Evaluating the Body; Establishing and Recording Decedent Profile

Information; and Completing the Scene Investigation. Excepted with minor edits (p. 22–47):

Section C. Documenting and Evaluating the Scene

1. Photograph Scene

Note: If evidence has been moved prior to photography, it should be noted in the report, but the body or other evidence should not be reintroduced into the scene in order to take photographs.

Summary: Photography allows for the best permanent documentation of the death scene. It is essential that accurate scene photographs are available for other investigators, agencies, and authorities to recreate the scene. Photographs are a permanent record of the terminal event and retain evidentiary value and authenticity. It is essential that the investigator obtain accurate photographs before releasing the scene.

2. Develop Descriptive Documentation of the Scene

Principle: Written documentation of the scene(s) provides a permanent record that may be used to correlate with and enhance photographic documentation, refresh recollections, and record observations...

Policy: Investigators shall provide written scene documentation.

Procedure: After photographic documentation of the scene and prior to removal of the body or other evidence, the investigator should:

A. Diagram/describe in writing items of evidence and their relationship to the body with necessary measurements.

B. Describe and document, with necessary measurements, blood and body fluid evidence including volume, patterns, spatters, and other characteristics.

C. Describe scene environments including odors, lights, temperatures, and other fragile evidence.

Note: If evidence has been moved prior to written documentation, it should be noted in the report.

Summary: Written scene documentation is essential to correlate with photographic evidence and to recreate the scene for police, forensic(s), and judicial and civil agencies with a legitimate interest.

3. Establish Probable Location of Injury or Illness

Principle: The location where the decedent is found may not be the actual location where the injury/illness that contributed to the death occurred. It is imperative that the investigator attempt to determine the locations of any and all injury(ies)/illness(es) that may have contributed to the death. Physical evidence at any and all locations may be pertinent in establishing the cause, manner, and circumstances of death...

Policy: The investigator shall obtain detailed information regarding any and all probable locations associated with the individual's death.

Procedure: The investigator should:

A. Document location where death was confirmed.

B. Determine location from which decedent was transported and how body was transported to scene.

C. Identify and record discrepancies in rigor mortis, livor mortis, and body temperature.

D. Check body, clothing, and scene for consistency/inconsistency of trace evidence and indicate location where artifacts are found.

E. Check for drag marks (on body and ground).

F. Establish post-injury activity.

G. Obtain dispatch (e.g., police, ambulance) record(s).

H. Interview family members and associates as needed.

Summary: Due to post-injury survival, advances in emergency medical services, multiple modes of transportation, the availability of specialized care, or criminal activity, a body may be moved from the actual location of illness/injury to a remote site. It is imperative that the investigator attempt to determine any and all locations where the decedent has previously been and the mode of transport from these sites.

4. Collect, Inventory, and Safeguard Property and Evidence

Principle: The decedent's valuables/property must be safeguarded to ensure proper processing and eventual return to next of kin. Evidence on or near the body must be safeguarded to ensure its availability for further evaluation…

Policy: The investigator shall ensure that all property and evidence is collected, inventoried, safeguarded, and released as required by law.

Procedure: After personal property and evidence have been identified at the scene, the investigator (with a witness) should:

A. Inventory, collect, and safeguard illicit drugs and paraphernalia at scene and/or office.
B. Inventory, collect, and safeguard prescription medication at scene and/or office.
C. Inventory, collect, and safeguard over-the-counter medications at scene and/or office.
D. Inventory, collect, and safeguard money at scene and at office.
E. Inventory, collect, and safeguard personal valuables/property at scene and at office.

Summary: Personal property and evidence are important items at a death investigation. Evidence must be safeguarded to ensure its availability if needed for future evaluation and litigation. Personal property must be safeguarded to ensure its eventual distribution to appropriate agencies or individuals and to reduce the likelihood that the investigator will be accused of stealing property.

5. Interview Witness(es) at the Scene

Principle: The documented comments of witnesses at the scene allow the investigator to obtain primary source data regarding discovery of body, witness corroboration, and terminal history. The documented interview provides essential information for the investigative process…

Policy: The investigator's report shall include the source of information, including specific statements and information provided by the witness.

Procedure: Upon arriving at the scene, the investigator should:

A. Collect all available identifying data on witnesses (e.g., full name, address, DOB, work and home telephone numbers, etc.).
B. Establish witness' relationship/association to the deceased.
C. Establish the basis of witness' knowledge (how does witness have knowledge of the death?).
D. Obtain information from each witness.
E. Note discrepancies from the scene briefing (challenge, explain, verify statements).
F. Tape statements where such equipment is available and retain them.

Summary: The final report must document witness' identity and must include a summary of witness' statements, corroboration with other witnesses, and the circumstances of discovery of the death. This documentation must exist as a permanent record to establish a chain of events.

Section D. Documenting and Evaluating the Body

1. Photograph the Body

Principle: The photographic documentation of the body at the scene creates a permanent record that preserves essential details of the body position, appearance, identity, and final movements. Photographs allow sharing of information with other agencies investigating the death…

Policy: The investigator shall obtain detailed photographic documentation of the body that provides both instant and permanent high-quality (e.g., 35 mm) images.
Procedure: Upon arrival at the scene, and prior to moving the body or evidence, the investigator should:
A. Photograph the body and immediate scene (including the decedent as initially found).
B. Photograph the decedent's face.
C. Take additional photographs after removal of objects/items that interfere with photographic documentation of the decedent (e.g., body removed from car).
D. Photograph the decedent with and without measurements (as appropriate).
E. Photograph the surface beneath the body (after the body has been removed, as appropriate).
Note: Never clean face, do not change condition. Take multiple shots if possible.
Summary: The photographic documentation of the body at the scene provides for documentation of the body position, identity, and appearance. The details of the body at the scene provide investigators with pertinent information of the terminal events.

2. Conduct External Body Examination (Superficial)
Principle: Conducting the external body examination provides the investigator with objective data regarding the single most important piece of evidence at the scene, the body. This documentation provides detailed information regarding the decedent's physical attributes, his/her relationship to the scene, and possible cause, manner, and circumstances of death…
Policy: The investigator shall obtain detailed photographs and written documentation of the decedent at the scene.
Procedure: After arrival at the scene and prior to moving the decedent, the investigator should, without removing decedent's clothing:
A. Photograph the scene, including the decedent as initially found and the surface beneath the body after the body has been removed.
Note: If necessary, take additional photographs after removal of objects/items that interfere with photographic documentation of the decedent.
B. Photograph the decedent with and without measurements (as appropriate), including a photograph of the decedent's face.
C. Document the decedent's position with and without measurements (as appropriate).
D. Document the decedent's physical characteristics.
E. Document the presence or absence of clothing and personal effects.
F. Document the presence or absence of any items/objects that may be relevant.
G. Document the presence or absence of marks, scars, and tattoos.
H. Document the presence or absence of injury/trauma, petechiae, etc.
I. Document the presence of treatment or resuscitative efforts.
J. Based on the findings, determine the need for further evaluation/assistance of forensic specialists (e.g., pathologists, odontologists).
Summary: Thorough evaluation and documentation (photographic and written) of the deceased at the scene is essential to determine the depth and direction the investigation will take.

3. Preserve Evidence (on Body)
Principle: The photographic and written documentation of evidence on the body allows the investigator to obtain a permanent historical record of that evidence. To maintain chain of custody, evidence must be collected, preserved, and transported properly. In addition to all of the physical evidence visible on the body, blood and other body fluids present must be photographed and documented prior to collection and transport. Fragile evidence (that which can be easily contaminated, lost, or altered) must also be collected

and/or preserved to maintain chain of custody and to assist in determination of cause, manner, and circumstances of death...

Policy: With photographic and written documentation, the investigator will provide a permanent record of evidence that is on the body.

Procedure: Once evidence on the body is recognized, the investigator should:

A. Photograph the evidence.
B. Document blood/body fluid on the body (froth/purge, substances from orifices), location, and pattern before transporting.
C. Place decedent's hands and/or feet in unused paper bags (as determined by the scene).
D. Collect trace evidence before transporting the body (e.g., blood, hair, fibers, etc.).
E. Arrange for the collection and transport of evidence at the scene (when necessary).
F. Ensure the proper collection of blood and body fluids for subsequent analysis (if body will be released from scene to an outside agency without an autopsy).

Summary: It is essential that evidence be collected, preserved, transported, and documented in an orderly and proper fashion to ensure the chain of custody and admissibility in a legal action. The preservation and documentation of the evidence on the body must be initiated by the investigator at the scene to prevent alterations or contamination.

4. Establish Decedent Identification

Principle: The establishment or confirmation of the decedent's identity is paramount to the death investigation. Proper identification allows notification of next of kin, settlement of estates, resolution of criminal and civil litigation, and the proper completion of the death certificate.

Policy: The investigator shall engage in a diligent effort to establish/confirm the decedent's identity.

Procedure: To establish identity, the investigator should document use of the following methods:

A. Direct visual or photographic identification of the decedent if visually recognizable.
B. Scientific methods such as fingerprints, dental, radiographic, and DNA comparisons.
C. Circumstantial methods such as (but not restricted to) personal effects, circumstances, physical characteristics, tattoos, and anthropologic data.

Summary: There are several methods available that can be used to properly identify deceased persons. This is essential for investigative, judicial, family, and vital records issues.

5. Document Post Mortem Changes

Principle: The documenting of post mortem changes to the body assists the investigator in explaining body appearance in the interval following death. Inconsistencies between post mortem changes and body location may indicate movement of body and validate or invalidate witness statements. In addition, post mortem changes to the body, when correlated with circumstantial information, can assist the investigators in estimating the approximate time of death...

Policy: The investigator shall document all post mortem changes relative to the decedent and the environment.

Procedure: Upon arrival at the scene and prior to moving the body, the investigator should note the presence of each of the following in his/her report:

A. Livor (color, location, blanchability, Tardieu spots) consistent/inconsistent with position of the body.
B. Rigor (stage/intensity, location on the body, broken, inconsistent with the scene).
C. Degree of decomposition (putrefaction, adipocere, mummification, skeletonization, as appropriate).

D. Insect and animal activity.
E. Scene temperature (document method used and time estimated).
F. Description of body temperature (e.g., warm, cold, frozen) or measurement of body temperature (document method used and time of measurement).
Summary: Documentation of post mortem changes in every report is essential to determine an accurate cause and manner of death, provide information as to the time of death, corroborate witness statements, and indicate that the body may have been moved after death.

6. Participate in Scene Debriefing
Principle: The scene debriefing helps investigators from all participating agencies to establish post-scene responsibilities by sharing data regarding particular scene findings. The scene debriefing provides each agency the opportunity for input regarding special requests for assistance, additional information, special examinations, and other requests requiring interagency communication, cooperation, and education...
Policy: The investigator shall participate in or initiate interagency scene debriefing to verify specific post-scene responsibilities.
Procedure: When participating in scene debriefing, the investigator should:
A. Determine post-scene responsibilities (identification, notification, press relations, and evidence transportation).
B. Determine/identify the need for a specialist (e.g., crime laboratory technicians, social services, entomologists, OSHA).
C. Communicate with the pathologist about responding to the scene or to the autopsy schedule (as needed).
D. Share investigative data (as required in furtherance of the investigation).
E. Communicate special requests to appropriate agencies, being mindful of the necessity for confidentiality.
Summary: The scene debriefing is the best opportunity for investigative participants to communicate special requests and confirm all current and additional scene responsibilities. The debriefing allows participants the opportunity to establish clear lines of responsibility for a successful investigation.

7. Determine Notification Procedures (Next of Kin)
Principle: Every reasonable effort should be made to notify the next of kin as soon as possible. Notification of next of kin initiates closure for the family, disposition of remains, and facilitates the collection of additional information relative to the case...
Policy: The investigator shall ensure that next of kin is notified of the death and that all failed and successful attempts at notification are documented.
Procedure: When determining notification procedures, the investigator should:
A. Identify next of kin (determine who will perform task).
B. Locate next of kin (determine who will perform task).
C. Notify next of kin (assign person(s) to perform task) and record time of notification, or, if delegated to another agency, gain confirmation when notification is made.
D. Notify concerned agencies of status of the notification.
Summary: The investigator is responsible for ensuring that the next of kin is identified, located, and notified in a timely manner. The time and method of notification should be documented. Failure to locate next of kin and efforts to do so should be a matter of record. This ensures that every reasonable effort has been made to contact the family.

8. Ensure Security of Remains
Principle: Ensuring security of the body requires the investigator to supervise the labeling, packaging, and removal of the remains. An appropriate identification tag is placed on the body to preclude misidentification upon receipt at the examining agency.

This function also includes safeguarding all potential physical evidence and/or property and clothing that remain on the body...

Policy: The investigator shall supervise and ensure the proper identification, inventory, and security of evidence/property and its packaging and removal from the scene.

Procedure: Prior to leaving the scene, the investigator should:

A. Ensure that the body is protected from further trauma or contamination (if not, document) and unauthorized removal of therapeutic and resuscitative equipment.
B. Inventory and secure property, clothing, and personal effects that are on the body (remove in a controlled environment with witness present).
C. Identify property and clothing to be retained as evidence (in a controlled environment).
D. Recover blood and/or vitreous samples prior to release of remains.
E. Place identification on the body and body bag.
F. Ensure/supervise the placement of the body into the bag.
G. Ensure/supervise the removal of the body from the scene.
H. Secure transportation.

Summary: Ensuring the security of the remains facilitates proper identification of the remains, maintains a proper chain of custody, and safeguards property and evidence.

Section E. Establishing and Recording Decedent Profile Information

1. Document the Discovery History

Principle: Establishing a decedent profile includes documenting a discovery history and circumstances surrounding the discovery. The basic profile will dictate subsequent levels of investigation, jurisdiction, and authority. The focus (breadth/depth) of further investigation is dependent on this information...

Policy: The investigator shall document the discovery history, available witnesses, and apparent circumstances leading to death.

Procedure: For an investigator to correctly document the discovery history, he/she should:

A. Establish and record person(s) who discovered the body and when.
B. Document the circumstances surrounding the discovery (who, what, where, when, how).

Summary: The investigator must produce clear, concise, documented information concerning who discovered the body, what are the circumstances of discovery, where the discovery occurred, when the discovery was made, and how the discovery was made.

2. Determine Terminal Episode History

Principle: Pre-terminal circumstances play a significant role in determining cause and manner of death. Documentation of medical intervention and/or procurement of antemortem specimens help to establish the decedent's condition prior to death...

Policy: The investigator shall document known circumstances and medical intervention preceding death.

Procedure: In order for the investigator to determine terminal episode history, he/she should:

A. Document when, where, how, and by whom decedent was last known to be alive.
B. Document the incidents prior to the death.
C. Document complaints/symptoms prior to the death.
D. Document and review complete EMS records (including the initial electrocardiogram).
E. Obtain relevant medical records (copies).
F. Obtain relevant ante mortem specimens.

Summary: Obtaining records of pre-terminal circumstances and medical history distinguishes medical treatment from trauma. This history and relevant ante mortem specimens assist the medical examiner/coroner in determining cause and manner of death.

3. Document Decedent Medical History

Principle: The majority of deaths referred to the medical examiner/coroner are natural deaths. Establishing the decedent's medical history helps to focus the investigation. Documenting the decedent's medical signs or symptoms prior to death determines the need for subsequent examinations. The relationship between disease and injury may play a role in the cause, manner, and circumstances of death...

Policy: The investigator shall obtain the decedent's past medical history.

Procedure: Through interviews and review of the written records, the investigator should:

A. Document medical history, including medications taken, alcohol and drug use, and family medical history from family members and witnesses.

B. Document information from treating physicians and/or hospitals to confirm history and treatment.

C. Document physical characteristics and traits (e.g., left-/right handedness, missing appendages, tattoos, etc.).

Summary: Obtaining a thorough medical history focuses the investigation, aids in disposition of the case, and helps determine the need for a post mortem examination or other laboratory tests or studies.

4. Document Decedent Mental Health History

Principle: The decedent's mental health history can provide insight into the behavior/state of mind of the individual. That insight may produce clues that will aid in establishing the cause, manner, and circumstances of the death...

Policy: The investigator shall obtain information from sources familiar with the decedent pertaining to the decedent's mental health history.

Procedure: The investigator should:

A. Document the decedent's mental health history, including hospitalizations and medications.

B. Document the history of suicidal ideations, gestures, and/or attempts.

C. Document mental health professionals (e.g., psychiatrists, psychologists, counselors, etc.) who treated the decedent.

D. Document family mental health history.

Summary: Knowledge of the mental health history allows the investigator to evaluate properly the decedent's state of mind and contributes to the determination of cause, manner, and circumstances of death.

5. Document Social History

Principle: Social history includes marital, family, sexual, educational, employment, and financial information. Daily routines, habits and activities, and friends and associates of the decedent help in developing the decedent's profile. This information will aid in establishing the cause, manner, and circumstances of death...

Policy: The investigator shall obtain social history information from sources familiar with the decedent.

Procedure: When collecting relevant social history information, the investigator should:

A. Document marital/domestic history.

B. Document family history (similar deaths, significant dates).

C. Document sexual history.

D. Document employment history.

E. Document financial history.

F. Document daily routines, habits, and activities.

G. Document relationships, friends, and associates.

H. Document religious, ethnic, or other pertinent information (e.g., religious objection to autopsy).
I. Document educational background.
J. Document criminal history.
Summary: Information from sources familiar with the decedent pertaining to the decedent's social history assists in determining cause, manner, and circumstances of death.

F. Completing the Scene Investigation

1. Maintain Jurisdiction Over the Body
Principle: Maintaining jurisdiction over the body allows the investigator to protect the chain of custody as the body is transported from the scene for autopsy, specimen collection, or storage...
Policy: The investigator shall maintain jurisdiction of the body by arranging for the body to be transported for autopsy, specimen collection, or storage by secure conveyance.
Procedure: When maintaining jurisdiction over the body, the investigator should:
A. Arrange for, and document, secure transportation of the body to a medical or autopsy facility for further examination or storage.
B. Coordinate and document procedures to be performed when the body is received at the facility.
Summary: By providing documented secure transportation of the body from the scene to an authorized receiving facility, the investigator maintains jurisdiction and protects chain of custody of the body.

2. Release Jurisdiction of the Body
Principle: Prior to releasing jurisdiction of the body to an authorized receiving agent or funeral director, it is necessary to determine the person responsible for certification of the death. Information to complete the death certificate includes demographic information and the date, time, and location of death....
Policy: The investigator shall obtain sufficient data to enable completion of the death certificate and release of jurisdiction over the body.
Procedure: When releasing jurisdiction over the body, the investigator should:
A. Determine who will sign the death certificate (name, agency, etc.).
B. Confirm the date, time, and location of death.
C. Collect, when appropriate, blood, vitreous fluid, and other evidence prior to release of the body from the scene.
D. Document and arrange with the authorized receiving agent to reconcile all death certificate information.
E. Release the body to a funeral director or other authorized receiving agent.
Summary: The investigator releases jurisdiction only after determining who will sign the death certificate; documenting the date, time, and location of death; collecting appropriate specimens; and releasing the body to the funeral director or other authorized receiving agent.

3. Perform Exit Procedures
Principle: Bringing closure to the scene investigation ensures that important evidence has been collected and the scene has been processed. In addition, a systematic review of the scene ensures that artifacts or equipment are not inadvertently left behind (e.g., used disposable gloves, paramedical debris, film wrappers, etc.), and any dangerous materials or conditions have been reported...
Policy: At the conclusion of the scene investigation, the investigator shall conduct a post-investigative "walk through" and ensure the scene investigation is complete.
Procedure: When performing exit procedures, the investigator should:

> A. Identify, inventory, and remove all evidence collected at the scene.
> B. Remove all personal equipment and materials from the scene.
> C. Report and document any dangerous materials or conditions.
> Summary: Conducting a scene "walk through" upon exit ensures that all evidence has been collected, that materials are not inadvertently left behind, and that any dangerous materials or conditions have been reported to the proper entities.

Implicit in these guidelines is a recognition that they are necessary—because competent training and practice continue to elude the practice of medicolegal death investigation nationwide (see generally Edwards & Gotsonis, 2009).

It bears mentioning that these guidelines have been around for almost 20 years now; everyone knows that they exist; and they are almost never followed. Students and professionals are trained with these guidelines, they go out into the world, and then that training is ignored by the political structure and policies of the agencies that employ them. Primarily because the prosecution does not want this wealth of information in the hands of the defense; they want to control information flow about the victim in the discovery process. So there is no accountability for medicolegal death investigators who ignore good science and best investigative practice when rendering their findings, so long as they remain police and prosecution friendly. Otherwise extensive decedent profile information, background, and other relevant history (e.g., victimology) would be collected and made available in every death investigation. Instead, it is generally ignored.

CASE EXAMPLE: *STATE MEDICAL EXAMINER, OKLAHOMA*

Consider the series of related scandals involving the State Medical Examiner's Office in Oklahoma. In 2009, it lost its NAME accreditation and was, at the same time, subjected to a Grand Jury Investigation. During the same timeframe, the Medical Examiner (Dr. Collie Trant) was fired; the interim Medical Examiner (Dr. Andrew Sibley) was investigated for sexual harassment; and the former Chief Investigator (Kevin Rowland) was charged with rape. As reported in Hoberock (2009):

> The state medical examiner's office has lost its accreditation with the National Association of Medical Examiners. Oklahoma had been accredited for 18 consecutive years, the association's executive director, Denise McNally, said Wednesday.
>
> The accrediting agency detected an excessive number of deficiencies, according to a letter sent to the medical examiner's office by Dr. Jeffrey M. Jentzen, chairman of the association's inspections and accreditation committee. "It should be noted that the majority of the deficiencies were related to the facility and staffing," the letter states. "The inspector recognized the quality of work done by your dedicated staff, when death investigations and autopsy pathology are performed, despite the deficiencies."
>
> Dr. Collie M. Trant, the state's chief medical examiner, said the grade is the result of underfunding, a lack of staffing, poor equipment and facilities…
>
> The agency has been the subject of a probe by the Oklahoma State Bureau of Investigation and the multicounty grand jury. It also has drawn criticism from some lawmakers, who have suggested the agency be moved into the OSBI or state Health Department.

The Grand Jury investigation into the Medical Examiner's Office revealed an agency in chaos, with employees both professionally lost and abused, and all staff being run roughshod over by the chief investigator. It reported the following and resulted in multiple indictments (MGJIR, 2009, p. 2–5):

> Over the past few months, this jury has heard testimony leading it to conclude that there has been either willful blindness or gross incompetence on the part of those responsible for administration of the office. Others who should have been limited in their scope of authority have been allowed to exercise apparent authority over the entire office overriding the agency's organizational chart. Ultimately, some staff members have suffered at the hands of another. The manner in which the Medical Examiner Office was run has resulted in the office falling short of its true calling. Mal administration has ultimately led to various existing and potential problems identified by the grand jury.
>
> In the State of Oklahoma, the top administrator for the Medical Examiner Office has always been a pathologist. The Medical Examiner Office occupies a position of utmost public trust. The office is given enormous responsibilities. Although the Chief Medical Examiner is the top administrator, for a number of years, many of the administrative duties have fallen to the person who served as chief investigator. One former Chief Medical Examiner testified that he was paid $235,000.00 a year to be the Chief Medical Examiner and that he only spent approximately 25% of his time performing in an administrative capacity.
>
> Based on the evidence collected by the grand jury, administrative duties such as overseeing the day to day operations of the physical offices for the Chief Medical Examiner, hiring and firing staff and setting office procedure and policy were delegated to the former chief investigator. The former chief investigator was used as the funnel through which all decisions were made by Chief Medical Examiners. The grand jury found that what resulted is an abuse of power by the person who served as chief investigator. The extent to which one employee was given unbridled authority is astounding to the grand jury. The grand jury understands Chief Medical Examiners dating back several years were made aware of brewing problems concerning the former chief investigator, however, he was allowed to continue the exercise of what can only be described as absolute power, control and authority over the entire office.
>
> The grand jury concludes that delegation of such a large degree of authority to one person who was obviously abusive was no less than derelict on behalf of Chief Medical Examiners. For some time, Chief Medical Examiners were made aware that the former chief investigator's behavior, in particular, was abrasive, sexually harassing and sometimes rose to violations of criminal law.
>
> The grand jury believes the former chief investigator's conduct could have been stopped by proper oversight. After listening to testimony, it became evident that comments were made to several women and men that were inappropriate and sexual in nature. Testimony showed that not only did the former chief investigator make the referenced comments, but he set the tone in the office for other males to feel comfortable making similar types of comments to female staff. Testimony indicated that sexual harassment and sexual battery were carried out within the office.
>
> A couple of witnesses testified that they filed grievances in reference to allegations of sexual harassment. The grand jury found that the handling of grievances by those working in human resources did not provide for creating and maintaining files in reference to formal grievances wherein such files would be kept in a secure location separate and apart from other personnel files. In fact, the grand jury learned that

documentation concerning the referenced grievances were either lost or stolen and could not be found in personnel files for either the accuser(s) Ot the accused.

The grand jury also found that nothing ultimately happened in reference to the formal grievances. The grand jury is left to wonder whether the former chief investigator's behavior would have escalated to criminal conduct had the grievances for sexual harassment been properly handled. Multiple other witnesses testified that they would have lodged complaints against the former chief investigator and/or others but decided their efforts would be futile because:

- There are no internal procedures for lodging formal complaints;
- Investigations of complaints are not carried out; *and*
- Some complaining parties feared retaliation from the former chief investigator;

In reference to virtually every aspect of the office's operations, there are scarce written policies and procedures for employee reference. Written policies are lacking as to personnel matters as well as protocol for how investigations or cases should be handled. Witnesses including investigators appearing before the grand jury advised that they have questioned why written policies and procedures do not exist in various areas. Some witnesses advised that the former chief investigator, in particular, served as close advisor to chief medical examiners and that the former chief investigator has been quoted as saying "if a policy is in writing then we would have to follow it." Witnesses testified that written policies and procedures don't exist in some areas because the former chief investigator did not want them to be in writing.

As a result of the absence of written policies and procedures, there is inconsistency in how routine practices are carried out by staff. Some individuals have developed best practice rules for self governance. However, even if the staff consists of a majority of individuals who tend to be methodical, leaving each individual to develop his or her own procedure runs the risk of inconsistency within the agency. Furthermore, the absence of written policy and procedure in reference to personnel matters can only result in inequity when resolving the same or similar matters.

It is the grand-jury's belief that misconduct and abuse of power incidents don't just happen out of the blue. It is fairly rare that one finds an inexperienced employee involved in misconduct of the magnitude and degree revealed to the grand jury in this investigation. The grand jury is of the opinion that the absence of structure and weak Chief Medical Examiner's for an extended period of time lead to misplaced authority within the Medical Examiner Office.

It is instructive to note that the Chief Investigator at the time, Kevin Rowland, was indicted for sex crimes by the Grand Jury. The resolution of his case was a winding road with an uncertain and politically brokered outcome, as reported in Braun (2011):

A first-degree rape charge was dismissed Wednesday against a former chief investigator of the state Medical Examiner's Office who was accused of raping a co-worker at a Tulsa hotel. The case was dismissed against Kevin Rowland within a month of a scheduled April 4 trial date.

Tulsa County District Judge William Kellough ordered the case dismissed based on a motion by state Attorney General Scott Pruitt and Assistant Attorney General Mykel Fry. The Attorney General's Office prosecuted the case and indicated in a court document that the dismissal was "pursuant to an agreement of the parties and in the best interest of justice."

A spokeswoman for the Attorney General's Office said the woman did not want to pursue the case further because of health reasons. "She just said after careful consideration and consultation with her family that it would be in her best interest, for her health and well-being, to not continue," the spokeswoman said...

Rowland resigned from his chief investigator's job in 2009. At an April 2010 preliminary hearing, Special Judge David Youll ordered Rowland bound over for trial on an allegation that he raped a woman in a hotel room in 2006. Rowland had been indicted in 2009 on four counts of sexual battery — alleged to have occurred in Tulsa County and involving two women — after an investigation by the state's multicounty grand jury.

At the time of the alleged offenses, the women worked at the Tulsa branch of the Medical Examiner's Office. The Attorney General's Office amended the charges in February 2010, alleging three counts of sexual battery and one count of rape. At the preliminary hearing, a prosecutor requested that the sexual battery counts be dismissed because of a statute of limitations that involved those counts but not the rape count.

In May, an Oklahoma County jury found Rowland not guilty of a charge of sexually battering a male employee of the Medical Examiner's Office in 2007.

Further details and consequences of this year's long series of scandals are reported in Clay (2012):

A longtime doctor at the Oklahoma medical examiner's office and two supervisors have been fired after an investigation. Dr. Andrew Sibley, investigator supervisor Brenda Kelley and administrative supervisor Ashley Hancock were fired July 12. The three Tulsa employees had been on administrative leave since late May when they were forced to leave work.

Officials called Tulsa police beforehand to assist, if necessary, with their removal in May, The Oklahoman was told. The new chief medical examiner, Dr. Eric Pfeifer, fired all three himself, first by phone and then by certified mail.

Kelley was fired for violations of an employee conduct policy and a discrimination and harassment policy, according to her two-page termination letter. "Acts of sexual harassment may include, but are not limited to...sexual kidding or other contact in an intimate or sexual way, sexual jokes or stories," Pfeifer wrote in the letter that provided no specifics about the alleged violations...

Kelley and Hancock could not be reached for comment.

Sibley said last week by phone from Canada that he has not seen his termination letter yet. He complained he does not know what accusations were made against him. He said he was never given a chance to respond before being fired. "This is terrible. This is terrible," Sibley said. "I have always thought that one should be given the opportunity to not only defend oneself against any allegations but, also, to at least know what the allegations are. ... I've not been asked any questions. I have no idea what the issue is," Sibley said. "A professional who has been with the agency for 12 years, through thick and thin, should be afforded a little bit more consideration than this," he said.

Sibley, 50, served as the interim chief medical examiner for months until the board that oversees the medical examiner's office hired Pfeifer in March 2011. The Board of Medicolegal Investigations offered Sibley the top position in November 2010, but he turned it down...

Before coming to Oklahoma in 2000, Sibley was accused in Arizona of harassing female employees at the medical examiner's office in Pima County. One female employee filed a sexual harassment lawsuit against Sibley and the county. Sibley was eventually dropped from the lawsuit, and the woman settled with the county. The amount was not disclosed.

> *A Pima County human resources investigation of the woman's complaints substantiated that "a sexually hostile working environment exists" at the medical examiner's office because the place had become permeated with sexual comments, stories, innuendo and jokes, records show.*
>
> *In Oklahoma, a former female investigator once alleged Sibley and others said "many inappropriate things of a sexual nature" to and around her, records show. The investigator worked in the Tulsa office from 2005 to 2007...*
>
> *The dismissals are a sign of continuing turmoil at an agency where officials have been working to overcome widely publicized problems. Gov. Mary Fallin said last year it was time for the agency to get past the challenges that have plagued it and "move to a new day."*

It should be mentioned that the one of the authors (Turvey) has worked multiple cases in Oklahoma, and has visited the OCME in Tulsa on at least two occasions for different capital murder investigations. Problems and politics can be said to persist.

AUTOPSY PROTOCOLS

All autopsies are not equal. Some are performed in hospitals by medical professionals with no forensic training, with aim to satisfy administrative requirements. Others are performed in a forensic context by medical examiners trained in the forensic sciences. For example, a gunshot victim who dies in a hospital may receive a limited autopsy from a hospital pathologist; and gunshot victim who dies in their home may receive a *medicolegal autopsy*, with their body sent directly to a medical examiner (e.g., a forensic pathologist).

THE NATIONAL ACADEMY OF SCIENCES REPORT

Perhaps the best description of what an autopsy involves, requires, and aims for is provided in Edwards and Gotsonis (2009):

> *An autopsy is the systematic external and internal examination of a body to establish the presence or absence of disease by gross and microscopic examination of body tissues. The pathologist makes a surgical incision from shoulder to shoulder and from the midpoint of the shoulder to shoulder incision to the pubic bone. The skin is reflected, and each organ in the chest, including the neck structures, abdomen, and pelvis is removed and carefully examined. An incision is also made from the mastoid bone on the right to the mastoid bone on the left, and the scalp is pulled forward and the bony cap removed to reveal the brain. The brain is removed and examined. The pathologist takes a small sample or biopsy of all tissues and archives them in formalin to maintain them for future reference.*
>
> *In medicolegal autopsies, all tissues other than the biopsies are replaced in the body, except for perhaps the brain or heart, which may be retained and examined by consultants for diagnoses causing or contributing to death. For*

hospital autopsies, depending on the list of permissions given by the person qualified to give permission, tissues and organs may be retained for study, research, or other investigations. The pathologist submits small 2 × 2 cm sections of tissue to the histology laboratory, where thin slices a few microns thick are subjected to chemical treatment to preserve them. The tissue blocks are shaved, so that a thin layer can be mounted on a glass slide and stained with dyes to differentiate cells. The pathologist can recognize diseases in the stained tissue.

Medicolegal autopsies are conducted to determine the cause of death; assist with the determination of the manner of death as natural, suicide, homicide, or accident; collect medical evidence that may be useful for public health or the courts; and develop information that may be useful for reconstructing how the person received a fatal injury.

This overview is generic, but instructive. What it implies is that a forensic autopsy is a thorough endeavor that is to be carried out by educated professionals. This must be spelled out because attorneys, and the courts, will want to have it both ways when it suits them—allowing or proffering testimony from incredible sources when it should not be permissible, and barring testimony from otherwise credible sources when it does not fit their predetermined narrative.

THE NATIONAL ASSOCIATION OF MEDICAL EXAMINERS STANDARDS

Perhaps the best autopsy protocols have been established by the NAME. These standards are comprehensive and easy to understand. We provide them here for reference, without significant edit (Peterson & Clark, 2006, pp. 7—14):

The purpose of this section is to establish minimum standards for the external examination of all bodies.

Standard D9 Preliminary Procedures

These standards underscore the need for assessment of all available information prior to the forensic autopsy to (1) direct the performance of the forensic autopsy, (2) answer specific questions unique to the circumstances of the case, (3) document evidence, the initial external appearance of the body, and its clothing and property items, and (4) correlate alterations in these items with injury patterns on the body. Just as a surgeon does not operate without first preparing a history and physical examination, so must the forensic pathologist ascertain enough history and circumstances and may need to inspect the body to decide whether a forensic autopsy is indicated and to direct the forensic autopsy toward relevant case questions.

Preliminary procedures are as follows:

D9.1 forensic pathologist reviews the circumstances of death prior to forensic autopsy.

D9.2 forensic pathologist or representative measures and records body length.
D9.3 forensic pathologist or representative measures and records body weight.
D9.4 forensic pathologist examines the external aspects of the body before internal examination.
D9.5 forensic pathologist or representative photographs, or forensic pathologist describes decedent as presented.
D9.6 forensic pathologist documents and correlates clothing findings with injuries of the body in criminal cases.
D9.7 forensic pathologist or representative identifies and collects trace evidence on clothing in criminal cases.
D9.8 forensic pathologist or representative removes clothing.
D9.9 forensic pathologist or representative photographs or lists clothing and personal effects.

Standard D10 Physical Characteristics

The external examination documents identifying features, signs of or absence of disease and trauma, and signs of death. Recording identifying features provides evidence for or against a putative identification. Recording signs of disease and trauma is a primary purpose of the forensic autopsy.
The forensic pathologist shall:
D10.1 document apparent age.
D10.2 establish sex.
D10.3 describe apparent race or racial characteristics.
D10.4 describe hair.
D10.5 describe eyes.
D10.6 describe abnormal body habitus.
D10.7 document prominent scars, tattoos, skin lesions, and amputations.
D10.8 document presence or absence of dentition.
D10.9 inspect and describe head, neck, thorax, abdomen, extremities, and hands.
D10.10 inspect and describe posterior body surface and genitals.
D10.11 document evidence of medical or surgical intervention.

Standard D11 Postmortem Changes

Recording rigor mortis documents a sign of death that cannot be captured by photography. Recording livor mortis helps to answer later questions about bruises and body position. Notation of postmortem artifacts is useful for interpretation of subsequent forensic autopsy findings. Each of these may be useful in estimation of the postmortem interval.
The forensic pathologist shall:
D11.1 describe liver mortis.
D11.2 describe rigor mortis.
D11.3 describe postmortem changes.
D11.4 describe evidence of embalming.
D11.5 describe decompositional changes.
…

Standard E12 Suspected Sexual Assault

Collection of swabs, combings, clippings, and trace evidence may be necessary to 1) determine if sexual assault occurred; 2) link multiple, apparently unrelated deaths; or 3) link the death to an assailant. DNA analysis is now the test of choice on swabs, hair, and fingernail clippings. These collections shall be performed in accordance with the requirements of the crime laboratory procedures.

The forensic pathologist or representative shall, prior to cleaning the body:

E12.1 collect swabs of oral, vaginal, and rectal cavities.
E12.2 collect pubic hair combings or tape lifts.
E12.3 collect fingernail scrapings or clippings.
E12.4 collect pubic and head hair exemplars.
E12.5 identify and preserve foreign hairs, fibers, and biological stains.

Standard E13 Injuries: General

Documentation of injuries may be necessary to determine the nature of the object used to inflict the wounds, how the injuries were incurred, and whether the injuries were a result of an accident, homicide, or suicide. Written, diagrammatic, and photographic documentation of the injuries may be used in court. Observations and findings are documented to support or refute interpretations, to provide evidence for court, and to serve as a record.

The forensic pathologist shall:

E13.1 describe injuries.
E13.2 describe injury by type.
E13.3 describe injury by location.
E13.4 describe injury by size.
E13.5 describe injury by shape.
E13.6 describe injury by pattern.

Standard E14 Photographic Documentation

Photographic documentation complements written documentation of wounds and creates a permanent record of forensic autopsy details. Photographic documentation of major wounds and injury shall include a reference scale in at least one photograph of the wound or injury to allow for 1:1 reproduction.

The forensic pathologist or representative shall:

E14.1 photograph injuries unobstructed by blood, foreign matter, or clothing.
E14.2 photograph major injuries with a scale.

Standard E15 Firearm Injuries

Documentation of firearm wounds as listed below should include detail sufficient to provide meaningful information to users of the forensic autopsy report, and to permit another forensic pathologist to draw independent conclusions based on the documentation.

The forensic pathologist shall:

E15.1 describe injuries.
E15.2 measure wound size.

E15.3 *locate cutaneous wounds of the head, neck, torso, or lower extremities by measuring from either the top of head or sole of foot.*
E15.4 *locate cutaneous wounds of the head, neck, torso, or lower extremities by measuring from either the anterior or posterior midline.*
E15.5 *locate cutaneous wounds of the upper extremities by measuring from anatomic landmarks.*
E15.6 *descriptively locate cutaneous wounds in an anatomic region.*
E15.7 *describe presence or absence of soot and stippling.*
E15.8 *describe presence of abrasion ring, searing, muzzle imprint, lacerations.*

Standard E16 Sharp Force Injuries
Documentation of sharp force injuries as listed below should include detail sufficient to provide meaningful information to users of the forensic autopsy report, and to permit another forensic pathologist to draw independent conclusions based on the documentation.
The forensic pathologist shall:
E16.1 *describe wound.*
E16.2 *measure wound size.*
E16.3 *locate wound in anatomic region.*

Standard E17 Burn Injuries
Documentation of burn injuries as listed below should include detail sufficient to provide meaningful information to users of the forensic autopsy report, and to permit another forensic pathologist to draw independent conclusions based on the documentation.
The forensic pathologist shall:
E17.1 *describe appearance of burn.*
E17.2 *describe distribution of burn.*

Standard E18 Patterned Injuries
Documentation of patterned injuries as listed below should include detail sufficient to provide meaningful information to users of the forensic autopsy report, and to permit another forensic pathologist to draw independent conclusions based on the documentation. Bite marks should be swabbed to collect specimens to use for DNA comparison with putative assailants.
The forensic pathologist shall:
E18.1 *measure injury size.*
E18.2 *describe location of injury.*
E18.3 *describe injury pattern.*
E18.4 *swab recent or fresh bite mark.*
…

Standard F19 Thoracic and Abdominal Cavities
Because some findings are only ascertained by in situ inspection, the thoracic and abdominal cavities must be examined before and after the removal of organs so as to identify signs of disease, injury, and therapy.

The forensic pathologist shall:
F19.1 examine internal organs in situ.
F19.2 describe adhesions and abnormal fluids.
F19.3 document abnormal position of medical devices.
F19.4 describe evidence of surgery.

Standard F20 Internal Organs and Viscera
The major internal organs and viscera must be examined after their removal from the body so as to identify signs of disease, injury, and therapy.
Procedures are as follows:
F20.1 the forensic pathologist or representative removes organs from cranial, thoracic, abdominal, and pelvic cavities.
F20.2 the forensic pathologist or representative records measured weights of brain, heart, lungs, liver, spleen, and kidneys.
F20.3 the forensic pathologist dissects and describes organs.

Standard F21 Head
Because some findings are only ascertained by in situ inspection, the scalp and cranial contents must be examined before and after the removal of the brain so as to identify signs of disease, injury, and therapy.
Procedures are as follows:
F21.1 the forensic pathologist shall inspect and describe scalp, skull, and meninges.
F21.2 the forensic pathologist shall document any epidural, subdural, or subarachnoid hemorrhage.
F21.3 the forensic pathologist shall inspect the brain in situ prior to removal and sectioning.
F21.4 the forensic pathologist shall document purulent material and abnormal fluids.
F21.5 the forensic pathologist or representative removes the dura mater and the forensic pathologist inspects the skull.

Standard F22 Neck
The muscles, soft tissues, airways, and vascular structures of the anterior neck must be examined to identify signs of disease, injury, and therapy. A layer-by-layer dissection is necessary for proper evaluation of trauma to the anterior neck. Removal and ex situ dissection of the upper airway, pharynx, and upper esophagus is a necessary component of this evaluation. A dissection of the posterior neck is necessary when occult neck injury is suspected.
The forensic pathologist shall:
F22.1 examine in situ muscles and soft tissues of the anterior neck.
F22.2 ensure proper removal of neck organs and airways.
F22.3 examine neck organs and airways.
F22.4 dissect the posterior neck in cases of suspected occult neck injury.
F22.5 perform anterior neck dissection in neck trauma cases.

Standard F23 Penetrating Injuries, Including Gunshot and Sharp Force Injuries

Documentation of penetrating injuries as listed below should include detail sufficient to provide meaningful information to users of the forensic autopsy report, and to permit another forensic pathologist to draw independent conclusions based on the documentation.

The recovery and documentation of foreign bodies is important for evidentiary purposes. Internal wound pathway(s) shall be described according to organs and tissues and size of defects of these organs and tissues.

The forensic pathologist shall:

F23.1 correlate internal injury to external injury

F23.2 describe and document the track of wound

F23.3 describe and document the direction of wound

F23.4 recover foreign bodies of evidentiary value

F23.5 describe and document recovered foreign body

Standard F24 Blunt Impact Injuries

Documentation of blunt impact injuries as listed below should include detail sufficient to provide meaningful information to users of the forensic autopsy report, and to permit another forensic pathologist to draw independent conclusions based on the documentation.

The forensic pathologist shall:

F24.1 describe internal and external injuries with appropriate correlations.

F24.2 describe and document injuries to skeletal system.

F24.3 describe and document injuries to internal organs, structures, and soft tissue.

Again, these protocols are not a gold standard; they are basic requirements. If the forensic pathologist is not abiding by the standards, then their work is substandard and related finings must be viewed with skepticism. If the person conducting the autopsy is not a forensic pathologist, then their findings must be considered suspect altogether. If the person conducting the autopsy is not aware of these standards, and that they exist, then they are not professionals and should not be conducting autopsies in any capacity.

CONTENTS

The autopsy report should be organized in such a fashion as to make findings clear, accessible, and unequivocal. Additionally, it should be clear who conducted all related examinations, when and what evidence was collected, where it was sent, whether it was tested, and by whom. The following is a content and section checklist for the forensic autopsy, adapted from Dolinak et al. (2005):

1. Name of examiners
2. Name of persons present during examination
3. Date and time of examination

4. Descriptive results of External Examination
5. Description of evidence of therapy and/or medical intervention
6. Description of evidence of injury, with trauma-grams (e.g., diagrams of the body with injuries and descriptions drawn in)
7. Descriptive results of Internal Examination
8. Descriptive results of Microscopic Examination
9. Descriptive results of Toxicological Examination
10. Evidence collected and submitted for analysis (e.g., clothing, fingernail scrapings, and sexual assault kit)
11. Summary of Findings
12. Cause and Manner of Death

An important concept in medicolegal examinations is negative documentation: establishing where there is an absence of injury. Attorneys enjoy pretending that this is not a forensic concept, or that this is scientifically unnecessary, especially when it does not align with their respective legal arguments. However, Dolinak et al. (2006) make the following observation (p. 69–70): "It is important to clearly state all of the injuries and other significant findings discovered at autopsy. However, it is equally important, and sometime evermore important to state *pertinent negatives* when they are deemed significant." This preserves a record of injury, and any lack thereof, to prevent others from implying its existence as part of a legal argument or a new allegation at a later time.

MEDICOLEGAL FAILURES: A TOP 10 LIST

To provide an initial sense of the challenges that were are continuously faced with in our investigative and forensic casework, the authors offer the following list of failures regularly encountered in the work of those charged with conducting medicolegal death investigations. This is not a list of pet-peeves, but rather it is a list of things that are supposed to be done every time, and generally are not:

1. Fraud, negligence, or absenteeism due to private practice casework. Many medical examiners and coroners work for the government, but also maintain private practices that are required to be wholly separate. The problem is that they are often not, and private fees are much more lucrative. Invariably their state work suffers because it can, while private clients will not be so forgiving. This means more hours, even days, away from state duties; hurried and incomplete state work; delayed reports, sometimes by months or even years; illegal use of state personnel and resources to satisfy private practice examinations, or to run personnel errands; illegal use of state vehicle used for private practice travel and accommodation, and double billing for time; and the improper use of government titles and positions for an unfair advantage a private practice (e.g., giving private practice testimony as a state medical examiner or coroner).

2. Uncritical reliance on law enforcement, EMS, or 911 dispatcher reports for case information that is unconfirmed. Too often, the cause and manner of death are determined by a caller during a 911 call, or by police officers reporting inaccurate, incomplete, or just plain biased information from the scene. These narratives are absorbed into official medicolegal death investigation reports; they are not investigated by anyone; and they are later repeated as fact from those reports as though they arose from and were validated by a formal investigation. This happens a great deal and is one of the common mechanisms by which false assumptions infect case theory as facts.
3. Failure to visit the scene and collect observations and photos separate from law enforcement. Law enforcement is not generally trained in death investigation and does not generally understand what that process requires. Attending the death scene is therefore a requirement to avoid missed evidence and contextual information.
4. Failure to document an objective victim history (e.g., medical, mental health, sexual history, hobbies, prior or recent injuries, timeline of last 24 h, etc.). This information provides context and is universally understood to be essential when forming conclusions about cause and manner of death. Certainly it is not ethical or competent to form medical conclusions without such information.
5. Failure to collect biological samples and submit them for toxicological analysis—prevents us from knowing whether the victim was drunk, on drugs, or even conscious. This decision helps preserve the image of a "chaste" and sympathetic victim, clearing the way for a clean prosecution, and is the direct result of police and prosecutorial influence.
6. Failure to take adequate photographs of injuries in context—prevents us from knowing where there injury actually is on the body; this kind of detail should also be in the autopsy report but often is not.
7. Failure to take overall photos of the body and provide negative documentation—this prevents conclusive review of the body to confirm the absence of injury; it also prevents the discovery of injury missed at the time of autopsy, which is common, and includes a failure to document hands, feet, and genitals.
8. Failure to collect a sexual assault kit when there is a sexual theme or context to the crime. This decision is too often based on assumption about the case rather than an investigation of the facts.
9. Failure to document whether wounds happened before or after death. Obviously this cannot always be done, but it is often intentionally avoided as a subject in the report to prevent interference with prosecutorial case theory.
10. Exaggerated credentials and opining beyond expertise. This is common among unqualified coroners and medicolegal death investigators attempting to pass themselves for forensic scientists in court. In reality, they are too often just cops in lab coats (see Turvey, 2013b).

The root cause here is generally a combination of two parts laziness, one part ignorance, and one part political expedience. The medicolegal death investigation is commonly a reflection of the desires, and even commands, of law enforcement and the prosecution in a given region. They are, after all, the immediate end user of the information. If they don't want certain information to be collected because they know it will get in the way case theory down the line, they will pressure those responsible not to collect or even document. The result is not a thorough or even objective forensic finding, but a series of cherry picked items that are susceptible to adaptation to prosecutorial case theory as needed.

CONCLUSION

The medicolegal death investigation is meant to be an independent scientific inquiry carried out by qualified investigative and medical personnel trained in forensic pathology. In reality, it is more often a muted effort, hampered by untrained personnel, political agendas, and an overall lack of examiner competence within a broken and underfunded system. Nationwide, the medicolegal death investigation system is plagued by systemic problems which impede truth seeking and can only enhance the problem of wrongful convictions.

Nationally accepted protocols for death scene investigation and forensic autopsies have been widely available and freely disseminated for the better part of the last 20 years. These are not gold standards, but rather represent fundamental requirements for reliable scientific and medical conclusions. Yet these protocols have failed to take hold and are widely ignored. The failure of law enforcement and prosecutorial agencies, along with judicial bodies, to require enforcement of these essential protocols suggests their complicity. That is to say, there is every reason to consider that death investigations remain fragmented, underfunded, and incomplete to some extent by design.

The authors see little hope of this changing in the future and continue to raise awareness to the extent possible in both the classroom and the courtroom.

ENDNOTES

1. One of the authors (Turvey) has worked many such cases over the years. One of three instances necessitates involvement. First, a law enforcement agency reaches out because they incorrectly believe they have a potential serial killer, given the victim bondage and apparatus present in the death scene; second, a defense attorney reaches out because law enforcement has arrested their client in relation to an autoerotic death or consensual sexual asphyxia; and third, a civil attorney or family member reaches out because an insurance company mistakenly claims that autoerotic death is an intentional act—and therefore a suicide (most insurance policies do not pay out benefits for a suicide).
2. This needs to be spelled out for the benefit of prosecutors, and other attorneys, who would ignore science and proceed with levying contrary allegations or charges. In such ways, the negotiation of legal findings is too often at odds with the physical and scientific evidence.

REFERENCES

Adelson, L. (1974). *The pathology of homicide*. Springfield, IL: Charles C. Thomas.

Black, H. C. (1990). *Black's law dictionary* (6th ed.). St. Paul, MN: West.

Braun, B. (March 9, 2011). Rape charge against former Medical Examiner's Office employee dismissed. *Tulsa World*. http://www.tulsaworld.com/archives/rape-charge-against-former-medical-examiner-s-office-employee-dismissed/article_053d061a-5078-5b4a-b535-060779235028.html.

CDC. (2003). *Medical examiners' and coroners' handbook on death registration and fetal death reporting*. Hyattsville, MD: U.S. Department of Health and Human Services, Centers for Disease Control.

CDC. (2015). *Understanding suicide*. U.S. Department of Health and Human Services, Centers for Disease Control. http://www.cdc.gov/violenceprevention/pdf/suicide_factsheet-a.pdf.

CDC. (2016). *Leading causes of death*. U.S. Department of Health and Human Services, Centers for Disease Control. http://www.cdc.gov/nchs/fastats/leading-causes-of-death.htm.

Clay, N. (July 22, 2012). Doctor, two supervisors fired from Oklahoma medical examiner's office. *The Oklahoman*. http://newsok.com/article/3694640.

DiMaio, D., & DiMaio, V. (2001). *Forensic pathology* (2nd ed.). Boca Raton: CRC Press.

Dolinak, D., Matshes, E., & Lew, E. (2005). *Forensic pathology: principles and practice*. Boston: Elsevier Science.

Edwards, H., & Gotsonis, C. (2009). *Strengthening forensic science in the United States: A path forward*. Washington, DC: National Academies Press.

FBI. (September 15, 2015). *Former Richmond county coroner sentenced to three years in prison for credit card fraud*. U.S. Department of Justice. Press Release https://www.fbi.gov/contact-us/field-offices/atlanta/press-releases/former-richmond-county-coroner-sentenced-to-three-years-in-prison-for-credit-card-fraud.

Hoberck, B. (July 2, 2009). *Oklahoma medical examiner loses rank by national group*. Tulsa World. http://newsok.com/article/3382323.

Hodsen, S. (May 27, 2015). *Ex-richmond county coroner Grover Tuten pleads guilty*. The Augusta Chronicle. http://chronicle.augusta.com/news/crime-courts/2015-05-27/ex-richmond-county-coroner-grover-tuten-pleads-guilty.

Hunter v. Astrue. (2009). U.S. Dist. LEXIS 92045 (D. Minn. August 4, 2009).

Kraker, D. (March 10, 2015). *After controversial autopsy attempts, medical examiner resigns*. MPRNews. http://www.mprnews.org/story/2015/03/10/medical-examiner-resigns.

Melinak, J. (September 9, 2015). 7 common mistakes regarding autopsy reports. *The Forensic Magazine*. http://www.forensicmag.com/article/2015/09/7-common-mistakes-regarding-autopsy-reports.

MGJIR. (2009). In the matter of the 12th multicounty, state of Oklahoma Supreme court case No. SCAD- 2009-18, District Court No. CJ-2009-1925; filed July 20.

NIJ. (1999). *Death investigation: A guide for the scene investigator*. Washington, DC: National Institute of Justice. Research Report NCJ 167568.

Peterson, G., & Clark, S. (2006). *Forensic autopsy performance standards*. Atlanta, GA: The National Association of Medical Examiners.

Turvey, B. (2011). *Criminal profiling* (4th ed.). London: Elsevier Science.

Turvey, B. (2013a). Autoerotic asphyxia. In J. Seigal, & P. Saukko (Eds.), *Encyclopedia of forensic sciences* (2nd ed.). San Diego: Academic Press.

Turvey, B. (2013b). *Forensic fraud*. San Diego: Elsevier Science.

CHAPTER 10

Forensic Interviews

Paul J. Ciolino[1], Brent E. Turvey[2]

Paul J. Ciolino and Associates, Inc., Chicago, IL, United States[1]*; Forensic Criminology Institute, Sitka, Alaska, United States and Aguascalientes, Mexico*[2]

CHAPTER OUTLINE

Terms and Definitions	262
Goals	263
Stakes and Consequences	264
Interview Preparation and Checklists	265
Investigative Tasks Prior to Any Interview	266
Documentation and Recording	267
Interview Protocols	269
Generic Interview Questions: A Starter Kit	270
General Interview Questions for All Witnesses	270
Eyewitness Questions	270
Alibi Witness Questions	271
Advice and Discussion	271
Physical Evidence	272
Conduct and Tone	272
Investigator Dress and Presentation	272
Number of Personnel	272
Length of Interviews and Interrogations	273
Evaluating a Witness	273
Promises	273
False Confessions	273
Continuing Education and Professional Development	275
Endnotes	275
References	275

The purpose of this chapter is to introduce readers to the concept of forensic interviewing. It will attempt to cover, from an applied perspective, the major constructs that such an endeavor requires and implies. While not all inclusive, readers are meant to appreciate that the forensic interview is a process, conducted by investigative and forensic professionals in concert. It is not likely to be anything that they would have seen before in film or on television, as such depictions have been almost entirely inaccurate.

Readers are also cautioned to accept that forensic interviewing is a skill that can and must be taught to every investigator. However, not just everyone has the patience, professionalism, and personal demeanor to conduct them effectively. That will become clear as we review the essential goals and protocols.

The bottom line is that good interviewers get solid statements on the record that are verified by the physical and documentary evidence. Substandard and inept interviewers get nowhere, or worse. Any related arrests get tossed, and any related convictions get overturned. That is because their results do not line up with the other evidence in the case. When other professionals are able to check their work (aka peer review—which is prevented by sloppy or deliberately opaque interviewing habits), errors become evident and incompetence is revealed.

In this chapter, readers will learn how a forensic interview should be conducted, why, and how to avoid common pitfalls.

TERMS AND DEFINITIONS

Forensic. Over the past three decades, there have been few words so improperly used, overused, and then spread like fertilizer throughout popular culture. In all likelihood, this is due in no small part to the poor and repetitive imaginations of screenwriters and producers, TV and film; fiction and nonfiction alike. We are bombarded daily with their ignorance, and then it is repeated as "reporting" by the news media. Everyone uses the word *forensic*, and few get it right.

These fictional conceptualizations of what it means to be *forensic* have, without question, bled into the fabric of our justice system. Colleges and universities have not always helped; they continually attempt to sell students of criminal justice something labeled "forensic"—marketed improperly as "police-only" science laced with the allure of violence and gore. These ignorant concepts, unchecked, have been carried into the courtroom.[1] Judges and juries have, over time, been literally brainwashed into believing that if the word forensic is employed, then science and certainty can be implied, but only when delivered by someone with a badge (see generally Cooley & Turvey, 2014; Turvey, 2013). Nothing could be farther from the truth.

So let us start by getting our basic terms and definitions right. *Forensic* is not a descriptor associated strictly with scientific practice; nor is associated solely with the efforts of law enforcement or the prosecution. According to Black's Law Dictionary, the word *forensic* means "[b]elonging to courts of justice" (Black, 2016).[2] In other words, it does not imply a scientific endeavor, nor does it imply special or secret knowledge. It refers strictly to court.

As explained in Turvey, Petherick and Ferguson (2010, p. xxxviii): "This is the forensic realm: the world of investigations, courts, and law." The work being done by a given professional is only considered forensic if it is intended for use in a courtroom. That is to say, courtroom testimony must be a regular and anticipated feature of a professional's work. Otherwise the word forensic has no place in descriptions of themselves or their efforts.

Consequently, a *forensic interview* is one that is conducted for the purposes of assisting an investigation, in a legally defensible manner, that meets the criteria for courtroom admissibility; it is also intended to be structured in such a fashion as to elicit specific types of information from the subject in order to achieve maximum integrity and accountability (see generally Newlin et al., 2015, pp. 1—18).

Put succinctly, conducting a forensic interview requires that the process be done in a specific fashion. Otherwise it may not be admissible in court. Other forms of interviewing, of insufficient quality, with insufficient corroboration, or with insufficient documentation, may not be admissible in court. And if it is not admissible in court, then it is not evidence.

GOALS

The interviews of witnesses and suspects are the bread and butter of an investigation. There is no greater source of information, and no faster route to a successful conclusion. The speed with which a good interview can lead to the truth is matched only by the certainty that a bad one will be riddled with deceptions and ensure investigative failure.

The goal of the forensic interview is to achieve an accurate and reliably documented statement from a *witness*[3]; this in order for it to be easily corroborated by other evidence and ultimately suitable for use in a courtroom. The pillars of a forensic interview are:

- Consistency
- Accuracy
- Documentation
- Reliability
- Corroboration
- Admissibility

Consistency: The forensic investigator asks the same kinds of questions, and establishes the same information, in every case, with bias or deviation.

Accuracy: The forensic investigator wants factual information that accords with reality; not the fantasies of the biased, the eager, or the obsessed.

Documentation: The forensic investigator takes great care to ensure that everything they do, and everything that the subject does, is recorded in such a manner as to ensure that it can be faithfully confirmed by any third party.

Reliability: The forensic investigator strives for trustworthiness in their process, which means transparency with respect to their methods, their findings, and even their own character.

Corroboration: The forensic investigator understands that the interview is one part of the investigative process and not the whole case. It must therefore stand the test against other witness statements, objective documentation, and the physical evidence. Consistency suggests veracity; variations suggest the need for continued investigation until reliable conclusions can be found.

Admissibility: Evidence is only evidence in court if a judge decides that it is so. In rendering these pillars honestly, firmly, and lawfully, the forensic interviewer can faithfully attest under oath that the court may accept their work.

Failing at any one of these pillars is sufficient cause to doubt the veracity of related interview results. Failing to accept these pillars as essential is a sign of poor training or bias on the part of the investigator. Ultimately, what the forensic interviewer should want is a truthful statement, legally obtained, that is worthy of the court; not a contrived, fabricated or coercively obtained assortment of assertions that are tailor-made to serve duplicitous motives.

Note: It should not need to be stated that reliable interviews and statements are *never ever* achieved under conditions that involve *coercion* or *torture*. This is something that every properly trained and ethical criminal justice practitioner understands. Unfortunately, many law enforcement agencies, prosecutors, and even judges in the United States can be found looking the other way when these circumstances are alleged or evident. However, a quick review of social media and cases matriculating through the civil justice system will reveal that such cases are all too common (e.g., Glawe, 2015; Goldberg, 2015; Ortiz; 2015; Spielman, 2016; Taylor, 2015; Worland, 2014). Certainly the casework and experiences of the authors can attest to these realities (e.g., Hughes, 2016; Woolsey, 2016).

In any event, the forensic interview process follows protocols meant not only to get to the truth, but also to demonstrate the reliability and the integrity of the interview itself; the health and cognitive awareness of the subject; and the absence of police misconduct, coercion or torture.

STAKES AND CONSEQUENCES

Forensic interviews are intended to serve as evidence in the courtroom. This anticipates the interviews being used as evidence in legal disagreement, whether immediate, eventual, or potential. Legal disagreements over actions and consequences, whether they are criminal or civil, can eventually become hotly contested courtroom battles. In civil trials, there are huge amounts of money at stake. In criminal trials, personal liberties and freedom are at stake. And in capital murder trials, should the state prevail, the defendant can be put to death. In other words, these are serious matters being initiated by very serious people who do this for a living. By the time things get to court, the stakes are unquestionably high: fortunes, freedoms, reputations, and lives.

Among the greatest mistakes that any investigator can make is to underestimate their role or importance in these legal contests. Those doing battle, specifically the lawyers for any opposing counsel, can be counted upon to scrutinize, criticize, and marginalize your reputation and work product. They will do this in order to minimize the damage it might cause their own theories of the case. When they cannot do it themselves, they will hire your peers to do it for them—as trial consultants or forensic experts.

A critique of your work in a given case may not happen right away. It might take as little as 6 months or as much as 20 years. It may take so long that you learn bad habits, thinking professionalism and competence to be unnecessary, all the while enjoying the protection of the court or benefiting from the lethargy of attorneys and colleagues in given region.

The point is that, one day, sooner or later, every forensic investigator will meet someone on a case with an agenda. That agenda may be legitimate, it may be political, or it may be egotistical. The motives will not matter. Their goal will be to investigate your work, your reputation, and your methods. Consequently, every pillar of every case that the forensic investigator helps to build must be strong enough to withstand this level of scrutiny. Whether your work is the target of a political witch-hunt or the object of a routine admissibility hearing, the goals must be the same. Attend to the pillars; attend to the facts and evidence; and in doing so build a reputation worthy of the courtroom. Otherwise your work and reputation will be easy targets for the motivated.

The stakes are high for everyone involved in a legal context, and the consequences of failure are often higher. Know the stakes; appreciate the consequences; and conduct every piece of work as though it will be scrutinized from top to bottom by your most ardent detractors. Because eventually it will; especially, if you become good at your work and develop a reputation for integrity. Skilled lawyers enjoy nothing more than eating an unprepared opposition witness for breakfast, whether in a deposition or during trial.

One sloppy case can destroy a reputation and end a career. Better to stave apathy with attentiveness. Better to take the time to do things right, every time.

INTERVIEW PREPARATION AND CHECKLISTS

Interview preparation is critical to its ultimate success. Without it, a thousand mistakes will be made, which are impossible to identify until well after the interview has been concluded. And by that time, it is of course much too late.

The forensic interviewer must therefore research the history, background and personality of any interview subject—to the extent possible. This is always an important consideration, but never more than when dealing with a primary suspect, a complaining witness (aka, an alleged victim), or some other key witness. There are often no second chances, and preparation is the best way to ensure that the first efforts are as complete, and informative, as far as possible.

Two enemies of professional competence are disorganization and distraction. To avoid both, investigators are admonished to compile sensible preliminary checklists;

use them as a guide and not so much a crutch; and use them until they become an automatic response and ultimately unnecessary. Write them up, follow them up, and save them for every case.

Consider the following checklist:

INVESTIGATIVE TASKS PRIOR TO ANY INTERVIEW

1. Complete criminal and civil background investigation on subject.
    a. Check all county courthouses where the subject has resided.
    b. Obtain records and transcripts of any criminal or civil actions, and related testimony.
    c. Check all records for family law matters, child support, and orders of protection.
    d. Check for business records, permits, corporate, and limited liability companies (LLCs) connections.
    e. Run database searches for relatives and known associates.
    f. Check federal records for bankruptcy, tax liens.
    g. If permitted obtain a credit check.
    h. Locate all vehicles owned or recently sold.
    i. If subject is former inmate or convict, locate all relevant available records.
2. Complete medical and mental health history on the subject.
    a. Names of all doctors and care facilities attended.
    b. All medical and mental health diagnoses.
    c. Prescription medications, past and current.
    d. Major surgeries and physical or mental disabilities.
    e. Recent or current injuries, no matter how minor.
3. Complete employment, social and educational history on the subject.
    a. Names of all schools, colleges and universities attended, areas studied, and levels of completion.
    b. Names of all current and past employers.
    c. Military history, if any.
    d. Names of all current and past intimate and/or marriage partners.
    e. Complete Internet database and social media investigation (e.g., Google, Facebook, LinkedIn, Instagram, etc.). Determine activities, interests, and connections to complete missing pieces of the employment, social and educational history.

This information may or may not be available, and provides the investigator with a starting point. It also provides questions, or topics of discussion, that need to be worked into the interview if unanswered prior.

DOCUMENTATION AND RECORDING

Nobody wants to see a bad convenience store quality security tape that is in black and white and without audio. Good equipment is inexpensive these days, and easy to use. It is not rocket science, and if you want to lose your audience before one word is spoken put up a poorly shot video with inadequate audio on the screen.

In the digital age, there is no subsequent excuse for failing to document any interview thoroughly. This means digital color video, with high resolution, and clear audio. As explained in Newlin et al. (2015, p.6):

> *Electronic recordings are the most complete and accurate way to document forensic interviews (Cauchi and Powell, 2009; Lamb et al., 2000), capturing the exchange between the [subject] and the interviewer and the exact wording of questions (Faller, 2007; Warren and Woodall, 1999). Video recordings, used in 90% of Children's Advocacy Centers (CACs) nationally (MRCAC, 2014), allow the trier of fact in legal proceedings to witness all forms of the child's communication. Recordings make the interview process transparent, documenting that the interviewer and the multidisciplinary team avoided inappropriate interactions with the child (Faller, 2007). Recorded forensic interviews also allow interviewers and others to review their work and facilitate skill development and integrity of practice (Lamb, Sternberg, Orbach, Esplin, & Mitchell, 2002; Price and Roberts, 2011; Stewart, Katz, & La Rooy, 2011).*

When recording any statement, have a backup recorder running. Prior to the interview, test the equipment. Make certain that you have backup batteries. Make certain that the lighting and recording settings are adequate and accurate. Check the audio levels. An investigator can take the greatest statement in the world, but if it is not properly documented then it did not actually happen.

In the absence of recording equipment, employ a court reporter's service. These are third party professionals who can assure the veracity of what is being done and said, with no investment either way. It can be costly, but it may well be worth it.

It should not be necessary to make clear the need for recording interviews, especially on the part of law enforcement. But until recently many federal agencies, including the Federal Bureau of Investigation (FBI), refused to do so. As reported in Johnson (2014):

> *Senior Justice Department officials have quietly notified U.S. attorneys and federal agents that they're establishing "a presumption" that agents will electronically record statements made by individuals in their custody.*
>
> *In a memo obtained by National Public Radio (NPR), Deputy Attorney General Jim Cole strongly encourages agents to videotape suspects in custody before they appear in front of a judge or magistrate on federal charges. The memo says FBI special agents in charge of field offices or U.S. attorneys can override the policy if they have good cause to set it aside…*

For years, the FBI has resisted recording confessions or interviews. In fact, the bureau had a formal policy barring any recordings unless authorized by a senior supervisor. The FBI policy dated March 2006 (http://www.nytimes.com/packages/pdf/national/20070402_FBI_Memo.pdf) says "the presence of recording equipment may interfere with and undermine the successful rapport building interviewing technique which the FBI practices." And later, that FBI policy notes that "perfectly lawful and acceptable interviewing techniques do not always come across in recorded fashion to lay persons as proper means of obtaining information from defendants".

The new policy, set to take effect July 11, is designed to align practices across the federal government, where some law enforcement agencies employ recordings and others don't. The memo has been sent to not only the FBI but also the Drug Enforcement Administration, the Bureau of Alcohol, Tobacco, Firearms and Explosives, the U.S. Marshals and the Bureau of Prisons.

A law enforcement source tells NPR that the impending change is already producing a flurry of activity, meetings and training sessions. Discussions about recording interrogations have been underway at the federal level since early in the Obama administration. And many state and city police already record interviews with suspects because of concerns about abusive practices that could railroad innocent or vulnerable individuals into false confessions.

For now, the new DOJ policy applies to cases where suspects are in federal custody. But Cole says he'd like agents and prosecutors to electronically record interviews they conduct as part of normal investigations, too. Cole says he favors electronic recordings but that audio recordings can serve as a substitute in certain cases.

Defense attorneys say they welcome the new approach. Jerry J. Cox, president of the National Association of Criminal Defense Lawyers, says the group is greatly encouraged by this important step. "As we have seen from data regarding wrongful convictions, coercive police techniques and compromised mental states can conspire to produce false confessions," Cox says. "Recording interrogations protects the accused against police misconduct, protects law enforcement against false allegations, and protects public safety by ensuring a verbatim record of the interrogation process and any statements".

Recorded interviews have been the community standard of care since the invention of the tape recorder. Now there is digital video and audio, making this kind of evidence easier to store, review, and share. Any interview that is conducted without this level of care and documentation should be considered substandard and essentially unreliable for courtroom purposes. This includes written statements, prepared otherwise; interview summaries; and transcripts without associated audio and video.

Resistance to recording interviews at any level should be met with skepticism by any forensic professional.

INTERVIEW PROTOCOLS

The authors also generally recommend the following guidelines with respect to interviews with witnesses, victims, and suspects, adapted from Savino and Turvey (2012, pp. 183–184):

1. Interviews should be done in private and without distractions.
2. Interviews must be done in a professional, sensitive and tactful manner—without threats or violence.
3. An interview conducted amid threats of inflicting harm or withholding necessities (e.g., food, bathroom, medical care, protection from retaliation) is not an interview at all, but more akin to hostage negotiation. Nothing that a person says in exchange for their safety or protection is reliable.
4. An interview conducted on a medicated or intoxicated person is not reliable. Establish whether this is the case at the outset of every interview. Determine the nature of any drugs being taken by the subject and their side-effects.
5. Interviewers should demonstrate nonjudgment and patience. Interviewers must strive to create an environment that allows the interviewee to make statements willingly and naturally. Taking time and having an open mind will yield more information in the long run.
6. Interview collaterals separately. Interviewing anyone with family, friends, boyfriend, parents, spouses, or others present may give someone an overt opportunity to control or taint subsequent responses. One may also be less likely to be forthcoming in the presence of another. If there is someone present, a victim may feel uncomfortable asking that person to leave. It is the investigator's responsibility to make this decision on the victim's behalf. If the interviewer speaks with each interviewee separately, he or she has a better chance of getting more complete and reliable information.
7. Avoid compound or multiple questions. Asking more than one question at a time encourages confusion, interrupts the flow of the interview, and allows the interviewee to dodge portions of the question.
8. Repeat questions. Asking the same question or variations of the same question at different times throughout the interview is a simple but useful interview strategy. Interviewees often disclose some aspects of their histories in response to questions that are posed early in the conversation and then add more details, information, and explanations if the questions are rephrased and reemphasized later on in a different context.
9. Do not tip your hand. Some interviewees will try to determine what the investigator knows about the offense and their personal history and will admit only to those facts. The investigator should inform the interviewee that a great deal is already known about the case, while at the same time remaining vague on the specifics until the interviewee has told the individual concerned's version of the story and has been encouraged to fill in any missing details. Giving the interview information about the crime can also induce a false confession.

10. Be open-minded. Do not focus on one theory and then ask questions only to prove that theory. Consider that the person being interviewed may know about conduct and motives unknown to investigators.
11. Use behavioral descriptors. Words such as "molester" or "rapist" mean different things to different people. Ask questions concerning the offender's specific behavior rather than using words or phrases that are prone to misinterpretation. Do not make the mistake of being vague.
12. Listen. It is very important to listen during interviews and interrogations. During interviews or interrogations, many investigators take the opportunity to engage in a kind of bizarre monologue to prove their insight or investigative virility. It is often comical, and certainly unprofessional. They would rather listen to themselves speak, and establish what they perceive as their authority, than to hear what the victim, witness, or suspect is trying to say. Investigators must remember the statement is the victim's, or the suspect's. It is not theirs. Interviews are not the place for diatribes, lectures, or monologues simply because the investigator has a captive audience. This is, in fact, a great way to kill a good interview and lose the respect, and trust, of the subject.

GENERIC INTERVIEW QUESTIONS: A STARTER KIT
GENERAL INTERVIEW QUESTIONS FOR ALL WITNESSES

1. Who do you think committed the crime?
2. Who have you talked to about this matter?
3. When and why did you have this conversation?
4. Who said what to whom?
5. Do you have any emails, text messages etc., from anyone regarding this?
6. When and how did you hear about this event?
7. What was your reaction to hearing the news?
8. Did you know the victim?
9. When was the last time you communicated with the victim?
10. Did the victim ever express fear of being killed or injured?

EYEWITNESS QUESTIONS

1. Where were you when you witnessed the crime?
2. What were the lighting conditions?
3. Were you alone?
4. What was the nature of your business there?
5. What was the weather like?
6. Do you wear glasses or contacts?
7. Have you ever had any type of eye surgery?
8. Have you ever witnessed another crime?

9. What did you hear?
10. Have you applied for any type of reward money?
11. Do you know any of the involved parties?
12. Are you related to any law enforcement personnel?
13. Do you have any drug, alcohol, or mental health issues?
14. Were you using any drugs, alcohol, or prescription drugs at the time of the incident? If you had a prescription who is Doctor who prescribed it?
15. Have you ever been arrested or convicted of a crime?
16. What is the highest level of education completed?
17. Have you read or saved any media accounts of this incident?
18. What did you do after you witnessed the incident?
19. What were you doing just prior to the incident?
20. How long did the event last?

ALIBI WITNESS QUESTIONS

1. How do you know this person?
2. Who else was present?
3. Have you discussed this matter with anyone? Under what circumstances?
4. Have you ever been an alibi prior to the event?
5. Where was your phone?
6. Was it turned on?
7. Did you take any photos with it?
8. Did you call anyone prior to or after the event?
9. What was the nature of the call?
10. What do you know about this matter?
11. What have you read or seen in the media?
12. Did you blog or write anything on social media about this matter?
13. When, where, and on what device?
14. What was the total elapsed time you were together?
15. During the course of your day with the subject was anyone using drugs or alcohol being consumed?
16. Was your phone ever turned off on the day of the event?
17. Did the subject use his phone? Who did he speak with?
18. Did anyone involved in this matter discuss this interview?
19. Has anyone offered you any money for your testimony?
20. Did you use your debit card or make any cash purchases on the day of the event? Do you have those receipts?

ADVICE AND DISCUSSION

In this section, the authors offer straightforward advice regarding specific issues raised by the interview protocols offered.

PHYSICAL EVIDENCE

Confessions are nice and they are often critical, but when there is an absence of other evidence to support a confession beware. As already warned, a confession must be corroborated. It cannot exist in vacuum, defying other evidence and statements.

Our best advice is this: in reality, if you follow the science you will seldom be wrong. When you ignore the science, it is a safe bet that your investigation is way off track. Good confessions lead to good physical evidence, and do not require you to ignore everything else.

CONDUCT AND TONE

Without exception, be respectful and appropriate. There are a number of reasons for treating all witnesses and suspects with a tone of respect and professionalism. The number one reason is that people respond better if they feel they are being treated fairly. It does not matter if you are talking to a medical doctor who just strangled his estranged wife, or a street junkie who just shot his dealer. If you treat them respectfully, and in a manner that does not degrade or humiliate them, things will progress in a manner more favorable to the open flow of information.

INVESTIGATOR DRESS AND PRESENTATION

In court, you must dress like a professional to be perceived as a professional—and to show the court the respect it deserves. This means at least a jacket, dress-shirt, necktie, and slacks. A suit is preferable (male and female alike). Too often state witnesses come to court looking like they are on a smoke break, with tight shirt sleeved shirts and khakis. This is, to be sure, an outfit which evidences an utter lack of seriousness and professionalism.

When conducting interviews, this is another matter. Old school thinking would have you dressed in a sports jacket and tie. This is still appropriate in some settings, but the new school of thought is more casual. Not sweat pants casual, but certainly jeans are an option. The trick is to not be so casual that your subject looks upon you as peer. You want to suggest a serious tone but not an over the top situation. Dress appropriate for the weather, neighborhood, and subject. Be clean shaven, or trim your beard and have your hair combed. Female investigators should dress similarly and appropriately (e.g., business casual).

Number of Personnel

Whenever possible, there should be two people present, one to take the statement and one to witness it. The secondary investigator is there to be a "prover." The prover's role is often critical when a witness denies making a statement or decides to change their testimony at a later date. Their role is limited to observing and documenting. These issues need to be worked out well in advance. There should never be without few exceptions more than two personnel present. Otherwise you may be accused of intimidation or some other form of trickery or deceit.

Length of Interviews and Interrogations

Whenever an interrogation or an interview has lasted beyond 5 or 6 h, beware. This is how coercive and false statements are made. Any evidence that is gathered after such a long period of time becomes questionable. The interview may even become worthless. Whenever we hear about a marathon interrogation that lasted 10 or 12 h, resulting in a confession, the first thought that comes to mind is—*false confession*.

Evaluating a Witness

The investigator should be constantly evaluating the individual that they are interviewing. The primary question: Are they being truthful?

The answer is usually no. They are often intentionally lying, or they are just mistaken as to what they saw, heard or witnessed for any number of reasons. There are a thousand variables that play into this evaluation, and it is exhausting if you think about it for any amount of time. Nevertheless that is what must be done. At the end of the day a successful investigation is an evaluation of all the evidence—and this means diligently checking the statement for errors against other evidence and statements. Failure to do so is nothing short of negligence.

PROMISES

As an investigator, there are very few times that you can guarantee anything to any witness. You generally do not possess the power to make deals and grant immunity. Lawyers negotiate these sorts of things, not investigators. Any promises made to a witness should be truthful, and within the realm of reality. Do not lie to witnesses, promising them the impossible against the reality of the probable.

Never say, "This is off the record." Anything a witness says to you will be reported. Never exchange drugs or alcohol for testimony from an informant. Always think before you make any promise to any type of witness. The only promise you should make is that you will treat everyone with respect, and you will not do anything that would jeopardize your reputation.

Failure to attend to the aforementioned protocols and concerns can lead to a false confession. These are to be avoided as anathema to justice.

FALSE CONFESSIONS[4]

Confession evidence is among the most powerful forms of proof that is used to suggest a defendant's guilt at trial. Judges rarely exclude it and juries almost never ignore it. It is the kind of evidence that can leave little doubt in the minds of those who hear it. As explained in Leo and Davis (2010, p. 19):

> *Confessions are universally viewed as extraordinarily persuasive evidence of guilt, particularly when they contain a plausible story line, a description of motives, explanations, crime knowledge, emotional expressions, and acknowledgments of voluntariness.*

In some instances, however, there is reason for doubt. Although it is difficult for some to believe, false confessions can and do occur "when a suspect's resistance to confession is broken down as a result of poor police practice, overzealousness, criminal misconduct, and/or misdirected training" (Leo and Ofshe, 1998).

Confronted with the problem, the most reasonable question that is asked about false confessions is why? Why would anyone confess to being a rapist, a murderer, or any other kind of criminal when they are in fact innocent? There are a number of circumstances that work alone or in concert to help elicit a false confession as listed:

1. Innocent suspects may be mentally disabled or disadvantaged in some way and therefore unable to understand the nature and consequences of what they are agreeing to.
2. Innocent suspects may be presented with fabricated evidence that makes the case against them seem hopelessly overwhelming. This can be as simple as phony claims that the suspect failed a polygraph or as involved as altered forensic reports.
3. An innocent suspect may be worn down by hours upon hours of uninterrupted, physically and mentally exhausting interrogation that breaks their will.
4. Innocent suspects may be physically threatened or abused by their interrogators, which can also break them down mentally and lead them to falsely confess.
5. Innocent suspects may give an ambiguous or equivocal statement that zealous investigators interpret incorrectly as a confession, such as a discussion about a dream related to the crime or holes in their memory around the presumed time of the crime.
6. Innocent suspects can give a confession while under the influence of drugs or alcohol.

Research has also found that false confessions are statistically more likely when the perceived consequences for failing to confess appear insurmountable; or when the pressure is higher on investigators to produce results, as it is with homicides and in cases of capital murder.

It is important to understand that children, teenagers, and the homeless are particularly susceptible to giving false confessions. Children and teenagers are more susceptible because of their lack of appreciation for the consequences of their statements. The homeless are more susceptible because of the associated frequency of mental illness, drug, and alcohol abuse within that group.

False confessions are most readily identified by a failure to accurately account for the circumstances of the crime. Moreover, they may even reflect law enforcement's misperceptions about how the crime occurred. In such ways, overzealous or incompetent investigators leave their mark on the confession that they have induced. Either they have purposefully led the suspect to confess to a false version of events or they have failed to establish the facts of the case adequately and competently and subsequently sign off on a confession to events that did not occur.

As explained in Leo and Davis (2010, p. 56): "there is no piece of erroneous evidence that if put before a jury is more likely to lead to a wrongful conviction than a false confession." Good interviewers know the power that they wield; they know that during some interviews, with some suspects, they can get them to agree with just about any set of facts. Such is their skill. However, responsible interviewers in search of the facts of a case will use their skill to understand and accept when they have reached this point and not abuse their power.

CONTINUING EDUCATION AND PROFESSIONAL DEVELOPMENT

There have been a number of books and treatises written on the subject of interviews and interrogation. The best investigators will read them all, and will not stop trying to learn from others. They will continually improve themselves by reading the latest textbooks, attending professional seminars, conducting their own research, and even publishing it when time permits. They will also talk with other professionals who do the same work, and keep up with the latest trends and technology. Experience is in fact the best teacher, as are the failures that it guarantees, but continuing education and involvement professional communities are what separate good investigators from the exceptional.

ENDNOTES

1. For example, if a student is being taught a forensic subject without an instructor that has a forensic background, this can be problematic without sufficient access guest lecturers and informed reference material.
2. It can also be a reference to formal debate. But that is not how it is used in relation to the law.
3. A witness may be defined as anyone that observed or experienced anything relevant to the case. This can include victims, suspects, friends, family members, accessories after the fact and disinterested third parties.
4. This section is adapted from Savino and Turvey (2012).

REFERENCES

Black, H. C. (2016). *Black's law dictionary* (2nd ed.) Online: http://thelawdictionary.org/letter/f/page/67/.

Cooley, C., & Turvey, B. (2014). *Miscarriages of justice: Actual innocence, forensic evidence, and the law.* San Diego: Elsevier Science.

Glawe, J. (May 15, 2015). *Talking to the journalist who uncovered police torture in Chicago.* Vice. http://www.vice.com/read/talking-to-the-journalist-who-uncovered-police-torture-in-chicago-515.

Goldberg, B. (October 13, 2015). *Former Louisiana police chief jailed for tasing inmates.* Reuters. http://www.businessinsider.com/former-louisiana-police-chief-jailed-for-tasing-inmates-2015-10.

Hughes, D. (April 28, 2016). *Witness says police tortured thacker, confessions in 2010 killing not backed up.* Arkansas Democrat-Gazette. http://m.arkansasonline.com/news/2016/apr/28/witness-says-police-tortured-thacker-co/.

Johnson, C. (May 21, 2014). *New DOJ policy urges agents to videotape interrogations.* NPR. http://www.npr.org/sections/thetwo-way/2014/05/21/314616254/new-doj-policy-calls-for-videotaping-the-questioning-of-suspects.

Leo, R., & Davis, D. (Spring—Summer 2010). From false confession to wrongful conviction: seven psychological processes. *Journal of Psychiatry & Law, 38,* 1—56.

Leo, R., & Ofshe, R. (Winter 1998). The consequences of false confessions: deprivations of liberty and miscarriages of justice in the age of psychological interrogation. *Journal of Criminal Law and Criminology, 88,* 429—496.

Newlin, C., Steele, L. C., Chamberlin, A., Anderson, J., Kenniston, J., Russell, A., et al. (September 2015). *Child Forensic Interviewing: Best Practices.* U.S. Department of Justice, Juvenile Justice Bulletin. https://www.ojjdp.gov/pubs/248749.pdf.

Ortiz, F. (May 06, 2015). *Chicago council approves reparations for police torture victims.* Reuters. http://www.reuters.com/article/us-usa-police-chicago-idUSKBN0NR1YA20150506.

Savino, J., & Turvey, B. (2012). Interviewing suspects and victims. In J. Savino, & B. Turvey (Eds.), *Rape investigation handbook* (2nd ed.). San Diego: Elsevier Science.

Spielman, F. (January 4, 2016). *Chicago pays $5.5M in reparations to 57 Burge torture victims.* Chicago Sun-Times. http://chicago.suntimes.com/politics/chicago-pays-5-5m-in-reparations-to-57-burge-torture-victims/.

Taylor, G. (October 13, 2015). *Cops almost got away with torturing Mathew Ajibade to death.* The Daily Beast. http://www.thedailybeast.com/articles/2015/10/13/cops-almost-got-away-with-torturing-matthew-ajibade-to-death.html.

Turvey, B., Petherick, W., & Ferguson, C. (Eds.). (2010). *Forensic Criminology.* San Diego: Elsevier Science.

Turvey, B. (2013). *Forensic fraud.* San Diego: Elsevier Science.

Woolsey, R. (February 10, 2016). *Sitka settles with tasered teen for $350,000.* KCAW. http://www.kcaw.org/2016/02/10/sitka-settles-with-tasered-teen-for-350000/.

Worland, J. (November 28, 2014). *U.N. panel sharply criticizes police brutality in U.S.* Time Magazine. http://time.com/3609811/police-brutality-united-states-un-ferguson-torture/.

CHAPTER 11

The Polygraph: Uses and Misuses

Michael McGrath

Forensic Psychiatrist, Unity Healthy Systems, Rochester, NY, United States

CHAPTER OUTLINE

The Test 278
Polygraph Research 280
Summary 289
Endnotes 290
References 291

Imagine your doctor trying to convince you to get a screening for a major illness. He or she tells you that the test has a scientific basis, yet you are aware that the test is not accepted by many reputable scientists and, in fact, a national scientific organization has written a book-long review of the test and pronounced it unreliable for screening purposes and problematic in case-specific scenarios. Now imagine that when you refuse to subject yourself to such a scenario, your doctor interprets the refusal as proof that you have the disease. Furthermore your doctor makes a living by administering these tests and if the test is positive (even if falsely so) there are grave consequences as to your employment and freedom. Also, you are aware that the test has been shown to miss a true disease state over and over again, and 20% of the time it does not even work. Would you take this test? I would not. But this is the state of polygraphy.

The reader might ask, how could this be? How could our federal government, police, and other agencies rely on a machine that has no solid scientific basis and yet can have serious repercussions both for the person being tested (if a false positive[1]) and the agency relying on the testing (if a false negative[2])? Would they really have faith in such a machine? Clearly, the answer is yes. They like it because they sometimes get people to confess to a crime or act during the course of the examination. Whether the confession is a valid one may not always be clear. Unfortunately many criminal investigation stop with a confession, regardless of its validity. As most know, a confession entered at trial will usually trump reason. Oftentimes people will confess to the matter at hand even before the actual polygraph testing begins. But you do not need a polygraph for that. All you need is someone who believes a machine can tell if they are lying.

There is an old story[3] of a crime investigation where the suspect was sitting in a chair with tinfoil on his head and a wire from the chair to a copier. Already prepared were pages that said *Lie* or *Truth* in bold letters. When asked his name and after the suspect gave it, a detective hit the copy button. After the light moved across the glass plate and the machine whirred a bit, a sheet of paper came out and was shown to the suspect. It said "Truth." After a few more questions that would be answered truthfully, similar sheets emerged from the copier. When asked if he committed the crime in question, the subject said no. The detective hit the copy button and since he had switched to the lie sheet that is what came out. It was shown to the subject, who then confessed, convinced the machine could read his mind. Would we say copy machines can tell a lie from the truth?

One would think that pseudoscientific ideas, tests, machines, etc., would be quickly identified and discarded. But one would be wrong. The list is long and includes things such as chiropractic, EMDR (eye movement desensitization and reprocessing) treatment for trauma and other ills, complimentary or alternative medicine[4] (such as acupuncture), etc. In a land where a large portion of the population cannot accept evolution as a fact should we be surprised that pseudoscience flourishes?

THE TEST

The polygraph is based on the premise that a heightened physiological response when answering a question is indicative of deception. The polygraph measures physiological arousal. That is all it does. Physiological arousal to answering a question could be due to lying; but it could also be due to other things, including anxiety about the situation. Current practice is to use a laptop computer to record and score the test, adding a veneer of authority and scientification[5] to the test.

The subject to be tested is interviewed and told the questions that will be asked.[6] The subject is "educated" about the polygraph, with the examiner attempting to convince the subject of the accuracy or infallibility of the machine. The subject is then hooked up to apparatus that measures the rate of breathing, blood pressure, pulse, and skin conductance (which changes when one sweats). These physiological parameters are graphed as questions are asked. Prior to the examination, the polygrapher describes the apparatus and how the exam will be conducted. The most common test is the CQT or control question test. The exam starts with control questions that are asked to set a baseline for both telling the truth and for lying. The subject will be asked questions with a yes or no response. Questions that the polygrapher knows are true set the baseline for truthful answers. For example, the subject could be asked their name (Are you Robert Smith?), address, workplace, etc. They are also asked questions to set the baseline for deceit, such as "Have you ever stolen anything? Have you ever lied?" which the examiner knows is a lie if the answer is no. They may also instruct the subject to lie. Once the examiner has set baselines for truth and deceit, he or she will ask relevant questions, such as "Were you involved in the theft of the money?" Increases above baseline of the control questions would be interpreted as indicative of deception.

The testing paradigm is problematic on many levels, not the least of which is that, despite the body of literature conducted by proponents of the polygraph, it has never been proven that the machine detects lies. It has been proven over and over that innocent people have been labeled as guilty and that guilty people have been labeled as truthful. Also, it is well known that a guilty subject can take countermeasures and pass the test. Such measures are easily available on the Internet. What is not suggested is that an innocent person might take countermeasures because they know they could be innocent and still fail the test.

If a subject reacts more strongly to relevant questions than control (baseline) questions they are considered to be deceptive. If more reactive to control questions than relevant questions they are considered to be truthful. If there is not enough difference between the reaction to the control and relevant questions the test is "inconclusive."

The CQT relies on the assumption that all people physiologically respond the same and that a subject will have more internal blushing[7], if you will, when lying to a relevant question (Did you kill your wife?) than when lying on a control question (Have you ever stolen anything?). The first assumption is simply wrong. The second is unproven and easily debunked. Imagine your spouse has been stabbed to death and you are innocent. You are asked to take a polygraph "So we can clear you." During the exam you are asked if you ever stole anything (control question) and you answer no, when in fact several times in your life you have stolen things, but nothing of much value. You are then asked (relevant question) if you killed your wife. You are innocent, but not sure if these people (polygrapher, police, etc.) will believe you. Would you bet your freedom on the expectation that the response to the relevant question will be lower than the control question?

A variant of the CQT is the guilty knowledge test, or GKT, where questions are asked in such a way that knowledge only a guilty person could possess[8] would lead to a change in the physiological parameters. For example, if a victim was killed with a knife, a polygrapher could ask "Did you kill your wife with a rope? A gun? A knife? A baseball bat?" The examiner will be looking for your response when the word "knife" is mentioned. This variant test is difficult to set up and suffers from situational influences[9] and lack of research.

Aside from the various tracing lines of the polygraph, there is room for the examiner to determine if a certain graph is a lie or not. Various polygraphers can grade a tracing differently, although they will claim that the computers they use minimize this. Regardless, even if 100 polygraphers read a tracing the same, all we can say is this speaks to reliability, not validity.

It is common practice for polygraphers to use the polygraph as a ruse[10]; for example, to claim that there is a "problem" with a particular answer and use this as an opening to interrogate the subject further. It should be noted that a polygraph examination is an interrogation. In investigations, the subject is presumed guilty,[11] otherwise they would not be tested. It is not uncommon for a person who "passes" a polygraph to be told they failed and coercive interrogation tactics used. A person will be expected to be anxious when feeling accused of something they did not do, but apparently this has no effect on the tracings. Circumstances where the subject may not be presumed guilty are when the polygraph exam is incident to being hired for certain sensitive jobs and require a security clearance, or routine follow-up exams for those in such jobs. For example, a CIA operative returning from an assignment in a foreign country may routinely be polygraphed and asked questions related to contact with foreign intelligence services. Interestingly the US government has passed laws prohibiting the use of the polygraph in employment screening due to concerns about its validity, but excludes from this law agencies such as the FBI, NSA, CIA, etc. In one well-known case of a CIA agent spying for The Soviet Union, Alrich Ames was passing polygraphs while actively spying over the course of 9 years (FBI). Part of the problem is that polygraphers confuse utility with accuracy, because they may get people to confess to something during a polygraph. This reinforces their belief that the machine "works."

The problems with the polygraph are twofold. First, the scientific basis for the machine is lacking; in other words the test is not valid. It does not measure what its proponents claim, i.e., lying. Secondly, while it may have good reliability,[12] there are problems with sensitivity and specificity. Reliability is getting the same, or similar result from a measurement. For example, you would not use a scale that changed the weight readout if you stepped back on the scale within seconds and it was off by an amount larger than an acceptable margin of error. Sensitivity is the ability of a test to find what it is looking for without making errors. If a test fails to find something that is there, it is a false negative. If a test finds something that is not there, it is a false positive, and suffers from poor specificity. In a polygraph examination, calling an innocent person a liar is a false-positive error. Calling a liar innocent is a false negative. The polygraph is weighted against the truth teller.

POLYGRAPH RESEARCH

The American Polygraph Association (APA) is the professional organization representing polygraphers in private practice as well as those employed by police, other governmental agencies, and some private companies.[13] Its website (www.polygraph.org) lists research on the polygraph among other trade issues. Since the polygraph's appearance, there have been thousands of studies, but only a small proportion of them actually involve research and an even smaller number meet scientific standards (Ekman, 1992). Problems with polygraph research include determining "ground truth" (knowing who is lying) and the base rate of lying. People do not realize that even if a machine is very accurate at detecting lying, if the base rate for lying is low,[14] there will be many false positives (Ekman, 1992).

Richard Leo (2008, p. 89) summarizes the research:

> *The claims of proponents of the polygraph that it is accurate 95 to 99 percent of the time are simply wild exaggerations with no empirical basis and have been discredited by scientific critics (Ekman, 1992; Kleinmuntz & Szucko, 1984; Lykken, 1998). In fact, the few methodologically sound studies of polygraphy suggest that the so-called lie detector is no more accurate than 60 to 75 percent of the time (Lykken, 1998). However, polygraph examiners are more likely to make false–positive errors (classifying a truthful subject as lying) than false-negative errors (classifying a lying subject as truthful). According to the leading scientific critics of the polygraph, an innocent subject stands a nearly 50 percent chance of failing the examination (Kleinmuntz & Szucko, 1984; Lykken, 1998)…*

When proponents are citing the thousands of studies done on the polygraph, they are referring to reliability studies that prove nothing as to the validity of the device, or accuracy studies that are flawed. As noted, there are very few studies that use acceptable methodology. Most accuracy studies do not include inconclusive test results, relying on passed or failed tests. But an inconclusive test is a test where the device did not work. It could not accurately tell whether the subject was lying or not. To exclude them inflates whatever accuracy scores are presented.

In the most recent issue of the APA Magazine (2015, p 124), a 32-page declaration of polygraph expert affidavit by Dr. David Raskin (2014), a strong proponent of the machine, was published. It is presumed the affidavit was to support a Daubert challenge. Dr. Raskin is among a small group of polygraphers who possess actual training and education in a scientific field. In the affidavit he describes his review of the scientific status of polygraphy, asserting that polygraphy is accepted as scientific by most scientists and its accuracy exceeds 90%.

The affidavit addresses the validity of polygraph testing by claiming that polygraphy has gained general acceptance in the fields of psychology and psychophysiology, and that it is has a scientific basis and "has been tested with the methods of science. Any conscious effort at deception by a rational individual causes involuntary and uncontrollable physiological responses through the nervous system that may include measurable reactions in blood pressure, …" (p. 3) Why hedge with *may*? If the expected changes *may* appear, that would mean they *may not*. He references "… numerous scientific tests during the past 30 years. The results of these scientific tests have been published in high quality peer-reviewed scientific journals."

Dr. Raskin states that there are known error rates from lab and field studies. In the lab it is easier to control things, such as who is lying and who is telling the truth (a.k.a. ground truth). The subjects are usually college students asked to either lie or tell the truth in relation to a minor crime. They have no reason to fear the outcome of the testing. To claim that this is applicable to a criminal suspect being accused of a rape or a murder would appear naïve at best. In support of his claim that such lab studies can be applied to the field, Dr. Raskin cites Anderson, Lindsay, and Bushman (1999) saying (Raskin, 2014, p. 4): "Laboratory research on credibility assessment has been criticized as lacking in realism. However, the level of realism in properly designed and conducted laboratory studies does not limit the ability of scientists to apply the laboratory results to real world—world settings." The Anderson et al. (1999) study was a metaanalysis of 38 research topic pairs of lab/field studies. These authors opined their findings supported the belief that lab studies produced valid results that could be generalized to other settings.

In 2015 Mitchell replicated the study using a larger database. He (p. 114) concluded "My results qualify the conclusion reached by Anderson et al. (1999): Many psychological results found in the laboratory can be replicated in the field, but the effects often differ greatly in their size and less often (though with disappointing frequency) differ in their directions." Whether the results of these two studies are valid or not, the papers did not have anything to do with the polygraph. Citing Anderson et al. (1999) as lending support to polygraph lab studies being as valid as field studies is unwarranted and arguably misleading. The reader should keep in mind that this information is being supplied to a court.

In addressing the problem of ascertaining ground truth in field studies of polygraphy, Raskin (2014) states that it is "generally agreed" that the use of polygraph-induced confessions is the best approach. In other words, if someone fails the polygraph and is interrogated and confesses, then that can be used as proof of the polygraph's accuracy. But, as pointed out by Lykken (1998), the paradigm is flawed. It selects for cases where confessions occurred. If a guilty person passes they are not questioned further, so the error is never caught. Also, the issue of false confessions[15] is ignored.

Raskin then lists (2014, Table 1, p. 7) 11 "high-quality laboratory studies" (Driscoll, Honts, & Jones, 1987; Ginton, Daie, & Elaad, 1982[16]; Honts, Raskin, & Kircher, 1994; Honts et al., 2003[17]; Honts, Devitt, Winbush, & Kircher, 1996[18]; Kircher & Raskin, 1988; Patrick & Iacono, 1989; Podlesny & Raskin, 1978; Podlesny & Truslow, 1993; Raskin, and Hare, 1978; Rovner, 1979[19]) opining that "overall, the CQT correctly classified 91% of the subjects and produced approximately equal numbers of false-positive and false-negative errors." The total number of subjects ranged from 15 to 100, with a cumulative n of 553. The inconclusive tests were 10% of the subjects who were guilty and 11% of the innocent subjects. A footnote advises that inconclusive tests were excluded because "they are not decisions," i.e., the polygraph could not determine whether the subject was deceptive or truthful. So in "high-quality" studies, the researchers are allowed to ignore when the machine does not perform. This would inflate the accuracy of the machine, would it not? Also, an inconclusive test will leave the subject under a cloud of suspicion, very possibly leading to enhanced questioning.

The studies referenced include *The accuracy of physiological detection of deception for subjects with prior knowledge* (Rovner, 1986), which was published in *Polygraph*, the APA trade journal, not a scientific peer-reviewed journal. Subjects received $7.50 to participate with a $10-bonus for those (guilty or innocent) who passed the polygraph. Twenty-nine percent of the original 84 possible subjects were excluded for various reasons (some of which would likely have affected performance during a polygraph[20]), leaving 60 subjects divided into guilty or innocent groups. Yet Table 1 (Raskin, 2014) lists two groups of 24 subjects. There were technical problems that caused other subjects to be excluded. Aside from that (according to Table 1) there were 16 inconclusive tests for the 48 subjects, one-third of the study. Rovner claims 95.5% accuracy in determining truth or lying, regardless of whether the subject was naïve to the test or educated prior to the test. That the percent accuracy would exactly match for both cohorts is interesting. Raskin (2014, p. 7) lists 82% (guilty) and 83% (innocent) for the Rovner (1986) study. At some point it simply does not matter as the study should not be cited anywhere. That this is offered as a "high-quality laboratory study" to a court borders on stunning.

The Podlesny and Truslow (1993) paper was a simulation study with roles of thief, accomplice, confidant, and innocent. They offered an 84.7% accuracy rate for guilty subjects and a 94.7% accuracy rate for innocent subjects. As usual, inconclusive tests were ignored, which averaged 19% for the two groups. Almost one-fifth of the exams were unable to discriminate lying from truth telling, but this does not affect accuracy? 91% and 89% overall accurate findings for the 11 studies fall to 82% and 83% if inconclusive tests are not excluded. That is, if one is willing to accept even those numbers. In the Patrick and Iacono (1989) study, 36% of the innocent subjects were identified by polygraph as guilty.

The Ginton et al. study (1982) included 21 Israeli policemen. We do not know on what basis they were chosen, other than they were taking a course. They were given an aptitude test and, because of the way the test was administered had a chance to cheat if they chose to, allowing Gitan et al. to know who had cheated and who had not. Several days later the subjects were advised that there were concerns that some had cheated and offered them a polygraph test to sort it out, with the subjects believing that the results of the test could affect their career. Seven of the original 21 (33%) had cheated. Although all subjects agreed to take the polygraph, only 15 (71%) eventually did.[21] The n for the guilty cohort tested was two. Could this possibly have any significance statistically? The n for the innocent cohort was 13. For the 13 innocent subjects the accuracy was 85%, giving a 15% false-positive rate. Is this level of error really acceptable? The means reported for accuracy, etc., in Table 1 (Raskin, 2014, p. 7) are the percentages from the studies totaled and divided by 11. So a study (Ginton et al., 1982) with a guilty n of two finding 100% accuracy carries the same weight as a study (Podlesny & Truslow, 1993) with a guilty n of 72 finding 69% accuracy (ignoring inconclusive tests).

Raskin (2014) then comments on the available four field[22] studies of the polygraph (Honts, 1996; Honts & Raskin, 1988; Patrick & Iacono, 1991; Raskin, Kircher, Honts, & Horowitz, 1988) that are acceptable to him, offering a 90.5% CQT accuracy rate, noting that in field studies nearly all the errors were false positives, i.e., calling a truthful person a liar. Yet these four studies have an inconclusive rate of 10% for 108 subjects believed guilty and 29% for 82 subjects believed innocent. That means for 180 tests, the machine was unable to give an answer for (11 plus 24) 35 subjects. So in 19% (essentially one in five) of the tests the researchers were unable to say whether a subject was lying or telling the truth, but (as usual) these results were simply excluded. Imagine trying to get a paper published (and apparently you can) and noting that 20% of your testing did not work so you will just ignore that fact? Why are inconclusive tests an issue that cannot be ignored? Because the subjects did not physiologically react according to the theory and assumptions put forth by the proponents of the polygraph.

The Raskin et al. (1988) study has never been published in a scientific peer-reviewed journal. Lykken (1998, pp. 130–32) reviewed what information he was able to piece together. A total of 2522 CQTs were administered by the secret service. Only 4% of the tests could be "verified" as guilty or innocent, with such verification being incomplete, being related many times to only one test question. Sixty-six tests were "verified" as deceptive and led to interrogation that led to a confession. The deceptive tests were then proven accurate. But the verification is not independent of the confession. According to Lykken (p. 131): "But these results are entirely compatible with the assumption that there is no relationship *whatever* between the veracity of the suspect and his score on the CQT!" (emphasis in original) He also points out that so-called corroborating physical evidence is not independent of test outcome, as has been noted above, as if one does not fail the CQT there is no confession and no further inquiry. The "independent" verifications are not independent.

The Honts, 1996 study selected 29 exams from one examiner ("first wave") and 12 ("second wave") from another performed as part of a criminal investigation. The first wave cases (evidence and exams) were reviewed for "confirmation"[23] by a "highly experienced (20 years) police investigator and polygraph examiner" and PhD psychologist who had been doing polygraph exams for 16 years (p. 314) using a 1–7 point scale. The ratings of the two evaluators were found to be "very similar" which tells us nothing about the polygraph itself. Because of the similarity in ratings only the psychologist reviewed the second batch. The results were 7 subjects were "no confirmation" (NC); 11 "weak confirmation" (WC); 10 "moderate confirmation"; 13 "strong confirmation" (SC). Of the NC group six were identified by polygraph as truthful, with the one left listed as inconclusive. For the 11 WC, 3 were truthful and 6 deceptive. The evaluators disagreed on the 1–7 scale on the two remaining WCs, so they were dropped from the study.[24] Of the six in the MC, four were deceptive and two truthful. For the 15 in the SC, the "evidence and a confession indicated that six suspects were truthful (there was a confession of guilt plus evidence provided by another suspect), and nine were deceptive." (p. 315). The reader will notice that the numbers do not tally. The SC cohort has increased by 2, from 13 to 15. The study started with 41 subjects and lost two to lack of agreement among the evaluators leaving 39 exams in the study. The sum of the remaining subjects listed in the four categories adds up to 36. Four exams were lost from the data between the 10 MC which are reported as 6 MC in the same paragraph with no explanation and the SC group suddenly increased from 13 to 15. Aside from the discrepancies regarding the numbers of subjects in each arm of the study, the selection of cases was not random and there is no way to know the quality of evidence evaluated as confirmation. Again, the polygraph exams are not independent of the criteria used to verify their accuracy. Any exam that led to a confession was "proven" correct and exams not felt to indicate deception would not have led to further search for a confession or evidence against that subject. Dr. Honts highlights reliability between evaluators, but this proves nothing. Polygraphers confuse reliability with accuracy in a distressingly consistent manner.

Honts and Raskin (1988) claim that the validity of the CQT has been established by laboratory research, when in fact that is far from the case. They claim that a directed lie can serve as a control for a lie. The study consisted of 25 criminal suspects, 12 of whom they believe were innocent and 12 "confirmed" as guilty. They claim 100% accuracy in determining guilt. This study suffers from small nonrandom sample size, and the fact that the outcomes are not independent of the teat result, as only those who fail the exam are subjected to further scrutiny. In essence, they find their successes and miss their errors.

Patrick and Iacono (1991)[25] attempted to address sampling bias pointing out that studies of CQT exams relying on confessions as ground truth are flawed As has been noted, a failed polygraph will lead to an interrogation and any subsequent confessions will "prove" the exam was accurate. Exams that are passed will not lead to an interrogation. Also the final opinion of the result of an exam may include observations of the examiner independent of the actual tracings. The authors reviewed all the cases available from the Vancouver RCMP from 1980 to 1984, a total of 402 polygraphs. Eighty-nine cases were verified guilty or innocent with maximum certainty, per the authors. Of 52 guilty subjects, 92% were reported as correctly categorized, 2% were wrong and 6% inconclusive. Of 37 innocent subjects, 30% were correctly categorized, 24% were wrong with 46% inconclusive. This study highlights the fact that the polygraph is weighted against the innocent.

Dr. Raskin quotes (2014, p. 20) the NAS 2003 report on lie detection in support of his opinion that the polygraph is a scientifically valid tool:

The National Research Council of the National Academy of Science recently reviewed the scientific research concerning the validity of the polygraph. Although they were critical of the use of non-specific issue polygraphs as a national security screening tool, they reached the following conclusions about specific issue polygraphs used in criminal cases: The available evidence indicates that in the context of specific-incident investigations and with inexperienced examinees untrained in countermeasures, polygraph tests as currently used have value in distinguishing truthful from deceptive individuals.No alternative techniques are available that perform better,....(p. 178)[26]

There is a sentence he left out. The full quote, with the missing sentence in italics, is (NAS, 2003, p. 178):

The available evidence indicates that in the context of specific-incident investigations and with inexperienced examinees untrained in countermeasures, polygraph tests as currently used have value in distinguishing truthful from deceptive individuals. However, they are far from perfect in that context, and important unanswered questions remain about polygraph accuracy in other important contexts. *No alternative techniques are available that perform better…*

Why was this sentence dropped from the quote? There is no ellipsis following "deceptive individuals" to indicate that text is left out, as was used at the end of the quote.

In a lab study the authors would probably prefer to forget about (Barland & Raskin, 1976) 72 "guilty" and "innocent" students were tested using the CQT paradigm. They were randomly assigned to three situations. One group was told the polygraph was an effective tool (positive), one group was told the machine was not working as it should (negative), and the third group was told nothing. The polygraph (CQT) was able to correctly identify the students 53% of the time. The error rate is given at 12% (4% false negatives and 8% false positives), and the inconclusive rate as 35%.

Another proponent of the polygraph is Dr. Charles Honts, a former student of Dr. Raskin. He testified as an expert witness on the polygraph in a *Daubert* hearing in September of 2005 in the US District Court in front of the Hon. Janet King, US Magistrate Judge. In October 2005, she issued her ruling denying the defendant's motion to admit polygraph evidence (US v Williams, 2005). The defendant, Williams, was charged with conspiring to rob an armored car. He was alleged to be the "inside" man regarding information, and was not present when the robbery took place. During the robbery a security guard was killed and another injured. The defense attorney hired a polygrapher to conduct a CQT polygraph exam.[27] The exam was not videotaped. Since the polygrapher said the defendant passed, the defense sought to have this fact introduced at trial and retained Dr. Honts as their expert witness. The following commentary is taken from Judge King's ruling:

- The court had serious concerns regarding Dr. Honts' testimony suggesting that he never met a polygraph exam that he did not like.
- According to Dr. Honts only studies and articles published by proponents of the polygraph are valid.
- "Also, although Dr. Honts struggled to avoid admitting the obvious, a recent report on the polygraph examination reliability and validity issued by the National Academy of Sciences ('NAS') questioned the quality of all the available studies—including those in which Dr. Honts participated or on which he relies." (p. 15)
- "Additionally, Dr. Honts is not above editing quotes or taking quotes out of context in his declaration to the court in order to support the arguments he makes as a proponent of the admissibility of polygraph evidence." (p. 16)[28]
- Referring to the omitted sentence from the NAS quote (see previous list): "If not intending to intentionally mislead the court, this omission at least exemplifies Dr. Honts' bias." (p.17)
- Although standards exist for polygraph examinations, there is no enforcement, and all compliance is self-imposed.
- Polygraph examinations for admission into evidence should be videotaped.
- There is no consensus that polygraph evidence is reliable.

A recent paper by Dr. Honts and Reavy (2015) reports on a lab study of a mock crime involving 250 subjects. In this study, the probable-lie (ex., Prior to 2013, did you ever lie to anyone? p. 16) question is replaced with a directed-lie (ex., Prior to 2012, did you ever tell even one lie in your entire life? p. 16) question. The essential difference is that with a probable-lie question the examiner asks a question he/she assumes the subject will answer with a lie, but is not 100% sure the answer is a lie. With a directed-lie question the subject is instructed to lie, so the examiner is sure the response is a lie. Aside from the philosophical issue that a directed lie is not a lie, it is incomprehensible that there is an expectation that such a directive will allow for the creation of a baseline for lying.

The polygraph examiners were blind to who was "guilty" and who was "innocent." The exams were score by humans and again by computer. The percent inconclusive was 14% for both human and computer, but these tests are jettisoned. No significant difference was found between the probable-lie and the directed-lie tests, which is hardly surprising since both are based on the same unsupported basis. I could find no discussion or listing of erroneous test results, i.e., false positives or false negatives in relation to the study subjects. Honts and Reavy (2015) cite the Anderson et al. (1999) study (see earlier), as well as a metaanalysis by Hartwig and Bond (2014) as support for extrapolating lab studies to the field. Neither study included any polygraph research, a point Honts admits for the Hartwig and Bond (2014) study, but neglects to mention for the Anderson et al. (1999) work. While the Hartwig and Bond 2014 metaanalysis dealt specifically with deception research, it ignores the polygraph and suggested a 67% accuracy rate for deception detection using multiple cues.

The National Research Council (National Academy of Sciences (NAS), 2003) report on the polygraph is an unbiased[29] examination of the state of the research in the area. By selectively quoting sections, proponents of the polygraph imply that the NAS has endorsed the polygraph, but, as noted earlier, this would be misleading. There is no question that the report does not recommend the polygraph as a screening tool (p. 3): "Scientific evidence for employee or preemployment screening is extremely limited. Only one field study, which is flawed, provides evidence directly relevant to accuracy for preemployment screening."

Regarding specific incident polygraphs[30] (p.3):

Of the 57 studies used to quantify the accuracy of polygraph testing, all involved specific incidents, typically mock crimes (four studies simulated screening in the sense that the incidents were followed by generic screening-type questions). The quality of the studies varies considerably, but falls short of what is desirable... Field studies have major problems with identifying the truth against which tests should be judged. In addition, they suffer from problems associated with heterogenicity and lack of control of extraneous factors and more generally, they have lower quality than could be achieved with careful study design. Moreover, most of the research, in both the laboratory and in the field, does not fully address key potential threats to validity. For these reasons, study results cannot be expected to generalize to practical contexts.

Estimates of accuracy from these 57 studies are almost certainly higher than actual polygraph accuracy of specific-incident testing in the field…

Furthermore "almost a century in scientific psychology and physiology provides little basis for the expectation that a polygraph test could have extremely high accuracy" (p. 212). One would be hard pressed to read such text as an endorsement.

More recently proponents of the polygraph have continued the search for a theory to validate the machine. Palmatier and Rovner (2015) propose that preliminary process theory (PPT) fits the bill. In their abstract (p. 3) they say "the term 'polygraph test,' particularly in a forensic context, is used to generally describe *diagnostic procedures* using a polygraph instrument to assess credibility" (emphasis added). The claim that they are diagnosing is problematic, but typical of attempts to make the machine sound scientific. They are not diagnosing anything and should not be using that word. Palmatier and Rovner review the orienting response[31] (OR) and PPT. The paper essentially says that when people lie they have to (cognitively) work harder by both lying and suppressing the truth. They believe that lying adds an emotional and cognitive load that they should be able to detect. That telling the truth can involve emotional and cognitive loads apparently never occurs to them.

They (Palmatier & Rovner, 2015) feel that polygraph researchers are hampering themselves by trying to prove either that CQT or CIT[32] tests are valid, as opposed to proving that both are. After decrying the fact that "a few academics" disagree with them, Palmatier and Rovner weave their opinions through a scientific sounding, but unfulfilling, description of why the polygraph can discern lying from truth telling and how OR and PPT are involved. In attempting to justify the polygraph, they arguably make the case for why it does not work (p. 10):

We believe that if the science relative to the instrumental assessment of credibility is to evolve, practitioners and scientists alike must be sensitive to a converging body of evidence that a human being is not an assembly of independent components responding in isolation, but rather a constellation of interdependent and interactive systems and subsystems (Churchland, 2007), which depending on situational circumstances, and individual differences, will call into play appropriate affective and cognitive responses (Cunningham & Brosch, 2012) to address whatever situation may present itself.

In invited commentary Elaad (2015) remarked on the Palmatier and Rovner (2015) article, opining that the CQT rests predominately on emotional processes while the CIT rests largely on cognitive processes (i.e., retrieval and assessment of memory) and that the same rationale should not explain both processes. While this is a reasonable approach, it too fails to elucidate to what degree various processes are assessed in different polygraph testing paradigms

Ben-Shakar et al. (2015)[33] suggest that (p16):

Palmatier and Rovner (2015) published an article attempting to establish the construct validity of the Comparison Question Test (CQT). By citing research ranging from modern neuroscience to memory and psychophysiology, they argue

that the available scientific evidence establishes a plausible theoretical construct that strengthens the practical application of the polygraph in forensic and other settings. In this comment we argue that: (1) Palmatier and Rovner's review of research on the Preliminary Process Theory (PPT) of the orienting response (OR) fails to specifically connect it to the CQT, and is therefore insufficient for construct validity. (2) PPT cannot account for observed differential heart rate responses found in deception research. (3) Neuroimaging studies on deception do not provide support for a stable and context-independent neural correlate of deception, nor do findings from this domain directly generalize to the autonomic responses measured in the CQT. Finally, (4) Palmatier and Rovner ignore the many other deficiencies of the CQT such as the lack of criterion validity as well as lack of proper control and standardization, which cannot be resolved by any psychological or psychophysiological theory.

Alder Vrij (2015), an internationally known credibility assessment researcher (BPS, 2004), offered invited commentary on the Palmatier and Rovner (2015) article. He applauded them for their efforts, but noted that they focused in their article on liars, failing to consider the tests in respect to truth tellers. Vrij (2015) believes the way a truth teller is protected from a false accusation differs between the CQT and the CIT tests believing the CIT test is more protective of the innocent. Vrij notes (p. 21) that Palmatier and Rovner (2015) cite high accuracy rates for the CQT, but fail to report the problems associated with the research. Vrij (2015) points out that confession-based studies inflate accuracy rates, noting (p. 21):

In other words, confessions are not appropriate to use to demonstrate that a CQT actually works and field studies need to be conducted that include ground truth exclusively based on real conclusive evidence. To my knowledge, such a field study does not exist, and in any case Palmatier and Rovner fail to cite such a field study.

Vrij (2015) also notes that the impression fostered by Palmatier and Rovner (2015) that only a few individuals have serious reservations over the CQT test is misleading.

SUMMARY

Although in use for decades, the polygraph is an unreliable way to determine if a particular individual is lying or truthful. The presumed scientific basis for it lacks a verifiable theory and the test lacks validity. It cannot tell us if tracings on paper are proof of a lie or the truth. The vast majority of the literature from the field is useless. Literature that employs an appropriate academic basis is limited and often suffers from sampling issues, lack of knowing ground truth, and examiner bias, to name only a few problems. The widespread selecting out of inconclusive test results falsely buoys exaggerated accuracy claims. What few field tests that exist are flawed. The machine is dangerous and no person, agency, or government should rely on it to make important decisions. As a screening tool it is very problematic, and for specific incident testing it is still problematic. There is no Pinocchio effect. The same physiologic responses can occur during both lying and truth telling. It is that simple. Diehard proponents of the polygraph are almost always financially dependent on it, and this will help perpetuate its use.

The plural of anecdote is not data, but an anecdote is illustrative. Gary Ridgway, known as the Green River killer, was killing women over a 20-year span in and around Seattle, Washington. Ridgway came to the attention of police on more than one occasion, due to his behavior with prostitutes. In 1984 he was given a polygraph test that he passed. He was never taken off the suspect list and was polygraphed again in 1987 and passed again. In 2001, due to advances in DNA technology, Ridgway was arrested and charged with the murders of several women.

As part of the investigation, an FBI criminal profile was done and it led police to suspect a local cab driver, Melvin Foster. In 1982 Foster agreed to take a polygraph test and failed, although he had no connection to the killings.

ENDNOTES

1. An innocent person being labeled a liar.
2. A liar being labeled innocent.
3. A scene from HBO's The Wire replicates the story, although without the wire and tinfoil. See: https://www.youtube.com/watch?v=DgrO_rAaiq0.
4. If so-called "complimentary" or "alternative" medicine worked, it would be called medicine.
5. A term coined by Brent Turvey to describe something done or added to a pseudoscientific paradigm to give it the veneer of science.
6. This description of a polygraph test is limited. For detailed descriptions see Lykken (1998).
7. A phrase coined by Lykken.
8. Many times such as "not known by the general public" information is known by the public. Also investigators often leak "guilty knowledge" to suspects, a major issue in false confessions.
9. As does the CQT test.
10. Like a glorified copy machine.
11. Unless it is a "friendly" test, one where the polygrapher is hired by the defense.
12. Different examiners reading the test results the same.
13. It is interesting that the organization is eager to debunk Voice Stress Analysis, another type of "lie detector" used by police that suffers from the same flaws as the polygraph. See: http://www.polygraph.org/review-of-voice-stress-based-technologies-for-the-detection-of-deception.
14. One could say that since everyone lies, the base rate should be high. But this is (or should be) a rate related to lying during the exam on a serious matter.
15. Not a minor issue. See: McGrath (2014).
16. Although the table lists 1984 as year of publication, the paper was published in 1982 and cited as such in references.
17. Although the table lists 2003 as year of publication, the paper was published in 2005 and is cited as such in references.
18. Although the table lists 1996 as year of publication, the paper was published in 1997 and is cited as such in references.
19. The article appears to have been published in 1986 and is listed as such in the references.

20. Of 84 initial possible subjects, 12 disqualified themselves for various reasons we are ignorant of. Four dropped out due to "moral problems" related to stealing, two due to anxiety about the whole thing, one due to lacking confidence that he could deceive the examiner, one due to fear of somehow getting in trouble, and one subject actually confessed the crime during the pretest! Three more were cut: (1) the examiner became aware of which cohort the subject was in, (2) one subject did not follow the instructions, and (3) one subject could not find the ring he was supposed to steal.
21. One guilty subject did not show for the test. Two (a guilty and an innocent) refused to take the polygraph and three guilty subjects refused to take the exam.
22. Is it surprising that only four of these studies are available yet this machine is apparently so highly regarded.
23. That is, the result of the polygraph examination was confirmed.
24. There was no explanation of how or why they disagreed or how this might or might not affect any results.
25. Dr. Iacono is often identified as a "polygraph critic" by polygraph proponents.
26. The #34 footnote in the earlier quoted text is to the NAS 2003 report, as is the page notation, 178.
27. This is known as a "friendly" examination. The examinee is advised by the polygrapher that he is under attorney—client privilege and the results of the exam would only be released if the attorney chose to do so. Clearly that would happen only if the defendant passed. Obviously such an arrangement decreases pressure on an examinee who would appear to have nothing to lose by taking the polygraph exam.
28. Judge King gives as an example the same NAS quote noted earlier in regard to Dr. Raskin where an important sentence is missing from the quote.
29. The researchers involved in the report had no prior experience researching the polygraph.
30. For example when investigating a theft or other crime.
31. Directing attention to a stimulus.
32. Another name for the guilty knowledge test.
33. The "few academics" noted in the Palmatier and Rovner (2015) article who interfered with the scientific assessment of the polygraph by polygraph proponents by utilizing critical thinking and an understanding of science.

REFERENCES

American Polygraph Association (APA) (http://www.polygraph.org).

Anderson, C. A., Lindsay, J. J., & Bushman, B. J. (1999). *Research in the psychological laboratory: Truth or triviality*.

Barland, G. H., & Raskin, D. C. (1976). *Validity and reliability of polygraph examinations of criminal suspects, (Report No. 76—1, Contract No. 75-N1-99-0000)*. Washington, DC: National Institute of Justice, Department of Justice.

Ben-Shakhar, G., Gamer, M., Iacono, W., et al. (2015). Invited commentary: preliminary process theory does not validate the comparison question test: a comment on Palmatier and Rovner (2015). *International Journal of Psychophysiology, 95*, 16—19.

British Psychological Society (BPS). (2004). *A review of the current scientific status and fields of application of polygraphic deception detection*. Available at: http://www.bps.org.uk/sites/default/files/documents/polygraphic_deception_detection_-_a_review_of_the_current_scientific_status_and_fields_of_application.pdf.

Churchland, P. M. (2007). *Neurophilosophy at work*. Cambridge, MA: Cambridge University Press.

Cunningham, W. A., & Brosch, T. (2012). Motivational salience: amygdala tuning from traits, needs, values, and goals. *Current Directions in Psychological Science, 21*(1), 54–59. http://dx.doi.org/10.1177/0963721411430832.

Driscoll, L. N., Honts, C. R., & Jones, D. (1987). The validity of the positive control physiological detection of deception technique. *Journal of Police Science and Administration, 15*(1), 46–50.

Ekman, L. (1992). *Telling lies: Clues to deceit in the marketplace, politics and marriage.* New York: WW Norton & Company, Inc.

Elaad, E. (2015). Invited commentary: cognitive and emotional aspects of polygraph diagnostic procedures: a comment on Palmatier and Rovner (2015). *International Journal of Psychophysiology, 95,* 14–15.

Federal Bureau of Investigation (FBI). www.fbi.gov https://www.fbi.gov/about-us/history/famous-cases/aldrich-hazen-ames.

Ginton, A., Daie, N., & Elaad, E. (1982). A method for evaluating the use of the polygraph in a real-live situations. *Journal of Applied Psychology, 67,* 131–137.

Hartwig, M., & Bond Jr, C. F. (2014). Lie Detection from Multiple Cues: A Meta-analysis. *Applied Cognitive Psychology, 28,* 661–676.

Honts, C. R., Devitt, M. K., Winbush, M., & Kircher, J. C. (1996). Mental and physical countermeasures reduce the accuracy of the concealed knowledge test. *Psychophysiology, 33,* 84–92.

Honts, C. R. (1996). Criterion development and validity of the control question test in field application. *The Journal of General Psychology, 123,* 309–324.

Honts, C. R., et al. (2003). Effects of outside issues on the control question test. *The Journal of General Psychology.*

Honts, C. R., & Raskin, D. C. (1988). A field study of the validity of the directed lie control question. *Journal of Police Science and Administration, 16,* 56–61.

Honts, C. R., Raskin, D. C., & Kircher, J. C. (1994). Mental and physical countermeasures reduce the accuracy of polygraph tests. *Journal of Applied Psychology, 79,* 252–259.

Honts, C. R., & Reavy, R. (2015). The comparison question polygraph test: a contrast of methods and scoring. *Physiology & Behavior, 143,* 15–26.

Kircher, J. C., & Raskin, D. C. (1988). Human versus computerized evaluations of polygraph data in a laboratory setting. *Journal of Applied Psychology, 73*(2), 291–302.

Kleinmuntz, B., & Szucko, J. (1984). Lie detection in ancient and modern times: a call for contemporary scientific study. *American Psychologist, 39,* 766–776.

Leo, R. (2008). *Police interrogation and American Justice.* Cambridge, MA: Harvard University Press.

Lykken, D. (1998). *Tremor in the blood: Uses and abuses of the lie detector.* New York: Plenum.

McGrath, M. (2014). Police interrogations and false confessions. In B. Turvey, & C. Cooley (Eds.), *Chapter in miscarriages of justice* (pp. 114–147). London: Academic Press.

Mitchell, G. (2015). Revisiting truth or triviality: the external validity of research in the psychological laboratory. *Perspectives on Psychological Science, 7*(2), 109–117.

National Academy of Sciences (NAS): National Research Council of the National Academies. (2003). *The polygraph and lie detection.* Washington, DC: The National Academic Press.

Palmatier, J. J., & Rovner, L. (2015). Credibility assessment: preliminary process theory, the polygraph process, and construct validity. *International Journal of Psychophysiology, 95,* 3–13.

Patrick, C. J., & Iacono, W. G. (1989). Psychopathy, threat, and polygraph test accuracy. *Journal of Applied Psychology, 74*(2), 347–355.

Patrick, C. J., & Iacono, W. G. (1991). Validity of the control question polygraph test: the problem of sampling bias. *Journal of Applied Psychology, 76*, 229–238.

Podlesny, J. A., & Raskin, D. C. (1978). Effectiveness of techniques and physiological measures in the detection of deception. *Psychophysiology, 15*, 344–358.

Podlesny, J. A., & Truslow, C. M. (1993). Validity of an expanded-issue (modified general question) polygraph technique in a simulated distributed-crime-roles context. *Journal of Applied Psychology, 78*(5), 788–797.

Raskin, D. (2014). Declaration of polygraph expert. *In APA Magazine, 2015, 48*(4), 105–136.

Raskin, D. C., & Hare, R. D. (1978). Psychopathy and detection of deception in a prison population. *Psychophysiology, 15*(2), 126–136.

Raskin, D. C., Kircher, J. C., Honts, C. R., & Horowitz, S. W. (1988). *A study of the validity of polygraph examinations in criminal investigation. (Grant No. 85-IJ-CX-0040, National Institute of Justice)*. Salt Lake City: University of Utah, Department of Psychology.

Rovner, L. (1979). *The importance of research to the polygraph examiner.* Texas Association of Polygraph Examiners Newsletter. February.

Rovner, L. I. (1986). The accuracy of physiological detection of deception for subjects with prior knowledge. *Polygraph, 15*, 1–39.

US v Williams. (2005). *District court for the Northern District of Georgia, Atlanta Division.* Crim. Case No. 1:03-CR-636-5-JEC. Available at: https://antipolygraph.org/litigation/williams/us-v-williams-daubert-report.pdf.

Vrij, A. (2015). Invited commentary: the protection of innocent suspects: a comment on Palmatier and Rovner (2015). *International Journal of Psychophysiology, 95*, 20–21.

CHAPTER 12

Investigating Allegations of Police Torture: Forensic Protocols and Psychological Assessment

Aurelio Coronado Mares[1], Brent E. Turvey[2]

Forensic Psychologist, Cienca Aplicada, Aguascalientes, Mexico[1]; Forensic Criminology Institute, Sitka, Alaska, United States and Aguascalientes, Mexico[2]

CHAPTER OUTLINE

- Prevalence 297
  - Torture by Government Agents in Mexico 297
    - The 43 Students 297
    - Interrogation in Ajuchitlan 299
  - Torture by Government Agents in the United States 302
    - Jon Burge, Chicago Police Department 302
    - Sitka Police Department—Sitka, Alaska 305
    - US Military, Abu Ghraib Prison, Baghdad, Iraq 306
- Role of the Forensic Investigator 310
- Defining Torture 312
- Coercive Interrogation v. Torture 312
  - Coercive Interrogation 313
  - Torture: The Rationale 313
- Behaviors Constituting Torture 314
- Diagnostic Categories Related to Torture 315
- The Psychological Effects and Impact of Torture 316
  - Cognitive and Behavioral Manifestations 316
- Torture: Forensic Interview Protocols for the Mental Health Professional 320
- Conclusion 325
- Endnotes 325
- References 326

Law enforcement agencies, and the military, are legally charged with investigating reports of crime and maintaining public order. These responsibilities require the cooperation, and the sometimes begrudging compliance, of citizens. Consequently, law enforcement and the military need lawful mechanisms for inducing citizen compliance when verbal requests fail. They are, therefore, given a variety of weapons and related training to lawfully exert force. They are further given legal mandates, and legal boundaries, within which to use the force deemed necessary as the need arises.

If this all sounds a bit murky or complex, it is meant to. The use of force by law enforcement and the military is almost always a judgment call made in the heat of the moment, based on best evidence, agency policy, and training, and sometimes a lack thereof.

The presumption is that government agents will be sufficiently educated and trained to use only lawful measures of force, and then only in service of the public good. The problem is this: those with power often come to believe that torture is acceptable as a means to an end. They may even come to believe, by virtue of culture, training, or supervisory decree, that it is acceptable to torture anyone deemed to be "evil," or anyone who has been otherwise dehumanized. This to say nothing of often being improperly educated or trained on matters of law, civil rights, and basic human rights. Suffice it to say, under certain conditions and under the worst leadership, acts of torture have been committed against citizens in just about every nation by agents of their own government.

In case there is any misunderstanding, let us be absolutely clear: the use of *torture* violates human rights, civil rights, and criminal statutes across the board. In other words, its use disregards everything that a criminal justice system must stand for. This is why civilized nations adopt clear prohibitions against it and set forth harsh consequences for transgressors. The use of torture is therefore both a legal and moral violation. Those that use methods of torture, advocate their use, or support their use by action or inaction are themselves criminals. And they have no place in positions of power or authority.

In Mexico, torture violations of a horrific nature have been a problem for a very long time. They have been part of the landscape for so long that they have become almost accepted as a cardinal feature of a justice system that no longer enjoys the public trust. In the United States, violations are common but not quite as severe. That is to say, when cases of torture occur, there is still public shock and even levels of disbelief. That is among most significant differences between our two nations on the issue. In Mexico, government-sponsored torture is so common that it is all but expected; in the United States it is believed to be less common and is generally met with degrees of revelation and disbelief.

No matter the country, and no matter the government, there will always be allegations of torture. Some will be true. Some will be false. It is the role of the forensic investigator to help make that determination, without passion or prejudice.

We recognize that this chapter is born of the Mexican experience. That is unavoidable given the casework and expert testimony of the primary author (Coronado). But the examples emerging from the United States cannot be denied. What's more, the psychological research and related assessment protocols are international. They are also universally applicable. So no matter where the forensic investigator lives, no matter the rule of law that governs their region, they will find this work of terrible relevance.

This chapter will provide readers a definition of torture; an understanding of the psychological effects on torture subjects; how this bears on the forensic reliability of any information gathered using methods of torture; and a basic psychological protocol for evaluating those that have been tortured, for courtroom purposes. The work of the United Nations, as well as the *Istanbul Protocols*, will feature prominently.

Case examples of police torture, from the United States and Mexico alike, will be presented as necessary.

PREVALENCE

The use of torture by law enforcement and the military is commonplace in both the United States and Mexico. The precise methods have varied, but not by much. In this section, we will discuss major case studies from each nation to contextualize the reality of the problem and make clear the subsequent necessity for related forensic investigative protocols.

TORTURE BY GOVERNMENT AGENTS IN MEXICO

In Mexico, confirmed allegations of suspect torture committed by the police and military are, again, all too common. It may even be argued that torture is the professional default of government agents in many Mexican states. Perhaps this is because torture is the easiest, first, and sometimes only tool in their respective investigative arsenal—to the point where it has become an accepted reality within the Mexican justice system.

Two recent high profile cases, publicized internationally, illustrate these points. The investigation into the missing 43 students, last seen in Iguala, in September of 2014; and the torture of a female suspect in Ajuchitlan, committed by female Military and Federal Police personnel acting together, caught on video in February of 2015.

The 43 Students

The first case involves the now infamous 43 students of the Raúl Isidro Burgos Rural Teachers' College of Ayotzinapa; they disappeared in Iguala, Guerrero in 2014. They were going to hold a protest at a conference that was being led by the mayor's wife. They were intercepted by local police and then at some point handed over to the local Guerreros Unidos ("United Warriors") cartel. Mexican authorities have reported that Iguala's mayor, José Luis Abarca Velázquez, and his wife, María de los Ángeles Pineda Villa, orchestrated or at the very least ordered the abductions and are responsible for their presumed murders.

More than 100 suspects have been arrested in connection with that case to date. Many of them were tortured by the police and the military, without consequence, as reported in the Associated Press (2016a):

> *There is strong evidence that Mexican police tortured some of the key suspects arrested in the disappearance of 43 students, according to a report released Sunday by an outside group of experts.*
>
> *The Inter-American Commission on Human Rights group of experts says a study of 17 of the approximately 110 suspects arrested in the case showed signs of beatings, including, in some cases, dozens of bruises, cuts and scrapes.*
>
> *One suspect said he was nearly asphyxiated with a plastic bag, and medical studies showed another had been slapped on the ears so hard his eardrums broke and his ears bled. The Mexican government recently released documents suggesting investigations had been opened against police and military personnel, but authorities have not answered requests about whether anyone has been arrested or charged.*
>
> *The 43 students at a radical teachers' college have not been heard from since they were taken by local police in September 2014 in the city of Iguala, in Guerrero state.*
>
> *The allegations of torture could put in danger any chance of convictions one of the highest-profile human rights cases in Mexican history, especially because the government's version of events — that corrupt police handed the students over to drug gang members who killed them and burned their bodies at a trash dump — hangs in large part on the testimony of some drug gunmen who now say they were tortured into confessing.*
>
> *"It is a lie the way they said they caught us," said Patricio Reyes Landa, alias "El Pato," said in testimony made public by the experts' report. "They went into the house, beating and kicking. They hauled me aboard a vehicle, they blindfolded me, tied my feet and hands, they began beating me again and gave me electric shocks, they put a rag over my nose and poured water on it. They gave me shocks on the inside of my mouth and my testicles. They put a bag over my face so I couldn't breathe. It went on for hours".*
>
> *…the "significant evidence of torture and abuse" of the suspects was the report's most damning element. For example, the medical reports on one suspect whose testimony was key for the government's case, Agustin Garcia Reyes, claimed he had one injury, a bruise, after marines took him into custody. But hours later when he was turned over to civilian prosecutors, they said he had 30 bruises, scrapes and scabs.*

The systemic failures identified in this case, which include government corruption and a concerted torture initiative, have caused many to question the last shreds of credibility enjoyed by the Criminal Justice System in Mexico. Brutality and injustice suspected in the local government were responded to with the same from those running the government investigation. In any event, the case remains largely unresolved, with more revelations certainly yet to come as the international community deepens its gaze.

Interrogation in Ajuchitlan

The second high profile torture case out of Mexico is more isolated, but no less disturbing. It involves the physical abuse of a female suspect by both female soldiers and female federal police officers during an interrogation, in February of 2015. Captured on video by one of those involved at the scene, this documentation of torture, and its acceptance by the government agents present, is undeniable. As reported in the Associated Press (2016b) (Fig. 12.1):

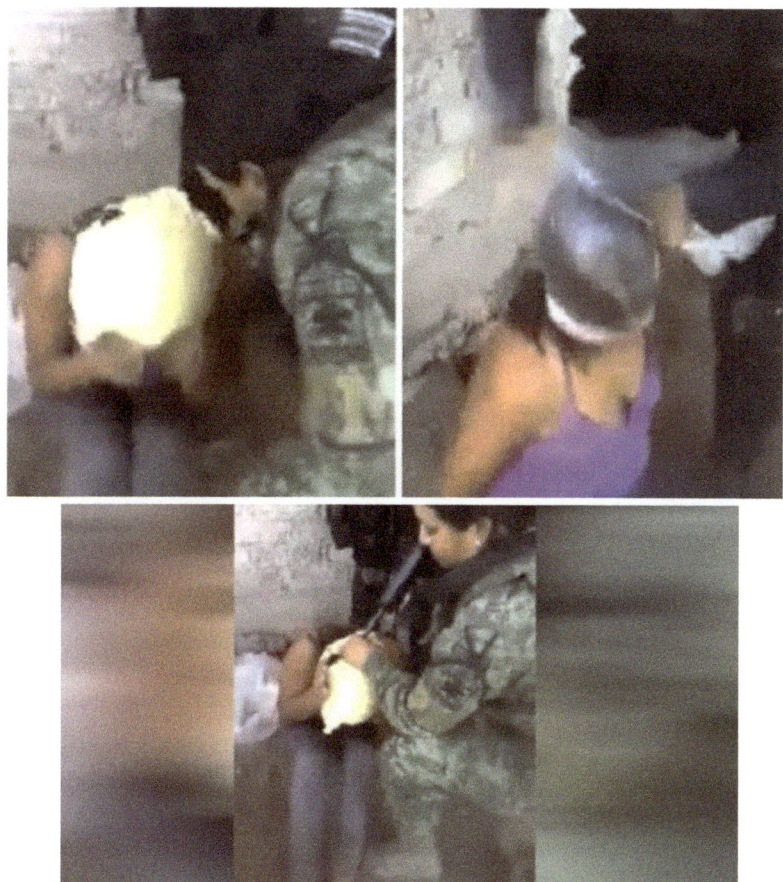

FIGURE 12.1

Female soldiers with the Mexican Army assist Federal Police with the torture and interrogation of a female suspect using threats of various torture methods, along with beatings, asphyxiation with a plastic bag, and a gun barrel against her head. The astonishing thing about this case is not that it happened, but that it was so well documented. And also that it involved female officers inflicting the torture, which goes against popular presumptions and stereotypes regarding police brutality. The video was taken with a cell phone by one of the officers at the scene, and then posted to social media.

> Two Mexican army soldiers face military charges after a video surfaced of them helping a federal police officer torture a female suspect. A female military police officer is seen in the video interrogating the woman. She pulls her hair and places the muzzle of her rifle against the woman's head.
>
> Within minutes the torment escalates as a blue-uniformed federal police officer puts her head inside a plastic bag and pulls it tight.
>
> The Defense Department says the events occurred February 4, 2015 in Ajuchitlan, a small mountain town in southern Guerrero state. Opium poppy plantations are common in the area where drug cartels operate.
>
> The federal police officer placed a plastic bag over the woman's head until she almost passed out. It is unclear if the police officer — apparently also female — faces charges.
>
> Mexico's army said Thursday that the two soldiers are in a military prison facing charges of failure to obey orders.
>
> The Defense Department said that civilian prosecutors had been advised of the incident. Under Mexican law, civilian prosecutors are supposed to investigate army abuses against civilians, but soldiers can also face simultaneous charges in military tribunals.
>
> The chilling, four-minute video shows the handcuffed woman sitting in the dirt, crying, outside a rural cinder-block house. The female soldier asks her repeatedly during and after the torture, 'Are you going to talk? Yes or no? Now do you remember?' 'Do you want more? Who is this damn Maria?'
>
> As the suspect lies inert on the ground, the female soldier asks her 'Do you remember now? Or do you want the bag again? Or water? Or (electric) shocks? Tell me what you want.'
>
> The military justice system acted much more quickly in the case than civilian prosecutors. The army said it found out about the video — apparently taped by a police officer or soldier at the scene — in December, and arrested the two soldiers in January.
>
> Civilian prosecutors could not say whether any charges had been filed against anyone in civilian courts.

This case reveals the problem of government torture as one deeply embedded in the Mexican culture. This is evidenced by the fact that it involves multiple government agencies acting illegally, and in concert, while also recording their crimes without fear of consequence; and also female officers committing brutal acts of torture, in defiance of any stereotype or presumption about the nature or corruptibility of their gender.

Both of these events serve to illustrate how common, systemic, and normalized torture has become in the Mexican Justice System. Also, that the government response is often a function of public exposure—and sometimes even that does not guarantee action. These and similar cases indicate an institutional pattern across Mexico, as reported in Pena (2016):

> *The now-infamous video of Mexican soldiers helping a federal police officer torture and interrogate a female suspect in Ajuchitlán del Progreso, Guerrero, this past February seems to be another confirmation that there are two classes of Mexicans. There are those who are exempt from consequences (politicians and the wealthy, including Mexico's military elite) who operate with impunity in Mexico. And then there are the rest of us, regularly policed by force with the active participation of Mexico's military and federal police in intimidation tactics and the violation of human rights.*
>
> *The world might rightly be shocked by the way the woman in the video was asphyxiated with plastic bags, by the way she screamed as the muzzle of a gun was pressed to her skull, but every Mexican knows that this single story of torture is part of a pattern.*
>
> *Just last week, Mexico's Comisión Nacional de los Derechos Humanos confirmed the involvement of two Mexican federal police in the disappearance of the 43 students in Ayotzinapa. In the 2014 Tlatlaya massacre, Mexican soldiers were allegedly ordered by senior officers to murder 22 civilians who had already surrendered to Mexican forces. Also that year, National Autonomous University of Mexico student and poet Sandino Bucio was arrested by plainclothes federal police, presumably for having participated in the 20 November march in Mexico City in support of the then recently disappeared Ayotzinapa students.*
>
> *Bucio said in an interview that after he was kidnapped and beaten, his captors threatened to disappear him by handing him over to the Guerreros Unidos cartel, the same cartel the municipal police in Iguala allegedly worked with to disappear the 43 Ayotzinapa students.*
>
> *In all of these cases, the federal police or military directly involved were punished, but no high-ranking officers responsible for overseeing their personnel were brought to justice. (President Enrique Peña Nieto is commander-in-chief of the Mexican armed forces).*
>
> *As is standard in the Mexican human rights abuses that have come to light, a mea culpa is offered as part of the public relations gameplan, but not before the victim is discredited in a smear campaign. Later, a high-ranking officer will apologize for the offense, some lowly officers will be sentenced as part of a peace offering to the public, and then the event is brushed aside…*
>
> *In its 2015 Human Rights Report on Mexico, the US Department of State… suggests in its executive summary that not only have torture and extrajudicial killings been used to intimidate dissenters, journalists and activists within Mexico, but it's been done with the collusion of armed gangs and cartels — as happened in the Ayotzinapa case, in which initial blame fell conveniently on the municipal Iguala police and Guerreros Unidos cartel.*

These cases are representative of the problems with the Justice System in Mexico, which are by now undeniable on the international stage. Documented on social media, many more such instances of government-sponsored torture and related abuses of power exist, and all one need do to find them is look.

However, suspect torture at the hands of government agents (e.g., police, prosecutors, military) is not a uniquely Mexican problem. It is a persistent, historical, and global phenomenon. No one nation is immune. Not even the United States. For those who might disagree, technology, and the use of social media, has advanced to the point where denials are no longer acceptable.

TORTURE BY GOVERNMENT AGENTS IN THE UNITED STATES

The authors of this chapter have worked together on cases that have involved government-sponsored torture in the United States. One of them (Turvey) has testified as a forensic expert on these and related subjects in US courts (crime reconstruction; physical evidence of torture; investigative procedure; police use of force; and the Istanbul Protocols). Both operate as independent forensic investigators and examiners, without a particular government affiliation or alliance.

One such case, which shocks the conscience of any ethical professional, is that of *Oklahoma v. Elvis Thacker*. It involves the shooting and torture of a homicide suspect by multiple police investigators, captured entirely on video, over the course of 40 min. This ordeal is detailed in *Chapter 14*. The facts of that case, involving multiple agencies and officers, are enlightening with respect to law enforcement culture in both Oklahoma and Arkansas. The precise details will not be repeated here, and readers are encouraged to make a study of that case as presented to form their own conclusions.

Additional cases involving similar behavior include the following:

Jon Burge, Chicago Police Department

The Jon Burge case involves the torture of more than 100 suspects, and multiple wrongful convictions, between 1972 and 1991. Former Commander Burge, whose attitudes and misconduct were emblematic of the Chicago Police Department at the time, was eventually sent jail for lying about his crimes during a civil deposition. He had been fired back in 1993, but it took years for his victims to get justice, and cost the city over a hundred million dollars in legal fees and settlements. He supervised a "ring" of corrupt officers who engaged in the illegal arrest, detention, and torture of primarily black suspects, as reported in Lee (2015):

> *A former Chicago police commander who for decades ran a torture ring that used electrical shock, burning and beatings on more than 100 black men has been released from federal prison after spending less than four years behind bars.*

> *Jon Burge was transferred to a Florida halfway house on Thursday, reigniting the nightmares of many of his victims. Burge and his crew of detectives terrorized the city's predominantly black South Side throughout the 1970s, 1980s and early 1990s.*

In 2010, long after the statute of limitations had expired for his many vile acts, Burge was convicted of perjury for lying about police torture that he oversaw. He was sentenced to four and a half years in prison for that charge alone…

Anthony Holmes told the Chicago Tribune *that he had been a former gang member arrested by Burge in 1973. He said he was taken to a police station where detectives hooked him up to an electrical box and had a bag pulled over his head. Holmes said the officers shocked him over and over again until he confessed to a murder he hadn't committed. Holmes, now nearly 70 years old, said he remembers Burge calling him the N-word and warning him not to bite through the bag over his head… Holmes eventually spent 30 years in prison for the killing he was tortured in to admitting.*

Last year, Mayor Rahm Emanuel officially apologized on behalf of the city, calling Burge's reign of terror a "dark chapter in the history of the city of Chicago." "All of us," Emanuel said, are "sorry for what happened."

Burge has cost the city and Cook County nearly $100 million in legal fees and settlements. The city last year alone approved a $12.3 million settlement to a pair of Burge's victims who are among the 120 known black victims of Burge's ring. So far, according to various reports, the city has paid about $67 million in settlements to 18 victims and more than $20 million in lawyers to defend Burge, former mayor Richard Daley and the city.

While Emanuel has described Burge as a "stain on the city's reputation," the 66-year-old ex-cop is still receiving a $4000-a-month pension from the city. The state attorney general recently challenged the city's pension board after it refused to take away Burge's pension. But the Illinois Supreme Court this summer ruled that the attorney general's office didn't have the legal authority to strip Burge of his pension…

Burge was fired from the police department in 1993. In 2006, following a 4-year investigation, a Cook County prosecutor found evidence of widespread abuses committed by Burge and his henchmen. But the prosecutor also acknowledged that the statute of limitations had passed. Federal prosecutors later nailed Burge for lying during testimony in a civil case where he denied any knowledge of abuse ever committed under his watch.

During his trial in 2010, many of Burge's victims lined up to describe the atrocities they had suffered during torture sessions. Their testimony included revelations that detectives had suffocated suspects with plastic bags and used cattle prods to shock their genitals.

This week an ordinance was introduced at City Hall to set aside a $20 million compensation fund for Burge's victims. The fund would provide paid tuition to city colleges for survivors and the establishment of a public memorial. It would also require the city's schools to teach lessons about the case.

This unprecedented series of cases related to a single individual and his subordinates resulted in a multimillion dollar fund setup by the city to provide reparations to his torture victims. As reported in Emmanuel (2015):

> More than 100 people who alleged they were tortured by former Chicago Police Cmdr. Jon Burge or officers under his command more than 20 years ago could be eligible for settlements under an agreement announced on Tuesday. The settlements would be paid from a $5.5 million fund to be set up by the City of Chicago.
>
> The settlements are part of a reparations package announced at a special session of the Chicago City Council Committee on Finance on Tuesday. The package also includes a formal apology to torture victims, as well as specialized counseling services, free enrollment at Chicago City Colleges and job training.
>
> If the ordinance passes, Chicago would become the first American city to enact a comprehensive reparations law for police misconduct, city officials and advocates for victims said…
>
> The reparations were the result of months of negotiations between representatives of the city, People's Law Office, Amnesty International, USA, and Chicago Torture Justice Memorials, a coalition of lawyers, activists, artists and educators that has been pushing for reparations for torture survivors. Stephen Patton, chief lawyer for the city, said an arbitrator will determine who is eligible.
>
> …Chicago Torture Justice Memorials praised the reparations package as a "historic agreement" that follows decades of organizing by a number of social justice organizations.
>
> Burge was sentenced to 54 months in prison followed by three years of supervised release for lying in a deposition in a civil case about torture and abuse of suspects by Chicago police officers. Burge, who joined the police department in 1970, was fired in 1993. The U.S. Department of Justice determined that Burge and detectives under his command systematically tortured more than 100 black men and women on the South and West sides from 1972 to 1991.
>
> Their methods included suffocation, electric shock and mock executions, according to the Department of Justice. Scores of victims were forced into false confessions and later convicted, advocates for the victims have said.

The details of this case reveal a racist policy of organized and institutionalized torture against black suspects by the Chicago Police Department and perjury by all of those officers involved to cover it up. These crimes were encouraged by the cardinal traits of law enforcement culture (see generally Turvey, 2013) and necessarily tolerated by (and therefore encouraged by) the local court system.

It is worth noting that Burge is reported to have used a homemade black box, with a hand crank and electrical leads, to manually generate current with which to torture suspects. Modern law enforcement wears precisely such a device on their standard issue utility belts. It is the Taser—which has been used to both torture and kill those upon whom it has been deployed.[1]

Sitka Police Department—Sitka, Alaska

In 2014, members of the Sitka Police Department (SPD) arrested, detained, and then proceeded to torture an 18-year-old high school student in a padded jail cell within the Sitka Police Department. The officers claimed that they were attempting to get Frank Hoogendorn, an Alaskan Native, to comply with their order to change his clothes. They forcibly disrobed him, held him down, and then "drive-tased" him at least 17 times over the course of a very few minutes. This technique is meant to achieve what is referred to as "pain compliance"—which is essentially torture, by any definition.[2] Officers ultimately left him half naked on the floor of the padded cell and provided no medical attention.

The case gained public attention when an internal departmental video of the incident was released on social media, as reported in Staff (2015):

> *The video, uploaded by school district employee, Alexander Allison, shows surveillance footage at the police station revealing the student, Franklin Hoogendorn of Koyuk, staggering, visibly inebriated, but compliant, being brought to the station, through the corridors, and ultimately into a cell, where three officers stripped him of his clothing and slammed him face-down onto the holding cell's mat. Through the entire footage, Hoogendorn showed no resistance to the officers.*
>
> *It was then that the officers ordered Hoogendorn to place his hands behind his back as one of the officers knelt on Hoogendorn's calf, then straddled the teen and the other officer punched Hoogendorn in the face. Then, Officer Jonathan Kelton, stepped back, brought out his tazer and stepped back in and began tazing the teen on the bare skin of his leg. Hoogendorn could be seen reacting and struggling from the effects of the tazer as Officer Kelton continuously administered the device, the sound clearly picked up on the recording.*
>
> *Hoogendorn could be heard hollaring "Ok, ok, ok…" but the tazing continued and the officers brought the teen's arms and legs up onto his back. Only then, did the officers release Hoogendorn and leave the cell. Hoogendorn could be seen lying motionless, facedown on the mat, as someone in the room says, "What a Douchebag!" and the footage ends.*
>
> *Officer Kelton, the officer administering the tazer, came to the Sitka Police Department in 2013 from the Roswell Police Department, where he left after being involved in the death of a 34-year-old man there after struggling with officers there. That man was also tazed by Kelton.*
>
> *Although that case was determined to be a homicide by the medical examiner in New Mexico, no charges were ever filed against the officers involved. Kelton has since left the Sitka Police Department…*

It should be noted that Officer Kelton was promoted to Detective in mid-2015, well after the tasing incident, and that an internal investigating by SPD supervisors had bizarrely cleared him of any wrongdoing. However, once the video was made public, and all charges against Hoogendorn were dropped, Kelton resigned from the department altogether.

As indicated, Sitka Police Chief Sheldon Schmitt initially claimed that the officer's use of force in this case did not violate departmental policy. Eventually, one of the authors (Turvey) and other members of the community in Sitka were able to convince the SPD to release its policy manual to the public—as it is not a protected document and older copies were already in wide circulation. An examination of the manual revealed no written policy on the use of drive-tasing, and nothing clear about Tasers. So while clearly negligent with respect to officer hiring, training, and supervision, Chief Schmitt was technically accurate if not also misleading in his initial public comments.

Regardless, once the video was made public, any suggestion that police officers had acted lawfully, or in good faith, was eradicated. Eventually, the City and the Department realized their fault and liability, settling with Hoogendorn out of court. This avoided the painful prospect of having any officers, or supervisors, go under oath about their involvement in incident. As reported in Woolsey (2016):

> *Sitka has settled out of court with a high school student who was tasered in the city's jail in 2014.*
>
> *Franklin Hoogendorn will be paid $350,000 by Sitka's insurance carrier. Hoogendorn was 18 years old, and attending Mt. Edgecumbe High School, when he was arrested in September of 2014 outside a Sitka bar where he had been attempting to buy a drink.*
>
> *Police took Hoogendorn into custody. A video of the arrest, (http://www.kcaw.org/2015/11/02/arrest-video-raises-questions-of-excessive-force-in-sitka-jail/) which went viral on social media last fall, shows Hoogendorn being forcibly restrained by a jailer and two police officers and repeatedly tasered as his clothes are removed.*
>
> *The settlement was negotiated between the Alaska National Insurance Company, on behalf of the City of Sitka, and the two legal firms representing Hoogendorn.*

As a result of a complaint filed by the Sitka Tribe of Alaska in the Hoogendorn matter, the Sitka Police Department remains, as of this writing, under investigation by the FBI for civil rights violations.

US Military, Abu Ghraib Prison, Baghdad, Iraq

This case involves the torture of male and female detainees by US Military personnel and civilian contractors at the Abu Ghraib Prison facility, just outside of Baghdad, Iraq. As reported in Bierman (2015):

> *Photos of Iraqi prisoners tethered to dog leashes and electrical wires dominated the news when they emerged in 2003 and 2004. The abuse scandal centered at the Abu Ghraib prison outside Baghdad aroused bipartisan shock at home and embarrassment abroad…*

Eleven U.S. soldiers were convicted in military trials of crimes related to the humiliation and abuse of the prisoners. A $5.3-million settlement two years ago with the parent company of L-3 Services Inc., which provided translation services at the prison, is the only known civil penalty imposed on a private firm.

Official reports documented the participation of contractors in several incidents in Abu Ghraib, but none has been prosecuted criminally, nor have any companies been barred publicly from subsequent government contracts, which have been worth hundreds of millions of dollars…

The men who brought the suit, which seeks unspecified damages, were held at different times between 2003 and 2008. None was part of the prior settlement with L-3, now a subsidiary of Engility Holdings Inc.

One of them, a 44-year-old Al Jazeera reporter named Salah Ejaili, said in a phone interview from Qatar that he was arrested in 2003 while covering an explosion in the Iraqi province of Diyala. He was held at Abu Ghraib for 48 days after six days in another facility, he said. "Most of the pictures that came out in 2004, I saw that firsthand — the human pyramid where men were stacked up naked on top of each other, people pulled around on leashes," he said in the interview, with one of his attorneys translating. "I used to hear loud screams during the torture sessions".

Ejaili says he was beaten, left naked and exposed to the elements for long periods, and left in solitary confinement, among other acts. "When people look at others who are naked, they feel like they're animals in a zoo, in addition to being termed as criminals and as terrorists," he said. "That had a very strong psychological impact".

The plaintiffs also say they suffered electric shocks; deprivation of food, water and oxygen; sexual abuse; threats from dogs; beatings; and sensory deprivation.

Taha Yaseen Arraq Rashid, a laborer, says he was sexually abused by a woman while he was cuffed and shackled, and also that he was forced to watch a female prisoner's rape. Ejaili said that his face was often covered during interrogations, making it difficult for him to identify those involved, but that he was able to notice that many of the interrogators who entered the facility wore civilian clothing.

His attorneys, citing military investigations into abuses at Abu Ghraib and other evidence, say the contractors took control of the prison and issued orders to uniformed military…

A report from Maj. Gen. Antonio M. Taguba recommended discipline for two CACI employees, including one who allowed or instructed military police to help in interrogation in a manner that "he clearly knew … equated to physical abuse."

A report by Maj. Gen. George R. Fay said CACI interrogators were not screened by the company and that "little, if any, training on Geneva Conventions was

308 CHAPTER 12 Investigating Allegations of Police Torture

presented to contractor employees." That report cited CACI employees for participating in abuse, including grabbing and pushing a handcuffed detainee off a vehicle, putting a prisoner in a dangerous "stress position" and joining soldiers in using dogs to threaten prisoners.

The lawsuits associated with government contractors operating at Abu Ghraib are ongoing, but evidence of torture continues to mount. The photographs of detainees being tortured, which are undeniable, were taken by those involved as trophies to share among themselves and their families. This is how the story was originally leaked back to the United States and eventually made its way to the press. Photos taken by those responsible, including former Corporal Charles Graner and Private Lynndie England (both of whom were convicted and served prison terms for their crimes), included depictions of the following acts of torture against male, female, and child detainees (Fig. 12.2).

  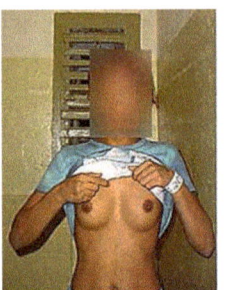

FIGURE 12.2

Charles Graner is pictured in the process of beating several nude male detainees with plastic bags over their heads, as they forced together in close proximity, softening them up for interrogation as he later explained. Lynndie England is pictured with a row of nude male detainees, all with plastic bags over their heads. She smiles while triumphantly coercing one of them to masturbate for the camera in front of other detainees. Also pictured, a female detainee is forced to show her breasts to male prison guards while being photographed.

1. Electric shocks
2. Sensory deprivation (e.g., blindfolded, bags over the head)
3. Oxygen deprivation (e.g., plastic bags over the head)
4. Sexual humiliation (e.g., forced nudity; bondage; photography of same)
5. Being smeared with human waste
6. Forced sex acts (e.g., rape, sodomy, and masturbation)
7. Forced to witness forced sex acts against other victims, including children
8. Threats and attacks using dogs
9. Extreme cold
10. Suspension
11. Stress positions
12. Physical abuse

Multiple acts of torture were used simultaneously against detainees. Sometimes they were alone, and sometimes they were tortured in groups to increase anticipation, fear, and humiliation. On more than a few occasions, these acts of torture resulted in the death of a detainee. Those involved even posed for photos with the victim's bodies.

It is important to understand that what happened at Abu Ghraib was not the act of a single individual. Rather, it occurred in a culture of dehumanization and cruelty that was created, nurtured, and openly bragged about by all of those who served there. As reported in Daily Mail Reporter (2011):

Charles Graner Jr., 42, was released from the U.S. Disciplinary Barracks at Fort Leavenworth, Kansas, on Saturday morning. He served nearly seven years of a 10-year sentence for his role in the abuse scandal at Abu Ghraib prison, spokeswoman Rebecca Steed said. She said Mr Graner will be under the supervision of a probation officer until Dec. 25, 2014…

Neither Mr Graner nor his wife - another Abu Ghraib defendant - have responded to interview requests from The Associated Press…. Mr Graner was an Army Reserve corporal from Pennsylvania, when he and six other members of the Maryland-based 372nd Military Police Company were charged in 2004 with abusing detainees at the Iraq prison.

The strongest evidence included photos of grinning American soldiers posing with naked detainees stacked in a pyramid or held on a leash. The images strained international relations for the U.S. and sparked a debate about whether harsh interrogation techniques amounted to torture. He was convicted of stacking prisoners into a pyramid, knocking one out with a head punch and ordering prisoners to masturbate for photos.

During his deployment, Mr Graner fathered a son with former Pfc Lynndie England of Fort Ashby, West Virginia. Miss England was given a three-year sentence for her role in the scandal. After his conviction, Mr Graner married another member of his unit, former Spc Megan Ambuhl of Centreville, Virginia. She was discharged from the Army after pleading guilty to dereliction of duty for failing to prevent or report the mistreatment. Seven guards and four other low-ranking soldiers were convicted of crimes at Abu Ghraib.

In a book about the scandal, Mr Graner was portrayed as a manipulative bully with the bad-boy charm to draw others into his sadistic games.

The most disturbing part of what happened there is not just the extent of the torture, but also the undeniable enjoyment of those responsible. Not only do they seem pleased with themselves in the photographs taken, but also they were eager to document their illegal activities and share them with others. This was likely a demonstration of power and conquest, not foreign to the theater of war.

The authors have found this to be common among those who commit acts of state-sanctioned torture, when there is no oversight and no immediate consequences for misconduct: they are proud of what they have done and what they believe they have accomplished; they are pleased with themselves for having done it; and they do not see themselves as having done anything morally wrong (quite the opposite, in fact).

These cases combine to demonstrate that torture by government agents is a genuine concern, whether dealing with law enforcement or the military, and their related institutional cultures. It can occur whether they are working for governments in Mexico City, Alaska, Oklahoma, Chicago, or Iraq. The problem is human in nature within confines of societal power structures, and therefore it is universal. Specifically, torture is "a massive and systematic fact that comes out from the concrete way of how society is governed" (Sánchez, 1989). When one group has power over another, and that power is not checked by any intervening authority, abuses are going to occur.

The tradition of suspect and dissident torture in both the United States and Mexico has long been considered an evil necessary for obtaining justice—permissible because of public faith in government institutions and public ignorance of the problems associated with it. However, the authors have observed that this faith is being questioned by the newest generation of policemen, psychologists, and criminologists. They are more educated than their predecessors, with more access to training and information. Consequently, they better understand and appreciate the importance of essential concepts such as human rights, civil rights, and due process. They also understand the need for objective scientific analysis in casework protocols, to ensure the scientific character, or even the reliability, of any related courtroom testimony.

Enter the courts, and the forensic investigator.

ROLE OF THE FORENSIC INVESTIGATOR

As explained clearly in the Istanbul Protocol (United Nations, 2004), the purpose of an investigation into allegations of torture is to gather the relevant facts and evidence, determine whether and how torture occurred, whether it is isolated or systemic, and provide the basis for any related criminal arrests and prosecutions (p. 17):

> The broad purpose of the investigation is to establish the facts relating to alleged incidents of torture, with a view to identifying those responsible for the incidents and facilitating their prosecution, or for use in the context of other procedures designed to obtain redress for victims. The issues addressed here may also be relevant for other types of investigations of torture. To fulfill this purpose, those carrying out the investigation must, at a minimum, seek to obtain statements from the victims of alleged torture; to recover and preserve evidence, including medical evidence, related to the alleged torture to aid in any potential prosecution of those responsible; to identify possible witnesses and obtain statements from them concerning the alleged torture; and to determine how, when and where the alleged incidents of torture occurred as well as any pattern or practice that may have brought about the torture.

In this context, the roles of the forensic investigator in cases of alleged torture are fairly straightforward.

First, the forensic investigator can serve as an educator. In this role, they can help train, or inform, government agents, attorneys, and the court. They can help them define torture, its elements, and explain its consequences in an objective fashion. They can also advise as to the kind of information and evidence that must be collected to make such determinations. With this information, informed decisions about related matters can be made by those that have been educated—whether regarding agency policy, official positions, or the law. This may be all that is required, and it is not an insignificant function.

Second, they may serve as an investigator or a forensic examiner. In this role they determine, or help to determine, whether or not the elements of torture are present in a given case. They might examine physical evidence, psychological evidence, or both when available. Their subsequent written findings can then be used to inform investigative and legal decisions.

Third, the forensic investigator may be asked to give expert forensic findings, cultivating in courtroom testimony. Under these circumstances, their findings about whether the elements of torture are present, and whether torture occurred, are considered evidence by the court. They are offered under penalty of perjury, and only in accordance with reliable scientific practice, to inform courtroom decisions.

As an ancillary to these roles, the forensic investigator may be asked to comment or opine on the quality and reliability of prior forensic findings. This secondary independent review provides the balance required in an adversarial system and is therefore among the most important functions that a forensic investigator or examiner can perform. Without a secondary review, referred to in science as a "peer review" or a "validation" inquiry, the original finding cannot really be trusted, especially when proffered by an entity (e.g., the government) with an investment in the outcome (see generally Edwards and Gatsonis, 2009).

Secondary review, independent of the original inquiry, is basic scientific practice that is essential to the reliability of any scientific finding. This means that any scientific finding must be rendered in such a fashion is to provide for, and encourage, independent review. Any argument to the contrary is admission that the original inquiry was not scientific and therefore may be considered less than scientifically valid.

Each one of these roles has tremendous value in the service of justice. The problem is not with understanding or wanting to serve these roles faithfully, however. The problem comes when political or institutional pressure is applied to coerce the forensic investigator away from being honest about what they have found. The government is generally the subject of the investigation, and the government generally has profound resources with which to influence even the most seasoned forensic professionals. This is why forensic examiners should be allowed to serve in a manner that shields them state sanctions (again, see generally Edwards and Gatsonis, 2009). Otherwise their findings cannot really be trusted.

DEFINING TORTURE

In Mexico, the word *torture* is a specific reference to any force used by government authorities with the objective of obtaining a confession, or any other information that incriminates a suspect, in a criminal case. Torture can be physical or psychological, involving actual or threatened harm.[3] Significant to the forensic investigator, confessions or statements made by detainees obtained as a result of torture are typically considered inadmissible in court.[4]

Internationally, the most commonly used definition of *torture* is found in Article 1 of the United Nations Convention Against Torture and other Cruel, Inhuman or Degrading Treatment or Punishment (UNCAT, 1987): "the term "torture" means any act by which severe pain or suffering, whether physical or mental, is intentionally inflicted on a person for such purposes as obtaining from him or a third person information or a confession, punishing him for an act he or a third person has committed or is suspected of having committed, or intimidating or coercing him or a third person, or for any reason based on discrimination of any kind, when such pain or suffering is inflicted by or at the instigation of or with the consent or acquiescence of a public official or other person acting in an official capacity. It does not include pain or suffering arising only from, inherent in or incidental to lawful sanctions."

This definition is important because it recognizes that pain and suffering can incidentally rise from the lawful actions of law enforcement and the military meant to protect life and ensure pubic safety. However, their actions become unlawful when they occur in violation of the law, due process, or civil rights. This includes acting with the intent to get inculpatory statements, punish, or intimidate.

This raises an important point. Torture is not only found in the context of criminal investigations. In 2015, the *Human Rights Practices* report on Mexico by the US Department of State confirmed that law enforcement and the military "intimidate, kill, and torture not just suspected criminals, but migrants, journalists, and those who try to defend human rights in the country" (Phippen, 2016).

COERCIVE INTERROGATION V. TORTURE

Police brutality is not a black-and-white concept; it exists on a continuum of unlawful behavior, within which there are varying degrees of force. It begins at the low end with *excessive force* (more than is lawful or necessary, e.g., threats and unnecessary escalation) and can rise to the highest levels, which include torture and/or lethal force. However, regardless of the level of brutality or unlawful force, any amount violates the civil and human rights of the arrested. And anything gained as result is tainted as both empirically unreliable and legally inadmissible.

For our purposes, it is helpful to categorize this kind of behavior in two different ways: *coercive interrogation* and *torture*.

COERCIVE INTERROGATION

Coercive interrogation involves deliberate and systematic detainee mistreatment that is intended to pressure compliance (e.g., lengthy interrogations; multiple interrogators; sleep deprivation; absence of legal counsel; selectively recorded interview sessions; and withholding essential needs such as a food, water, and environmental controls). Typically, this will also occur in the context of wanting the detainee to confirm existing investigative theories by feeding them suggestive information. Ultimately, the coercion is obvious and the information documented is unreliable.

Torture, as already suggested, involves inflicting pain and suffering with the intent of breaking the detainee's physical and psychological will. In these cases, the authorities want compliance—whether that means signing confessions, making admissions, or implicating others in whatever crimes at issue.

Criminal investigators are commonly trained to engage in particular styles and methods of interview and interrogation (e.g., cognitive interviewing, the Reid Technique, voice stress analysis, and polygraphy). This arises from the mistaken belief that such methods increase the probability of obtaining a confession, or merely criminalizing the person who has been arrested. Many studies, however, suggest the opposite is true. But we continue to believe because we see them used on TV and in movies. They are also hyped in over priced law enforcement only seminars, taught by former law enforcement investigators with very little actual knowledge of human psychology.

Improper use of any interview or interrogation method can increase the likelihood of a false statement or confessions. This is to say nothing of the fact that submitting anyone to the stressful conditions of an interrogation will actually decrease the quality, and reliability, of any of the information that has been obtained. Investigators must be mindful of these realities and that they can induce a false or unreliable statement without necessarily knowing it.

Instead of focusing on getting confessions and making arrests, investigators should be focused on getting reliable information during interviews and assessing the credibility of any future testimony. This is why forensic psychologists have developed so many protocols for interviewing those involved in or associated with criminal investigations: to ensure that accurate and reliable information is properly obtained and documented.

There is a principal rule to attend in this endeavor: the fewer the restrictions that exist during the interview, the more reliable the information that is gathered. The more the restrictions are, the less the reliability is. And the only mechanism for confirming that information is through an examination and comparison of other witnesses and the physical evidence. Failure to cross-corroborate interviews is an investigative choice that all but ensures unreliable information, time lost, and unnecessary expense.

TORTURE: THE RATIONALE

Earlier in this chapter, we defined torture (see generally UNCAT, 1987). We also explained that torture is illegal, inhumane, and most importantly does not produce reliable results. Given that these things are true, why does its use persist? Why do torture detainees when it does not result in useful information?

Despite continued scientific evidence that torture produces biased and inaccurate information, the factors that contribute to its ongoing use are many. The first is ignorance, fed by films and television. They offer an endless supply of fictionalized accounts in which torture is used successfully by heroic government agents (e.g., the Dirty Harry films; and more recently 24, Homeland, and Zero Dark Thirty[5]). These accounts are emotionally packaged propaganda, suggesting anecdotal evidence of the necessity and effectiveness of torture without a basis in fact.

Other reasons include lack of training in proper criminal investigation and interview methods; ignorance of the law; lack of foundational education and literacy; personal vendettas; the aggressive and retributive stance of police and military culture; religious beliefs; and institutional, societal, or cultural pressure to meet cruelty with cruelty.

To be clear, and to repeat: torture does not produce reliable or legally admissible results (see generally: Costanzo, Gerrity, & Lykes, 2007; McCoy, 2006; O'Mara, 2015; Turvey, 2011). Anyone that engages in torture is a criminal; morally bankrupt; ethically bereft; and should go to jail. There is no gray area here and no acceptable rationale.

BEHAVIORS CONSTITUTING TORTURE

There are many behaviors that constitute and are even quite obviously torture. Unfortunately, too many in law enforcement and the military have become acclimated to using all the force at their disposal. We know this is true because they require specific laws, policies, and guidelines to act with restraint. Instead of viewing themselves as peace officers, and keepers of the peace, they view themselves as warriors or as instruments of righteous vengeance.

Specifically, among the most common methods of torture, documented by the Amnesty International (2015), include:

- Punches and strikes with boots, rifle butts, sticks;
- Introducing, through the nose of the arrested, water mixed with gas or chili;
- Death threats;
- Electric shocks, often to the toes or testicles;
- Simulated execution (e.g., dry-firing guns to the head);
- Threats of kidnapping;
- Suffocation with plastic bags, wet cloths;
- Water torture, including submersion and waterboarding;
- Sexual humiliation and assault.

Readers will note that this list of behaviors reflects the reality that criminal laws relating to torture have traditionally focused on the inflection of physical injury (Echeburrua, Corral, & Amor, 2002). As already suggested, the fields of scientific inquiry related to the evaluation of torture have evolved beyond physical classifications and embrace an understanding of associated human psychology. This conforms with the Istanbul Protocols, which explains (United Nations, 2004, p. 45):

> *One of the central aims of torture is to reduce an individual to a position of extreme helplessness and distress that can lead to a deterioration of cognitive, emotional and behavioural functions. Thus, torture is a means of attacking an individual's fundamental modes of psychological and social functioning. Under such circumstances, the torturer strives not only to incapacitate a victim physically but also to disintegrate the individual's personality. The torturer attempts to destroy a victim's sense of being grounded in a family and society as a human being with dreams, hopes and aspirations for the future. By dehumanizing and breaking the will of their victims, torturers set horrific examples for those who later come in contact with the victim. In this way, torture can break or damage the will and coherence of entire communities.*

Once we understand this aspect of torture, we can realize that it puts the victim in a highly vulnerable and even suggestive state. It makes them easy to manipulate, easy to exploit, and highly unreliable.

DIAGNOSTIC CATEGORIES RELATED TO TORTURE

Torture causes psychological damage. This means inflicting physical and/or psychological abuse using a wide variety of potential methods. The common results include not only evidence of physical injury, but also trauma-related mental disorders (United Nations, 2004, p. 48–49):

> *While the chief complaints and most prominent findings among torture survivors are widely diverse and relate to the individual's unique life experiences and his or her cultural, social and political context, it is wise for evaluators to become familiar with the most commonly diagnosed disorders among trauma and torture survivors. Also, it is not uncommon for more than one mental disorder to be present, as there is considerable co-morbidity among trauma-related mental disorders. Various manifestations of anxiety and depression are the most common symptoms resulting from torture. Not infrequently, the symptomatology described above will be classified within the categories of anxiety and mood disorders.*

The most common trauma-related mental disorders resulting from torture are similar to those found in victims of sexual assault and include posttraumatic stress disorder (PTSD), major depression, and enduring personality changes.

Just as any physical evidence of torture is best established and interpreted by a properly trained forensic scientist, psychological manifestations of torture are best established and interpreted by properly educated and trained behavioral scientists (e.g., psychologists and psychiatrists). It is not an assessment to be conducted by those working for the accused governments; and it is certainly not to be conducted by those with an inherent bias, such as law enforcement, military personnel, or victim advocates.

Also, it is important to understand that a baseline must be constructed of the alleged victim in each case with respect to their behavior a psychological traits prior to the alleged time frame of torture. That baseline becomes the most significant point of comparison for behaviors occurring after the alleged time frame of torture. The changes that can be documented suggest the appropriate diagnostic categories. They can also provide a framework for discovering potential trauma unrelated to torture allegations and even malingering (e.g, false reporting).

THE PSYCHOLOGICAL EFFECTS AND IMPACT OF TORTURE

The psychological damage caused by torture is emotional injury beyond a victim's capacity to accept and mentally adjust to what is happening. That is exactly what torture is about: taking someone beyond their physical and psychological limits—until they break by complying or giving authorities what they want. This includes providing information, making a confession, or compliance with commands (e.g., the performance of sex acts; political statements; or changing undesirable behavior).

COGNITIVE AND BEHAVIORAL MANIFESTATIONS

Emotional strength and stability are meaningless in the face of torture, no matter how much the victim possesses. They will eventually break; it will just take longer and therefore be more traumatic. Esbec (1994) identifies the following as primary behavioral evidence of psychological damage related to torture:

- Negative feelings: humiliation, shame, guilt, or anger
- Anxiety
- Continual worries about the trauma, tending to remake the incident
- Depression
- Progressive loss of self-confidence as a consequence of the experimented feelings of defenselessness and faithlessness
- Decrease of self-steam
- Loss of interest and concentration in old gratifying activities
- Changes in the values system; especially confidence in others and the belief of a fair world
- Hostility, aggressiveness
- Drug abuse
- Modification of relationships (emotional dependence, isolating)
- Increase of the vulnerability being afraid of living in a dangerous world and loss of own life's control

- Drastic change in the lifestyle, being afraid of going to habitual places, prior need to change their address
- Disturbances on the rhythm and the content of the dream
- Sexual dysfunction

These signs and symptoms are corroborated in Hauksson (2003), in his rendering of psychological effects adapted from the Istanbul Protocols (p. 5–6):

Common Psychological Responses (adapted from the Istanbul Protocol)

1. *Re-experiencing the trauma*
    a) *Flashbacks or intrusive memories, i.e. the subjective sense that the traumatic event is happening all over again, even while the person is awake and conscious.*
    b) *Recurrent frightening dreams or nightmares that include elements of the traumatic event(s) in either their original or symbolic form.*
    c) *Physiological or psychological stress reactions at exposure to cues that symbolize or resemble the trauma. This may include lack of trust and fear of persons of authority, including physicians and psychologists. In countries or situations where authorities participate in human rights violations, lack of trust, and fear of authority figures should not be assumed to be pathological.*
2. *Avoidance and emotional numbing*
    a) *Avoidance of any thoughts, conversations, activities, places, or people that arouse recollection of the trauma*
    b) *Profound emotional constriction*
    c) *Profound personal detachment and social withdrawal*
    d) *Inability to recall an important aspect of the trauma*
3. *Hyperarousal*
    a) *Difficulty falling or staying asleep*
    b) *Irritability or outbursts of anger*
    c) *Difficulty concentrating*
    d) *Hypervigilance*
    e) *Exaggerated startle response*
    f) *Generalized anxiety*
    g) *Shortness of breath, sweating, dry mouth, dizziness*
    h) *Gastrointestinal distress*
4. *Symptoms of depression*
    a) *Depressed mood*
    b) *Markedly diminished interest or pleasure in activities*
    c) *Appetite disturbance and resulting weight loss, or weight gain*
    d) *Insomnia or hypersomnia*
    e) *Psychomotor agitation or retardation*
    f) *Fatigue and loss of energy*
    g) *Difficulty in attention, concentration and memory*

      h) Feelings and thoughts of worthlessness, guilt and hopelessness
      i) Thoughts of death and dying, suicidal ideation, suicide attempts
5. Damaged self-concept and foreshortened future
      a) A subjective feeling of having been irreparably damaged and of having undergone an irreversible personality change
      b) A sense of foreshortened future: not expecting to have a career, marriage, children, or a normal life span
6. Dissociation, depersonalisation and atypical behaviour
      a) Dissociation: a disruption in the integration of consciousness, self-perception, memory and actions. A person may be cut off or unaware of certain actions or may feel split in two and feel as if observing him or herself from a distance.
      b) Depersonalisation: feeling detached from oneself or one's body
      c) Impulse control problems, resulting in behaviours that the survivor considers highly atypical with respect to his or her pre-trauma personality. A previously cautious individual may engage in high-risk behaviour.
7. Somatic complaints

Somatic symptoms such as pain and headache and other physical complaints, with or without objective findings, are common problems among torture victims. Pain may be the only presenting complaint. It may shift in location and vary in intensity. Somatic symptoms, such as pain of all kinds, may be a direct physical consequence of torture, or of psychological origin, or both.

The chronic pain syndrome is exacerbated by a vicious circle of inactivity, insomnia and use of analgesics. Typical somatic complaints include:
      a) Headaches: a history of beatings to the head and other head injuries are very common among torture survivors. These injuries often lead to posttraumatic headaches that are chronic in nature. Headaches may also be caused by or exacerbated by tension and stress.
      b) Back pain
      c) Musculoskeletal pain and tenderness, diffuse and non-specific
8. Sexual dysfunction

Sexual dysfunction is common among survivors of torture, particularly among those who have suffered sexual torture or rape, but not exclusively. It can be linked to depression and posttraumatic stress disorder, but can be a direct result of an assault. Hypnotics or alcohol abuse can occur in this context.

9. Psychosis

Cultural and linguistic differences may be confused with psychotic symptoms. Before labelling someone as psychotic, one must evaluate the symptoms within the individual's unique cultural context. Psychotic reactions may be brief or prolonged. The psychotic symptoms may occur while person is detained and tortured as well as afterwards. The following is a list of possible findings:
      a) Delusions
      b) Hallucinations: auditory, visual, tactile, olfactory

c) Bizarre ideation and behaviour
   d) Illusions or perceptual distortions
   e) Paranoia and delusions of persecution
   f) Recurrence of psychotic disorders or mood disorders with psychotic features may develop among those who have a past history of mental illness.
10. Substance abuse
   Alcohol and drug abuse often develops secondarily in torture survivors as a way of obliterating traumatic memories, regulating affect and managing anxiety.
11. Neuropsychological impairment
   Torture can involve physical trauma that leads to various levels of brain impairment. Blows to the head, suffocation, and prolonged malnutrition may have long-term neurological and neuropsychological consequences that may not be readily assessed.

The manifestation of these effects, and their intensity, will depend a great deal on the intensity of the torture that was suffered and the victim's individual vulnerability. These are collectively referred to as *protective factors*. There are many, and they may be characterized as internal (arising from within the individual) and external (arising from the context and the environment).

Protective factors include variables such as the existence of personal coping and defense mechanisms; social and family support networks; the nature and extent of the torture suffered; and the distance in time from the victim's experience being tortured (see generally Fernández-Ballesteros, 2001). As further reported in Hauksson (2003, p. 16):

There seems to be a higher rate of PTSD among tortured non-activists than in those politically active. A study compared 55 tortured political activists and 34 torture survivors with no history of political activity, commitment to a political cause or expectations of arrest and torture and were thus presumed to be less "psychologically prepared" for torture. Non-activists were subjected to relatively less severe forms of torture but had significantly higher prevalence of current PTSD (58% vs. 18%) and current depression (24% vs. 4%) and higher levels of psychopathology on most measures.

Prior knowledge of and preparedness for torture, strong commitment to a cause, immunization against traumatic stress as a result of repeated exposure, and strong social supports appear to have protective value against PTSD in survivors of torture. On the other hand, survivors who have stronger feelings of injustice arising from the impunity enjoyed by the perpetrators of human rights violations, have more severe psychological problems subsequent to torture. Both loss of control and fear of further persecution are critical to the survivor's reaction to the impunity of the perpetrators. Torture has long-term psychological effects independent of those related to uprooting, refugee status, and other traumatic life events in a politically repressive environment.

> *Obviously, this means that every case, and every victim allegation, must be investigated and examined independently to discover the presence or absence of protective factors. And to establish the mental health baseline discussed in the prior section. This information can then be used to interpret those behaviors and cognitive functions reveled at the time of the forensic assessment.*

TORTURE: FORENSIC INTERVIEW PROTOCOLS FOR THE MENTAL HEALTH PROFESSIONAL

As already mentioned, determining whether there is psychological damage to an alleged victim caused by torture requires a psychological assessment by properly educated and trained forensic mental health professionals. This means a formal and structured interview, aimed at gathering and objectively documenting specific information to contextualize findings. Failure to gather and document this information will result in findings that are either unreliable or unsupportable in a court of law.

The interview itself can be a traumatic event for the victim; consequently the Istanbul Protocols offer the following guidelines (United Nations, 2003, p. 50):

> *The clinician should introduce the interview process in a manner that explains in detail the procedures to be followed (questions asked about psychosocial history, including history of torture and current psychological functioning) and that prepares the individual for the difficult emotional reactions that the questions may provoke. The individual needs to be given an opportunity to request breaks, interrupt the interview at any time and be able to leave if the stress becomes intolerable, with the option of a later appointment. Clinicians need to be sensitive and empathic in their questioning, while remaining objective in their clinical assessment. At the same time, the interviewer should be aware of potential personal reactions to the survivor and the descriptions of torture that might influence the interviewer's perceptions and judgements.*

What these advise is an overall demeanor that is cognizant of the harm that might be caused by retraumatizing the victim and contaminating the information being gathered; while also being patient. Moreover, the interviewer must avoid appearing salacious or voyeuristic their questions—this can be ameliorated by a professional and caring demeanor which does not judge or become excited. Ultimately, an interview such as this is about building trust and making the subject feel safe. Anything acting as an obstacle to these can prevent them from being honest or forthcoming, which negates the purpose and overall value of the interview.

Specific interview guidelines are taken directly from the Istanbul Protocols and enjoy the confidence of the international forensic mental health community—

consequently they are presented here in nearly their entirety for context (United Nations, 2003, pp. 52—54):

> The introduction should contain mention of the referral source, a summary of collateral sources (such as medical, legal and psychiatric records) and a description of the methods of assessment used (interviews, symptom inventories, checklists and neuropsychological testing).
>
> (a) History of torture and ill-treatment
> 276. Every effort should be made to document the full history of torture, persecution and other relevant traumatic experiences (see chapter IV, sect. E). This part of the evaluation is often exhausting for the person being evaluated. Therefore, it may be necessary to proceed in several sessions. The interview should start with a general summary of events before eliciting the details of the torture experiences. The interviewer needs to know the legal issues at hand because that will determine the nature and amount of information necessary to achieve documentation of the facts.
>
> (b) Current psychological complaints
> 277. An assessment of current psychological functioning constitutes the core of the evaluation. As severely brutalized prisoners of war and rape victims show a lifetime prevalence of PTSD of between 80 and 90 per cent, specific questions about the three DSM-IV categories of PTSD (re-experiencing of the traumatic event, avoidance or numbing of responsiveness, including amnesia, and increased arousal) need to be asked.113, 114 Affective, cognitive and behavioural symptoms should be described in detail, and the frequency, as well as examples, of nightmares, hallucinations and startle response should be stated. An absence of symptoms can be due to the episodic or often delayed nature of PTSD or to denial of symptoms because of shame.
>
> (c) Post-torture history
> 278. This component of the psychological evaluation seeks information about current life circumstances. It is important to inquire about current sources of stress, such as separation or loss of loved ones, flight from the home country and life in exile. The interviewer should also inquire about the individual's ability to be productive, earn a living, care for his or her family and the availability of social supports.
>
> (d) Pre-torture history
> 279. If relevant, describe the victim's childhood, adolescence, early adulthood, his or her family background, family illnesses and family composition. There should also be a description of the victim's educational and occupational history. Describe any history of past trauma, such as childhood abuse, war trauma or domestic violence, as well as the victim's cultural and religious background.
> 280. The description of pre-trauma history is important to assess mental health status and level of psychosocial functioning of the torture victim prior to the

traumatic events. In this way, the interviewer can compare the current mental health status with that of the individual before torture. In evaluating background information, the interviewer should keep in mind that the duration and severity of responses to trauma are affected by multiple factors. These factors include, but are not limited to, the circumstances of the torture, the perception and interpretation of torture by the victim, the social context before, during and after torture, community and peer resources and values and attitudes about traumatic experiences, political and cultural factors, severity and duration of the traumatic events, genetic and biological vulnerabilities, developmental phase and age of the victim, prior history of trauma and pre-existing personality. In many interview situations, because of time limitations and other problems, it may be difficult to obtain this information. It is important, nonetheless, to obtain enough data about the individual's previous mental health and psychosocial functioning to form an impression of the degree to which torture has contributed to psychological problems.

(e) *Medical history*

281. The medical history summarizes pre-trauma health conditions, current health conditions, body pain, somatic complaints, use of medication and its side effects, relevant sexual history, past surgical procedures and other medical data (see chapter V, sect. B).

(f) *Psychiatric history*

282. Inquiries should be made about a history of mental or psychological disturbances, the nature of problems and whether they received treatment or required psychiatric hospitalization. The inquiry should also cover prior therapeutic use of psychotropic medication.

(g) *Substance use and abuse history*

283. The clinician should inquire about substance use before and after the torture, changes in the pattern of use and whether substances are being used to cope with insomnia or psychological/psychiatric problems. These substances are not only alcohol, cannabis and opium but also regional substances of abuse such as betel nut and many others.

(h) *Mental status examination*

284. The mental status examination begins the moment the clinician meets the subject. The interviewer should make note of the person's appearance, such as signs of malnutrition, lack of cleanliness, changes in motor activity during the interview, use of language, presence of eye contact, ability to relate to the interviewer and the means the individual uses to establish communication. The following components should be covered, and all aspects of the mental status examination should be included in the report of the psychological evaluation; aspects such as general appearance, motor activity, speech, mood and affect, thought content, thought process, suicidal and homicidal ideation and a cognitive examination (orientation, long-term memory, intermediate recall and immediate recall).

(i) *Assessment of social function*

285. Trauma and torture can directly and indirectly affect a person's ability to function. Torture can also indirectly cause loss of functioning and disability, if

the psychological consequences of the experience impair the individual's ability to care for himself or herself, earn a living, support a family and pursue an education. The clinician should assess the individual's current level of functioning by inquiring about daily activities, social role (as housewife, student, worker), social and recreational activities and perception of health status. The interviewer should ask the individual to assess his or her own health condition, to state the presence or absence of feelings of chronic fatigue and to report potential changes in overall functioning.

(j) *Psychological testing and the use of checklists and questionnaires*

286. Little published data exist on the use of psychological testing (projective and objective personality tests) in the assessment of torture survivors. Also, psychological tests of personality lack cross-cultural validity. These factors combine to limit severely the utility of psychological testing in the evaluation of torture victims. Neuropsychological testing may, however, be helpful in assessing cases of brain injury resulting from torture (see section C.4 below). An individual who has survived torture may have trouble expressing in words his or her experiences and symptoms. In some cases, it may be helpful to use trauma event and symptom checklists or questionnaires. If the interviewer believes it may be helpful to use these, there are numerous questionnaires available, although none are specific to torture victims.

(k) *Clinical impression*

287. In formulating a clinical impression for the purposes of reporting psychological evidence of torture, the following important questions should be asked:

(i) Are the psychological findings consistent with the alleged report of torture?

(ii) Are the psychological findings expected or typical reactions to extreme stress within the cultural and social context of the individual?

(iii) Given the fluctuating course of trauma-related mental disorders over time, what is the time frame in relation to the torture events? Where is the individual in the course of recovery?

(iv) What are the coexisting stressors impinging on the individual (e.g. ongoing persecution, forced migration, exile, loss of family and social role)? What impact do these issues have on the individual?

(v) Which physical conditions contribute to the clinical picture? Pay special attention to head injury sustained during torture or detention;

(vi) Does the clinical picture suggest a false allegation of torture?

288. Clinicians should comment on the consistency of psychological findings and the extent to which these findings correlate with the alleged abuse. The emotional state and expression of the person during the interview, his or her symptoms, the history of detention and torture and the personal history prior to torture should be described. Factors such as the onset of specific symptoms related to the trauma, the specificity of any particular psychological findings and patterns of psychological functioning should be noted. Additional factors should be considered, such as forced migration, resettlement, difficulty of acculturation, language problems,

unemployment, loss of home, family and social status. The relationship and consistency between events and symptoms should be evaluated and described. Physical conditions, such as head trauma or brain injury, may require further evaluation. Neurological or neuropsychological assessment may be recommended.

289. If the survivor has symptom levels consistent with a DSM-IV or ICD-10 psychiatric diagnosis, the diagnosis should be stated. More than one diagnosis may be applicable. Again, it must be stressed that even though a diagnosis of a trauma-related mental disorder supports the claim of torture, not meeting criteria for a psychiatric diagnosis does not mean the person was not tortured. A survivor of torture may not have the level of symptoms required to meet diagnostic criteria for a DSM-IV or ICD-10 diagnosis fully. In these cases, as with all others, the symptoms that the survivor has and the torture story that he or she claims to have experienced should be considered as a whole. The degree of consistency between the torture story and the symptoms that the individual reports should be evaluated and described in the report.

290. It is important to recognize that some people falsely allege torture for a range of reasons and that others may exaggerate a relatively minor experience for personal or political reasons. The investigator must always be aware of these possibilities and try to identify potential reasons for exaggeration or fabrication. The clinician should keep in mind, however, that such fabrication requires detailed knowledge about trauma-related symptoms that individuals rarely possess. Inconsistencies in testimony can occur for a number of valid reasons, such as memory impairment due to brain injury, confusion, dissociation, cultural differences in perception of time or fragmentation and repression of traumatic memories. Effective documentation of psychological evidence of torture requires clinicians to have a capacity to evaluate consistencies and inconsistencies in the report. If the interviewer suspects fabrication, additional interviews should be scheduled to clarify inconsistencies in the report. Family or friends may be able to corroborate details of the story. If the clinician conducts additional examinations and still suspects fabrication, the clinician should refer the individual to another clinician and ask for the colleague's opinion. The suspicion of fabrication should be documented with the opinion of two clinicians.

(l) Recommendations

291. The recommendations resulting from the psychological evaluation depend on the question posed at the time the evaluation was requested. The issues under consideration may concern legal and judicial matters, asylum, resettlement or a need for treatment. Recommendations can be for further assessment, such as neuropsychological testing, medical or psychiatric treatment, or a need for security or asylum.

It is important to note that the interview protocols here are presented as a forensic inquiry, not a foregone conclusion. In other words, no ethical forensic professional makes the assumption that findings of torture will be validated. Validation and refutation of allegations are both potential outcomes of the assessment process. The psychologist's investigation, like any other investigation, must be conducted with an open mind and with the understanding that the truth must be revealed by the evidence not assumed as part of it from the outset.

CONCLUSION

When acts of torture are used, sponsored, or tolerated by government agents, it is an abuse of authority. What's more, it is an effective demonstration of cruelty evidencing cultural and institutional tyranny. This is perhaps why there is no better mechanism for inducing resentment, mistrust, and then active resistance from those who suffer its effects. It also renders any information subsequently gathered completely unreliable—to include accusations and confessions alike. The results of torture are not just lawfully inadmissible, but empirically untrustworthy.

Those conducting assessments of the use of force by government agents, including allegations of torture, must therefore be educated in the basic principles of human psychology and human rights; trained on the various mechanisms and effects of torture; and sufficiently independent from the government to avoid bias or coercion when gathering evidence and rendering expert findings. They must also ask the right questions and properly document the answers. In the absences of these conditions, use of force assessments is itself unreliable and should be viewed with all of the skepticism that good science mandates.

ENDNOTES

1. As reported in CBSNEWS (2007): "A United Nations committee said Friday that use of Taser weapons can be a form of torture, in violation of the U.N. Convention Against Torture" with "proven risks of harm or death".
2. One study found that at least 8 of 48 Taser-related deaths involved the practice of so-called "drive-stunning," as reported in Thompson and Berman (2015):

   More than half of the 48 suffered from mental illness or had illegal drugs in their system at the time. At least 10 were Tasered while handcuffed or shackled… Deaths after Taser usage by police are relatively rare, accounting for a fraction of the people who die during or after encounters with officers, according to a comprehensive study by the National Institute of Justice. Research shows that when used correctly, the devices are generally safe and prevent injuries to both police officers and civilians. But when Tasers are used excessively or if officers don't follow department policy or product guidelines, the risk of injury or death can increase, according to company product warnings and police experts. Tasers are best known for their ability to incapacitate individuals while used in "probe mode," when they fire two barbs that deliver an electric current along wires, causing the muscles to lock up. When

> placed against a person's body in "drive-stun" mode, as happened in the Ajibade case, Tasers do not incapacitate but cause localized pain that can be used to control dangerous individuals. Pain compliance, police call it.
>
> At least nine of the 48 cases this year involved individuals who were Tasered in the drive-stun mode. Taser International has issued product warnings to law enforcement about drive-stunning, noting the need for caution and restraint when using the technique on people with mental illnesses. "Drive-stun use may not be effective on emotionally disturbed persons or others who may not respond to pain due to a mind-body disconnect," the company warned in 2013. "Avoid using repeated drive-stuns on such individuals if compliance is not achieved."

In other words, drive-stunning or drive-tasing has no purpose other than to inflict pain; and it cannot induce compliance in someone that is mentally ill or intoxicated. Moreover, the Taser advises that if it does not work immediately, stop doing it. Meaning that its only real value is in satisfying the emotional needs that officers often have for retribution against a noncompliant detainee.

3. Common examples include threats of physical violence, rape, and murder directed at the detainee, or at their loved ones.
4. This would be why denying allegations of torture is commonplace even when it is obvious. The consequences to the state's criminal cases can be catastrophic, even completely ruinous.
5. Numerous complaints have been made regarding the film Zero Dark Thirty because it depicts the use of torture as a key element in helping US agents locate and kill Osama Bin Laden. In fact, just about everyone involved disputes this notion as fiction, and anger toward the film among those in government has been well documented (Baram, 2015).

REFERENCES

Amnesty International. (November 2015). *What is torture?*. https://www.es.amnesty.org/stoptortura/la-tortura/.

Associated Press. (April 24, 2016). *Mexican police tortured suspects in case of missing students, report says*. Los Angeles Times. http://www.latimes.com/world/mexico-americas/la-fg-mexico-torture-20160424-story.html.

Associated Press. (April 24, 2016). *Mexican soldiers arrested for torturing woman after horrific video emerged of them helping a police officer suffocating helpless detainee with plastic bag*. The Daily Mail. http://www.dailymail.co.uk/news/article-3540172/Mexican-soldiers-face-charges-apparent-torture-woman.html.

Baram, M. (May 21, 2015). *A US senator walked out of 'Zero Dark Thirty' after 15 minutes because it was so 'false'*. Business Insider. http://www.businessinsider.com/a-us-senator-walked-out-of-bin-laden-raid-movie-zero-dark-thirty-because-it-was-so-false-2015-5.

Bierman, N. (March 17, 2015). *Few have faced consequences for abuses at Abu Ghraib prison in Iraq*. Los Angeles Times. http://www.latimes.com/nation/la-na-abu-ghraib-lawsuit-20150317-story.html.

CBSNEWS. (November 25, 2007). *UN: Tasers are a form of torture*. CBSNews.com. http://www.cbsnews.com/news/un-tasers-are-a-form-of-torture/.

Costanzo, M., Gerrity, E., & Lykes, B. (2007). Psychologists and the use of torture in interrogations. *Analyses of Social Issues and Public Policy, 7*(1), 7−20.

Daily Mail Reporter. (August 6, 2011). *Last suspect in Abu Ghraib prison abuse scandal released from jail early*. Daily Mail. http://www.dailymail.co.uk/news/article-2023222/Charles-Graner-Ringleader-Abu-Ghraib-prisoner-abuse-scandal-released-jail-early.html.

Echeburrua, E., Corral, P. D., & Amor, P. J. (2002). Evaluating of psychological damage on victims of violent crimes. *Psicothema*, 139–146.

Edwards, H., & Gotsonis, C. (2009). *Strengthening forensic science in the United States: A path forward*. Washington, DC: National Academies Press.

Emmanuel, A. (April 14, 2015). *Chicago to create fund to compensate victims of Burge police torture*. The Chicago Reporter. http://chicagoreporter.com/chicago-to-create-fund-to-compensate-victims-of-burge-police-torture/.

Esbec, E. (1994). Victims of violent crime: general and forensic victimology. *Legal and Forensic Psychiatry, 2*.

Fernández-Ballesteros, R. (2001). Behavioural Assessment. In M. J. Smelser, & B. S. Baltes (Eds.), *International encyclopedia of the social & behavioral sciences*. New York: Pergamon Press.

Hauksson, P. (November 6, 2003). *Psychological evidence of torture: How to conduct an interview with a detainee to document mental health consequences of torture or ill-treatment*. Strasbourg: Council of Europe. http://www.cpt.coe.int/en/working-documents/cpt-2003-91-eng.pdf.

International Rehabilitation Council for Torture Victims. (2007). *Psychological evaluation of torture allegations: A practical guide to the Istanbul protocol*. Copenhague: IRCT.

Lee, T. (June 9, 2015). *Jon Burge, ex-Chicago cop who ran torture ring, released from prison*. MSNBC.com. http://www.msnbc.com/msnbc/jon-burge-ex-chicago-cop-who-ran-torture-ring-released-prison.

McCoy, A. (2006). *A question of torture: CIA interrogation, from the cold war to the war on terror*. New York: Metropolitan Books/Henry Holt.

O'Mara, S. (2015). *Why torture doesn't work: The neuroscience of interrogation*. Boston: Harvard University Press.

Pena, D. (April 19, 2016). *Torture of ordinary Mexicans may be shocking, but it's not surprising*. The Guardian. http://www.theguardian.com/commentisfree/2016/apr/19/mexico-citizen-torture-shocking-video-soldiers-police-suspect.

Phippen, J. W. (April 20, 2016). *Tortured at the hands of Mexican police*. The Atlantic. http://www.theatlantic.com/international/archive/2016/04/mexico-torture/479124/.

Sánchez, D. (1989). *Torture: A social approach. Torture: Medical, psychological and social aspects: Prevention and treatment*. Santiago, Chile: Mental Health Team-DITT Committee of Defense of the Rights of the People (CODEPU).

Staff. (November 4, 2015). *Sitka police excessively tazing student YouTube video goes viral!* Alaska Native News. http://alaska-native-news.com/sitka-police-excessively-tazing-student-youtube-video-goes-viral-19981.

Thompson, C., & Berman, M. (November 26, 2015). *"Improper techniques, increased risks: Deaths have raised questions about the risk of excessive or improper deployment of Tasers"*. Washington Post. http://www.washingtonpost.com/sf/investigative/2015/11/26/improper-techniques-increased-risks/.

Turvey, B. (2011). *Criminal profiling* (4th ed.). London: Elsevier Science.

Turvey, B. (2013). *Forensic fraud*. San Diego: Elsevier Science.

UNCAT. (1987). *Convention against torture and other cruel, inhuman or degrading treatment or punishment, adopted and opened for signature, ratification and accession by general assembly resolution 39/46 of 10 December 1984.* http://www.ohchr.org/EN/ProfessionalInterest/Pages/CAT.aspx.

United Nations. (2004). *Istanbul protocol: Manual on the effective investigation and documentation of torture and other cruel, inhuman or degrading treatment or punishment.* Geneva: Office of The United Nations High Commissioner for Human Rights.

Woolsey, R. (February 10, 2016). *Sitka settles with tasered teen for $350,000.* KCAW. http://www.kcaw.org/2016/02/10/sitka-settles-with-tasered-teen-for-350000/.

CHAPTER 13

Forensic Investigations for Court: Probation, Sentencing, Mitigation Issues in Capital Cases

Ronald J. Miller
Behavioral Forensics, Washington State, United States

CHAPTER OUTLINE

Juvenile Court Probation Systems 330
Adult Probation 332
Capital Murder Mitigation Investigations 336
References 342

The challenge for the courts (and juries in capital cases) is continually trying to better assess and assign appropriate sentencing to criminal offenders of all ages and all crimes. Such an endeavor is indeed challenging and this chapter provides a small window into that enormous task. In the 21st century, we are challenged with an ever-growing population, cyber crime, and international drug trafficking and terrorism. The question has always been and will always be "how do we protect society, punish the offender, and yet do so in a manner that is fair to all"? Like Quixote, we will likely continue refining this process forever as society changes and as the resources diminish or increase. It is a moving target. Yet fundamental to today's concept of justice, individual factors of each defendant, victim, and circumstance must be evaluated.

This discussion will assign the forensic investigator, involved in sentencing, into three general and the most common areas of practice:

- Juvenile court probation
- Adult presentencing and probation/parole
- Capital murder penalty phase trial mitigation investigations

The depth of inquiry, goals for investigation, and training and expertise of the investigator vary with each of these specialties.

The descriptions or these functions may vary from jurisdiction because of varying law and practice. With the exception of death penalty, mitigation investigations, and those presentencing investigations in federal court, there are no clear national standards. Much is left up to the local court jurisdictions or various statutory sentencing guidelines for each state.

JUVENILE COURT PROBATION SYSTEMS

This challenge of appropriate sentencing begins with children, entering the juvenile court system as minors. Usually it starts with minor infractions; theft, running away, drugs, alcohol, fighting, and then frequently escalating to various felonies paralleling the adult world to include aggravated murder.

As a culture, we believe that the "early years" are critical for healthy development into responsible, contributing adults and hold juveniles to standards that account for the varying and dynamic changes taking place in their developmental and maturation progress to adulthood. This is particularly challenging due the variances in background, maturation rates, socioeconomic resources, and other factors. This is evidenced by the strict child abuse and neglect laws present in every Western society.

The agency of jurisdiction of the juvenile court may vary from state to state. Generally, minors by definition are under the age of 18 years. However, in some jurisdictions they may be held to a higher standard of accountability beginning at age 14 years or 16 years. Depending on the nature of the offense alleged and other factors in their background, on petition by the state prosecuting attorney, these minors can be tried and sentenced in adult court. This is known as a "remand" process. Minors, regardless of any remand, cannot be subject to capital punishment (Roper v. Simmons, 543 US. 551 2005).

Children under the age of pubescence, typically around 10 years or less maybe held to different accountability standards than older children. There may be a hearing process to determine the competency and reliability of younger children as witnesses and defendants. Again this varies by jurisdiction and may be regulated by a combination of statute or case law.

The variances in the maturation and developmental progress of a juvenile offender has resulted in a great deal of research as to how to assess what is in the best interest of the public and the minor in the hopes of protecting both the public and increasing the possibility of rehabilitation. The goal in juvenile probation is first to protect the public but a second and similarly high priority is the goal to rehabilitate the child to prevent recidivism during a period of personality development and increased social responsibility.

To accomplish this goal, over the years a number of assessment tools have been developed in an effort to determine what is in the best interest of the child and the public. The degree to which these assessments and evaluations are conducted is greatly dependent on the resources and cultural attitudes of that jurisdiction. An example of an early tool to evaluate a juvenile and plot a course toward rehabilitation and reduction of recidivism is the "Manual For The Structured Assessment Of

Violence Risk In Youth" (SAVRY) (Borum et al., 2002). The SAVRY is an attempt to combine early efforts at clinical evaluations (psychological and mental health assessments) and more systematic empirical investigations based on specific risk and supportive factors in the life of the juvenile (Borum et al., 2002, p. 3). This combined approach utilizes the general better performance of statistical and actuarial data over pure clinical data yet include the ever-changing dynamic factors, which may be more evident in a clinical evaluation. Because juveniles are in a continual state of dynamic personality development, pure actuarial models have their limitations.

The SAVRY includes data collected in the following domains:

- Historical risk factors—these are based on past behavior or experiences such as prior episodes of violence. They are generally static and appear to be not subject to change over time. There is a high association with violence risk recidivism.
- Social/contextual risk factors—these include social and contextual risk factors that influence interpersonal relationships and connection to social institutions. These might include peer delinquency, peer rejection, stress and poor coping skills, poor parental management, and lack of personal or social support and community disorganization.
- Individual risk factors—these include aspects of psychological and behavioral functioning such as negative attitudes, risk taking and impulsivity, substance abuse and use difficulties, anger management problems, social adaptations problems, attention deficit disorder and hyperactivity problems, poor compliance, and low interest or commitment to school.
- Protective factors—the presence of one or more risk factors do not in themselves predict that violence is certain to occur. Just as there are factors which increase the likelihood of violence there also individual and contextual protective factors that can reduce the negative impact of a risk factor. Protective factors are important to them mitigate the appraisal of risk and are important to consider in treatment and reinforcement during the probation or rehabilitation process. Protective factors can include supportive family, supportive social organizations such as church, involvement in athletics, employment, community service, and other activities which support and encourage healthy relationships between people and improved problem-solving and conflict resolution. Strong attachment and bonds to primary caregivers are very important. A mentor in the community or even a social service agency can make a huge difference. A probation officer can facilitate the linkage between such a supportive person and a probationer. A strong commitment to school and the development of a resilient personality are skills which are extremely influential on the developing psyche of an adolescent (Borum et al., 2002, p. 8–10).

Whatever assessment tools are utilized, and there are many, they must have components of the risk and protective factors which help guide juvenile court judges and probation counselors and attempting to optimize rehabilitation as opposed to recidivism or "graduating to adult crimes." Sadly, these tools and institutions using them are frequently limited in the influence for those children whose lives are dominated by risk factors.

A dedicated and sincere juvenile court probation counselor can have a tremendous positive influence on a young person. It is a career that is rewarding in many cases and sadly disappointing in others.

The training and educational requirements for a juvenile court probation officer combine those of a good parent, social worker, football coach, and police officer. Most such probation counselors have training and bachelor's degrees in related fields such as social work, sociology, administration of justice, psychology, and education. The ability to objectively evaluate and collect data relevant to each probationer and to develop a probation plan which can be amended as needed is paramount. This requires an impartial evaluation of the situational life circumstances of each individual juvenile dispassionately. The balance between commitment to the ideal of rehabilitation and the realities of recidivism can be stressful and a source of cynicism if the juvenile probation officer does not engage in good self-care. This is a role in which the desire to help, shape, and be a positive influence dominate the relationship along with the ever present authority to hold the youth accountable to the requirements of the court. Maintaining professional boundaries and realistic acceptance is paramount to avoid burn out.

ADULT PROBATION

Once a juvenile graduates into adulthood or is remanded to adult court to be tried as an adult, the focus and goals of sentencing and rehabilitation change fairly dramatically. Once that magic age is attained, responsibility for one's actions enter a whole new domain.

In most jurisdictions, a juvenile is "found" to be accountable for the actions for which they are accused. The terminology may change but generally juveniles are not deemed to be "guilty" or "not guilty." As an adult that changes. Just as in juvenile court, the criteria and depth of studies conducted by an adult probation officer for the purposes of a presentencing memorandum or a postconviction memorandum to assist in sentencing vary greatly with respect to the breadth and depth of the inquiry conducted.

The adult probation officer conducting the presentence or postsentencing study is more akin to be affiliated with the prosecutorial side of the process. As such, depending on the philosophy and culture of that particular probation officer, these reports tend not to show the accused or convicted in the best or most optimistic light. Again, standardized criteria and investigative policy and procedures vary greatly from agency to agency and state to state.

The American Probation and Parole Association (APPA) has recommended that presentence reports are intended to provide the sentencing court with a succinct and purposeful collection of data on which to base a reasonable sentencing decision. In some states, there are sentencing statutes which require that the sentencing magistrate remain within a range of possible sentences. In such cases, these presentencing reports may or may not have much influence on the final outcome. They are, however, in valuable to the sentencing magistrate where such flexibility occurs. These reports are also helpful if the defendant is sentenced to a custodial institution that is not familiar with him or her, with some background as to appropriate placement in and supporting resources in an institutional setting.

The APPA stresses that the probation officer conducting the analysis of data regarding the individual must maintain a high degree of independence if justice is to be served. Therefore, except for when required by law, the independence of the evaluator should be maintained without any influence of persons or agencies directly or indirectly on his or her recommendations. The court has ultimate authority over what should be considered in the sentencing process. This can include additional information for consideration or information in the report to be excluded in the sentencing.

Ideally, such a presentence investigation and report should be conducted in every case where an individual is possibly facing incarceration or extremely structured probation. The ability to conform to this ideal is limited by resources, funding and caseload. In a perfect world, each defendant would have a complete and thorough presentence evaluation prior to final disposition at sentencing. This does not always occur.

With the exception of probation officers assigned to the federal court, there is no nationwide standard for the preparation of these studies in subsequent reports and recommendations. In some jurisdictions misdemeanor convictions and crimes are handled by local County probation departments and felonies are handled by parole officers from the state Department of Corrections. This is likely because misdemeanor convictions result in only County jail time or local probation whereas a felony will likely result in either extended County jail time or incarceration in the State Bureau of Prisons. Hence, all felony convictions in some states fall under the authority of the state Department of Corrections. Again, this variance is jurisdiction dependent.

Just about every jurisdiction has established guidelines for the sentencing of offenders who are convicted of crimes. These guidelines are dependent on criteria established by the state legislatures which establish maximum and minimum terms of confinement or parole for various categories of crimes. There is usually a formulation via an "offense grid" which is used by the court to determine an appropriate sentence. This grid would include such items as "points" for previous convictions, aggravating factors in the crime and possession of weapons in the commission of the crime. Entering the collection of data into the "grid" defines the parameters by which the court may sentence the individual. The intent, is to reduce the amount of arbitrary sentencing that might occur and provide predictability for all concerned as to the potential outcomes of the case should the defendant be convicted. Given the "grid" scores, many defendants can be motivated to plea bargain their case for a lower predictable "grid score." A presentencing memorandum includes the data by which to compute a potential grid score. Some states may have mandated sentences for some crimes with very little discretion on the sentencing judge, others may be extremely broad where persons could be sentenced to probation or very minimal custody time for such crimes as vehicular manslaughter. Age and location of offense are huge variables on the sentence.

The APPA recommends that presentence reports be flexible in format; reflect the difference in the backgrounds and individuality of different offenders in use resources available to them as completely as possible to gain as much information as reasonable for the purposes of their study. These reports should have the following characteristics and include the following information:

- A complete description of the offense and circumstances of the offense. This description should not be limited as to the specific aspects developed for the purposes of establishing guilt and the subsequent judicial process.
- A high priority is given to the victim of the offense. The victim should be allowed to either make a statement to the court or include a statement in the presentencing memorandum as to the personal impact on them. A complete description of that person or persons, their status, the losses that they have incurred in the impact that the offense has had on their lives. This includes, but is not limited to, psychological, physical, and financial harm done to the victim.
- A complete history of the subject's prior criminal record and the nature of the crimes committed in the past and patterns of behavior following those convictions in and out of custody. This would include the compliance with previous probation or parole.
- A full and complete description of the offenders' educational history and special training including military history.
- Offenders employment background and stability, financial status at the time of conviction and abilities to make restitution to the victim and the state.
- A social history of the offender should include his or her marital status, family relationships, responsibilities to children in and out of wedlock, ties to the community, history of residential stability and other community ties.
- The presentencing investigator must have the skills and insights to identify those environments in which he/she is least likely to offend should he/she be granted probation or on release from incarceration as a parolee.
- The report should include the basis for an opinion which would find that confinement to a correctional facility was necessary for the safety of the public from future criminal activity.
- The medical and psychiatric history of the defendant is very important. This would likely have significant influence on the placement in a correctional institution or the advantage of a noncustodial probation status where possible.
- Previous presentencing reports and relevant information from correctional institutions, drug and alcohol treatment facilities, and other social service agencies which had a relationship with the offender can be very relevant.
- In the course of this investigation, it may become apparent that the offender would benefit from various training programs, treatment programs, specific

rehabilitation programs, and other specific programs that the offender could participate in that would increase his/her employability and hopefully reduce recidivistic behavior on release from the custodial institution.
- A brief but thorough summary should be provided to give a concise since the succinct body of information that can be evaluated by the sentencing magistrate.

Probation is generally accepted as the preferred disposition for offenders if the circumstances of each case, the crime, and previous criminal history, the character of the offender, and available community and institutional resources are considered. Most courts will seriously consider probation if the following issues are not evident in the presentencing report:

- Confinement is necessary to protect society.
- Correctional treatment can be most effectively provided when confined.
- The seriousness of the offense dictated that probation was not reasonable due to the gravity of the crime.
- Statutory rules and laws require confinement.

A presentencing study should also include those conditions which are recommended should the offender be granted probation. Such conditions might include the following:

- Close supervision
- Inpatient drug and alcohol treatment
- Attendance and participation in an anger management program
- Participation in a specific treatment program for low-level sex offenders
- Maintaining family obligations financially and socially
- Participate in and continue medical or psychiatric treatment as necessary
- Engage in higher education or vocational training
- Maintaining a residence in a restricted facility or group home specifically designed for the character of the offender and offense
- A prohibition in associating with persons convicted of felonies or crimes related to the offenders unlawful past
- Making restitution and reparation for losses and damages caused by his/her offense
- Timely payment of fines and other financial obligations resulting from his/her conviction
- Requiring submission to search and seizure of person, vehicles, and residence for contraband or evidence of additional crimes
- Requiring submission to drug and alcohol tests as required by the probation officer
- Submission of samples for DNA registration
- Any other requirements that the probation officer felt would reduce the likelihood of recidivistic behavior and encourage successful completion of probation (APPA, Position Statement, January 1987).

Although these studies are usually done by agents of the state, there is a growing trend for defense counsel to conduct similar studies in cases where they feel that there are circumstances which would benefit their clients in either the plea bargaining process or trial and sentencing. These studies by a defendant's attorney would utilize a forensic investigator knowledgeable and skilled in unearthing relevant data. Such a study by the defense of course is dependent on the financial resources available to the client. If the client does not have the money to engage in such an endeavor, they must rely on the generosity of the indigent defense program for their jurisdiction. The variance in such resources is very wide but the more enlightened programs realize that the pursuit of justice for all, including the defendant, is an ethical and moral obligation.

The educational and special training for adult probation and parole officers can be different than those for juvenile probation counselors. The adult probation and parole officer is more of an enforcement body with some social work skills. Although it is advantageous for the adult probation officer to maintain a good working relationship with his/her probationer, the probation or parole officer's primary job is to keep the offender on track and operating within boundaries as dictated by the law and the court. Most states and jurisdictions require that adult probation and parole officers be classified as "correctional officers." They may have certain statutory authority over there caseloads and frequently must attend state-certified academies related to their statutory function. In some states corrections officers are duly-appointed specially commissioned peace officers with arrest powers and are frequently armed. These correctional officers frequently have persons on their caseloads who have committed serious and dangerous felonies. Their histories may be such that the likelihood of recurring criminal behavior is very high. As such, the correctional officer works in an environment which is frequently at a much higher risk than those of a juvenile probation officer. Also any juvenile probation officer who works in the inner city with gang-affiliated youth will tell you that their risk is very high. This is not to say that a juvenile probation officer is frequently exposed to risk and danger, it is just that their caseload may have a different emphasis and a different clientele. There is a huge difference in caseload characteristics between a rural community in Wyoming and East Los Angeles County.

Most correctional officers have at least a bachelor's or master's degree in administration of justice, criminology, psychology, sociology, or relevant field. Many field correctional officers have had previous employment working in a penitentiary or other correctional institution. In that environment they learn much about the population that they would someday be monitoring on the "outside." This experience is invaluable to effectively supervise and monitor a population, many of whom are habitual offenders and experts at manipulating people, especially their parole officers.

CAPITAL MURDER MITIGATION INVESTIGATIONS

The pinnacle of casework for a forensic investigator specializing in the psychological and sociological backgrounds of persons is that of a "mitigation specialist." The function of such assignments is to complete a very in-depth psychological, educational, sociological, genealogical, family systems, and other relevant history and factors relating specifically to the defendant. This is a pretrial function primarily, however, also occurring in various stages of postconviction appeal. The time frame for one of these cases typically takes 18 months to 2 years preparation and frequently involves national or even international travel to interview potential witnesses and collect data and records.

The function of the mitigation specialist is a relatively recent component in the judicial system. Subsequent to a series of United States Supreme Court decisions regarding a defendant's right to due process under the Constitution, the role has evolved significantly since 1972. A brief history of the sequence and development of the mitigation role is important to understand the progression and recognition of the critical importance of this work. Unlike the previous discussions on probation and parole presentence investigations, in death penalty cases the sentence when carried out is irrevocable. From 1973—2015, there have been 156 exonerations of death row inmates awaiting execution. That is an average of three exonerations per year from 1973 to 1999 and five exonerations per year from 2000 to 2011 (Death Penalty Information Center, "Facts about the Death Penalty", December 9, 2015).

It is likely that some innocents have been executed, however, that is difficult to pursue officially as the courts are generally reluctant to continue an appellate or investigative process once an execution occurs. It is thought that perhaps as many as 40 such innocents have been executed (Death Penalty Information Center, "Executed But Possibly Innocent", January 2016).

The most seminal United States Supreme Court cases affecting the responsibility of defense counsel and the court to provide due process with respect to defendant background descended from the following cases:

- Furman v. Georgia 408 US. 238, 92 S. Ct. 2726; 33L. Ed. 2d 346; (1972)
  - The court held in Furman that the arbitrary and inconsistent imposition of the death penalty violated the Eighth and Fourteenth Amendments and constituted cruel and unusual punishment. This decision mandates the treatment of each defendant as an individual and that those individual traits must be considered.
- Lockett v. Ohio 438 US. (1978).
  - The court held in a 7—1 decision in favor of Lockett that the Eighth and Fourteenth Amendments required in all but the rarest cases that triers of fact must consider mitigating factors concerning the defendant before deciding whether or not that person should be executed. Such factors might include the defendant's "character or record and any applying circumstances of the offense proffered as a reason for a sentence less than death."
- Ake v. Oklahoma 470 U.S. 68 (1985)
  - In Ake, the court ruled that to provide a "meaningful access to justice" that a defendant was entitled to psychiatric evaluation and assistance in the course of their defense.

- Ford v. Wainwright 477 U.S. 399 (1986)
  - In Ford, the court ruled that to be consistent with "the progress of a maturing society" that executing an insane person did not serve any penological goals and that there must be adequate procedures for determining competency of the defendant. The court ruled that the Eighth Amendment barred states from capital punishment of insane and incompetent persons.
- Atkins v. Virginia 536 US. 304 (2002)
  - In Atkins, the primary issue dealt with intellectual disability. The court ruled that executing people with intellectual disabilities violated the Eighth Amendment's ban on intellectual disability, commonly referred to at the time as "mental retardation." The data on which the Supreme Court relied on was primarily limited to standard intelligence quotient testing. In this case the defendant Daryl Atkins had an IQ of 59. Atkins was sentenced to death and the court reversed.
- Hall v. Florida 134 S. Ct. 1986 (2014).
  - Hall is a derivative case of Atkins in which the court expanded Atkins and thus the more broad definition of intellectual disability to include three functions: (1) "subaverage intellectual functioning" means low IQ scores; (2) a lack of fundamental social and practical skills; and (3) the presence of both conditions must exist prior to age of 18 years. This eliminates the "Bright Line Standard" of an IQ of 70 which was implied by the Atkins decision. This allows for cases in which the individual may have an IQ which is low but above 70 and yet still has an extremely low social or occupational functioning as a result of intellectual defects.

These decisions by the United States Supreme Court and decisions following these emphasize the absolute critical nature of conducting mitigation investigations in a death penalty trial. In 1976, the United States Supreme Court in *Woodson v North Carolina* (428 U.S. 153 1976) stated clearly:

Death, in its finality, differs more from life imprisonment than a 100 year prison term differs from one of only a year or two. Because of that qualitative difference, there is a corresponding difference in the need for reliability in the determination that death is the appropriate punishment in a specific case.

This decision continued the trend in American judicial history that death worthiness in a capital murder case required that there needed to be an individualized determinative process rather than being an automatic death sentence for a given crime without due consideration and evaluation by the sentencing jury.

This individualized requirement is accomplished by an in-depth study of the defendant with respect to previously mentioned inquiries. As Cunningham so aptly defines the role of mitigation in the determination of moral culpability, the role of the mitigation specialist is clearly defined.

Accordingly, what constitutes "mitigation" or lessening of death worthiness maybe anything that a given juror determines is mitigating. Each juror is free to make an independent moral judgment of the sentence that is deserved. The jurors need not be unanimous that a factor is mitigating or agree on the weight to give the factor. The scope of evidence and argument that the defense may assert mitigation is thus exceedingly broad (Cunningham, 2010, p. 31).

The determination of moral culpability is a process by which one takes into account all of the damaging and risk factors that the defendant was subjected to in life up to the point of the offense and how those factors affected the defendant's choice. The greater number of damaging factors results in an increased impairment in the ability to make moral choices. Hence, the lower ability to make a moral choice reduces moral culpability. This is the function of the jury—to make a judgment as to the degree of impairment of the defendant's moral culpability based on his or her psychological, sociological, physiological, or genetic deficits considering the presence of or lack of protective factors in the defendant's life persons with low moral culpability may be held to a different standard that a person who had a higher moral culpability and thus made a much clearer and knowledgeable choice regarding the taking of another human life. There has to be an element of fairness in any sentencing scheme. That fairness is the exclusive providence of the jury (Cunningham, 2010, p. 38).

In 2008, the American Bar Association (ABA) defined the expectations for a capital defense team. These guidelines were devised under the guidance of Russell Stetler, a nationally known Mitigation Specialist. The supplemental guidelines were adopted by the ABA to supplement the guidelines for counsel in death penalty cases (American Bar Association, 2003).

These guidelines thoroughly and succinctly as possible define the role of the forensic investigator as a mitigation specialist and the defense team:

All capital defense teams must be comprised of individuals who, through their experience, training and function, strive to fulfill the constitutional mandate that the sentencer consider all evidence in support of a sentence other than death. Mitigation evidence includes, but is not limited to, compassionate factors stemming from the diverse frailties of humankind, the ability to make a positive adjustment to incarceration, the realities of incarceration and the actual meaning of a life sentence, capacity for redemption, remorse, execution impact, vulnerabilities related to mental health, explanations of patterns of behavior, negation of aggravating evidence regardless of its designation as an aggravating factor, positive acts or qualities, responsible conduct in other areas of life (e.g. employment, education, military service, as a family member), any evidence bearing on the degree of moral culpability, and any other reason for a sentence less than death (Stetler, 2008, p. 679).

In the ABA guidelines, Stetler describes the broad responsibilities of each member of the defense team including the mitigation specialist:

It is counsel's duty to provide each member of the defense team with the necessary legal knowledge for each individual case, including features unique to the jurisdiction or procedural posture. Counsel must provide mitigation specialists with knowledge of the law affecting their work, including an understanding of the capital charges and available defenses; applicable capital statutes and major state and federal constitutional principles; applicable discovery rules at the various stages of capital litigation; applicable evidentiary rules, procedural bars and "door opening" doctrines; and rules affecting confidentiality, disclosure, privileges and protections (Stetler, 2008, p. 681).

The defense team must include individuals possessing the training and ability to obtain, understand and analyze all documentary and anecdotal information relevant to the client's life history. Life history includes, but is not limited to: medical history; complete prenatal, pediatric and adult health information; exposure to harmful substances in utero and in the environment; substance abuse history; mental health history; history of maltreatment and neglect; trauma history; educational history; employment and training history; military experience; multi-generational family history, genetic disorders and vulnerabilities, as well as multi-generational patterns of behavior; prior adult and juvenile correctional experience; religious, gender, sexual orientation, ethnic, racial, cultural and community influences; socio-economic, historical, and political factors.

Mitigation specialists must be able to identify, locate and interview relevant persons in a culturally competent manner that produces confidential, relevant and reliable information. They must be skilled interviewers who can recognize and elicit information about mental health signs and symptoms, both prodromal and acute, that may manifest over the client's lifetime. They must be able to establish rapport with witnesses, the client, the client's family and significant others that will be sufficient to overcome barriers those individuals may have against the disclosure of sensitive information and to assist the client with the emotional impact of such disclosures. They must have the ability to advise counsel on appropriate mental health and other expert assistance.

Team members must have the training and ability to use the information obtained in the mitigation investigation to illustrate and illuminate the factors that shaped and influenced the client's behavior and functioning. The mitigation specialist must be able to furnish information in a form useful to counsel and any experts through methods including, but not limited to: genealogies, chronologies, social histories, and studies of the cultural, socioeconomic, environmental, political, historical, racial and religious influences on the client in order to aid counsel in developing an affirmative case for sparing the defendant's life.

At least one member of the team must have specialized training in identifying, documenting and interpreting symptoms of mental and behavioral impairment, including cognitive deficits, mental illness, developmental disability, neurological deficits; long-term consequences of deprivation, neglect and maltreatment during developmental years; social, cultural, historical, political, religious, racial, environmental and ethnic influences on *behavior; effects of substance abuse and the presence, severity and consequences of exposure to trauma. Team members acquire knowledge, experience, and skills in these areas through education, professional training and properly supervised experience.*

Mitigation specialists must possess the knowledge and skills to obtain all relevant records pertaining to the client and others. They must understand the various methods and mechanisms for requesting records and obtaining the necessary waivers and releases, and the commitment to pursue all means of obtaining records (Stetler, 2008, pp. 682–683).

Failure to perform these standards adequately can be the basis for overturning a conviction (guilt phase) or sentencing (penalty phase) of a person convicted and sentenced under the United States Supreme Court case "*Strickland v Washington*" (466 U.S. 688 1984).

In *Strickland*, the Supreme Court held that a defendant in a capital murder trial has the right to the "effective assistance of counsel." If there is a claim that counsel was ineffective then, there are two components, both of which must be present to render such a claim as "ineffectiveness of counsel." The two components consist of the following:

- First, counsel's performance was "deficient," such that counsel's errors were so serious that counsel was not functioning as the "counsel" guaranteed to the defendant by the Sixth Amendment.
- Second, the deficiency or "ineffectiveness" of counsel's performance was so egregious so as to prejudice the defendant's ability to receive a fair trial.

Counsel has a duty under Strickland and subsequent case law, to "reasonably" engage in a mitigation investigation. As described in the ABA guidelines, such a mitigation investigation is extensive and in depth. Research into at least three generations of family members for all the factors previously described is necessary to be completed as best as possible.

"Ineffectiveness of counsel" is frequently the most common claim in postconviction appellate proceedings. The forensic investigator who acts as a mitigation specialist in these proceedings must have all of the skills and knowledge base of the mitigation specialist that acted at the trial level but also has the increased burden of doing so with cases that may be 20 years old or older. A typical mitigation investigation at both the trial and postconviction appeal level can take thousands of hours.

The forensic investigator specializing in these areas must be dedicated, compassionate, an obsessive researcher and have excellent people skills. Performing as a mitigation specialist requires the ability to not become emotionally involved yet have a deeply trusting relationship with the defendant, knowing the perhaps someday, that person who you have come to know and understand probably better than their parents may suffer the ultimate punishment. This is not a career to enter into lightly.

REFERENCES

American Bar Association. (Summer 2003). 'The guiding hand of counsel': ABA guidelines for the appointment and performance of defense counsel in death penalty cases. *Hoftstra Law Review, 31*(4).

American Probation and Parole Association. (January 1987). In *"Probation pre-sentence investigation", position paper.* www.appa-net.org.

Borum, R., Bartel, P., & Forth, A. (2002). *Structured assessment of violence risk in youth.* (SAVRY) University of South Florida.

Cunningham, M. (2010). *Evaluation for capital sentencing.* Oxford University Press.

Death Penalty Information Center. (December 9, 2015). *Facts about the death penalty.* http://www.deathpenaltyinfo.org/documents/FactSheet.pdf.

Death Penalty Information Center. (January 2016). *Executed but possibly innocent.* http://www.deathpenaltyinfo.org/executed-possibly-innocent.

Stetler, R. (2008). Supplementary guidelines for the mitigation function of defense teams in death penalty cases. *Hofstra Law Review, 36*, 677.

CHAPTER 14

Oklahoma v. Elvis Thacker: Evaluating Victimology, Victim Sexual Assault Evidence, Suspect Torture by Law Enforcement, and the Quality of a Forensic Investigation

Brent E. Turvey

Forensic Criminology Institute, Sitka, Alaska, United States and Aguascalientes, Mexico

CHAPTER OUTLINE

The Plea and the Confession 345
The Evidence, the Confession, and Suspect Torture.. 345
The State of the Case 385
Endnotes 385

In this chapter, we provide forensic reports related to the case of *Oklahoma v. Elvis Thacker*. He and his older brother, Johnathan, have both been convicted of first-degree murder in the sexual homicide of Briana J. Ault. In fact, Jonathan made a plea deal to testify against his brother, in exchange for his life. It is not unreasonable to suggest that his confession, and eventual testimony, served as the primary basis for Elvis' conviction, despite the fact that no physical evidence supported the confession, or Elvis' involvement in the murder, whatsoever.

Briana Ault was no stranger to the Thacker brothers, who were essentially homeless methamphetamine dealers. To be blunt, rumors of Briana's romantic involvement with Elvis surrounded the case, as did questions about her involvement in their business. But the police refused to investigate and disclose that history, instead painting a very different public picture—as though she were all but a stranger to the brothers Thacker. In the process of failing to investigate the victim and any related evidence, and in their zeal to arrest the Thackers, police and prosecutors lost sight of everything that they swore to uphold.

The truth of this case, revealed in a careful examination of the facts and the evidence, has been distorted and abused. But our study of the record can provide an instructional example in the importance of victimology, forensic evidence, and the value of forensic investigation. It can also teach us much more about the role of the police, the reliability of confession evidence, the elements that constitute suspect torture, and suspect rights.

Briana Ault was a 22-year-old white female. At the time of her death, she worked the door at *The Electric Cowboy*, a country themed dance club and bar in Ft. Smith, Arkansas. She worked the door with other employees and was friends with several of her coworkers.

Briana had a prior marriage to Curtis D. Willhite. They married in January of 2009 and divorced in July of 2010. She was also known to have had a prior intimate relationship with Brian Walls, with some witnesses reporting that she had possibly intended to meet with him the night that she was killed.

According to law enforcement interviews with Lacey Ebarb—On September 12, 2010, Lacey Ebarb received a text from Briana Ault at about 11 p.m. Briana was at the Electric Cowboy, and she wanted Lacey to come join her. Lacey arrived at the Electric Cowboy on September 13, 2010, at about 12:15 a.m. They were both at the Electric Cowboy until about 1:15 a.m.

They both left the Electric Cowboy and went to Rooster's Bar, located on Garrison Avenue, also in Fort Smith, Arkansas. Briana drove Lacey to Rooster's Bar in her 2005 orange Chevrolet Cavalier.

At about 2 a.m., Briana told Lacey she had received a text from an ex-boy friend, who needed a ride. Briana told Lacey that her ex-boy friend was going to give her $50.00 to give him a ride. Briana explained to Lacey that she would be back to Rooster's Bar in 15 or 20 min. Lacey said he received a text from Briana's phone at about 4:07 a.m. The text said that Briana's friend got another ride and she was going home to go to bed. Briana's nude body was found in a local pond the next day; her throat had been cut and there were slash marks on her back. Details are reported in Kiger (2012)[1]:

> *Johnathen, 23 along with his older brother Elvis Aaron Thacker, 24, were charged with first degree murder on Sept. 20, 2010 for the Sept. 13, 2010 murder of Briana Jane Ault whose body was found naked in a pond on Texas Road in Pocola.*
>
> *According to affidavits filed in the case, the pair were arrested in Fort Smith, Ark. on Sept. 15, 2010 on an unrelated warrant. During the arrest, Elvis, stabbed Fort Smith Police Department Detective James Melson and was subsequently shot by FSPD Det. Jeff Carter. Reportedly after he was shot, Elvis, told agents with the Oklahoma State Bureau of Investigations who were at the scene, that, "I had Briana's car, so I know I'm f****ed. Yeah I did it."*
>
> *The court documents say that on the following day agents interviewed Johnathan who told them that Elvis had Ault pick the brothers up and drive them to Texas*

> Road where he told her to pull over. Johnathen allegedly stated that Elvis then pulled a knife and forced Ault to take off her clothes and perform sex acts on him. The affidavit goes on in detail about Elvis forcing Ault to wash away evidence in the pond before asking Johnathen to help him drown her. Reportedly Johnathen refused and walked back to the car. He then said Elvis returned to the car alone with blood on his clothing and said he had cut Ault's throat with his knife. The court documents go on to say the brothers then drove to Cedarville, Ark. where they threw the murder weapon and changed their clothes before returning to Fort Smith where they allegedly set Ault's car on fire.

During the law enforcement investigation, Elvis Thacker's cell phone number was found on Briana's call log. This proved that his phone had been in contact with her phone prior to her leaving Rooster's Bar. However, it was determined that both Elvis Thacker and his brother Johnathan had access to the phone in question. This makes it impossible to prove who actually used the phone and when.

The arrest and detention of Johnathan and Elvis Thacker, which occurred on September 15, 2010, is described in the forensic reports that follow.

THE PLEA AND THE CONFESSION

Johnathan's plea agreement, reached in 2014, required that he provide testimony against his brother at trial. This in exchange for dropping forcible sodomy charges against Johnathan and not seeking the death penalty. He testified that he and his brother both raped and murdered Briana Ault on the edge of a pond, in the mud, to include a violent anal assault, in the dark, despite the absence of any supporting physical evidence and despite multiple evidentiary contradictions.

In fact, law enforcement and prosecutors avoided the investigation of the physical evidence in this case almost entirely, likely owing to the circumstances of Elvis Thacker's arrest, which involved deliberate torture.

THE EVIDENCE, THE CONFESSION, AND SUSPECT TORTURE

The author was retained by the defense in this case to conduct a reconstruction of the crime and testified as a forensic expert during the trial of Elvis Thacker. This was reported in Hughes (2016)[2]:

> Confessions Elvis Aaron Thacker made in the 2010 murder of Briana Ault were unreliable because there was no physical evidence to verify them, a private criminologist retained by the defense team testified Wednesday.

Brent Turvey accused the Oklahoma State Bureau of Investigation of "professional abandonment" of the physical evidence gathered by investigators in Ault's murder.

Thacker is charged with first-degree murder and forcible sodomy in the Sept. 13, 2010, death of Ault, 22. Oklahoma is seeking the death penalty for Thacker.

Turvey said once Thacker confessed to cutting Ault's throat and leaving her nude body at a secluded pond just across the state line in Pocola, Okla., agency investigators became disinterested in the physical evidence and made no effort to corroborate Thacker's confessions with the evidence.

Turvey told jurors he was the first person to go through Ault's pockets when he did his assessment of the Oklahoma State Bureau of Investigation's investigation. "That's shocking," he said.

Turvey said in his assessment of the investigation, there was no evidence two perpetrators were involved in the murder as the state alleges. There was no multiple DNA found at the murder scene, no multiple use of weapons, no evidence Ault was restrained, and the sexual nature of the crime wasn't the type that would have multiple perpetrators, he said.

Turvey also accused the Fort Smith Police Department of torturing Thacker by letting him suffer with two gunshot wounds for more than 30 minutes without offering any aid while trying to get him to give a dying confession.

Turvey said he was obligated to report Thacker's treatment by police to the U.S. Department of Justice and to the United Nations under the Istanbul Protocols of 1999, which bars torture and inhuman or degrading punishment. He said he planned to file that report after his testimony. Any confession Elvis Thacker made is invalid because of the torture, Turvey said.

The reports and complaint that follow, supported by multiple forensic experts, are intended to enlighten readers as to the importance of thorough forensic reporting relating to the evaluation of victimology; victim sexual assault evidence; confession evidence; and suspect torture. This is an extreme case, involving extreme behaviors. But its lessons need not be wasted.

FORENSIC EXAMINATION REPORT

Forensic Solutions, LLC
P.O. Box 2175
Sitka, Alaska 99835
Ph: (907) 738-5121

Examiner: Brent E. Turvey, MS, PhD

For: Gretchen Mosley, Attorney
Oklahoma Indigent Defense System (OIDS)
610 South Hiawatha
Sapulpa, OK 74066-4650
Ph. (918) 248-5026

Date: December 30, 2015

Case: *Oklahoma v. Elvis Thacker, Case No. CF-2010-312*

Victim: Briana J. Ault, Jr. (22, WF)

PURPOSE
The purpose of this report is to provide results relating to the forensic examination and analysis of physical evidence in the homicide of 22 YO Briana J. Ault. Her body was found in a pond East of HWY I-12 on Texas Road in Pocola, Oklahoma. Her body was found on Sept. 13, 2010 at 1800hrs, by a fisherman.

As a related matter, this report will also evaluate associated law enforcement crime scene investigation and reconstruction efforts.

DISCOVERY MATERIAL
Starting in mid July of 2014, this examiner was provided with, and relied upon, at least the following discovery materials relating to this case, provided by Attorney Gretchen Mosley of OIDS:

1. Various Oklahoma State Bureau of Investigation investigative (OSBI) reports and summaries;
2. Various Ft. Smith Police Dept. reports and summaries;
3. The Autopsy and Toxicology Report of Briana Ault;
4. Crime scene photos taken by law enforcement and the ME's office;
5. Autopsy photos taken by the ME's office;
6. Law enforcement photos and video of Briana's burned vehicle;

7. Security video (from Greene's Energy Group) from the area near Briana's burned vehicle;
8. Law enforcement videos taken on the night of Elvis and Johnathan Thacker's arrest;
9. Taser video recorded on the night of Elvis and Johnathan Thacker's arrest;
10. Law enforcement photos of the area around the abandoned house (an A-Frame) associated with Elvis and Johnathan Thacker;
11. Various OSBI Crime Lab reports;
12. Photos taken by the defense during in custody evidence examinations;
13. Pretrial hearing transcripts.

It should be noted that this examiner visited the Office of the Medical Examiner in Tulsa, Oklahoma with Gretchen Mosley specifically to examine evidence and retrieve investigative reports and photographs not provided to the defense in discovery. This because the prosecution had apparently failed to request or examine these materials as of that date (e.g., ME Investigate Reports, scene photos, and autopsy photos). This occurred in October of 2014 - meaning that law enforcement investigators and prosecutors had yet to examine or consider this evidence as of that date, some four years after the victim's murder.

It should also be noted that this examiner inspected and photographed much of the physical evidence collected and retained by law enforcement agencies in this case. Much of the evidence inspected, all of which was in police custody, had not been previously opened or examined since the time of its collection. This means that law enforcement investigators and prosecutors had yet to examine or consider this evidence.

The failure to examine and consider the evidence by law enforcement investigators and prosecutors, effectively amounts to forensic abandonment across the board. It further prevents its consideration in the formulation of case theory and the levying of criminal charges. This examiner has not encountered an investigative or forensic lapse to this degree in 18 years of casework.

RELEVANT BACKGROUND
This sections provides contextual background information relevant to the reconstruction of physical evidence analyzed by this examiner.

Victimology
Briana J. Ault was a 22 year old white female (pictured on the right). At the time of her death, she worked the door at *The Electric Cowboy*, a country themed dance club and bar in Ft. Smith, Arkansas.

Briana had a prior marriage to Curtis D. Willhite. They married in January of 2009 and divorced in July of 2010. She was also known to have had a prior intimate relationship with Brian Walls, with some witnesses reporting that she had possibly intended to meet with him the night that she was killed.

On p. 2 of the investigative summary prepared by Robert Walden, the following background information is provided as being generally accurate:

> "On September 12, 2010, [LACEY] EBARB received a text from BRIANA [AULT] about 2300 hours. BRIANA was at the Electric Cowboy and wanted EBARB to come join her. EBARB arrived at the Electric Cowboy on September 13, 2010, about 0015 hours. BRIANA and EBARB were at the Electric Cowboy until about 0115 hours. BRIANA and EBARB left the Electric Cowboy and went to Rooster's Bar, located on Garrison Avenue, Fort Smith, Arkansas.
>
> BRIANA drove EBARB to Rooster's Bar in BRIANA'S 2005, orange, Chevrolet Cavalier. About 0200 hours, BRIANA told EBARB she had received a text from an ex-boy friend, who needed a ride. BRIANA told EBARB that her ex-boy friend was going to give her $50.00 to give him a ride. BRIANA told EBARB she would be back to Rooster's Bar in fifteen or twenty minutes. EBARB said she received a text from BRIANA'S phone about 04:07 hours. The text said that BRIANA'S friend got another ride and she was going home to go to bed. End of information provided by LACEY EBARB.
>
> On September 14, 2010, BRIANA'S Cell Phone Records were requested from her Cell Phone Carrier. On September 15, 2010, the records were received. ELVIS THACKER'S Cell Phone Number was on BRIANA'S Call Detail Records. ELVIS THACKER'S phone had been in contact with BRIANA'S phone prior to BRIANA leaving Rooster's Bar."

Both Elvis Thacker and his brother Johnathan had access to, and used, the cell phone owned by Elvis.

It is known that Briana Ault had a pre-existing relationship with the Thacker brothers that goes back some time, however the precise nature and duration of that relationship does not appear to have been questioned, investigated or established by law enforcement investigators.

Jonathan Thacker Plea Agreement
In April of 2014, Johnathan Thacker plead guilty to the first degree murder of Briana Ault. Johnathan's statements implicate his brother Elvis in that murder. Johnathan's plea agreement requires that he provide testimony against his

brother at trial. This in exchange for dropping forcible sodomy charges against Johnathan and not seeking the death penalty.

The state is seeking first degree murder and forcible sodomy charges against Elvis Thacker. The state is also seeking the death penalty.

EXAMINATIONS

Between October 3-5, 2014, this examiner met with Attorney Gretchen Mosley and others from her office in Poteau, OK. We subsequently visited defendant Elvis Thacker's places of residence, and additionally drove associated routes to the Electric Cowboy, Rooster's Bar, and the pond where the victim's body was ultimately found. This to gain a perspective on distances and spatial relationships. The crime scene was also visited after dark, in order to gain a perspective on lighting and the subsequent ability to drive or walk around under those conditions.

On March 11-12, 2015, this examiner met with Attorney Gretchen Mosley and others from her office to inspect and document the physical evidence in police custody.

FINDINGS

The findings in this case have been made in comportment with the literature on proper scientific methodology for the recognition, preservation, documentation, collection, transportation, testing and interpretation of physical evidence (see generally Edwards and Gotsonis, 2009; Kirk, 1974; NAS, 2002; NAS, 2009; and NIJ, 1999). It is also supported by the education, training, research, publications, and experience of this examiner (see generally Chisum & Turvey, 2012; Crowder & Turvey, 2013; and Turvey, Petherick, & Ferguson, 2010).

The findings are organized as follows:

1. Crime Scene Evidence
2. Evidence of Sexual Assault Related Injury
3. Aunt Vehicle Scene Evidence
4. Suspect Residence (Abandoned A-Frame)
5. Crime Scene Investigation: Nature & Quality
6. Forensic Assessment of Suspect Statements

1. CRIME SCENE EVIDENCE

The crime scene processed in relation to the homicide in this case was an outdoor location adjacent to a wooded area. Briana Ault's body was found in a pond, East of HWY I-12 on TEXAS Rd in Pocola, Oklahoma on Sept. 13, 2010 at

Texas Rd
Pocola, OK 74902

1800hrs. This location is off the main road, accessible by vehicle to a point, in a wooded area near the Arkansas border (general location pictured at the top of the next page; source: Google Maps).

Briana Ault's body was discovered floating face up in a shallow area of the pond. Her throat had been cut by a sharp force weapon. She was nude apart from wearing black socks.

Her body was found at least 31ft. and 7 inches from the side of the narrow dirt road above the pond. A steep path from that road down a muddy embankment is the only means of accessing the pond to reach that location. To be clear, the pond itself cannot be reached by vehicle; one must walk down the embankment, on a steep and uncertain path of mud, to enter the pond water. The depth of the pond is not known, but the bottom is a silty mud.

The following findings can be made in association with the crime scene in this case:

1.1 METHOD OF KILLING
The victim in this case was executed by virtue of having her throat cut. This was accomplished without apparent victim resistance. The available evidence suggests that the victim was surprised by this attack (see discussion in section 2 of this report), and did not see it coming. There is no physical evidence that the victim was involved in a fight or struggle prior to her death.

1.2 LOCATION OF THE DISPOSAL SCENE
The general area of, and the multiple access roads to, the pond would need to be known in advance by anyone traveling there; this location could not easily be found without foreknowledge.

1.3 DISPOSAL METHOD
Precautionary acts refer to behaviors that an offender commits before, during, or after an offense that are consciously intended to confuse, hamper, or defeat investigative or forensic efforts. Precautionary acts are intended to conceal the offender's identity, their connection to the crime, or the crime itself.

The disposal method in this case, dumping the body in a shallow pond in a remote wooded area, suggests a precautionary act. This is based on the following evidentiary considerations:

a. The selection of a secluded location known only to those in the area and difficult to access, increasing the amount of time required to find the body and reveal the homicide.

b. Removing the victim's clothing from the area where the body was found, increasing the amount of time required to locate, identify, and test it for evidence (if this happens at all).

c. Disposing of the body in water, washing away transfer evidence in the hopes of obliterating it.

1.4 TRANSPORT OF THE BODY
There is no evidence that the victim was dragged down the steep path to the pond (e.g., no rolled up socks; drag mark injuries to high points of body/scratches; soil and vegetation ground into hair; or drag marks on the path leading down to the pond); therefore she either walked down naked (in her socks only) or was carried.

There is no evidence that the victim walked down the path herself (e.g., no clothing near the pond; soil and vegetation ground into her socks; scratch marks on her ankles; or injuries to the bottom of her feet).

Given the available evidence, the offender would need to be physically capable of walking down the path to the pond, possibly carrying the victim. This would require an individual capable of navigating the steep angle, the mud, the tree branches, and the constant unpredictable changes in footing. All of this would also need to have been accomplished in the dark.

2. EVIDENCE OF SEXUAL ASSAULT RELATED INJURY

Nudity must always be explained when it is found in association with a crime. In this case, Briana Ault's throat was cut by a sharp force weapon. She was also found nude apart from wearing black socks. In addition, clothing was found on the access roads associated with the pond, but it is not clear whether it belonged to her.

However, the available physical evidence cannot be used to support the conclusion that a forcible sexual attack took place. This finding is based on the areas discussed in this section.

2.1 BODY

There is no evidence of injury on the victim's body that would suggest a forcible sexual attack. This includes the following evidentiary considerations:

a. There is no evidence anal or vaginal trauma.

b. Vaginal swabs taken from the victim were negative for semen.

c. Oral swabs taken from the victim were positive for P30 (semen), but negative for sperm. This indicates the possibility of sexual activity, but without evidence of force. This is consistent with recent consensual sexual activity with an unknown male.

d. There is no evidence of bruising on the victim's arms or legs to suggest that she had been bound, restrained, or held in any fashion.

e. There is no evidence of bilateral blunt force injury to the victim's inner thighs, sometimes associated forcible vaginal penetration.

f. There is no evidence of injury to the victim's face or mouth, to suggest that her mouth had been forcibly covered or that she was forcibly gagged.

g. There is no evidence of injury to the victim's knees, which would be expected if she was on her knees in the woods at night performing oral sex.

h. There is no evidence of defensive injuries to the victim. This means no evidence that she fended off an attacker, armed with a knife or otherwise. This includes an absence of sharp force and blunt force trauma injuries that are expected to the forearms, hands, fingers and fingernails.

i. There is no evidence that the victim struggled with an attacker, either in the water or out of it. This includes an overall absence of blunt force trauma injuries to the victim's body; the absence of defensive injuries; the absence of restraining injuries; the absence of injury to her hands; and the fact that her many piercings (e.g., ear, bellybutton, and eyebrow) are still intact.

j. There is no evidence that the victim aspirated any foreign material into her airway (e.g., water, soil or vegetative material); or that drowning was in any way associated with her cause of death. Additionally, there is no evidence of neck trauma or injury to her face (see autopsy report and crime scene photos). This, along with the overall absence of injury otherwise detailed in this section, combines to indicate that the victim was not forcibly held under water by her attacker in an attempt to drown her.

2.2 BREAST CONTUSION
As described in the autopsy report, there is a "7 x 4 cm red contusion is on the underside of the left breast". However, this injury by itself, in the absence of any other injuries associated with a forcible sexual assault, is not remarkable. It could easily be an artifact associated with the removal of the victim's clothing post-mortem. Certainly this type of injury could result from removing a bra that was still fastened during the pre or postmortem interval.

2.3 INCISED WOUNDS
As described in the autopsy report, "there are three superficial linear incised wounds on the back with minimal to no evidence of hemorrhage" (pictured below left, at the scene). These injuries do NOT appear to correspond with the cuts made to a pink plaid bra (Size 34C) that was found near the pond (pictured below right, during defense evidence viewing, labeled Evidence Item E-1). This is because those cuts would need to be on the victim's front shoulder, or on the shoulder, to correspond with the location of the cut bra straps. It is also important to note that cutting the bra straps would not accomplish the removal of the victim's bra, and that the bra itself was still fastened.

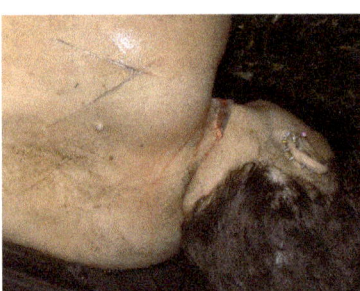

In any event, the absence of hemorrhaging associated directly with the incised wounds, and the lack of defensive injury suffered by the victim, suggest that they were inflicted after the victim was dead. They were also inflicted after the victims bra was removed, otherwise there would be associated cutting to that garment (lower back position) on at least the left strap.

2.4 CLOTHING
It is important to note that a number of items of clothing were collected from alongside the roads leading up to the pond off Texas Road. This entire area was literally a dumping ground for all manner of household and automobile related refuse. Items that can be observed in crime scene photos include carpeting, appliances, vehicle parts, plastic bottles, empty beer cans, blankets, and household garbage. It also includes a variety of discarded clothing items and footwear at multiple spots. This area was not fully photographed or documented, and the collection of clothing from it by law enforcement seems selective. It is ultimately clear from scene photos that much more could be observed than was documented or collected.

Of interest to this examiner is clothing Item E-1, the bra; and clothing item E-3, the black "No Boundaries" tank top, size Large (pictured at the right, during defense evidence viewing). The cuts to these items generally correspond to each other, being generally in the same location. However, this examiner is not aware of definitive evidence that these items belonged to, or were in fact worn by, the victim.

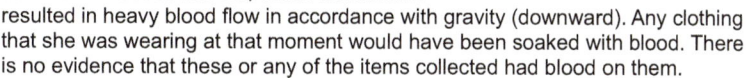

If these items of clothing had been worn by the victim on the night that she was murdered, they would need to have been removed prior to her death. This because of a lack of evident bloodstains on either. The victim's throat was cut, which would have resulted in heavy blood flow in accordance with gravity (downward). Any clothing that she was wearing at that moment would have been soaked with blood. There is no evidence that these or any of the items collected had blood on them.

It is important to stress, however, that while law enforcement records indicate that these and other items of clothing belong to the victim, there is no evidence that this has been confirmed. Not by witnesses and not by physical evidence testing. Therefore, regarding any of these items of clothing as necessarily the victim's is not permissible from a scientific standpoint.

3. AULT VEHICLE SCENE EVIDENCE

Briana Ault's vehicle was driven to a non-residential area. It was driven off the road and subsequently caught fire. It was burned extensively. This examiner visually inspected the evidence collected from this vehicle in police custody and took related photographs.

The available related security video shows only one individual walking, unhindered and without noticeable defect, away from the area where Briana Ault's burning vehicle was found.

The removal and disposal of Briana Ault's vehicle to a non-residential area, and driving it off road, are consistent with a precautionary act. If intentional, the burning of this vehicle would be consistent with a precautionary act as well.

4. SUSPECT RESIDENCE (ABANDONED A-FRAME)

There is no direct physical evidence connecting Elvis Thacker to the murder of Briana Ault. This includes consideration of items of evidence collected from the abandoned A-Frame house searched in relation to both of the Thacker brothers. This is a location where both brothers resided for a period of time prior to the murder.

It is important to note up front that items of clothing were found at this location. However, this examiner is not of the opinion that these items of clothing were worn recently. This given where they were found (outside and exposed to the elements); and their overall state (e.g., covered with mud and vegetation).

4.1 THE JEANS

Two pairs of jeans were pictured and recovered from this location. One was blue, found outside on the ground. The other was grey, found outside hanging from a tree. There is no evidence or indication suggesting any connection with the murder of Briana Ault. This examiner visually inspected these items in police custody, and took related photographs.

This examiner is not aware of any physical evidence associated with these items that connects them to the homicide of Briana Ault.

4.2 THE KNIFE

A folding pocket knife was collected from this location (pictured right). It was located outside, on the ground, with the blade folded out. This examiner visually inspected this item in police custody, and took photographs.

a. The weapon used by the offender to cut Briana Ault's throat inflicted at least two deep incised wound, which would have resulted in heavy blood flow acting in accordance with gravity.

b. The knife collected in association with the location (pictured) was tested by law enforcement for blood. The results were negative.

c. In a case involving heavy blood flow such as this, the suspects hand would be covered with blood, as would be the knife handle and blade. That blood would find its way inside the folding handle of the knife; in-between any metal parts; in-between any metal to wood parts; into any pits or cracks; and it would also soak into the wood itself. There is no evidence of this.

d. Barring immersion in industrial strength cleaner (which would be evident) it is not generally possible to clean this kind of knife such that all traces of blood would be removed under the known circumstances.

e. The blade of this knife is dull along the entire length of the blade. The sharp force weapon used to cut Briana Ault's throat, and back, was actually well sharpened, as indicated by the nature of the wounds.

To sum, there is no physical evidence that this knife was used in relation to the murder of Briana Ault, and some doubt that it could have been used to inflict the woulds on her body at all. Moreover, if it were used in this crime, such evidence would be revealed during a forensic examination.

5. CRIME SCENE INVESTIGATION: NATURE & QUALITY

The nature and quality of the crime scene investigation in this case was poor, and sunk to the level of professional abandonment. Crime scene investigation encompasses crime scene processing efforts, physical evidence examination and testing efforts, and crime reconstruction efforts. There was, ultimately, no effort by police or prosecutors to examine or test the majority of physical evidence in this case, which precludes the ability to accurately reconstruct the crime. This is based on the following facts and evidence (see also NIJ, 1999):

a. Many agencies apparently responded to this crime scene. It is not clear who was at or in the scene at any given time. Or who was allowed in that should not have been. This demonstrates an overall improper professional attitude towards the value of crime scene investigation and physical evidence - crime scene and evidence integrity were not considerations. Lots of agencies were represented and lots of people are pictured at the scene walking around on areas of potential evidence. This becomes more problematic when one considers the limited access points to the scene.

b. Numerous items of potential evidence are undocumented and uncollected (e.g., additional clothing located at the scene). It is, ultimately, unclear why some items of evidence were collected and others were not.

c. The victim's alleged clothes were not examined for trace evidence by law enforcement investigators. In fact they were not examined at all. This examiner was apparently the first to open and examine these items in police custody, subsequent to their collection. This would be years after the fact.

d. The victim's laptop was collected by law enforcement and not examined for related digital evidence.

e. The suspect clothing collected from Elvis and Johnathan Thacker by law enforcement investigators was not examined for trace evidence. This examiner was apparently the first to open and examine these items in police custody, subsequent to their collection. This would be years after the fact.

f. The suspect cell phones collected by law enforcement investigators were not broadly examined for digital evidence subsequent to their initial collection. Records were subpoenaed, but the devices themselves were not subject to a forensic examination. This examiner was apparently the first to open, power, and examine these devices in police custody, subsequent to their collection. This would be years after the fact.

g. This examiner is unaware of any effort by law enforcement to document cell tower information in relation to suspect cell phones collected by law enforcement investigators. This would be helpful to establish the general regions of suspect movement during times associated with suspected criminal activity, especially given then distance between the area where the victim's body was found and the abandoned house searched by law enforcement associated with the suspects.

h. The medical examiner's photos, along with related investigative reports and photos, were apparently not sought out and considered by law enforcement with respect to reconstructing events. This examiner traveled to and received them directly from the ME's office along with defense counsel. This extraordinary step was taken because this forensic evidence had apparently not been requested by the prosecution to be subsequently discovered to the defense. This would be years after the fact.

i. There was no formal attempt by any qualified forensic examiner to reconstruct this homicide prior to leveling charges against the defendant. Rather the physical evidence apparently took a back seat to inculpatory statements made by the defendant's brother, a charged and convicted co-conspirator, as well statements made by the defendant himself.

j. The suspect statements have not generally been investigated or compared to the physical evidence in this case, as majority of the physical evidence has remained unexamined by law enforcement investigators. This

6. FORENSIC ASSESSMENT OF SUSPECT STATEMENTS

Physical and documentary evidence are considered the most reliable and objective data for use in any reconstruction of a crime. Statements made by witnesses, suspects, and even victims are also of value, but only when they are found to comport with, or can be tested against, the known physical or documentary evidence. Consequently, before any statement can be accepted as sufficiently reliable for use in a scientific reconstruction of events, it must be evaluated for quality and context - as is true with any form of evidence.

The quality and context of statements made by Elvis Thacker in police custody, outside of the presence of legal counsel, are such that they are not reliable for use in a scientific reconstruction of events. This period of scientific unreliability begins from the moment that law enforcement approached and breached the residence of Floyd and Carolyn Jones at 5042 South 32nd, Tulsa Square Apartments, Apt. #4, on September 15, 2010.

This determination of scientific unreliability is based on the following facts and circumstances, much of which was recorded in real time (with audio) by a TASER cam, a law enforcement officer cam, and Axon video:

a. Law enforcement approached the residence that evening "under the guise" of being OG&E Employees. They were not dressed in police uniforms. There is further no clear documentary evidence that they identified themselves as being law enforcement prior to or during the breach of the residence.

b. During the breach, Elvis Thacker apparently defended himself against what he believed to be unknown intruders entering through the door, and also through one of the windows, with a knife. He is reported to have injured one of the officers during the breach. The officer received a non-fatal cut wound to the neck which was immediately treated with first aid outside of the apartment.

c. During the breach, Elvis Thacker was shot in the abdomen by law enforcement; tackled and taken to the floor; and also TASED by two separate officers. From that moment, he was in police custody having suffered a potentially mortal wound.

d. Elvis Thacker can bee seen at all times in related videos wearing a metal leg brace. This leg brace was part of the treatment he was receiving for a broken leg, which he apparently suffered in an accident a few weeks prior. The metal brace and related broken leg limited his range of motion, and limited his ability to walk or drive. This examiner inspected the brace, as it was collected as evidence and is currently in police custody.

e. It would be about 30 minutes from the moment of the breach before EMS personnel would enter the residence to give Elvis Thacker medical attention. It is of note that the wounded officer received first aid immediately for a superficial wound during this interval, and Elvis Thacker received no first aid at all. This makes it clear that first aid was available, and that it was apparently withheld for some reason.

f. At all times during this interval, Elvis Thacker was hooked with two separate sets of TASER leads. The distinctive electrical sound of a TASER cycling can be heard on video at multiple points during this interval.

g. Over the next 30 minutes, Elvis Thacker was repeatedly questioned and pressured by different members law enforcement to make inculpatory statements regarding the murder of Briana Ault.

h. At no time during this interval did Elvis Thacker receive either medical attention or basic first aid from law enforcement or anyone else. He lay on the floor bleeding and holding his wound. He appeared, on the video, to go in and out of consciousness. Law enforcement, standing over him, made several verbal attempts to keep him from doing so.

i. During this interval, Elvis Thacker was told by law enforcement that his injuries were likely mortal. On multiple occasions during this interval, law enforcement could also be heard speculating amongst themselves that Elvis Thacker would likely die of his injuries — meaning that this was not an extension of any ruse.

j. One set of TASER leads can been seen being removed from Elvis Thacker when EMS personnel were given entry. Another set of TASER leads were reported to have been identified and removed in the ambulance.

k. This interval of unreliability includes any statements made during Elvis Thacker's transportation to the hospital, prior to receiving the legal counsel.

In the context of having received a mortal wound and no medical care or first aid; being in the immediate custody of armed law enforcement; being hooked up to at least two separate live TASERs; and being repeatedly pressured to make inculpatory statements while also being told that the wounds inflicted are mortal; and all of this occurring over a period of 30 minutes while lying on the floor bleeding - it is not reasonable to accept any statements that are made by defendant under such circumstances as being true or correct. In other words, the quality of these statements is dubious because the environment was threatening to say the least.

The need to compare statements made against the objective record made by the physical evidence becomes all the more important under these kinds of circumstances, as an investigative and forensic consideration. Failure to do so is, to risk repetition, abandonment of both investigative and forensic responsibility.

Should new evidence become available, this examiner would necessarily reconsider any of the related findings in this report.

Brent E. Turvey
MS - Forensic Science
PhD - Criminology

REFERENCES

Chisum, W.J. & Turvey, B. (2012) *Crime Reconstruction*, 2nd Ed., San Diego: Elsevier Science.

Crowder, S. & Turvey, B. (2013) *Ethical Justice: Applied Issues for Criminal Justice Students and Professionals*, San Diego: Elsevier Science.

Kirk, P. (1974) *Crime Investigation*, 2nd Ed., New York: John Wiley & Sons.

NIJ (1999) *Death Investigation: A Guide for the Scene Investigator*, Research Report NCJ 167568. National Institute of Justice, Washington, DC.

Turvey, B., Petherick, W., Ferguson, C. (2010) *Forensic Criminology,* San Diego: Elsevier Science.

FROM THE DESK OF
BRENT E. TURVEY, PHD

May 6, 2016

Criminal Section - Civil Rights Division
U.S. Department of Justice
P.O. Box 66018
Washington, D.C. 20035-6018

Re: *Excessive force, civil rights violations, and human rights violations by agents of law enforcement and public officials in* <u>Oklahoma v. Elvis Thacker (CF-2010-312)</u>

My name is Brent E. Turvey. I am a forensic scientist in private practice, and a published author in the subjects of sex crimes investigation, crime reconstruction, and violent serial crime, among others. I have testified as a forensic expert in dozens of cases, all over the United States. I consult for and provide training to law enforcement agencies not only in the United States, but around the world. I hold a Master's of Science in Forensic Science, and a PhD in Criminology.

The following is a complaint of public corruption, civil rights violations, excessive force, and suspect torture to coerce a confession pursuant to my examination and expert testimony in the above mentioned case. This complaint involves agents of law enforcement from multiple agencies and jurisdictions. Therefore, this complaint necessitates attention from the United States Department of Justice, as well as from the international organizations and State agencies referenced in the CC list provided at the end of this document.

COMPLAINT
On September 15, 2010, agents of the *Oklahoma State Bureau of Investigation* (OSBI); the *Ft. Smith Police Department* (FSPD, Arkansas); and the *Ft. Smith Emergency Medical Service* (EMS; Arkansas) forcibly entered the residence of Floyd and Carolyn Jones in Ft. Smith, Arkansas. They did not identify themselves as law enforcement, but rather were posing as Oil, Gas, and Electric employees. This ruse was used in order to locate, detain and interrogate Elvis Thacker, and his brother Jonathan, as suspects in connection with the September 13, 2010, murder of Briana Ault. No warrants were produced to the suspects at the scene; and law enforcement did not have a no-knock warrant to breach the premises.

The audio and video evidence in this case, recorded by two separate Taser cameras and an Axon body camera, is unequivocal. When law enforcement entered the Jones residence, Elvis Thacker apparently attempted defended himself against intruders that were at the time unknown to him. He injured Det. James Melson in the neck (non-life threatening) with a small knife. He was immediately Tasered. While the Taser was deployed, and while Elvis Thacker was being jolted, he was subsequently shot twice in the abdomen by Det. Jeff Carter. He was not standing when he was shot.

Over the next 40 minutes, various agents of law enforcement entered and exited the scene under the supervision of, and with the awareness of, Agent Shawn Ward of the OSBI. He stood over Elvis Thacker during the majority of the video. No medical attention was provided to Elvis Thacker as he lay on the floor; no first aid was rendered by those present; and the Taser leads remained attached to his body - with the Taser pointed directly at him. During this same timeframe, agents of law enforcement repeatedly told Elvis Thacker that he was going die; and that he should confess to his involvement in the murder of Briana Ault. As he would lose consciousness, law enforcement can be heard rousing him to make a confession.

Those present at the scene believed, and later testified to the belief, that Elvis Thacker was going to die on the floor that day from his wounds. They further testified that the situation was urgent and life threatening, and that they hoped to get a confession from him about his involvement in the death of Briana Ault before he died. In other words, they were primarily concerned with obtaining a "death-bed" confession.

Also seen on the Axon video is Det. James Melson, standing only a few yards outside of the apartment where Elvis Thacker lay near death. He can be observed only minutes after the shooting receiving first aid for his injury by no fewer than three individuals. At trial, Det. Melson testified he was also given quick-clot (or some) variant by, and from the first aid kit of, OSBI Agent Shawn Ward. This negates any suggestion that EMS was unavailable to treat Elvis Thacker during the 40 minutes of video that was shot in the apartment.

Mr. Thacker survived these events and was arrested. Subsequently, there was a concerted effort by law enforcement to conceal the video evidence in this case from the defense and the public; as well as to conceal their failure to identify themselves as law enforcement and render aid to Mr. Thacker. This was done by virtue of courtroom testimony and statements made to the public about the existence of, and eventual content of, the law enforcement videos in this case.

This forensic examiner was hired by Defense Attorney Gretchen Mosley of the Oklahoma Indigent Defense System (OIDS) to examine the investigation, evidence, and suspect statements in this case. Subsequent expert testimony was offered at the trial of Elvis Thacker in April of 2016 which asserts and expands upon the evidence provided with this complaint. However, this examiner delayed making this formal external complaint until the conclusion of Mr. Thacker's trial in order to preserve due process, and to await any additional testimony or evidence from law enforcement that might explain their conduct when arresting and interrogating Elvis Thacker. And to allow other mandated reporters in this case the opportunity to come forward. None of this was forthcoming, necessitating this complaint.

Contextually, it should be noted that a number of the OSBI agents involved in this case were previously employed by the Ft. Smith Police Department. Furthermore, the Ft. Smith Police Department currently has numerous whistleblower complaints and lawsuits filed against it from former officers, as well as numerous recent scandals associated with officer misconduct. To be clear, even the most superficial inquiry reveals a department with integrity problems across the board.

The case of Elvis Thacker involves excessive force, torture, and false or misleading testimony from law enforcement and prosecutors. This resulted in civil rights and human rights violations against Mr. Thacker, evidencing systemic public corruption across multiple law enforcement agencies in Oklahoma and Arkansas.

EXPERT FINDINGS
Attached to this report are the findings and professional CVs of three forensic examiners. They are are as follows:

1. Forensic Examination Report by Brent E. Turvey, PhD (Forensic Scientist; court qualified in the United States as an expert in criminology, crime reconstruction, crime scene analysis, and related areas);

2. Forensic Psychologist's report by Aurelio Coronado Mares (Forensic Psychologist from Aguascalientes, Mexico; court qualified in Mexico by the Supreme Court in Forensic Psychology, Torture Evaluations, and related areas);

3. Investigative and Forensic Report by Lic. Manuel Esparza Navarrete (Former attorney general's prosecutor and law enforcement investigator from Juarez, Mexico with experience working with U.S. Law enforcement agencies such as the FBI; and experience presenting reports to the Inter-American Human Rights Commission within the *Organization of American States* in Washington, D.C.).

The reports collectively outline the specific nature of the physical and psychological *torture* inflicted on Elvis Thacker; the psychological elements, context and consequences of the *torture* evident in this case; the investigative and forensic consequences of using *torture* to induce a confession in this case; and the international human rights violations that are evident in this case.

From these reports, the extent of civil rights violations related to The United States Constitution and related State Constitutions becomes immediately apparent.

LAW ENFORCEMENT AGENCIES AND ACTORS

One of the purposes of this memo is to identify the agencies and individuals responsible for *torturing* Elvis Thacker, as well as those that have helped to obscure related events in the following years through false or misleading testimony; and false or misleading information provided to the public through the media. They include at least the following, whose pretrial and/or trial testimony in this case, and/ or statements to the press, and related conduct, should be investigated:

- Agent Shawn Ward, OSBI
- Agent Tammy Ferrari, OSBI
- Agent Beth Green, OSBI
- Officer Kyle Story, FSPD
- Det. James Melson, FSPD
- Det. Jeff Carter, FSPD
- Det. Michael Warren, FSPD
- Cpl. Eric Williams, FSPD (former; left FSPD on "bad" terms)
- Sgt. Dawn Sprayberry, FSPD
- Veronica Harris, Ft. Smith EMS, Arkansas
- Daniel Shue, Prosecutor, Sebastian County, Arkansas
- Jeff Smith, LeFlore County District Attorney, Oklahoma
- Margaret Nicholson, Oklahoma Office of the District Attorney, 16th Dist.

MATERIALS PROVIDED

It is requested that the DOJ open an independent inquiry into the shooting and subsequent *torture* of Elvis Thacker, given the multiple states and jurisdictions involved; and also given that no independent review of this shooting has occurred to date that is inclusive of examining the available testimony of officers at the scene, in conjunction with *all* of the video evidence. In fact, it seems clear that every effort has been made to keep this from happening on the part of law enforcement; and that false statements have been made to the public, via the media, regarding the content and the existence of the videos, by those involved. To that end, please find the following included with this complaint:

1. Pretrial hearing transcripts in *Oklahoma v. E. Thacker*;

2. Multiple taser-cam videos recorded by law enforcement on the night of Elvis Thacker's arrest and detention;

3. Axon video recorded by law enforcement on the night of Elvis Thacker's arrest.

4. The Forensic Examination Report and CV of Brent E. Turvey, PhD, dated 12/30/15; admitted as evidence with corresponding expert testimony in *Oklahoma v. Elvis Thacker*.

5. The Forensic Psychologist's report on the torture and interrogation of Elvis Thacker by Aurelio Coronado Mares, dated 5/5/16.

6. The Investigative and Forensic Report on the torture and interrogation of Elvis Thacker by Lic. Manuel Esparza Navarrete, dated 5/4/16.

Trial transcripts should also be requested and examined, though these are not available to my office as of this date.

PUBLIC DISCLOSURE
This documentation, including the aforementioned expert forensic reports and the videos of the shooting and torture of Elvis Thacker (one of which has already been released to the media by the prosecution), have all been simultaneously provided to the media. They have also been made available to the public via social media as of the date of this complaint. This in no way violates any restrictions on the material as it has been made public via Elvis Thacker's criminal trial, and admitted as evidence in that case along with my expert testimony and report. This has been done to ensure mutual transparency and accountability.

Please do not hesitate to contact me with any questions, or to inquire about further documentation and evidence that may be available.

Respectfully,

Brent E. Turvey
MS - Forensic Science; PhD - Criminology

CC list:

Office of the Inspector General, U.S. Department of Justice, 950 Pennsylvania Avenue, N.W., Suite 4706, Washington, D.C. 20530-0001

FBI Field Office - Oklahoma City, Attn: Civil Rights Division, 3301 West Memorial Road, Oklahoma City, OK 73134-7098

FBI Field Office - Little Rock, Attn: Civil Rights Division, 24 Shackleford West Boulevard, Little Rock, AR 72211-3755

Scott Pruitt, Oklahoma Attorney General's Office, Attn: Civil Rights Division, 313 NE 21st Street, Oklahoma City, OK 73105

Leslie Rutledge, Attorney General's Office, Attn: Civil Rights Division, 323 Center Street, Suite 200, Little Rock, Arkansas 72201

Inter-American Human Rights Commission, Organization of American States, 1889 F St. N.W., Washington, DC, U.S.A. 20006

Human Rights Council, Office of the United Nations High Commissioner for Human Rights (OHCHR), Palais des Nations, CH-1211 Geneva 10, Switzerland

Attorney Gretchen Mosley, Oklahoma Indigent Defense System (OIDS), 610 South Hiawatha, Sapulpa, OK 74066-4650 (Attorney for Elvis Thacker)

Forensic Psychological Analysis

Proyecto Ciencia Aplicada
Fco. I. Madero #333 Int. #301
Zona Centro 20020
Aguascalientes, Ags., México

For:
    Brent E. Turvey, PhD
    Forensic Solutions, LLC
    P.O. Box 2175   Sitka, Alaska 99835
    Ph: (907) 738-5121
    Email: bturvey@ forensic-science.com

Examiner:
    Aurelio Israel Coronado Mares
    Private Forensic Expert;
    Director - Applied Science Project
    Ph: +52 (449) 189 9978
    Email: aureliocoronado@hotmail.com

Date: May 05, 2016

Case:
    Oklahoma v. Elvis Thacker, No. CF-2010-312

PURPOSE

I'm a Forensic Psychologist with ten years of experience working with victims of violence; five of them have been dedicated to participating as an expert witness in cases of torture where police and military are involved. These assessments have been carried out according to the *Istanbul Protocols*. **This is the definitive international guide issued by the** United Nations for the effective investigation and documentation of *torture and other cruel, inhuman or degrading treatment or punishment.*

In my practice, I specialize in the psychological aspects of torture: on the effects of those who have suffered it; the psychosocial dynamics that support it; and the variables involved in the testimony or confessions obtained under related interrogations. In this regard, I am co-author of a book that approaches this and related matters (*Protocols of Criminal Investigation*, Forensic Press, 2016). I am also regularly invited to give lectures and training by the Supreme Court pf Mexico related to these Protocols, for those who administer justice in matters that involve the constitutive acts of torture and degrading treatment throughout the country.

Currently, I'm also working on the development of a protocol for the forensic psychological evaluation of torture with the National Board of Forensic Psychology in Mexico.

As a result of my publications, casework, and testimony, Brent Turvey Ph.D. asked me to review the material related to the arrest and detention of Elvis Thacker. This with respect to the events which took place on September 15, 2010. He asked me to conduct this assessment when we met in Atlanta in early April of 2016.

MATERIALS

I was provided with, and relied upon, at least the following materials:

1. Pretrial hearing transcripts in Oklahoma v. E. Thacker;
2. Two different taser-cam videos recorded by law enforcement on the night of Elvis Thacker's arrest;
3. Axon Video recorded by law enforcement on the night of Elvis Thacker's arrest;
4. The Forensic Examination Report of Brent E. Turvey, PhD, dated 12/30/15 (admitted as evidence along with Dr. Turvey's expert testimony in Oklahoma v. Elvis Thacker in late April of 2016).

FORENSIC PSYCHOLOGICAL FINDINGS

From the analysis of the material, and in light of the scientific literature, and best practices in forensic psychological assessment, it is possible to affirm the following:

1. The actions of the officers involved constitute *torture* against Elvis Thacker.

Torture is defined as any form of intentional damage caused, and the violation of the Human Rights of individuals, in order to obtain information or induce confessions. Torture is therefore an activity engaged in by authorities aimed to break the will and the ability of decision-making, in order to force the victim into saying or doing something to help authorities achieve their purposes.

From the *Convention against Torture and other Cruel, Inhuman or Degrading Treating or Punishments* (1984) the term torture is defined as:

> **Any act by which severe pain or suffering, whether physical or mental, is intentionally inflicted on a person for such purposes as obtaining from him or a third person information or a confession,** punishing him for an act he or a third person has committed or is suspected of having committed, or intimidating or coercing him or a third person, or for any reason based on discrimination of any kind, when such pain or suffering is inflicted by or at the instigation of or with the consent or acquiescence of a public official or other person acting in an official capacity. It does not include pain or suffering arising only from, inherent in or incidental to lawful sanctions.

Threatening harm or death constitutes torture; deliberate postponement of medical care constitutes torture; and using or threatening to use devices that give electrical shocks (e.g., a Taser gun) constitutes torture.

In the arrest of Elvis Thacker it can be seen on video that the following occurred:

a. There is a violent breach into a residence performed by police forces.
b. **There is a major disadvantage of strength between the officers and Elvis Thacker,** who is exceeded in number and physical abilities since he was wearing a metal prosthesis on one leg due to a recent injury when the breach occurs.
c. Elvis Thacker is subjected to violent verbal and physical attacks including the use of TASERS GUNS, the use of which remained steady over about 30 minutes causing visible injuries.
d. During the breach, Elvis Thacker attempted to defend himself, causing injuries to an officer who immediately received paramedical attention and was pulled to safety. Such paramedical care was restricted to Elvis Thacker for a period of approximately 30 minutes.
e. During the period between the submission and the paramedics arrival, Elvis Thacker lay dying on the floor. At times he lost consciousness and could barely

breathe. Meanwhile, he was interrogated by the investigators who made suggestive questions based on incriminatory information, for which they were seeking confirmation.

f. Aware of the seriousness of the health status of Elvis Thacker, officials conditioned medical attendance in exchange for a confession, saying repeatedly: "…This is your chance, take this chance…".

In summary, law enforcement from multiple agencies interrogated a man lying on the floor attached to two Tasers, with two critical gunshot wounds, having suffered electrical shocks, and withheld medical care from him - all while telling him repeatedly that he would not likely survive. This is precisely the definition of torture. The Istanbul Protocols note that: Perpetrators often attempt to justify their acts of torture and mistreatment by the "need" to obtain information. And that's what happened for 30 minutes. The agents involved insisted on treating Elvis Thacker like he was in any reasonable condition to answer their questions while he was, according to their own perception: "about to die". There is no legal, logical or ethical justification for this behavior.

2. Any information or "confession" which might come from Elvis Thacker during these events may not be reliable as evidence to be used later in a trial.

Torture produce psychological effects that rule out the usefulness of anything the victim says under that condition. The deep state of helplessness causes into the individual a loss of the thinking skills and the willingness to resist to what is being asked. In other words, torture activates mechanisms related to survival. Anxiety blocks the thought processes and consciousness and lead to erratic behavior characterized by submission to the other (O'Mara, 2015).

The sensation of imminent danger (aka - fear) caused by thinking about the legitimate and imminent possibility of dying, such as the fact that you have been shot twice by your captors and realizing what they want is a "confession", generates states of behavior related to survival (Mobbs, 2007). This instead of the evocation of memory or consciousness of past acts. In other words, a victim of torture is in immediate fear for their life and will do whatever it takes to survive, telling those responsible anything that they want to hear in order to survive.

We can represent the different types of behaviors and emotional reactions related to threatening situations as follows:

	Type of threat		
	Potential	**Remote**	**Actual**
Behavior	Risk estimation	Freezing	Scape/fight
Emotion	Anxiety	Fear	Panic

Panic is a state of extreme anxiety before a serious death threat and expresses with clinical indicators included in DSM-IV such as:

1. Palpitations, pounding heart, or accelerated heart rate
2. Sweating
3. Trembling or shaking
4. Feeling of choking or shortness of breath,
5. Feeling of choking,
6. Chest pain or discomfort,
7. Nausea or abdominal discomfort,
8. Instability, dizziness or fainting;
9. Derealization or depersonalization,
10. Fear of losing control or going crazy,
11. Fear of dying,
12. Paresthesias

In accordance with what we know about torture and related anxiety about the fear of imminent death, Elvis Thacker was hardly understanding what was asked by his interrogators. This is why he did not answer the majority of their questions. He was reacting in a disorganized fashion with his limited resources to the questions and requests being made. While his interrogators were focused on solving their murder case, Elvis Thacker could only react to the fear and anxiety he suffered as the result of what he believed to be his imminent death. Additionally, his injuries were critical to the point of causing him to lose consciousness repeatedly, making his ability to comprehend, comply or respond even less reliable.

In this case, there was physical injury-related pain. Of that there can be no question. But let us suppose for a moment that this physical pain was not present; that everything was circumstantial. Yet there were threats of imminent death, officials announced that he would die, and Elvis Thacker was receiving information - while he was in shock - that he was not get out of that room alive. Contemporary research tells us that such situations generate psychological effects that invalidate any statement that could be issued during and after the process, because fear and anxiety from and threats generate the same effects as physical torture (Reyes, 2007).

Finally, the effects of torture are not limited to the moments of detention and interrogation. The transition from the state of helplessness to the recovery of normal cognitive abilities is not immediate subsequent to release from captors. After being in such state of helplessness, danger of death, and shock, those subjected to torture must receive impartial medical and psychological care (Somnier, 1992). Until this occurs, none of what they say can be trusted on its own.

Therefore, law enforcement, prosecutors, and the courts recognize what ethical psychologists have established in the literature cited throughout this report: we cannot rely on statements from victims of torture, especially if they have not been protected by legitimate legal representation. This is because their condition of physical and mental instability, which necessarily results from physical and/or psychological suffering. As a consequence, confessions coerced under such circumstances must be considered unworthy as evidence for a trial.

CONCLUSIONS

1. The actions taken, and not taken, by officers in this case constitute t*orture* according to the UN's definition because of the extreme suffering imposed on Elvis Thacker in order to obtain inculpatory statements.

2. There is a total lack of reliability with respect to the statements provided, since Elvis Thacker was agonizing and often unconscious when the interrogation was performed by law enforcement. From the evidence provided in the videos, there is not guarantee of minimum level of mental capability to make reliable depositions by Elvis Thacker. It is not only ridiculous and even criminal to interrogate someone under these circumstances, but completely unethical to suggest that any resulting statements are reliable for courtroom purposes.

Should further evidence and information become available, this examiner would necessarily examine it for the purposes of revisiting and revising the opinions expressed in this report.

Aurelio Israel Coronado Mares

REFERENCES

O'Mara, S. (2015). *On the Imposition of Torture, an Extreme Stressor State, to Extract Information From Memory. Zeitschrift für Psychologie.*

Reyes, H. (2007). *The worst scars are in the mind: psychological torture.* International Review of the Red Cross, 89(867), 591-617.

Mobbs, D., Petrovic, P., Marchant, J. L., Hassabis, D., Weiskopf, N., Seymour, B., ... & Frith, C. D. (2007). "When fear is near: threat imminence elicits prefrontal-periaqueductal gray shifts in humans". *Science*, 317(5841), 1079-1083.

Somnier, F., Vesti, P., Kastrup, M., & Genefke, I. K. (1992). *Psycho-social consequences of torture: current knowledge and evidence.*

Investigative and Forensic Analysis

Institute of Forensic Investigation and Criminal Profiling
Canal de la Mancha 296
Fracc. Magnolias
Juarez, Chihuahua, Mexico 32424

For: Brent E. Turvey, PhD
Forensic Solutions, LLC
P.O. Box 2175
Sitka, Alaska 99835

Ph: (907) 738-5121
Email: bturvey@ forensic-science.com

Examiner: Lic. Manuel Esparza Navarrete
Prosecutor, Attorney General's Office - Chihuahua (retired);
Director - Criminal Investigation Program,
Institute of Forensic Investigation and Criminal Profiling

Ph: 011.52.656.418.7390
Email: mesparza@investigadoresforenses.com

Date: May 4, 2016

Case: Oklahoma v. Elvis Thacker, No. CF-2010-312

PURPOSE

I am a former prosecutor with 12 years of experience at the Attorney General´s Office in the State of Chihuahua, México. In my position, I conducted criminal investigations and prosecutions for several different units within the AG´s Office. This includes the Women´s Homicide Unit and the Organized Crime Homicide Unit. I also served as a supervisor to multiple Prosecutors, Investigators, and Forensic Scientists at the State Crime Lab in Juarez.

While working as Investigations Coordinator for the Women´s Homicide unit in Juarez México, I also filed and presented reports in person before the Secretary of Exterior Relations in Mexico City and the Inter-American Human Rights Commission of the *Organization of American States* in Washington, D.C. related to these particular cases, assisting the Chihuahua Attorney General.

I have extensive experience working with law enforcement, and within the Justice System, in the United States. From 1995 to 1998, I served with the Legal Attaché's Office for the Attorney General of Mexico, stationed in El Paso, Texas. From 1995 to 2014, I further served as the liaison for the AG´s Office with multiple Federal, State, and Local Law Enforcement Agencies in the United States - including the Federal Bureau of Investigation (FBI).

I have worked with Dr. Turvey for the past two years in his capacity as Director of the Criminal Profiling Program at the Institute of Forensic Investigation and Criminal Profiling. We have also co-authored a textbook on the subject of applied investigative and forensic analysis together.

In March of 2016, I was contacted by Dr. Turvey in his capacity as caseworker with Forensic Solutions, LLC, to examine the facts and evidence related to the arrest and detention of Elvis Thacker. This event occurred on September 15, 2010, when law enforcement breached the home of Floyd and Carolyn Jones at 5042 South 32nd, Tulsa Square Apartments, Apt. #4 in Ft. Smith, Arkansas. The purpose of this report is to relate my investigative, forensic and other related legal opinions.

MATERIALS
I was provided with, and relied upon, at least the following materials from the office of Brent E. Turvey, PhD of Forensic Solutions, LLC:

1. Pretrial hearing transcripts in *Oklahoma v. E. Thacker*.

2. Two short taser-cam videos recorded by law enforcement on the night of Elvis Thacker's arrest.

3. The Axon Video recorded by law enforcement on the night of Elvis Thacker's arrest.

4. The *Forensic Examination Report* of Brent E. Turvey, PhD, dated 12/30/15.

INVESTIGATIVE AND FORENSIC FINDINGS
After reviewing the aforementioned videos, it is evident that, Elvis Thacker was shot at twice by law enforcement. He was subject to electric shocks from at least two different taser guns - one before and one while he was being shot. This occurred without law enforcement identifying themselves to Mr. Thacker prior to a forced breach.

1. **Elvis Thacker should have been given immediate medical attention subsequent to being shot multiple times and shocked with a taser;**

medical attention was intentionally withheld from him by law enforcement.

In my experience, after he was shot and tased, law enforcement personnel at the scene had a duty to immediately procure medical attention for Mr. Thacker. Unfortunately, it is evident in the video that he did not receive any first aid or medical attention until more than a half an hour after he was critically injured. Worse, law enforcement left the taser probes attached to him while he was then interrogated.

Police officers can even be heard saying that Mr. Thacker "Is not going to make it", referring to the fact that he might die. All this while rescue personnel are right outside the residence tending to a person that can be seen standing up and conscious.

2. **Elvis Thacker's life was intentionally placed at risk by the actions of law enforcement in order to coerce a "deathbed confession".**

The actions of law enforcement personnel at the scene placed Mr. Thacker's life at risk. Whether intentional, due to ignorance, or due to a lack of training, they created the circumstances for a deathbed confession at the expense of Mr. Thacker's health, risking his life. However, these circumstances were CREATED by law enforcement personnel.

Instead of getting Mr. Thacker medical attention, which can be observed to be available just outside his apartment, multiple law enforcement agents took advantage of these circumstances in an attempt to coerce a confession. Mr. Thacker had to endure violence, pain, stress, shock and risk of death in exchange for information. There is no excuse for such behavior on the part of any ethical agent of law enforcement.

3. **Any statements made under the conditions observed, which include physical and psychological torture, are not reliable, and furthermore should not be considered admissible in any court of law. This is basic procedural knowledge that any investigator or prosecutor can be expected to be aware of.**

This is in accordance with *Article 1*, paragraph 1 of the *United Nations Convention against Torture and Other Cruel, Inhuman or Degrading Treatment or Punishment* (UNCATOCIDTP), which describes the elements of torture.

UNCATOCIDTP Article 1

"1. For the purposes of this Convention, the term "torture" means any act by which severe pain or suffering, whether physical or mental, is intentionally inflicted on a person for such purposes as obtaining from him or a third person information or a confession, punishing him for an act he or a third person has committed or is suspected of having committed, or intimidating or coercing him or a third person, or for any reason based on discrimination of any kind, when such pain or suffering is inflicted by or at the instigation of or with the consent or acquiescence of a public official or other person acting in an official capacity. It does not include pain or suffering arising only from, inherent in or incidental to lawful sanctions."

The presence of these elements should render any related statements or confessions from Mr. Thacker inadmissible in Court.

4. **The severity of the conduct observed requires any law enforcement agent or prosecutor that observed this event, or became aware of it in the course of their official duties, to open or refer the actions of those involved to independent administrative and criminal inquiries. This cannot be reliably accomplished with an internal investigation.**

If a situation like this had taken place under my supervision, or if this case had been presented to me as a prosecutor, I would not have risked taking such evidence before a Judge. This because the video evidence in this case clearly shows law enforcement agents torturing Mr. Thacker. I would have been obligated to make an official complaint against the officers and investigators involved for not providing immediate medical attention to the suspect and for prolonging his pain and suffering in order to coerce information from him.

5. **The actions of law enforcement and prosecutors this case are in violation of at least Articles 1, 2, 5, 7 and 11 paragraph 1 of the *Universal Declaration of Human Rights (UDHR)*.**

UDHR - Article 1.
The actions of law enforcement at the scene demonstrate that Elvis Thacker's life was not considered as, or treated as, equal to that of others present. He was denied medical care, and basic first aid, for at least 40 minutes. This despite life threatening injuries that law enforcement believed would result in his death. However, medical care was given to Officer Melson for non-life threatening injuries by at least three individuals. All of this during the same timeframe.

This is a violation of *Article 1*, which states: "All human beings are born free and equal in dignity and rights. They are endowed with reason and conscience and should act towards one another in a spirit of brotherhood."

UDHR - Article 2.
During his arrest Mr. Thacker was shot, tased and left without medical attention for more than a half an hour after sustaining life threatening injuries.

This violates his right to security of person, per *Article 2*, which states: "Everyone has the right to life, liberty and security of person."

The psychological mistreatment, pain, shock and suffering being endured by Mr. Thacker while being questioned to obtain information, and also while withholding medical attention, definitely show he was subjected to torture by Law Enforcement - depriving of his liberty and security in an attempt to deprive him of his life.

UDHR - Article 5.
There can be no question that withholding medical attention in exchange for a confession, in the context of being connected to multiple taser leads, being told that you are going to die, and without legal representation, constitutes torture.

Consequently, law enforcement violated *Article 5*, which states: "No one shall be subjected to torture or to cruel, inhuman or degrading treatment or punishment."

UDHR - Article 7.
Law enforcement agents and then prosecutors should have provided Elvis Thacker with the protection of law. This did not happen since he was abused and tortured when arrested. Matters were made worse by prosecutors taking this case to trial, with evidence obtained in violation of the law as well as in violation of his basic human rights.

In doing so, law enforcement and prosecutors violated *Article 7*, which states: "All are equal before the law and are entitled without any discrimination to equal protection of the law. All are entitled to equal protection against any discrimination in violation of this Declaration and against any incitement to such discrimination."

UDHR - Article 11.
According to Article 11, "Everyone charged with a penal offence has the right to be presumed innocent until proved guilty according to law in a public trial at which he has had all the guarantees necessary for his defense."

The conduct of law enforcement and prosecutors at all times in this case suggests that he was never considered anything but guilty, which seems to have emboldened their behavior with respect to violating his civil and human rights. By admitting his coerced statements as evidence, and by seeking to deprive the defense of evidence that might suggest his innocence, the police and prosecution have violated this presumption and its related legal guarantees.

6. **The actions of law enforcement and prosecutors this case are in violation of at least Articles 2, 10, 11, 12 and 15 of the United Nations Convention Against Torture and Other Cruel, Inhuman or Degrading Treatment or Punishment (UNC).**

    UNC - Article 2.
    The article reads: "1. Each State Party shall take effective legislative, administrative, judicial or other measures to prevent acts of torture in any territory under its jurisdiction. 2. No exceptional circumstances whatsoever, whether a state of war or a threat of war, internal political instability or any other public emergency, may be invoked as a justification of torture. 3. An order from a superior officer or a public authority may not be invoked as a justification of torture."

    Whether with intent, omission, gross negligence or under orders from a supervisory agent, torture was performed on Mr. Thacker's person, even though there are laws in existence to prevent and punish this kind of conduct.

    UNC - Article 10.
    The article reads: "1. Each State Party shall ensure that education and information regarding the prohibition against torture are fully included in the training of law enforcement personnel, civil or military, medical personnel, public officials and other persons who may be involved in the custody, interrogation or treatment of any individual subjected to any form of arrest, detention or imprisonment. 2. Each State Party shall include this prohibition in the rules or instructions issued in regard to the duties and functions of any such person."

    At the scene, agents of multiple law enforcement agencies can be observed walking in and around Elvis Thacker as he lay suffering and near death on the floor. None seem concerned or burdened with exigent purpose to locate or render any kind of immediate medical attention. Rather, they focus on coercing a confession. The fact that this seems normal to all present, and not a cause for concern, demonstrates that they have had no formal training in what torture is and why to avoid employing it on criminal suspects. Quite the opposite seems true, in fact.

    UNC - Article 11.
    The article reads: "Each State Party shall keep under systematic review interrogation rules, instructions, methods and practices as well as

arrangements for the custody and treatment of persons subjected to any form of arrest, detention or imprisonment in any territory under its jurisdiction, with a view to preventing any cases of torture."

I have experience dealing with Law Enforcement Agencies in the United States, and having received training from several of them. I´m therefore quite aware that there is education, training and protocols as to the lawful execution arrests, detention and imprisonment of individuals. As well as for in custody interrogations and the treatment that those in custody may be subjected to in these situations.

The actions carried out against Mr. Thacker by law enforcement cannot be justified as resulting merely from lack of knowledge or training on part of Law Enforcement. That is, unless they are willing to admit that their officers are poorly trained in such matters across the board, which would lead to the conclusion that they are unfit to interact with the general public they are supposed to protect and serve.

UNC - Article 12.
The article reads: "Each State Party shall ensure that its competent authorities proceed to a prompt and impartial investigation, wherever there is reasonable ground to believe that an act of torture has been committed in any territory under its jurisdiction."

To the best of my knowledge, at the time and date this report was written, there have not been any independent or impartial investigations into the actions and omissions of law enforcement personnel, with respect to bringing potential charges against them for the attack that they committed against Mr. Thacker's person. An internal investigation appears to have been performed by Ft. Smith Police, but this is akin to someone grading their own homework. It does not meet the criteria for impartial.

UNC - Article 15
The article reads: "Each State Party shall ensure that any statement which is established to have been made as a result of torture shall not be invoked as evidence in any proceedings, except against a person accused of torture as evidence that the statement was made."

During investigation and trial, the statements coerced from Mr. Thacker were used and presented as a valid and admissible confession. This occurred despite clear evidence that these statements were coerced under conditions that constitute torture - being shot, tased, and told he was going to die while denying medical attention. These facts alone, in accordance with International Law, should have rendered his statements or any alleged "confession" inadmissible. To say nothing of being spurned by any reputable prosecutor's office.

7. **The actions of law enforcement and prosecutors this case are in violation of at least Articles 1, 2, 3, 5 and 6 of the *United Nations Code of Conduct for Law Enforcement Officials (UNCCLEO)*.**

   UNCCLEO - **Article 1.**
   The article reads: "Law enforcement officials shall at all times fulfill the duty imposed upon them by law, by serving the community and by protecting all persons against illegal acts, consistent with the high degree of responsibility required by their profession."

   Law enforcement Officials failed to provide Mr. Thacker with the basic protections any individual should expect from them, whether they are a victim or a suspect. This by virtue of torturing him and denying him medical attention.

   UNCCLEO - **Article 2.**
   The article reads: "In the performance of their duty, law enforcement officials shall respect and protect human dignity and maintain and uphold the human rights of all persons."

   Mr. Thacker's basic human rights were violated with the actions of Law Enforcement Officials with respect to torturing him, and by failing to hold those among their ranks who coerced his statements to any account.

   UNCCLEO - **Article 3.**
   The article reads: "Law enforcement officials may use force only when strictly necessary and to the extent required for the performance of their duty."

   In my view, law enforcement's use of force on Mr. Thacker case should be deemed excessive, since he can be seen on video wearing a full leg brace which restricts full mobility. This because of his recently broken leg. He was shot twice, but after already being tased once. Then tased a second time. Most of this happened after he was already down. Three officers responded with three different levels of force one after the other, suggesting a lack of training, planning and unity of purpose.

   To put it another way, once Elvis Thacker has been tased, it seems excessive to shoot and tase him again, since he was already down.

   UNCCLEO - **Article 5.**
   The article reads: "No law enforcement official may inflict, instigate or tolerate any act of torture or other cruel, inhuman or degrading treatment or punishment, nor may any law enforcement official invoke superior orders or

exceptional circumstances such as a state of war or a threat of war, a threat to national security, internal political instability or any other public emergency as a justification of torture or other cruel, inhuman or degrading treatment or punishment."

We have already established that Mr. Thacker was tortured by Law Enforcement to coerce statements from him. However, all subsequent Law Enforcement officials, including all subsequent prosecutors, tolerated these acts to the point of presenting Mr. Thacker´s statements as evidence in Court. This is unacceptable, and emboldens law enforcement to do this kind of thing again in the future.

UNCCLEO - Article 6.
The article reads: "Law enforcement officials shall ensure the full protection of the health of persons in their custody and, in particular, shall take immediate action to secure medical attention whenever required."

There is no doubt after watching the video footage that Mr. Thacker´s health was not a priority for the officers keeping him in custody. And that medical attention was intentionally withheld to coerce a confession, based on all the facts and information already discussed about available first aid.

8. **The actions of law enforcement and prosecutors this case are in violation of at least Articles 4, 5, and 10 of the *United Nations Basic Principles on the Use of Force and Firearms by Law Enforcement Officials (UNBPUFFLEO)*.**

UNBPUFFLEO - Article 4.
The article reads: "Law enforcement officials, in carrying out their duty, shall, as far as possible, apply non-violent means before resorting to the use of force and firearms. They may use force and firearms only if other means remain ineffective or without any promise of achieving the intended result."

Even after Mr. Thacker, wearing a full leg brace, was tased, an officer deemed it necessary to shoot him, not only once, but twice. Then he was tased a second time. There was no need to breach the residence, nor was there any legal authority for doing so. This clearly contradicts the directive above.

UNBPUFFLEO - Article 5.
The article reads: "Whenever the lawful use of force and firearms is unavoidable, law enforcement officials shall: (a) Exercise restraint in such use

and act in proportion to the seriousness of the offence and the legitimate objective to be achieved; (b) Minimize damage and injury, and respect and preserve human life; (c) Ensure that assistance and medical aid are rendered to any injured or affected persons at the earliest possible moment; (d) Ensure that relatives or close friends of the injured or affected person are notified at the earliest possible moment."

No restraint was shown on part of Law Enforcement when subduing Mr. Thacker during his arrest. In fact, their actions accomplished precisely the opposite goal of the article. Especially with respect to preserving human life, which was clearly not a priority in their treatment of Elvis Thacker.

UNBPUFFLEO - Article 10.
The article reads: "…law enforcement officials shall identify themselves as such and give a clear warning of their intent to use firearms, with sufficient time for the warning to be observed, unless to do so would unduly place the law enforcement officials at risk or would create a risk of death or serious harm to other persons, or would be clearly inappropriate or pointless in the circumstances of the incident."

On video, we can observe that there was no clear verbal identification on the part of officers entering the residence where Mr. Thacker was arrested. Nor were any of those who conducted the breach wearing uniforms. Nor was there a warning of their intent to use lethal force. They breached without identifying themselves as law enforcement to Elvis Thacker, and without warning that lethal force was imminent.

9. **The actions of law enforcement and prosecutors this case are in violation of Articles 11 and 12 of the *United Nations Guidelines on the Role of Prosecutors (UNGRP)*.**

    UNGRP - Article 11.
    The article reads: "Prosecutors shall perform an active role in criminal proceedings, including institution of prosecution and, where authorized by law or consistent with local practice, in the investigation of crime, supervision over the legality of these investigations, supervision of the execution of court decisions and the exercise of other functions as representatives of the public interest."

    The fact that the prosecution presented a coerced confession in Court clearly shows lack of supervision over the legality of investigations performed by Law Enforcement on Mr. Thacker's case. The fact that the videos clearly show Mr.

Thacker being touted by law enforcement, and that prosecutors ignored and obfuscated this fact, is a further violation.

UNGRP - Article 12.
The article reads: "Prosecutors shall, in accordance with the law, perform their duties fairly, consistently and expeditiously, and respect and protect human dignity and uphold human rights, thus contributing to ensuring due process and the smooth functioning of the criminal justice system."

The use of torture to obtain a confession from Mr. Thacker is by itself a clear violation of due process. But the fact that it was tolerated by the prosecution, who passed it off as valid and admissible in Court, shows no respect for human rights. And perhaps even no understanding of them.

10. **The actions of law enforcement and prosecutors this case are in violation of Article 18 of the** *United Nations Declaration of Basic Principles of Justice for victims of Crime and Abuse of Power.*

Mr. Thacker was a suspect according to the investigation carried out by Law Enforcement Officials on this case. However, he then became a victim of torture and abuse of power who was subjected to psychological and physical violence with no regard for his well being or even his life. He was not given immediate medical attention, and his condition was taken advantage of to obtain a confession. The violation of his human rights is therefore not just in the form of physical and psychological violence. It is also shown to be evident when due process is violated.

Mr. Thacker's due process violations are therefore a violation of *Article 18*, which states: "'Victims' means persons who, individually or collectively, have suffered harm, including physical or mental injury, emotional suffering, economic loss or substantial impairment of their fundamental rights, through acts or omissions that do not yet constitute violations of national criminal laws but of internationally recognized norms relating to human rights."

Should further evidence and information become available, I would necessarily examine it for the purposes of revisiting and revising the opinions expressed in this report.

Lic. Manuel Adolfo Esparza Navarrete

REFERENCES

1. **UNIVERSAL DECLARATION OF HUMAN RIGHTS**
   http://www.un.org/en/universal-declaration-human-rights/

2. **UNITED NATIONS CONVENTION AGAINST TORTURE AND OTHER CRUEL, INHUMAN OR DEGRADING TREATMENT OR PUNISHMENT**
   http://www.ohchr.org/EN/ProfessionalInterest/Pages/CAT.aspx

3. **UNITED NATIONS CODE OF CONDUCT FOR LAW ENFORCEMENT OFFICIALS**
   http://www.ohchr.org/EN/ProfessionalInterest/Pages/LawEnforcementOfficials.aspx

4. **UNITED NATIONS BASIC PRINCIPLES ON THE USE OF FORCE AND FIREARMS BY LAW ENFORCEMENT OFFICIALS**
   http://www.ohchr.org/EN/ProfessionalInterest/Pages/UseOfForceAndFirearms.aspx

5. **UNITED NATIONS GUIDELINES ON THE ROLE OF PROSECUTORS**
   http://www.ohchr.org/EN/ProfessionalInterest/Pages/RoleOfProsecutors.aspx

6. **UNITED NATIONS DECLARATION OF BASIC PRINCIPLES OF JUSTICE FOR VICTIMS OF CRIME AND ABUSE OF POWER**
   http://www.un.org/documents/ga/res/40/a40r034.htm

THE STATE OF THE CASE

As of this writing, the Thacker cases are under appeal; the DOJ investigation into the Oklahoma State Bureau of Investigation and the Ft. Smith Police Department are in their initial phases; and the Human Rights violations have only just been reported to the United Nations.

ENDNOTES

1. Kiger, S. (September 25, 2012). Thackers to Appear in Leflore County Court in Ault Homicide Case — Oklahoma Welcome. *Oklahoma Welcome*.
2. Hughes, D. (April 28, 2016). Witness says police tortured Thacker, Confessions in 2010 killing not backed up. *Arkansas Democrat Gazette*. http://www.nwaonline.com/news/2016/apr/28/witness-says-police-tortured-thacker-co/.

Index

'*Note*: Page numbers followed by "f" indicate figures.'

A

Adult probation, forensic investigations
  American Probation and Parole Association, 332–333
  characteristics, 334–335
  correctional officers, 336
  County probation departments and felonies, 333
  data analysis, 333
  defense counsel, 335–336
  educational and special training, 336
  financial resources, 335–336
  presentence/postsentencing study, 332
  presentencing report, 335
Adversarial system
  defense, 23–24
  definition, 23
  prosecution, 23
Alaska Council on Domestic Violence and Sexual Assault, 185–187
American Bar Association (ABA), 339–341
American Polygraph Association (APA), 280
American Probation and Parole Association, 332–333
Authority appeals, 82–83
Autopsy protocols, 249–250

B

Behaviors constituting torture, 314–315
Brady violations, 126

C

Coercive interrogation, 313
Corpus delicti, 106–107
  burglary crime, 4
  comprehensive investigation, 4
  homicide crime, 5
  legal authority, 3
  rape/sexual assault, 4
Crime reconstruction, 162, 345–346
  case study, 101–105, 102f
  definition, 99
  digital evidence, 100–101
  forensic disciplines, 100–101
  physical evidence, 101
  police investigation, 101
  sexual assault examination
    Alaska Council on Domestic Violence and Sexual Assault, 185–187
    National Institute of Justice (NIJ), 185
    objective process, 182
    physical evidence, 182–183
    State Attorney General's Office, 183
    State Department of Public Safety, 183
    team members, 183–185
    team structure, 185–187
    uncritical acceptance, 183
Crime scene analysis (CSA), 92, 105
Crime scene investigation (CSI)
  crime reconstruction. *See* Crime reconstruction
  crime scene analysis (CSA), 92, 105
  FBI effect
    Evidence Response Team, 98
    interview and interrogation, 97
    murder and sex crimes investigation, 96
    myths series, 95–96
    professional law enforcement agency, 97
    scientific practice and evidence examination, gold standard, 97
    secret, high-tech database access, 97
    special training, 96
  food forensics, 91
  forensic relevance
    case study, 112–120
    corpus delicti, 106–107
    crime scene witness, 109
    evidence collection, 105–106
    investigative leads, 112–120
    modus operandi, 107
    signature behavior, 108
    suspects identification, 110–112, 111f
    victim suspect, 109
    witness and victim statements, 109–110
  forensic science community, 95
  forensic science reality and TV shows, 93–94, 93f
  goal of, 99
  investigation component, 98
  laboratory testing, 92
  physical evidence, 95
  show-makers and script consultants, 92
  TV crime lab myths, 94–95
  unrealistic imagery and expectations, 92
Crime scene processing
  biased forensic testimony, 126
  Brady violations, 126
  comprehensive investigation, 127
  definition, 126–127, 131–132

Crime scene processing (*Continued*)
  documentation, 133
  dumpsite/disposal site, 129–131, 130f
  forensic field tests, 137–140, 137f
  intermediate crime scene, 129
  law enforcement, 133
  legal authority, 126
  locate and protect physical evidence, 132
  National Academy of Science (NAS), 126, 132
  primary crime scene, 127–129, 128f
  problem and solution, 132
  protocols
    barrier tape, 140–141
    checklists, 140
    evidence collection and preservation. *See* Evidence collection and preservation
    evidence documentation. *See* Evidence documentation
    evidence recognition. *See* Evidence recognition
    evidence transportation, 154
    National Institute of Justice (NIJ). *See* National Institute of Justice (NIJ)
  secondary crime scene, 129
  tertiary crime scene, 131
  tiered system
    classifications and inherent limitations, 134–140
    convergent factors, 134
    law enforcement agencies control, 134
    prosecutors control, 134
    shield law enforcement from criticism, 134
  types, 127
Crime scene witness, 109
Criminal justice system
  academia, 21
  accused and convicted criminals, 20
  corrections, 22–23
  forensic services, 21–22
  judiciary, 22
  law enforcement, 21
  nonlaw enforcement, 20
  nonprosecutorial components, 20

D
Data integrity, 10
Due process
  federal and state constitutional rights, 31
  forensic examinations, 32–33
  history, 32
  moral requirements, 31
  personal ideas and emotions, 33

Duty of care
  case study, 56–59, 56f–57f
  comprehensive investigation, 53
  employers, 54
  Federal law enforcement agencies, 52
  fitness, 54
  Fitness-For-Duty Evaluation (FFDE), 55–59
  forensic investigator, 54
  law enforcement agency, 52
  legal responsibilities, 54–55
  primary responsibilities, 52–53
  red flags/indicators, 55

E
Emotional appeal, 84
Evidence collection and preservation
  biological material, 153–154
  cross-contamination, 152
  evidence storage, 154
  examination and testing, 151–152
  technicians and training, 152
  volatile material, 152
Evidence documentation
  forensic investigator, 148
  photography, 148–149
  sketching, 150–151
  videography, 149–150
Evidence recognition
  latent evidence, 147
  macroscopic evidence, 147
  microscopic evidence, 147
  physical evidence, 146–147
Evidence Response Team, 98
Evidence transportation, 154

F
False authority appeal, 83
False impression, 1–2
Federal law enforcement agencies, 52
Federal Rules of Evidence (FRE, 2011), 28–30
Fitness-For-Duty Evaluation (FFDE), 55–59
Forensic, definition, 7–8
Forensic examiners, 8–9
Forensic facts *vs.* political reality
  FBI agents, 12–13
  Michigan State Police Crime Lab, 15–16
  political landscape, 16
  political pressure, 14
  United States Department of Justice, 12–13
  Washington DC Department of Forensic Sciences Crime Lab, 13–14

Forensic interviews
　accuracy, 263
　admissibility, 264
　checklist, 266
　coercion/torture, 264
　conduct and tone, 272
　consistency, 263
　continuing education, 275
　corroboration, 264
　disorganization and distraction, 265–266
　documentation, 263
　　and recording, 267–268
　false confessions, 273–275
　fictional conceptualizations, 262
　interview preparation, 265
　interview questions
　　alibi witness questions, 271
　　eyewitness questions, 270–271
　　witnesses, interview questions, 270
　investigative tasks, 266
　investigator dress and presentation, 272–273
　physical evidence, 272
　professional development, 275
　promises, 273
　protocols, 269–270
　reliability, 263
　stakes and consequences, 264–265
　witness, 263
Forensic investigations, court, 10–11
　adult probation. *See* Adult probation, forensic investigations
　capital murder mitigation investigations
　　American Bar Association (ABA), 339–341
　　appellate/investigative process, 337
　　death penalty trial, 338
　　due process, 337–338
　　"effective assistance of counsel", 341
　　"ineffectiveness of counsel", 341
　　mitigation specialist, 336–337
　　moral culpability determination, 339
　　United States Supreme Court decisions, 337
　justice concept, 329
　juvenile court probation systems. *See* Juvenile court probation systems
Forensic Medical Examination and Evidence Collection Procedures, 192
Forensic necessity, 5–7
Forensic polygraph examination, 12
Forensic science, 8
Forensic scientists, 8–9
Forensic victimology
　behavioral indicators, 159
　death investigation, 159
　goals
　　case linkage, 163
　　crime elements, 161
　　crime reconstruction, 162
　　deification, 163
　　investigative suggestions, 162
　　offender modus operandi development, 162
　　offender motive development, 162
　　offender's exposure level, 162–163
　　public safety response, 163
　　suspect pool, 161–162
　　timeline development, 161
　　victim exposure, 164
　　victimization, contextualizing allegations, 162
　　vilification, 163–164
　guidelines
　　checklist, 174–175
　　court package, 177
　　digital package, 176
　　employment package, 177
　　financial package, 177
　　medical package, 177
　　objective packages, 175
　　personal package, 175–176
　　relationship package, 176–177
　　residence package, 176
　　timeline creation, 178–179
　guiding principle, 159
　international protocols, 158
　National Institute of Justice (NIJ) protocols, 158
　　guidelines, 160
　pervasive social and cultural belief systems, 157–158
　postassault activities, 160
　scientific method, 161
　sex crime investigators, 159–160
　victim exposure. *See* Victim exposure
　victim history, 160
Fragmented forensic science community, 71

G

Government agents torture
　in Mexico
　　brutal acts, 300
　　Justice System, 302
　　physical abuse, 299–300, 299f
　　public exposure, 300–301
　　43 students, 297–299
　in United States
　　independent forensic investigators and examiners, 302

Government agents torture (*Continued*)
  Jon Burge case, 302–305
  Sitka Police Department (SPD), 305–306
  US Military personnel and civilian contractors, 306–310, 308f

H
Homicide crime, 5

I
Intermediate crime scene, 129
Investigation, definition, 9
Investigative ethics
  bias
    case study, 60–62, 60f
    forensic community's affiliation, 60
    professional suicide, 59
  degree of opacity, 46
  dilemmas
    case study, 48–51
    immediate v. future, 48
    individual v. group, 47
    justice v. compassion, 48
    no-win situation, 47
    truth v. loyalty, 47–48
  duty of care. *See* Duty of care
  ethical canon, forensic investigator, 62–64
  "forensic" designation, 45
  and morality, 46–47
  professional ethics, 51–52
Investigators
  "after this, therefore because of this", 85
  argumentum ad hominem, 84
  authority appeals, 82–83
  availability heuristic, 76
  benefits, 76–77
  breed confidence, 77
  circulus in probando, 85
  critical thinking
    definition, 72
    evidence/theories, 72–73
    FBI, 74–75
    polygraph, 73–74
    problem, 75–76
  cum hoc, 85
  definition, 9
  emotional appeal, 84
  ergo propter hoc, 85
  false authority appeal, 83
  false precision, 86–87
  forensic neutrality, 68
  fragmented forensic science community, 71
  government-funded crime labs, 71–72
  hasty generalizations, 86
  individual professional compass, 72
  logical fallacies, 81–87
  logic of failure, 87
  metacognition, 69–70
  metacognitive dexterity, 70
  physical evidence, 68
  post hoc, 85
  preemptory attack, 82
  quality and substance experience, 77
  reflection, 69
  responsibilities, 68
  science
    falsification, 79–81
    vs. scientific method, 77–78
  suppressed evidence/card stacking, 82
  sweeping generalization, 86
  tradition appeal, 84
  witnesses dishonesty, 68
Istanbul Protocols, 310, 317–319

J
Juvenile court probation systems
  assessment tools, 330–331
  developmental and maturation progress, 330
  jurisdiction agency, 330
  SAVRY, 331
  social responsibility, 330
  training and educational requirements, 332

L
Law and evidence
  adversarial system
    defense, 23–24
    definition, 23
    prosecution, 23
  case-related decisions, 26
  chain of custody, 27
  constitutional rights, 30–41
    due process. *See* Due process
    U.S. Supreme Court. *See* U.S. Supreme Court
  criminal justice system. *See* Criminal justice system
  expert evidence
    Federal Court, 27
    Federal Rules of Evidence (FRE, 2011), 28–30
  justice, definition, 19–20
  legal reality, 27
  scientific fact *vs.* legal truth
    forensic practitioners, 25

objective and analytical deliberation, 24–25
trier-of-fact, 26
Lifestyle exposure
  afflictions, 166
  careers, 165–166
  extreme-exposure victims, 167
  factors, 165
  high-exposure victims, 168
  low-exposure victims, 168
  medium-exposure victims, 168
  personal traits, 166–167

M

Medicolegal death investigation
  autopsy
    case study, 229–230
    definition, 227
    forensic interpretations and opinions, 229
    investigative and forensic responsibilities, 227
    logical and comprehensible, 227–228
    NAME, 228–229
    statutory authority, 228
  body documentation and evaluation, 237–238
  case study, 235–236, 236f
  cause of death, 230–231
  chain of custody, 233–236
  contents, 233, 255–256
  coroner, 226–227
  decedent profile information, 242–244
  failures, 256–258
  forensic investigator, 223
  forensic pathology, 225–226
  manner of death
    accidental, 231
    classifications, 231
    homicide, 231–232
    natural, 231
    suicide, 232
    undetermined, 232–233
  medical doctor, 225
  medical examiner, 226
  medical opinions, 225
  medicolegal, definition, 223–224
  NAS Report, 224
  National Academy Of Sciences Report, 249–250
  National Association Of Medical Examiners (NAME), 225. *See also* National Association Of Medical Examiners (NAME) Standards
  NIJ, 233
  objective scientists and competent investigators, 222
  scene documentation and evaluation, 237–238
  scene investigation, 244–245
Michigan State Police Crime Lab, 15–16
Modus operandi, 107

N

National Academy of Science (NAS), 126, 132, 249–250
National Association Of Medical Examiners (NAME) Standards
  standard D10 physical characteristics, 251
  standard D11 postmortem changes, 251
  standard D9 preliminary procedures, 250–251
  standard E17 burn injuries, 253
  standard E15 firearm injuries, 252–253
  standard E13 injuries, 252
  standard E18 patterned injuries, 253
  standard E14 photographic documentation, 252
  standard E16 sharp force injuries, 253
  standard E12 suspected sexual assault, 252
  standard F24 blunt impact injuries, 255
  standard F21 head, 254
  standard F20 internal organs and viscera, 254
  standard F22 neck, 254
  standard F23 penetrating injuries, 255
  standard F19 thoracic and abdominal cavities, 253–254
National Institute of Justice (NIJ), 158
  guidelines, 141, 160
  preliminary documentation and evaluation, 145–146
  protocols, 142–146
National Research Council, 287

O

Oklahoma v. Elvis Thacker
  case study, 344
  crime reconstruction, 345–346
  forensic examination report, 347–361
  forensic psychological analysis, 367–373
  investigative and forensic analysis, 375–385
  law enforcement investigation, 345
  plea and confession, 345
  sexual homicide, 343

P

Physical evidence, 1
Police torture
  behaviors constituting torture, 314–315
  biased and inaccurate information, 314

Police torture (*Continued*)
  coercive interrogation, 313
  cognitive and behavioral manifestations
    primary behavioral evidence, 316–317
    protective factors, 319–320
    signs and symptoms, 317–319
  excessive force, 312
  forensic investigative protocols, 297
  forensic investigator, 310–311
  government agents torture. *See* Government agents torture
  law enforcement agencies, 295–296
  mental health professional
    guidelines, 320–324
      psychological assessment, 320
      validation and refutation, 325
  physical evidence, 315–316
  physical/psychological abuse, 315
  torture, definition, 312
  torture violation, 296
Polygraph
  American Polygraph Association (APA), 280
  CIA agent, 279–280
  CIT tests, 289
  CQT, 279
  criminal investigation, 284–285
  deceptive individuals, 286
  diagnostic procedures, 288
  emotional process, 288
  error rates, 281–282
  false confessions, 282
  federal government, 277
  high-quality laboratory study, 282–283
  inconclusive tests, 281, 283–284
  Judge King's ruling comment, 286
  lie detection report, 285
  National Research Council, 287
  physiological response, 278
  preliminary process theory (PPT), 288
  probable-lie and directed-lie tests, 287
  psychological results, 282
  sampling bias, 285
  testing paradigm, 279
Preliminary process theory (PPT), 288
Public facts, 2

S

Sex crime investigators, 159–160
Sexual assault examination
  bruise
    aging bruises, 210
    blunt force blow, 205
    breasts, 209
    hands and forearms, 206–207
    inner thighs, 206
    knees, 209
    ligature pattern, 208–209
    physical restraint and bindings, 206
    symptoms and physical signs, strangulation, 207–208
  clothing, 214
  crime reconstruction
    Alaska Council on Domestic Violence and Sexual Assault, 185–187
    National Institute of Justice (NIJ), 185
    objective process, 182
    physical evidence, 182–183
    State Attorney General's Office, 183
    State Department of Public Safety, 183
    team members, 183–185
    team structure, 185–187
    uncritical acceptance, 183
  examination reports, 217
  false positives, 215–216
  Forensic Medical Examination and Evidence Collection Procedures, 192
  forensic nursing
    consent forms, 189–191
    definition, 188
    intake form, 191–192
    sexual assault examination, 187–188
    time constraints, 188–189
  full body photos, 204
  genital examination, 210–211
  history
    collection, 195–197
    components, 193
    drug abuse, 194
    patient examination, 193
    postassault activities, 194
    recent consensual sexual activity, 194
    victim background information, 193
  NIJ guidelines, 197–204
  physical examination, 197
  physical injuries, 204–205
  sexual activity evidence
    acid phosphatase, 212
    condoms, 213–214
    DNA, 213
    fecal matter, 213
    P30, 212
    saliva, 213
    semen, 212

sperm, 212
victim history, 211
toxicology
  mental incapacity, 216
  substance abuse, 217
victim history, 218
Signature behavior, 108
Sitka Police Department (SPD), 305–306
Situational/incident exposure
  alcohol issue, 168
  care and supervision, 170
  drug and alcohol use, 170
  firearms usage, 168–169
  high-exposure victims, 170
  location of occurrence, 169
  low-exposure victims, 171–174
  medium-exposure victims, 170–171
  mind/perception, victim state, 170
  number of potential victims, 169
  proximity to criminal activity, 169
  time of occurrence, 169
  weapons availability, 169–170
State Attorney General's Office, 183
State Department of Public Safety, 183
State of Oregon's Attorney General's Sexual Assault Task Force, 2–3
Suspects identification, 110–112, 111f

T

Tradition appeal, 84

U

United States Department of Justice, 12–13
U.S. Supreme Court
  Brady V. Maryland (1963)
    prosecutorial misconduct, 34–35
    right to "effective" counsel, 35–37
    trial by ambush, 33–34
  Melendez-Diaz (2009)
    adversary system, 37–38
    federal agencies, 38
    government crime labs, 39–40
    government-employed forensic practitioners, 38
    pretrial evidentiary hearings, 39
    video depositions and phone testimony, 40–41

V

Victim exposure
  analysis, 164–174
  case study, 171–174
  classification
    lifestyle exposure, 165–168
    situational/incident exposure, 168–174
Victim suspect, 109

W

Washington DC Department of Forensic Sciences Crime Lab, 13–14